something like
stories
volume three

Jay Bell Books

www.jaybellbooks.com

Did you buy this book? If so, thank you for putting food on our table! Making money as an independent artist isn't easy, so your support is greatly appreciated. Come give me a hug!

Did you pirate this book? If so, there are a couple of ways you can still help out. If you enjoy the story, please take the time to leave a nice review somewhere, such as an online retail store (my preference), or on any blog or forum. Word of mouth is an unbeatable form of advertising, so if you can recommend this book to friends with more cash to spare, that would be awesome too!

Something Like Stories: Volume 3 © 2020 Jay Bell/Andreas Bell

ISBN: 978-1-7338597-6-9

ALL RIGHTS RESERVED. This book may not be reproduced in whole or in part without permission. This book is a work of fiction and any resemblance to persons, living or dead, or events is purely coincidental.

Cover art by Andreas Bell: www.andreasbell.com

-=Books by Jay Bell=-

The Something Like… series
#1 Something Like Summer
#2 Something Like Autumn
#3 Something Like Winter
#4 Something Like Spring
#5 Something Like Lightning
#6 Something Like Thunder
#7 Something Like Stories - Volume One
#8 Something Like Hail
#9 Something Like Rain
#10 Something Like Stories - Volume Two
#11 Something Like Forever
#12 Something Like Stories - Volume Three

The Loka Legends series
#1 The Cat in the Cradle
#2 From Darkness to Darkness

Other Novels
Kamikaze Boys
Hell's Pawn
Straight Boy

Other Short Stories
Language Lessons
Like & Subscribe
The Boy at the Bottom of the Fountain

Acknowledgements

Writing always involves a certain amount of gambling. An author spends months (if not years) working on a book without knowing if the audience will enjoy the story, or if those long lonely hours will be magically spun into gold. That's why I appreciate the financial and emotional support of the following people, who through Patreon, have generously taken some of the dreadful uncertainly out of an otherwise delightful occupation. Please join me in recognizing the following heroic personas:

Joseph Acosta ♥ Almost Alex ♥ Jake Allman ♥ Mark Andrews ♥ Daniel Attaway ♥ Kevin Arvizu ♥ The Bird and the Jet ♥ The Boys at By George Farm ♥ Kevin Bowling-Swan ♥ Jos Bowmaster ♥ KJ Brethauer ♥ John Burnside Jr. ♥ Chris & Kai Burton ♥ Cory Chamberlin ♥ Matthew Christian ♥ Matthew Cliburn ♥ Andy Corvin ♥ Neil Courtney ♥ Jim Cox ♥ Dee Damiano ♥ Chantal de Pessemier ♥ Corey Dobbs ♥ Iain Docherty ♥ Todd Doty ♥ Mark Edwards ♥ Shannon Everyday ♥ Evy ♥ Shannon Farnsworth ♥ Tallian Fisher ♥ Zac Ford ♥ Jeremy Friend ♥ Jim Frier ♥ Tom G ♥ James Gies ♥ Alex Gonzales ♥ Roman Gradinar and Irina Kirdun ♥ Tiffany C. Graham ♥ Devin Greenlee ♥ David Alan Griffin ♥ Sal Guenette ♥ Jeff Hall ♥ Felisha Height ♥ Robert Helms ♥ Jim and John Hertwig Perez ♥ Florian Heym ♥ Stephen Hurwitz ♥ Jarter ♥ Jason Jermyn ♥ Leigh Juhlke ♥ Ingrid Birgitta Karlsson ♥ Melissa Kidd ♥ Shaun King ♥ Felyx Lawson ♥ Jonothon Laycock ♥ Brittany Rose Lewis ♥ Lisa Lieurance ♥ Robert Lucas ♥ Marc Anthony Maestre ♥ David Manfredi ♥ Cat Marie ♥ Tony Marquardt ♥ Vince Marsters ♥ Merryl Martin ♥ Cory MB ♥ Susen McBeth ♥ Jini McClelland ♥ Michael & Koda ♥ Lindsay Moffat ♥ Carol Molinari ♥ Julia and Sam Morris ♥ Josh Oliff ♥ LaCole Ofosu ♥ Michael Oaks ♥ Olivier Ochin ♥ Zara Park ♥ Scott Pearson ♥ Matthew Perry ♥ Matthew Richards ♥ Ryan Riebeling ♥ Joshua Rivera ♥ Dayis R ♥ Jason Robertson ♥ Russell and Somyos ♥ Lee Short ♥ John Smeallie ♥ Kathie Smestad ♥ Heather Somma ♥ Muyang Song ♥ Jo Sowerby ♥ Fabian Stamm ♥ Stephanie Sullivan ♥ Michael Swearingen ♥ Holly Trebing ♥ Urban ♥ David W. Van Zyl ♥ Brian Verwiel ♥ Peter VH ♥ Michael Wallace ♥ Kelly Walker ♥ Jon and Will Wilder ♥ David Wood ♥ Paige Yodanis

Table of Contents

1. Something Like Home 1
2. Something Like Love 6
3. Something Like Friends 11
4. Something Like Vacation 16
5. Something Like Enemies 22
6. Something Like Then 37
7. Something Like Me 48
8. Something Like Bones 96
9. Something Like Spirits 104
10. Something Like Snow 125
11. Something Like Pride 138
12. Something Like Her 151
13. Something Like Stars 165
14. Something Like Us 226
15. Something Like Him 323
16. Something Like Family 335
17. Something Like Goodbye 362
18. Something Like Heaven 412

Foreword

Welcome to the final book in the *Something Like...* series! I know, I know. I made that claim before when publishing *Something Like Forever*. It really was my intent for that to be the end. The book you are reading now was never planned. It happened by accident. Deciding to end this series was more difficult for me than expected. Moving on was never the issue. I've written other unrelated books since then and had a great time while doing so, but I love Ben and his extended family. Letting go of them wasn't easy. The ongoing *Something Like Summer* comic became my emotional crutch, allowing me to revisit everyone I missed. Mostly. I grew impatient waiting to reunite with Jace, Victor, and others who hadn't made it into the comic yet. So I turned to the artist, Cassy Fallon, and asked if we could do a special series of illustrations. She agreed!

Over on Patreon we began polling supporters, asking them which pair they would most like to see. William and Jason, Kelly and Nathaniel, Marcello and Eric, and so on. At one point I decided it would be fun to write a little scene to accompany each illustration. Not a proper story with conflict and resolution. Just a tender or lighthearted moment featuring those characters. You'll recognize those in this collection when reading a story that seems unusually short. The more of them I wrote, the longer the "scenes" grew until they became full-fledged stories. At one point I stopped kidding myself, made a bucket list of everything I never got around to including in the main series, and started writing *intentional* short stories again. Enough to fill a nice fat collection, although I still wasn't planning to release another book. Only when I took a step back and shuffled the stories around did I see what a satisfying compilation they would make.

With the stories arranged in chronological order, this book takes us on a sightseeing trip through the entire series and beyond. We get to witness teenagers in love again, watch them grow up, suffer heartbreak, and bounce back heroically. Best of all, we get closure on many characters' lives. No matter who you want to see more of, there's a good chance you'll find them here. I like to think of this book as one giant epilogue to the series, reminding us of how long the journey has been while providing a glimpse into the future. I hope you laugh, cry, and mourn these characters all over again, because I truly do expect this to be the final book in the series. The story will always live on though, not only as a comic, a movie, or who knows what else, but in the heart of a silly old fool like me, and with any luck, the hearts of many of you as well. Thank you so much for allowing me this one last dance, even though the DJ has gone home and the janitor is mopping up around our feet.

-Jay Bell
Chicago, 2020

Something Like Stories: Volume Three

Something Like Home

by Jay Bell

Warrensburg, Missouri
1991

Jace only pretended to watch the fire. The stars above twinkled in a midnight sky, the trees still bare from their long winter slumber. The weather had warmed up in recent weeks, enough for his wild boy to return to the comforting embrace of Mother Nature. As always, Jace followed along behind him, his heart ever loyal. Now they were back in the clearing where so much had transpired. Jace glanced to his left to where Victor sat, focusing on the fire while wearing a serene smile. Jace thought of the cats his mother kept, how snow and ice would force them to remain inside and how increasingly agitated they became as cold weather persisted. Once spring finally arrived, the cats would scarcely come indoors, too happy to finally be outside again. He supposed he'd be spending a lot of time in the woods himself, if he wanted to see his boyfriend.

Jace angled his head forward, but his eyes remained on Victor, who generally had plenty to say, but sometimes liked to silently think instead. Moments like these drove Jace crazy. He was desperate to know each and every thought hidden behind those mismatched eyes. He tried to be patient and let Victor speak when he was ready, but his curiosity won out. He would pry. With subtlety, he hoped, but he would pry nonetheless.

"What do you see in the flames?" he asked. "The future?"

Victor took a few seconds to answer, as if needing to return from a far-away place. "That's right. I'm looking into the future."

"And what do you see?" Jace asked.

"A campfire, slow nights, and good company."

In other words, more evenings like this one. Jace frowned, which was odd, because he enjoyed their surroundings too. But... "For how long exactly?"

Victor glanced over at him, the confused expression short-lived. He always seemed to understand what Jace was getting at, even before he knew himself. "Until nights like these no longer happen, I suppose. What you'd really like to know is what comes after."

He nodded. "Where do you see yourself in five years?"

Victor gave it serious thought, even if his answer didn't seem grounded in reality. "Next to a river."

Jace groaned. "I mean it!"

"So do I." Victor tilted his head to one side. "I'm not talking about the creek we follow to get here, or even the lake. I'm picturing big rapids filled with salmon that leap into the air!"

"You can't stand fishing. We tried, remember?"

"Then let's hope a grizzly bear takes pity and shares his dinner with me." Victor reached over to run his fingers through Jace's hair. "Just like my lion does now."

As endearing as he found this, it was hardly an honest answer. "You must have some sort of plan."

Victor sighed. "I really don't. People who focus too much on their goals get tunnel vision and miss everything else that life has to offer. I don't intend to restrict myself that way."

"No limits?" Jace asked.

Victor nodded. "Exactly."

Jace returned his attention to the crackling timber, wanting to prove that he was just as carefree and aimless, but he couldn't let the subject drop. "You must have had plans at one time. What about when you were little? What did you want to be then?"

"An astronaut," Victor said instantly.

"Really?"

"Yup."

Jace thought about it and laughed. "I should have known."

Victor considered him, and for once, seemed unable to read his mind. "What's so funny about that?"

"Nothing. Just that you managed to choose the one occupation that's even more isolated than what you do now. Outer space is *way* more secluded than living in the woods, and about as far away from the system as you can get. No territory lines, no laws. Nothing but the remotest, most untamed corners of the natural world."

Victor looked intrigued. "Think it's too late to sign up?"

"I'm not rocketing into space with Tang and freeze-dried ice cream every time I want a kiss. Knowing you, it won't even be a planet. Those are too analyzed by astronomers, too labeled. No, you'll insist on living on some tiny asteroid hidden behind an undiscovered sun."

"Traveling has never sounded so good before."

Jace laughed and shook his head. "What are you so eager to get away from?"

"Nothing," Victor said, leaning his weight against him briefly. "I'm happy right where I am. In this moment."

Jace allowed himself to enjoy it too. While he was able. He possessed a curious mind, and before long it prompted him to ask another question. "What about me? What's my future?"

"Shouldn't you be the one to answer that?"

Jace shook his head. "I want to hear your version."

"Okay." Victor exhaled. "Let's see. You always talk about wanting to leave Warrensburg, so you won't be here. I picture you living in Kansas City."

"How come? Why not Seattle or Boston?"

"Too far," Victor said. "You'll want to stay close in case you miss your family. Or other people."

Jace grinned. "Good point. So what's my life in Kansas City all about?"

"You're the owner of a pizza place."

He scoffed. "Why pizza?"

"You speak Italian, don't you? I realize that's not very useful when running a fast-food restaurant, but you love any excuse to show off. You're always referring to the ingredients by their Italian names. The same with greetings and goodbyes. All in Italian. Your customers find it annoying, but luckily you've got a secret recipe that no one can resist."

"Hm. What's the name of my restaurant? I'm thinking Jace's Aces. The capital "A" in the sign will be a stylized pizza slice, obviously."

"Not bad," Victor said musingly. "You might have a future in graphic design. I've got a better name though. How about Jace's Crusty Pie?"

He shook his head and made sure he sounded disappointed. "And to think I named my most popular pizza after you."

"You did?"

"Yup. It's called Victoroni Pepperoni. The toppings are wild mushrooms, canned beans, and cigarette butts."

"All my favorites!" Victor grinned. "Sounds delicious.

Although it doesn't deliver on the promise of pepperoni. Tell your marketing team that. And can I make a request? Have the mushrooms be of the psychedelic variety."

"No way," Jace said, shaking his head. "I'm never doing that again."

"Wild mushrooms are fine then," Victor said. "I'll gather them during the day and be your supplier. That way you'll have an excuse to come visit me and my grizzly bear roommate at our river-side hut."

The mental image was cute, although Jace felt an unexpected pang of sorrow. "Be serious. I know you don't plan your future like most people do, but you must imagine it sometimes."

Victor nodded. "Occasionally."

"You don't have to tell me every detail. Just one." He swallowed, disliking how the smoke—or was it emotion?—made his eyes sting. "Do you think—"

"You're a part of that future," Victor said, not needing to hear the full question.

"How though? Will we live together? If so, will it be here in Missouri? In a house? I keep thinking if I buy some land—"

"Build the best life for yourself that you can," Victor interrupted. "Whatever shape that takes, I'll still be there."

"In what way?"

"Does it matter?"

"Yes! What's the point of any of this if we don't last?"

Victor was quiet before answering. "There are times, when I'm sitting out here all alone, that I hear the echo of your laughter. I imagine how you might reply to one of my thoughts, or I remember how good your hand feels in mine. You're with me each and every day, in the same way that I'll always be with you, no matter where we end up. Nothing can change that. I promise."

Jace stared at him in wonder. Then he nuzzled his nose against Victor's ear, gently kissed him on the temple, and turned his attention to the fire, content to stare into the flames and dream of a future that was anything but lonely.

Something Like Love

by Jay Bell

The Woodlands, Texas
1997

Ben pressed his back to the bedroom door and bit his bottom lip to stop himself from smiling. He would have to give in eventually, considering who was sprawled out in his bed. Tim's legs were hanging over the edge of the mattress, his body reclined and twisted to one side so he could read the back of a CD case. Alice in Chains, if Ben wasn't mistaken. Okay, so he knew exactly which CD it was and had left it lying around intentionally after Tim had teased him about listening to girl music. Whatever that meant. Was it Ben's fault that women had the best voices? Karen Carpenter for instance. No man possessed the voice of an angel like she did. Whitney Houston, Stevie Nicks, Nina Simone. The list went on and on. Ben felt no shame in worshiping these women, nor did he feel the need to defend his masculinity, but he did want to prove that his musical tastes were varied, and *Facelift* was one beautifully produced album. That's why Ben had chosen it. Now he regretted doing so because Tim was still absorbed in the album art.

Ben casually reached behind himself to push a button on the doorknob. This caused a metallic clink, which was enough for Tim to raise his head. He knew what that sound implied! Or maybe not.

"Why are you locking the door?" Tim asked.

"Why do you think?" Ben replied, sauntering forward. The weather was heating up, and for whatever reason, that always made him hornier than usual.

"Your parents are home," Tim said, eyes widening with trademark paranoia.

Ben shrugged. "So?"

"So they could hear us."

"Oh no," Ben deadpanned. "Like they haven't heard us a million times already. We might be a secret to your parents, but mine know all about us. Besides, they're cooking dinner together. We've got half an hour of guaranteed privacy, maybe more."

"It's a mood killer," Tim persisted.

"Or an appetite enhancer," Ben said. "I was hoping for some Mexican sausage myself." He stopped his approach and made a face. "Does something like that exist?"

"Chorizo," Tim said with a laugh. "And if mine looked anything like that, I'd have you drive me to the emergency room again."

Ben exhaled, feeling rejected. "Fine, have it your way. Wanna see what's on TV?"

Tim didn't answer the question. Instead he looked Ben over, like he often did when in the mood. "It *is* kind of hot in here."

"Totally!" Ben replied eagerly. Hormones don't hold a grudge. "Way too hot for all those clothes. Here, let me help you out of them."

Tim grinned, tossed the CD aside, and sat up, making it easier for Ben to strip off his shirt. Once it was off, Tim leaned back and casually tensed the muscles of his torso. Yum! Ben was about to fall to his knees and reach for a zipper when Tim spoke.

"Now show me yours."

"My what?" Ben said demurely.

"Your muscles."

Ben rolled his eyes. "You know I don't have any."

"You've got little tiny ones," Tim said. "Take off your shirt."

"Stop making fun of me and maybe I will," Ben retorted.

Tim looked confused. "I wasn't making fun of you. I love your body."

Ben froze. Was that the L-word? The one that Tim had never ever spoken, or at least never applied to him before. The nearest exception was two months ago on Valentine's Day, when Tim had seemed to teeter on the verge of saying the magical word. But he hadn't.

"I mean it," Tim insisted. "You turn me on. That's gotta be obvious by now, right?"

"Of course," Ben said, trying to play it cool. He stooped and shrugged out of his shirt, letting it drop to the floor. Then he attempted to flex, but instead of a gasp, he heard laughter. Ben glared in response. "You're such a dick!"

"That's right," Tim said, still chuckling. "I *am* a dick. A big fat hard one."

God that sounded delicious! Ben pounced, Tim lying flat to

accommodate him. As horny as Ben was, he didn't go straight for the jeans. Instead he pressed his lips to Tim's, his mind drifting to the weighty implications of that word again. *Love*. Ben knew from experience that he couldn't force Tim to say it. He shouldn't be so greedy anyway. This time last year he'd been alone and worried that he would never find a boyfriend. Now he had one who just happened to be the hottest guy in school. At least Ben thought so. His boyfriend was one of the popular kids too! Never had he dreamt of such a thing. And yet, he still wanted more.

Ben pulled back, breaking contact. "Do you feel like you knew me, even before we met?"

"Sure," Tim said, craning his neck for another kiss.

"Seriously!"

"Knew you before we met," Tim murmured to himself. Then the back of his head hit the mattress. "That doesn't make sense."

"It doesn't have to."

Tim furrowed his brow and shrugged. "In that case, yes. Now keep kissing me."

That was a request Ben couldn't deny, but after a few halfhearted smooches, he pulled back again. "Do you sometimes hear my heartbeat, even when we're not together?"

Tim looked incredulous. "No! That would scare the hell out of me!"

Ben tried again. "Or maybe you say my name just before you fall asleep. Or right when you wake up?"

Tim shook his head. "Have you gone crazy?"

Ben rolled over to one side. "Never mind."

"What? I don't get it."

"It doesn't matter."

"It must, because things were getting hot, but now you've gone cold."

Ben exhaled. "It's just that... Ronnie says the nicest things to Allison."

"Like how he can hear her heart from miles away?" Tim snorted. "That's one useless superpower."

"It's romantic!" Ben grumped. "You could learn a thing or two from him."

"I just told you that I love your body!"

"Yeah, but that's sexual." Ben looked away. "You never say what else you love."

Tim groaned. "Not this again."

"Yes, this again! I don't get why it's such a big deal."

Tim sat upright and reached for his shirt. "They're just words, Benjamin. They don't mean anything."

"Then it shouldn't matter. Just say it!"

"Fine." Tim dropped the shirt and turned to face him. "You know who I love? Do you have any idea who I want to spend the rest of my life with? The guy I'm talking about is my soulmate. He means everything to me. I love him more than anyone."

Ben's heart was thudding. "Who?"

"Bryce Hunter."

Ben stared. Then he started to climb out of bed until Tim grabbed an ankle to stop him. "Let go!"

"Nope." Tim did release him, but only to loop an arm around his waist. Then he yanked, pulling Ben back into bed.

"We're so over," Ben said, struggling to get free, but it was no use, because Tim climbed on top to pin him down. "Go back to Krista, I don't care. I'm dating Ronnie Adams now."

"You're dating me," Tim said.

"Nope. I don't date jerks."

"I was trying to show you how empty words are," Tim said. "Anyone can say whatever springs to mind—whatever they know the other person wants to hear—but that doesn't make it true."

"So what is the truth?" Ben asked, feeling vulnerable.

Tim lowered himself. "Can I show you?"

"No," Ben said, pushing against his chest.

Tim ducked his head beneath Ben's arms. "Please. Let me show you how I feel."

Ben hesitated. "So you *do* feel something?"

Tim's face came closer to his own. "Can't you tell?"

Ben stared into silver eyes, trying to discover the truth there. He thought he saw it too but couldn't be sure. Maybe he was only seeing what he wanted to. Perhaps no one ever knew what the other person truly felt. Tim wasn't attempting to kiss him anymore. He wasn't grinding against him and trying to take things further. He simply held himself above Ben, his gaze never wavering, like a promise that what they had together would never falter. As if it would last forever.

"Okay," Ben said, wrapping his legs around Tim's waist. "Show me everything."

Something Like Stories: Volume Three

Something Like Friends

by Jay Bell

Houston, Texas
1998

"What are ya watchin'?"

Jace scrambled for the remote to turn off the television, but the damn couch had a habit of eating anything smaller than a hardback book. The lush cushions were to blame for that. He was shoving his hand between them in a frantic search when he looked up and saw an equally panicked expression on Greg's face.

"Oh shit," his friend said. "You were about to whack it, weren't you?" Greg walked closer on bare feet and craned his neck to see the television. On the screen, two guys were peeling wet T-shirts off each other, the rain pummeling their exposed skin as they kissed. "Definitely gay porn," Greg said, starting to inch away. "I'll go for a walk. How long do you usually take?"

"It's not gay porn!" Jace huffed. His fingers finally sifted through enough spare change and paper cookie fortunes to locate the VCR remote. He pulled it free, pointed it at the screen, and the two lovers froze.

"Sure looks like porn to me," Greg said, flopping down on the couch next to him.

Despite his embarrassment, Jace couldn't help smiling. Ever since moving to Texas, he and Greg didn't see each other often. Only when Jace went home to Warrensburg, or times like now, when Greg flew to Houston for a visit. The studio apartment Jace lived in didn't provide much privacy, but he'd insisted that a hotel wasn't necessary. Neither one of them had wanted that, but now he was starting to regret their decision. Just a little. "It's not porn," Jace said again. "It's romantic."

"*Romantic?*" Greg said in disbelief before sticking out his tongue. "Blech! Since when do you watch that stuff?"

"There's more to life than action movies," Jace retorted.

"All right then." Greg nodded at the television. "Let's see."

"No way," Jace said. "You'll hate it."

"I won't," Greg said, his expression solemn. "Really. I'm an open-minded guy."

"Fine." Jace pressed the play button, wanting to fast forward past the sex. The scene wasn't graphic. It wasn't even clear how far the characters went, but he still felt awkward watching it with a straight guy.

"I'll never let them take you from me," one of the characters breathed. "Not ever!"

"How can they when you're already so deep inside of me?" the other responded.

Greg snorted. "Just how deep? Seven inches? Eight?"

Jace held up the remote and hit the stop button. "I knew this was a bad idea."

"Huh? We *always* make fun of movies together! Why take this one seriously?"

"Because this is all I get!" Jace pinched the bridge of his nose, breathed out, and let his hand drop. "You don't realize how often you see yourself reflected in the world. Every movie and TV show is filled with straight people falling in love, but how often do you see someone like me?"

"Not often enough," Greg said, never hesitant in his support. Jace knew he still felt bad for things he had said as a teenager, but Greg had more than made up for them over the years. "So uh, you've always watched stuff like this in secret?"

"Not really," Jace answered. "It's more of a recent thing because... Never mind."

Greg's brown eyes widened. "Tell me! We don't keep things from each other, remember? We never have."

That wasn't entirely true. Jace had some regrets himself, such as not trusting his best friend enough to talk about his sexuality when they were younger. He too had tried making up for the past by being more open in the present. Like now. "Sometimes I wonder if I missed my chance."

"Huh?"

"Victor. Maybe he was the one. My soulmate."

"Oh." Greg sighed and slumped into the couch. "You miss him."

"Yeah. More than that." Jace gestured to the blank television screen. "I miss having someone who makes me feel like I can't breathe when they're not around. And sometimes I wish Victor had acted that way with me instead of being so cool all the time. It would be nice if *any* guy lusted after me. I'm starting to get insecure."

"What?" Greg nudged him. "You're a helluva catch! Are you kidding me?"

Jace rolled his eyes. "You're not the best judge in this situation."

"You're hot," Greg said. "I might be straight, but I can tell. It doesn't hurt that you look so much like your sister. Would I have married her if I didn't think she was sexy? In fact, I've been missing her lately. Maybe you can help with that." Greg's voice had grown husky, his eyes half-lidded as he leaned closer. "Damn, Jace! It doesn't matter that I'm straight. Not with a guy like you."

"What?" Jace squeaked. He cleared his throat and tried again. "Have you lost your mind?"

"That's right." Greg reached over to place a hand behind Jace's head. "You're driving me crazy." His lips puckered up as they neared, but a little too much, like a cartoon character about to plant a big wet smacker on someone.

"Would you get off!" Jace said, but it was no use. Greg was stronger and still determined to reach him with those lips. Only when Jace used his arm like a crowbar to lever him away did Greg start laughing.

"You're hot, man," Greg said, ruffling his hair before leaning back again. "If I was into guys, I'd beg to be with you. Literally. Like this." He slid off the couch and onto his knees. Then he clasped his hands together as if praying. "Jace, please be my sweet little sugar plum fairy! I'd do anything for you. I'll never look at another girl again. Guy! Sorry. I'll never look at another guy again. You're smart, funny, and we've had enough sleepovers that I've seen what you're packing."

"Dude!"

Greg guffawed. "You're the complete package! *Including* your package."

"Please stop," Jace said. His face was burning now, but it had worked. He no longer felt as sorry for himself.

Greg got to his feet and flopped on the couch again. "You really are amazing," he said. "You'll find the right guy. Victor wasn't the only one for you. There's someone else out there."

"You can't know that."

Greg shrugged, unshaking in his confidence. "I'm right. Just you wait and see. Until then, you've always got me. I can't be everything to you. Just your best friend." He held up a fist for him to bump.

Jace took one look at it, and the incredible man the hand was attached to, and decided to believe that the best was yet to come. For now, he wouldn't be alone or feel unloved. Not by far, so he bumped fists. With his best friend.

———

Something Like Vacation

by Jay Bell

Rome, Italy
2000

"Nrrrrrrrrrgh," Ben said, smacking dry lips and burying his head deeper in the pillow. Just as he was drifting off again, hands returned to shake his body, so he raised his head slightly. While keeping his eyes closed, he added, "Nuh-uhhhhh!"

"You don't have to get up," he heard Jace say. "I just want you to know that I'm leaving you. That little old lady who's always hanging out in the hotel lobby? She just pinched my butt. In the elevator. I'm moving on to grayer pastures."

Ben compromised by opening one eye. "Did she really? Because I will take her down!"

"That's more like it," Jace said, patting him through the sheets before standing. "If you want to fight for me, you better get up. Come on now."

This ruse didn't work. Ben let his head land on the pillow again. "I'm too tired."

"Too tired for vacation? You're being ridiculous. Get up."

"Tired from walking," Ben said. "Nobody told me there would be so much!"

"Actually, I did."

"We've already seen Rome." Since they had arrived, Jace had dragged him through the city day after day, and while it was spectacular, spring break was supposed to be about partying, not exercising. "Besides, this room is probably expensive. Shouldn't we get our money's worth by actually spending time here?"

When he didn't get a response, he opened both eyes. Jace was standing over the bed with his arms crossed, looking uncharacteristically grumpy, which was kind of hot. Ben smiled and reached out. "Come get *your* money's worth."

Jace snorted. "First of all, that makes you sound like a rent boy. Secondly, I got this room using points, so I'm not losing any money. And finally, you stink."

Ben wasn't dissuaded. "Wanna get in the shower with me?"

Even though Jace was fully dressed and had clearly already bathed, he let his arms drop and nodded. "Fine. If that's what it takes."

"Yay!" Ben threw off the sheets and hopped naked out of bed. Okay, so maybe he wasn't *that* tired, but his leg muscles really were sore and his feet remained tender. His knees could still handle some abuse, which was good, because he already planned to be down on them. Jace led him to the bathroom, adjusted the shower water to the right temperature while Ben peed, and then guided him to the tub, holding open the curtain.

"In you go," Jace said, still fully dressed.

"But—" Ben tugged at his shirt in protest.

Jace sighed and started unbuttoning it. That was enough to encourage Ben to climb inside. He got beneath the stream of hot water, wanting to freshen up a little before things became really steamy. Except when he turned around again, the shower curtain was closed and he was alone.

"Hey!"

"I'll be right back," he heard Jace call from the other room. "With a surprise."

"It better not be that old lady!" Ben hollered, but he didn't hear a response. Resigned to his fate, he showered and got dressed. He was sitting on the edge of the bed and beginning to get bored when the door to the room opened again.

Jace entered, empty-handed except for a plastic cup filled with orange juice from the buffet downstairs.

"That's it?" Ben asked when this was handed to him. "I was hoping for donuts. With sprinkles."

"You're in Italy and you want donuts for breakfast?" Jace shook his head. "I have a much better idea. Put on your shoes."

Ben didn't move right away. Instead he weighed just how much he could get away with. A tantrum? He and Jace hadn't been together long. Three months, that was all, and he had already pushed his luck before this trip. Time to prove he was mature enough to date an older man. Ben chugged the juice, grabbed a pair of socks and his shoes, and was out the door in under five minutes. Jace rewarded him with a kiss in the elevator. Wanting to prove he could compete with a certain senior citizen, Ben reciprocated by pinching his butt.

"The juice wasn't the surprise," Jace said as they walked

through the lobby, "although it *is* the same color. See if you can spot what I'm talking about."

"I spy with my little eye..." Ben murmured as they walked outside. He didn't have to search far. Parked next to the lobby door was an orange and white moped. Ben nearly cried out in relief.

"No more walking?"

"Not *as much* walking," Jace corrected. "You aren't the only one with sore feet. I could use a break too. And maybe a foot rub later."

"Deal," Ben said, walking around the vehicle and laughing. "Mopeds are so cute! Do you know how to drive one?"

"Technically it's a scooter. Mopeds have pedals. And no, I can't drive one. I was hoping you knew how."

Ben looked at him sharply. "Me? No way! You saw me on ice skates. Balance has never been one of my strengths."

"Then I'll try my best," Jace said. "Ready?"

Ben wasn't. "Are you sure about this?"

Jace didn't seem to hear. Instead he sat on the scooter, passed him a helmet, and worked on buckling his own. He could be infuriatingly patient at times. Ben eyed the moped with uncertainty, cautious as he got on. The long, shared seat was comfortable, but he couldn't relax. As soon as the engine started and the scooter moved forward, Ben clung to Jace for dear life. Then he stopped clenching his eyes shut because, so far, the ride was smooth. He looked around when they reached the first stop sign, feeling more at ease. Then again, their hotel was outside the city, and the streets wouldn't stay this calm for long.

"Won't it be dangerous in Rome?" he shouted over the wind.

"That's not where we're going," Jace shouted back. "Another surprise."

That sounded great! No more cramming into a shuttle bus with other tourists or riding a packed subway. Having their own mode of transportation would be liberating, and so much easier on his legs. Ben took in the scenery until they reached the main road. Then he rested his cheek against Jace's back, hugging him until he felt the vehicle slow again. The road was ascending, providing them with a view of charming farms and distant green hills—a welcome sight after so many days spent in a hectic city.

They turned on a curve, passing through a small town. As

the scooter breezed past boutique stores, Ben decided he could handle more walking if it meant an opportunity to shop, but this didn't seem to be their destination. Soon they entered what resembled a narrow alley, but as it continued and branched off into other directions, he realized it was the standard system for roads here. Old stone homes walled them in from each side, a cobbled path providing just enough room for pedestrians. He was glad they weren't in a full-sized car. The street was barely wide enough for any sort of vehicle, resulting in one-way traffic only, but he liked how it didn't remind him of anywhere back home.

They entered a market square—a large courtyard surrounded by massive buildings. Flowers blossomed from hanging baskets and planters, a sun-baked man sold produce from a cart, and three scraggly musicians played their instruments on a corner, steadily earning coins. In the center of it all were tables, each with its own umbrella to shield café customers from the hot sun. Jace stopped near this, parking the scooter with expert skill. No way was this his first time driving one!

"Where are we?" Ben asked as they disembarked.

"Tivoli," Jace said. "You're going to love it here. We'll see the Renaissance gardens of the *Villa d'Este*, stroll across the *Ponte Gregoriano* to check out the waterfall, and then I'll take you to *Villa Adriana*. That belonged to Emperor Hadrian, who was gay. If you don't know his story, then I'll tell it to you over a picnic. It's very romantic. And tragic. He lost the love of his life much sooner than he should have."

Ben chuckled and shook his head. "This is your angle, huh? You whisk boys away to Italy to show off with your fancy foreign words, history lessons, and scooter driving skills, just so they'll fall in love with you."

Jace smiled. "Is it working?"

Yes. Most definitely, but Ben didn't rush into relationships as fast as he once had. He still sped along, but when it came to his heart, he was more cautious about who he gave it to. Although if this kept up, he wouldn't have a choice. Instead of answering the question with words, he kissed Jace. Then he looked around once more. "So… What's next?"

"*Gelato*," Jace said, pronouncing the word with a perfect Italian accent, but for once, Ben didn't need a translation.

"Ice cream," he said.

Jace nodded. "Yup. Beats donuts."

"For breakfast?"

Jace grinned. "Yeah!"

"Ice cream for breakfast," Ben repeated, shaking his head. "Is that even a thing?"

Jace wrapped an arm around his shoulders and guided him forward. After placing a kiss on his cheek, he whispered in Ben's ear, "A few months ago, we weren't a thing either. But now we are. Right?"

Ben tried to pull away, the breath in his ear tickling, but there was no getting away from that grip. Oh yes, they were most definitely a thing! Ben's legs protested, but he ignored them. The way he was feeling now, he would gladly walk around the entire globe, as long as he could do so with Jace at his side.

———

Something Like Enemies

by Jay Bell

Houston, Texas
2006

-rumble rumble-

Caesar pulled his head from beneath the pillow, swiped his hair back so he could see better, and groped around for his phone. Then he brought it close and squinted until the screen came into focus. Without his glasses, he practically needed to press his nose to the phone, but that was okay. If he couldn't wake up next to Nathaniel, this was the next best thing to a good-morning kiss. Although something was a little off today. The text message in particular.

good night my darling prince

Caesar grinned despite already having read this before falling asleep. Where was the text message that had awakened him? Then he heard another rumble, this one strong enough to shake the house. A storm. *That's* what had roused him from sleep. Caesar flopped back into bed, deciding to snooze a little longer. Then another idea occurred to him. Sitting up in bed, he reached for his glasses. The old red-framed ones that he wouldn't be caught dead in. Literally. Maybe he should let his parents know these wishes, just in case he checked out sooner than expected. *If the funeral is open-casket, make sure the undertaker puts in my contacts first.* He didn't care if that made practical sense. The idea amused him too much. Once the glasses were on his nose, he stared at the screen, his attention darting between the time at the top and the empty white space where a text message should be. Like clockwork, it came.

I'm up and already thinking about you

Which parts of you are up, Caesar replied, *and what sort of thoughts are you having?*

He let one of his hands snake beneath the sheets in anticipation of the answer, already imagining it was Nathaniel's touch he felt instead.

"Honey? Are you awake?" These words were followed by a light rapping on his bedroom door.

Caesar stifled a groan. His hands were already above the covers again, the mood instantly killed.

"Breakfast is ready. It's your favorite!"

"Thanks, Mom," Caesar called in return. "I'll be right down."

He rose and pulled on flannel pajama bottoms and an old T-shirt. He made use of the private bathroom attached to his room, already knowing he would soon miss such luxuries. Then he put in his contacts and grabbed his phone on the way out. He paused while walking down the hallway to read Nathaniel's response.

wanna know how bad I miss you? I think I could hammer a nail into the wall with this thing.

Caesar bit his bottom lip. Could he get away with sexting while at the breakfast table? He hated to leave Nathaniel hanging, but the idea of trying to hide his own arousal while his brothers and sisters slowly chewed on sausage links and scrambled eggs... Nope. He couldn't do it.

You're on your own. Sorry. Mom is already getting clingy.

Nathaniel would understand why. Caesar considered providing him with a few helpful suggestions on what he could do to himself, but before he could, another door in the hall opened. Jason's hair was a mess from sleep, his eyes wide when he spotted Caesar. Then his expression became steely as he marched across the hall to the bathroom, slamming the door behind him.

"Good morning to you too," Caesar said with a sigh.

He wasn't surprised by this behavior. Caesar only had himself to blame. Ever since Jason had shown up at the campus library to catch him and Nathaniel kissing, things had been uneasy between them. To put it mildly. The news that would break today would either make the situation better or worse. He wasn't sure, but he intended to defuse that bomb now. Or at least let it detonate in a controlled environment.

Caesar knocked on the bathroom door. "Jason? Hey. You got a second?"

He listened, only hearing intentional silence. It had to be. Nobody was that quiet in the bathroom.

"If you're on the pot," Caesar said, trying humor, "pinch it off and finish later. We need to talk."

He heard the shower curtain being ripped to one side and the water coming on. Caesar sighed again. He'd tried. That's all he could do, short of picking the lock and— He stopped, knowing where such thoughts would lead. He wasn't over Jason. Caesar still found him adorable, still wanted to hold him close, brush the bangs from his forehead, and make those sad eyes a little happier with each kiss. He still felt an overwhelming urge to watch over him. Jason was like a lost puppy wandering the streets. Only a monster wouldn't try to help. And yet, the kind of help Caesar had provided only seemed to do more harm than good.

With this in mind, he continued down the hall and descended the stairs. His worries were easier to forget when he smelled french toast. His mother, Constance, stopped him on the way to the table to kiss his cheek and murmur how proud she was of him. That was nice. The envious glare from Peter wasn't, but Caesar shrugged it off and sat.

"What's keeping Jason so long?" his mother complained, looking toward the stairs. "Todd, would you go up there and—"

"His stomach is upset," Caesar said before his father could rise. "Jason said we should start without him."

Constance pursed her lips. Then she nodded and moved to begin serving. Caesar hopped to his feet and grabbed the tray of toast before she could, putting slices on his parents' plates first and dishing out more to his siblings. Including his younger brother.

"Suck up," Peter mumbled under his breath.

"Learn from the master," Caesar murmured, a grin plastered on his face. He didn't have to fake it. He was excited. In truth, today would be a day like any other. The only difference would be an acknowledgement of how things were going to change, and they would all be happier because of it. Even Peter.

"Thanks, Mom!" Caesar said when he was seated again. "This looks great!" He swiped the bottle of syrup out of Amy's hands, and when her angelic little face started to crumple, he poured some on her toast in the shape of a heart. Then he doused his plate and began stuffing himself, covertly checking his phone to see what Nathaniel had to say.

the hammer experiment was a success. nails are in the wall, photos are hung. so am I. you're really missing out.

And another.

now I want to see if I can shoot a hole through a phone book.

Caesar snorted and coughed, claiming that he had swallowed wrong when his mother became concerned. That's when Jason showed up, hair damp from the shower.

"Is your stomach feeling better?" Constance asked.

Before Jason could look too puzzled, Caesar interjected with, "Those must have been some bad stomach cramps. Your face was all twisted up."

"I'm fine," Jason mumbled. Then he turned to Amy. "My face always looks like that." He scrunched it up and stuck out his tongue, to her delight.

Constance seemed to relax too. She encouraged Jason to load up his plate while there was still toast left, and once he had, she cleared her throat. "It's Saturday morning, and you all know what that means."

"Chore rewards," Peter said dutifully. "I'll vacuum."

More like he would run the vacuum behind closed doors while playing a handheld video game. Caesar didn't begrudge him that indulgence, since he himself was rarely expected to do more than get good grades and keep his room tidy.

"We have an extra special reward today," Constance continued. "We'll be going to the Downtown Aquarium for a family outing." Her eyes were shining when she focused on Caesar. "All of us."

He smiled back, making sure her attention was elsewhere before he dared to look at Jason. They were rarely in the same room together. Since the fallout, they had an unspoken truce to avoid each other as much as possible. Meals were the one exception. Those couldn't be avoided, although Caesar had seen Jason burn through a number of strategies. The first was to eat as quickly as possible and then ask to be excused. This was repeatedly denied, so Jason switched to clearing plates away the second he was done eating, like an over-eager waiter. When this drew complaints from his parents, Jason settled on eating slowly and deliberately, his concentration locked on his food at all times. Caesar tried to help by not talking as much, or by excusing himself early whenever he could. Not today though. They would be together, and that no doubt weighed heavily on both their minds.

"Do they have dolphins at the aquarium?" Amy asked.

"I don't think so," Caesar replied. "We'll make it work anyway. It'll be a lot of fun, I promise."

He hoped these words weren't lost on Jason. Rather than make him uncomfortable with further glances, Caesar focused on his food. As soon as Peter began dominating the conversation—which he always got around to eventually—he felt free to look back down at his phone.

no luck on the phone book experiment, Nathaniel had texted, *although I think I've begun my career as an artist. ever heard of Jackson Pollock?*

That sounded familiar. Caesar googled the name to be sure. Then he sent back his response. *Next time, I want to be your canvas.*

He was grinning at his own cleverness when he heard Jason say something about his stomach. By the time Caesar looked up, the chair where he'd been sitting was empty.

The Downtown Aquarium seemed to suffer from an identity crisis, unsure if it wanted to be a theme park, a restaurant, a zoo, or as the title suggested, an aquarium. The variety it offered made it the ideal choice. Caesar had been allowed to choose the venue for today and had thought little of his own needs, aware of how his adopted siblings viewed him. He was the spoiled biological child—the heir apparent—with his own lenient set of rules. That they didn't despise him completely was a miracle. The bias in his favor wasn't his own creation, and although he didn't resist it, he did try to set the balance right when he could. Like today.

Amy was easy. She was still young enough that anything bright and colorful made her happy. This included exotic fish, and even better, a ride on the Shark Voyage Train, which drove straight into the middle of a massive aquarium. Not through the glass, thankfully, but rather a tunnel that passed through the bottom center, creating the illusion that they were moving along the ocean floor. Peter's mood always improved around electronics, so he was ecstatic about the arcade, and Carrie enjoyed the carnival rides, which must have provided the perfect music video visuals to the tunes constantly pumping through her headphones. That just left one person, who Caesar only wished he could make happy. Although Jason *did* perk up during an outdoor portion of the train ride, just as they were passing by a lake and an animatronic shark broke the surface. While the robotic beast gnashed its teeth, Jason glanced over at Caesar, perhaps hoping the shark would swallow him whole so they would never have to be around each other again. If so, he'd get his wish soon enough.

They ended the afternoon at the white tiger exhibit. The environment was supposed to resemble some sort of temple in India, but there was no lush grass here or warm sunlight. Instead the exhibit was located in a basement with concrete floors and a few murky pools. Peter banged on the glass wall and laughed when this agitated one of the tigers. Amy and Carrie were pensive. Jason looked downright miserable. He had a soft spot for animals. Caesar moved toward him, just in case he needed someone to complain to. Or something else to focus on that he disliked even more. Caesar hadn't even reached his side before Jason noticed him coming and walked away.

"This is certainly… interesting," Constance said, not seeming pleased herself. "Who's ready for dinner?"

"I am!" Caesar said, mostly to get the others going.

"We haven't done the stingray reef yet," Peter complained. "They let you pet them!"

He felt a shiver run down his spine. "I am *not* touching one of those things."

"You don't have to," Peter shot back. "I'll do it. I'm not a wimp!"

"No one will be petting those poor things," Constance said. "Come along. It's time to eat."

"Will there be a birthday cake?" Amy asked.

"It's not anyone's birthday," Caesar said, tickling her on the way out.

"They should stick to proper aquariums and nothing more," Constance whispered to her husband. "First tigers and now stingrays. This is shameful."

Jason overheard this and smiled.

Caesar fell back a few paces, watching his family from a distance and recognizing that this was how it would be from now on. Six people instead of seven. He was okay with that, but he wanted to be sure it would work for Jason. Seeing him smile just now was a hopeful sign.

Caesar entered the restaurant in high spirits. The place

reminded him of the gimmicky Rainforest Café that Amy adored so much, except this one had an underwater theme. The walls were sculpted to resemble coral reefs, massive aquariums set into them that illuminated the dining area in a blue glow. Lamps shaped like fish hung from the ceiling—providing a warm ambience. The effect was impressive, their shared wonder lasting for most of the meal. Once the main courses were cleared away, everyone was pressured to order dessert, and when these arrived, Caesar braced himself for embarrassment. Sure enough, his mother stood up.

"As you know," she began, "Caesar applied to ten different colleges." She held up an envelope that had already been opened. "This isn't the only acceptance letter he received, but it's the only one that matters to this family." She looked at her husband.

Todd stood too, taking the envelope from her. "Probably a local community college," he joked. "A shame, because I was hoping you would follow in my footsteps." As he pulled out the letter, he did a credible job of appearing surprised. His parents already knew. Of course they did. They had practically watched the mailbox in shifts. "There must be some mistake," Todd said, shaking his head. "This letter is from Yale. And they've accepted you."

His parents sat again. The table was silent, but after an awkward pause, someone did start clapping. Caesar looked over at Jason, who he could swear was glaring behind those long bangs before a smile broke out.

"That's awesome," Jason said, almost sounding like he meant it.

"Isn't it?" Constance enthused. She looked at her other children, who began clapping too.

All except Amy. "Where's Yale?" she asked.

"Connecticut," Caesar replied, and before she could ask where that was, he put it in terms she could understand. "You would have to drive an entire day and night to get there."

Her little brow furrowed. "You're moving away?"

"Afraid so, kiddo. This is good though. Someday you'll move away too. Maybe to Connecticut. Then we can be roommates!"

Amy began to sulk. "But I don't want you to go!"

Jason's chair was shoved backward as he stood. "Can I be excused? I want to look at the rain forest exhibit again."

"Sit down!" Constance snapped. "You haven't even touched your dessert." Her gaze softened when she looked to Caesar. "We won't have many more family meals like this. Not with everyone here."

Jason sat and started spooning ice cream into his mouth while looking miserable. Amy followed his example. His other siblings were apathetic to his departure, so Caesar focused on his own dessert while discussing his future with his parents. He kept sneaking glances at Jason, whose mood only seemed to worsen, so once their plates were cleared away, he tried to do something about it.

"I want to see that rain forest area again too," Caesar said. "It was really cool. Mind if Jason and I go check it out?"

He was already on his feet, not waiting for an answer.

"I want to go back to the arcade," Peter said.

"Not on your own," Constance said.

"I'll go with him!" Amy chimed in.

"That's not what I meant," Constance replied.

Caesar looked at Carrie, staring at her until she pulled one of the buds from her ears.

"Huh?"

"Can you take Peter and Amy to the arcade?" he asked, expression pleading. "That way Mom and Dad can have some alone time. Why not order a bottle of wine?" he said, turning to them. "Make it romantic."

"I don't know," Constance said, her head already starting to shake.

"It'll be fun," Todd said, reaching to place a hand over hers. "Just a glass each."

His mother's cheeks grew rosy. That was as good as permission!

Caesar jerked his head toward the exit, only going that way when certain Jason would follow. "Don't worry," he said as soon as they were out of earshot. "You don't have to hang out with me. Once we're around this corner…"

Jason picked up the pace. When he rounded the corner, he didn't slow down. Caesar did, although he made sure to stay within visual range. Jason really did seem interested in the rainforest room, walking up to one of the tanks. Caesar hung back and pulled out his phone. He'd missed a text from Nathaniel.

come see me. tonight.

If only that were possible! Normally he would wait until his family was asleep and sneak out, but with his mother feeling sentimental, he could imagine her knocking on his door late at night, just to tuck him in. Embarrassing, but part of him would miss her affectionate little gestures.

Tomorrow, he wrote back. *I promise. What do you want to do? Besides the obvious.*

He leaned against a wall and waited. Nathaniel wasn't responding. That happened on occasion, when he got busy. Caesar grew increasingly bored. He stopped looking at the screen and switched to watching Jason as he moved along the glass. He didn't seem as tense now. Caesar glanced back down at his phone, and when it still didn't have anything to offer, he pocketed it and pushed away from the wall.

"Pretty cool," he said. "Isn't it?"

Jason spared him the briefest glance before returning his attention to an underwater world. "Yeah."

Caesar walked closer. "I thought you would be happier. With the news. I'll be out of your life soon. That's what I wanted to talk to you about this morning."

Jason swallowed and said nothing.

"You should put a claim on my room before Peter does," Caesar said, standing at his side and watching an eel wriggle by. "Tell him it's because you're older. I don't think Carrie will want it. She's planning on moving out with her boyfriend. Just wait until Mom finds out about that."

"I agree with Amy," Jason mumbled.

"Huh?"

"Nothing."

Did he mean... Caesar thought it through a few times, just to be sure, and was unable to find any other interpretation. "You don't want me to go?"

"That doesn't mean I like you!" Jason shot back.

Caesar laughed, but only because he was happy. "Huh. I thought you hated me."

Jason shrugged.

"Can't we be friends?" Caesar spoke quickly in case Jason

tried to escape. "If only for the rest of the night. I'm leaving anyway. What difference would it make? Give me the next half hour. Or better yet, as long I'm still in Texas. Please."

Jason swallowed again and looked over at him. "Why?"

"Because part of me doesn't want to go. Because I like you. Because..." Caesar shook his head. "I don't want it to end this way, with us not talking. You can hate me all you want. Just wait until I'm gone."

"I don't keep my distance because I hate you," Jason croaked.

Caesar sighed. "That's not why I stay away from you either." His stomach sank when Jason walked away, but he only moved to the opposite wall. Caesar followed cautiously. "You really like it here, huh?"

Jason nodded. "It's beautiful. And sad."

"What do you mean?"

"That school of fish," he said, nodding to where a dozen orange bodies slid gracefully through the water. "I wish I knew how that felt."

Caesar made a face. "You don't know how to swim?"

"I do, it's just..." Jason touched his hands to the glass. "They're synchronized. They all want the same thing and are going in the same direction. I've never felt that way. With anyone."

Caesar was about to claim that nobody did, but then he thought of his parents, and how content he was to follow their guidance as a child. When he outgrew them, he found like-minded friends instead. And then there were the people he had fallen in love with. Nathaniel. Steph. The guy standing right in front of him. He hated to think that Jason had never felt that sort of connection. How lonely that must be. Or maybe he simply hadn't recognized it.

"We had that," Caesar said, moving closer. He reached around Jason, placing his palms against the cold glass, and murmured in his ear. "Remember?"

Jason spun around, his back against the aquarium, but he didn't try to escape. "What are you doing?"

"Reminding you," Caesar said. "You'll find this again with someone else. Until then, don't forget, because if you got there once, you can do so again."

Jason's eyes were vulnerable, his bottom lip starting to tremble. "I won't find it."

"You will, and you won't be alone until then." Caesar let his arms drop. "You fit into this family. My parents can be a pain, I know, but they love you. So does Amy, and you get along with Peter better than I ever did. Those schools of fish look graceful from the outside, but I bet when you're in the middle of it all, it feels crowded. Just imagine those other fish telling you what to do and where to go, when all a guy wants is to make his own way in the world. That's family. It only looks harmonious from the outside."

Jason managed a smile. Then he turned around again, just in time for a massive turtle to swim by. "That's me," he said, nodding at it. "The only home I have is on my back, and I take it with me when I go."

Caesar snorted. Then he threw an arm around Jason's neck, yanking him closer in a playful headlock. "You're so dramatic! I think I get it now. You *want* to be seen as a loner."

"It's not an act," Jason pouted. Then he managed a subtle smile. "I'm just that cool. Admit it."

"You're the coolest," Caesar replied. "Come here." He pulled Jason close for a hug. "It's going to be okay. Take my place when I'm gone. My parents will be sad, and you can be their golden boy. Don't let Peter rule the roost. Promise me! I can't stand the idea. Make it your home. You deserve that."

"I'll try," Jason's muffled voice replied.

Caesar rubbed his back, intending to comfort him. Then his hand moved up to the messy hair. Caesar's body was reacting, but so was his heart. It never seemed to run out of love. He felt plenty now. For Jason. Caesar knew he needed to think of Nathaniel too, but one never seemed to cancel out the other like it did for most people. He wasn't sure why. All he wanted was to make sure Jason understood how special he was, no matter if that took words or something more. Caesar pulled back just enough to move his hand around to Jason's cheek. Their eyes met, their lips drawing near...

"Hey. Guys."

Caesar released Jason and spun to face the voice. It was only Carrie. She understood. Caesar had covered for her on numerous occasions too. They could both keep a secret. Her head tilted toward the hallway behind her, where Peter and Amy could be heard arguing. Caesar nodded his thanks. Carrie put her earbuds back in and returned to her own private soundtrack.

"What do you think?" Caesar said in low tones. "Can we be friends again?"

Jason's smile was tight. "Only if you agree to pet a stingray."

"Anything but that!" Caesar said in mock terror. He smiled at Amy and Peter when they entered the room. "Come on, guys. We're going to do that thing that Mom forbid us to." He led the way to the aquarium's glorified petting zoo, already dreading what would happen there, but he would play along. If it made Jason happy, even for just one night, then it was worth it. By the time he felt his phone vibrate again, Caesar had already decided to leave it in his pocket.

-rumble rumble-

Caesar forced himself to sit up in bed, blinked against the brightness of the morning, and reached for his glasses. He could tell from the light outside that there wasn't another storm, so he reached for his phone, discovering a text message from Nathaniel. Three in fact.

are you here yet?
are you here yet?
are you here yet?

Caesar laughed and shot a message back. *Don't make me pull this car over!* After a mighty yawn he added. *Breakfast with my family. Then I'll be on my way. Have you showered yet?*

no.

Good. Wait for me.

He yawned again and went through his usual morning rituals. He thought about the night before, how much fun he had hanging out at the aquarium. Like old times, or maybe even better, since everyone had gotten along so well. Caesar had talked his parents into another round of drinks, promising he would drive everyone safely home. While they sat in the restaurant together sipping wine, the rest of them returned to the amusement park area, playing games and hitting the rides. Best of all, he and Jason were talking again. At least until they came home, when Jason disappeared into his room and didn't come out. Caesar wasn't sure what to make of that, but he was eager to see where they stood today.

He was the first one at the breakfast table, his attention pulled away from his phone each time someone entered the room. Jason was the last to arrive. He didn't make eye contact. Maybe he was tired. As the meal neared its end, Caesar had his answer. Jason participated in conversation, but never replied to him directly or looked in his direction. The only exception happened while Caesar was responding to a text from Nathaniel. He'd tried to do so without anyone noticing, and when he saw Jason grimace, he put away the phone entirely. Not that it seemed to make a difference. Jason was the first to leave the table, as soon as he was allowed.

Caesar was in the upstairs hallway, returning to his bedroom, when the door to Jason's room opened and he was greeted with a muted, "Hey."

"Hey!" Caesar replied, feeling a burst of optimism. "How's it going?"

"I can't do it," Jason blurted out. "I can't be your friend. Or your brother. Or… anything else. Not with him around. It's too hard."

Caesar felt like the wind had been knocked out of him, but he nodded his understanding, because he wasn't sure he could keep up the act either. He loved Jason. Pretending otherwise would be impossible. "So back to how it was before?"

"Yeah," Jason said. "Sorry."

"I am too," Caesar said. "Not for what we had. I liked that. But I do regret hurting you."

Jason rolled his eyes. "Stop being nice. It doesn't help."

"Okay then," Caesar said, standing upright. "In that case, I'm going to sell my room to Peter for fifty bucks. I figure you won't be able to handle being in there, since the place is positively soaked in my sexy man energy."

"Stop being charming too," Jason said. "Go back to being an asshole. It makes it easier to pretend that I don't like you."

"*Back* to being an asshole?" Caesar said in mock offense. He felt his phone vibrate. That's when he knew what he needed to do. He pulled it out and pretended to read the text. "Nathaniel," he confided, as if any explanation was needed. "I need to get ready so I can go see him. Have fun at church."

Jason looked hurt, but he nodded and in a strained voice said, "Thanks."

Caesar didn't reply. He kept his attention on his phone until he was in his bedroom. Then he shut the door and exhaled. After collecting himself, he sent a text.

I can't wait to get out of here.

that bad?

No. That good. Otherwise this would be easy. Caesar comforted himself with the vision he'd had yesterday. A house full of foster kids without him as competition, and in one case, without a constant reminder of what could have been. As for Caesar, he would finally be free to love who he wanted. Despite his heavy heart, he reminded himself that this was for the best. A happy ending for those he would leave behind, and for himself, a new life where anything was possible.

Something Like Stories: Volume Three

Something Like Then

by Jay Bell

Austin, Texas
2008

Piece of you. Piece of me. Too worn down to recognize.

Allison's car swerved, the tires going over the curb before hitting the street again. When Ben looked out the window, he almost expected to see his childhood home there. He could easily imagine they were teenagers again, driving through his hometown of The Woodlands. That had everything to do with the events of the night, which began with a guilty-pleasure meal of fast food picked up from the drive thru. They had eaten this in her car, like they used to when wanting to avoid high school bullies. Or certain ex-boyfriends. Allison always had more of those than Ben did, but the one serious relationship he'd managed... Well, it was memorable, to say the least. It was hard not to think of Tim now, especially while this song was playing. *Milford Lake*, a B-side from the *Hedwig and the Angry Inch* soundtrack. Ben was tempted to skip to *Wicked Little Town* next, since that song really brought back those old feelings.

Then again, why stew on the past when the evening had been so awesome? After their deep-fried indulgence, they had taken in a lighthearted movie. Then they had driven around while singing—a karaoke bar bouncing through downtown Austin on four wheels. No alcohol was involved. They got enough of a buzz from belting out tunes together. Although a drink didn't sound so bad now.

"Do you want to come inside?" Ben asked, turning down the stereo at the end of the song.

"A nightcap?" Allison asked, pretending to be scandalized. "What would my darling husband say?"

She wiggled the fingers of her left hand so her ring would catch the light. Then she pulled her hand away again just as quickly, sandwiching it between her thigh and the car seat.

"Sorry," she said. "Dumb joke."

Ben snorted. "Why? Are you seriously worried that I'll think you're hitting on me?" Then, in a stage whisper, he added, "Or has Brian bugged the car? Is he that controlling?"

"No," Allison said. "It's just... Never mind. Do you need me to come inside?"

Ben stared at her. Why was she acting so weird? "Need is putting it strongly. I thought a glass of wine would be nice. Then again, we both have to work in the morning."

"True. But I can stay if you want."

If she felt like staying longer, she would be out of the car by now. He knew that Allison was in a good place with Brian. There was talk of them starting a family. Maybe she was eager to return home so they could get that going. He wasn't about to ask her if he was right, so instead he said, "You can walk me to my door. Just don't try to kiss me. My mother is probably watching us as we speak."

Allison laughed and shut off the engine. "Deal!"

After they left the car, she took his arm as they strolled across the overgrown lawn. Ben had once again forgotten to mow it, and speaking of being behind, he could already see letters sticking out of the mailbox next to the door. Bills, no doubt, in a variety of pretty colors to remind him how late he was on paying each. He decided to ignore them for tonight, listening instead to Allison sing under her breath. That was beautiful. And comforting. Spending time with her was his favorite thing in the world. How nice that, after so many years—over a decade, in fact—some things remained the same.

"I hope you never outgrow me," he said.

Allison laughed, like he was being silly. "That year we spent apart when you were in Chicago was the worst. So you better hope you never outgrow me, because I'm not going anywhere. I'll stalk you, Ben. If you refuse to see me, I'll break into your house and sleep beneath your bed every night, just to listen to you breathe."

Now it was Ben's turn to laugh. "That's so creepy. I love it! Can we do that anyway? Just once?"

"What makes you think I haven't already?" Allison said as they reached the porch.

They stopped there to face each other. Now it really did feel like a date, including the awkward pause where a kiss would fit perfectly.

"I guess this is it," Ben said, leaning toward her. "I had a wonderful night..."

Allison put her stamp of approval on their date by kissing

him. On the cheek, of course. When she pulled back, her eyes were watery.

"Sorry," Allison said, wiping at them.

"Are you okay?"

"Yeah! Are you?"

Ben shrugged. "Why wouldn't I be?"

"No reason. It just makes me happy to see you doing so well. I'm proud of the man you've become."

Ben snorted. "Thanks, Mom."

Allison laughed and shook her head to show that she was serious. "You've come a long way. We both have. Look at us, all grown up, steady jobs, houses of our own…"

Ben glanced over at the bills before remembering his intent to ignore them. "Do you feel grown up?" he asked. "Because I still feel like I'm faking it."

"I have those moments too. But I remember being upset a lot when we were teenagers, and worrying that things wouldn't work out. The future was a lot scarier then."

"Definitely," Ben said, nodding his agreement.

"Now things are steady. You know? Do you feel that way too?"

It was a complicated question with a simple answer, because this was his life, and yeah, he didn't ever see it changing. Not significantly. He would continue to wake up, go to work, borrow money from his parents when necessary and pay it back in installments even when they insisted he didn't have to. The system wasn't perfect, but it worked.

"Yeah. Things are nice and steady."

"Good!" Allison said, squeezing him with a hug. "You know where to find me if it ever gets crazy, right?"

"Sure do," Ben said, pulling away. "Is there something you're not telling me? Are you okay?"

"I'm fine. It's just been an emotional day. And I love you."

"I love you too," Ben replied. "Now I'm cutting you off from the wine before you've had a single sip. You've always been a weepy drunk, but this is a new record for you."

"What?" When Allison spoke next, her words were dripping with attitude. "I've *always* been able to handle my booze. *You're* the one who would be a mess after the first drink. Remember that time I had to disconnect the phone and hide it in the closet so you couldn't use it to call you-know-who?"

"Nope," Ben said, breaking eye contact. "I don't remember that at all."

"And when you found out where I'd hidden the phone, I believe your exact words were 'I'm going back in the closet! It's the only place where we can be together!'"

Ben fought down a smile. "Doesn't ring a bell, sorry. Maybe you're thinking of someone else."

"Oh, my *other* gay best friend from high school. That must be it." She shook her head. "There's only one way to settle this. Tequila shots, next weekend, you and me."

"You've got it!" Ben said, already knowing he would lose. It would be fun anyway. He tilted his head toward the front door. "I better start training."

"Okay," Allison said. "I'll probably be up for another hour or two, if you want to talk."

"You're giving me permission to drunk dial you?" Ben asked. He didn't wait for an answer, or need to, since they were too similar, and he would be fine with her calling under those circumstances. Especially since it usually resulted in drunken confessions that he could tease her about later. "Text me when you get home."

"I will."

They hugged again and said goodbye. He waited until she was in her car before he turned and unlocked the front door. He was greeted by a series of frantic meows. Samson was looking up at him, as if demanding an explanation.

"Were you eavesdropping?" Ben asked. "Wondering why your daddy was standing on the other side of that door and ignoring you, huh?"

Samson meowed again, firmly, as if his point had been made.

Ben kicked the door shut behind him and bent over to pick up Samson. "Okay, big boy. Let's get you fed."

He walked into the kitchen and set the cat down on the counter, where he normally ate. Ben took a plate out of the cupboard and a can from the pantry, Samson weaving between his arms and getting in the way during the entire process. Ben didn't complain, even when the tip of a tail brushed against his nose and almost made him sneeze. The instant the cat food landed on the plate, Ben was forgotten as Samson scarfed down what the can described as a fisherman's feast. Ben pitied the poor sailor who had to eat cat food for dinner or any meal.

Parental duties complete, he was free to open a bottle of wine. The fancy kind that cost less than five bucks. He couldn't afford more, and anything expensive would be wasted on him anyway. Ben only had the smallest appreciation for the taste. A warm buzz was the main draw for him. What better way to end the weekend? He grabbed his phone and carried his drink to the living room. Then he sat on the couch and raised his glass to Jace's photo on the end table. The one of him in his full flight attendant uniform, complete with jacket.

"Cheers, baby!" Ben said.

He took a sip and set down the glass so he could check his phone, in case Allison had made it home already. That's when he noticed that he hadn't turned it back on since the movie. He pressed the power button, and once the phone had booted up, received a voicemail notification. From his mom. She usually called during the day, not at night. Worried that something bad had happened, Ben played the message back.

"Hi, honey! I just wanted to check in. I know today was probably rough. You've always been my brave little boy, so I know you're fine. I still worry though. You can always call me if you need to, okay? I love you." After a ruffling sound, the voice on the recording became much deeper. "I love you too, son. Come see us soon, okay?" More muffled noises accompanied his father saying, "Do I just hang it up? Oh. Which button? Yes, I'm serious. Your phone is completely different from mine! I miss the old kind."

A beep finally signaled the end of the message. Ben laughed while feeling confused. Why would his mother think that today would be hard for him? Then it clicked. His dentist appointment! That would indeed be a traumatizing event for him, and yeah, normally he would call to whine about it, although she had the dates wrong. His appointment was next week, but he'd already decided to cancel. He wasn't having any dental problems, making the checkup an unnecessary expense. If he had any hidden cavities, he'd deal with them when they started hurting.

Putting the issue out of mind, he set down his phone, grabbed the glass of wine, and angled himself so he could see Jace's photo better.

"I had a nice day," Ben said. "I went over to Allison's place for lunch and to help her sort through her clothes. She's getting rid of a bunch of stuff, which seems crazy to me, because most of it was perfectly fine, but no longer in style. Being a guy is easier that way. I could wear the same sweater every winter for twenty years, and I bet nobody would notice. Assuming it wasn't falling apart. Fashion doesn't change for us guys very much, does it? Lucky you, or else I'd have to tape little outfits to your photo. Sort of like a paper doll." Ben thought about it while taking another swig. "I would love that actually. A tiny cut-out Jace I could dress up."

Samson wandered in from the kitchen to sit on the floor in front of him, licking a paw and using it to clean his whiskers as he listened.

"Anyway, the good news is that she's giving her old clothes away, so it's not like they'll go to waste. And if you're wondering, yes, she made me try on most of them and took a bunch of photos while laughing her ass off. I don't know why I love her so much. I tried to make her feel guilty by pointing out that it's hateful to mock people who enjoy crossdressing. Allison agreed and said it's only funny when I do it."

Jace would probably find that amusing. How nice it would be to hear him laugh again. Ben sighed. If anyone else was here, he would ignore the photo, or at least not speak to it. He knew that Jace couldn't actually hear him. Probably. But this was all they had left. He supposed it would be a sad sight for another person to witness, but hey, at least he wasn't completely alone. He patted his lap, hoping Samson would take the hint, but the cat wasn't done grooming yet.

"Don't get jealous," Ben said, still addressing the photo, "but Allison took me out on a date to thank me for helping her. I had a very *very* healthy salad, of course. I'm always watching my figure for you! Afterwards we went and saw *Wall-E*. You would have loved it. There's this cute little robot in a post-apocalyptic world and— That part is just okay. It gets really good when he reconnects with humanity. Talk about looking in the mirror. Or more like a crystal ball, because that's totally where our civilization is headed. I'm not doing the story justice, but it's a way better movie than *Cars*. Did you see that? When did it come out?"

Ben grabbed his phone to check. *Cars* was released in early two-thousand six, which means they could have seen it together, because Jace hadn't died until—

The events of the day rearranged themselves. Allison keeping him busy. Each of her concerned expressions that she quickly hid. Brian's upbeat tones that had seemed forced when he greeted Ben. The comfort food, the uplifting movie, the cathartic singing afterwards, and his mother... *You've always been my brave little boy.*

Ben felt like someone had not only ripped out his heart, but reached down his throat to do so. Everyone had remembered. Everyone but him, the person who should never forget that Jace had died on this date. And what had he done to pay tribute to his deceased husband? Ben's stomach turned. He'd had a carefree day, like none of it mattered. What's worse, he *had* thought about a long-lost love. Just not the right one.

Ben glanced at the clock. It wasn't too late. The day wasn't over yet.

"I'm sorry," he spluttered, his lip quivering when he turned back to the photo. "Today should have been about us. And it will be! I'll stay up all night if I have to. Um... Oh! I know!" Samson was trying to climb onto his lap, but now wasn't the time. Ben stood and went to the bedroom, returning with two scrapbooks and a box filled with photos and keepsakes. Then he sat on the floor, grabbing Jace's framed photo so it could join him. Which was silly, because as he opened the box and spread out the loose photos, he was *surrounded* by Jaces. Most of them smiled at him. Others had an arm around him, or kissed his hair, or ate birthday cakes, or posed in front of monuments. Jace laughed with his sister, his best friend, his parents. He lived dozens of little moments, each trapped in time. Ben stared at them all and wept. He finished one glass of wine and poured another. And another. Ben rose to put on music, the songs they liked to listen to, or those that Jace always asked him to sing. He couldn't tonight. Singing for him would hurt too much. Instead he returned to the small area of the carpet that remained clear. Samson climbed onto his lap as Ben touched little mementos from their past. Jace's old nametag from work. The hand-written letter he had left on Ben's pillow one Valentine's Day. Or even a miniature version of the Eiffel tower, the generic souvenir conjuring up memories of their trip to Paris as Ben ran his fingers along the textured surface. Being surrounded by so much of their relationship felt good, but it also stung, so he was disappointed after reaching again for the bottle of wine to discover it was empty.

That wouldn't do. Not one bit.

Ben gently lifted Samson and set him on the couch. Then he stood, patting his pockets for his keys, which he didn't have. Did he really need them? He was too drunk to drive, and a convenience store was just a few blocks away. It couldn't be more than a ten-minute walk in mild weather. Ben stumbled outside, walked down the street, and then doubled back when he realized he didn't have his wallet. He wanted to take Jace with him when leaving again, but he didn't truly need anything from the mess on the living room floor. The memories were powerful enough to accompany him on his walk: The scent of Jace's skin, the whispered promises, the feel of lips pressing against the back of his neck to wake him each morning.

Ben lurched through his neighborhood, glaring at the houses with warm glowing windows, and despairing at those that were dark, because that's what he had become. An empty home. A fireplace that was no longer lit. He had tried to keep the flames stoked, but it was getting harder. How could he forget this pain? Even for one second!

He reached the main road, the convenience store a neon beacon across the street. Another bottle of wine would kill the pain. Ben hit the button for the pedestrian crosswalk. He stood there and swayed while waiting for the signal to change, streaks of white and red lights making him blink as each car blew past. He was waiting now like he had been for the past two years. Waiting for the ache inside to stop, and for the brave heart that everyone spoke of to finally manifest. Now that it had, he felt terrible about it.

He was *supposed* to hurt! The pain proved how much he loved Jace. Moving on from that was the ultimate betrayal. And yet, if he was honest, Ben didn't want to always feel so tortured. It sapped the joy from life, put a strain on his friends and family, and made him think drastic thoughts, because it was too hard to go on living without him. And now that Ben had a taste of what life was like on the other side of that loss, he didn't want that either. There was no solution. He had died along with Jace. It had only taken him this long to finally realize the truth.

The pedestrian signal hadn't changed yet, not that it mattered. No more waiting. Ben closed his eyes and stepped out into the street.

He felt a warm hand wrap around his own. Long fingers and

a gentle grip. Jace had always done that when they crossed a street together. Every single time, like keeping Ben safe was his highest priority. Ben hadn't thought of that in ages. Probably not since Jace had died. He opened his eyes again, expecting to see him there, but Ben was alone. His hand was empty, and the car that was approaching him coasted to a gentle stop. The pedestrian light had changed from orange to white, so Ben crossed the street, trying to remember what that hand felt like again. It wasn't difficult. Ben kept imagining it, all the way to the other side of the street, and when the hand finally let go...

He tried to also.

"Here's what I've got," Ben said, after closing the front door behind him. Samson was dutifully sitting in the entryway, like he'd been waiting. "One of those honey buns that Jace liked so much. I'm going to eat it to soak up whatever wine is still sloshing around in my stomach. Then I'll wash it down with this neon-green Gatorade so I'm not too hung over in the morning. Don't worry. I didn't buy any more wine."

Samson yawned, as if not impressed. Or maybe it was just the increasingly late hour.

"I got canned chicken for you," Ben continued. "Maybe we should save that for breakfast, since you just ate. They also had this mouse, which they claim is a cat toy, even though it's so big that a dog would struggle to get its mouth around it. Anyway, the package says the mouse has catnip inside, and I'm totally willing to cut it open so you can get at the good stuff."

Ben shook the package, which attracted Samson's attention enough that the cat put his front paws on Ben's leg.

"We're going to celebrate Jace this time," Ben said, his chin starting to tremble before he got himself under control. He looked at the living room floor, which was still a mess, and sighed. "Within reason."

After fulfilling his promise to Samson—the cat rolling around in mouse guts made of cotton and catnip—Ben returned to the living room and crouched down to start picking up the photos. He was halfway through this process when he glanced up to see the framed photo of Jace, which he then returned to the end table.

"I really hope you can't see me," Ben said. "I know I usually hope for the opposite but..." He sighed. "I take it back.

Embarrassing or not, I wish you were here. You really did a number on me, you know that? It'll never be the same again. Not without you. I can't go back to who I used to be, but maybe I can still change. Just a little. Enough to get by, because if I'm honest, I don't want to die. I want to meet Allison's children and be an amazing uncle to them. And maybe I'll come home afterwards and let myself feel sad and miserable, but not all the time. I might forget to do that on occasion, and that's fine, because I don't think you would have liked seeing me this way."

Ben kept his head down while picking up the last of the photos. Once they were all back in the box, he sat on the couch and forced down the honey bun, shaking his head after each bite.

"How did you eat these things? And while we're on the subject, what kind of person thinks that fortune cookies actually taste good? They're a desperation dessert when there's no other choice."

Jace stared back, smiling shamelessly at him.

"Okay," Ben said as he rose. "Time for me to get some sleep."

He grabbed the photo and pressed sticky lips to Jace's face before setting it down again. Then he carried the scrapbook and memory box to the bedroom, returning them to the closet. He took out his phone and set it on the nightstand before he got undressed. Ben was under the covers for mere seconds before the mattress dipped and he felt a heavy weight settle against his legs. He reached down to scratch Samson behind the ear, the purrs that came in response a welcome comfort. Ben was on the verge of drifting off when he opened his eyes again and reached for his phone. He needed to send a text before he went to sleep. To Allison.

I hope this doesn't wake you, but I wanted to say thanks for making today so easy. And I thought you might like to know that—

Ben thought about it, wanting to be sure. And he was.

I'm okay. Everything is going to be all right.

Something Like Me

by Jay Bell

**Houston, Texas
2014**

"*You can be whatever you want. It's entirely up to you. Just promise me one thing…*"

Emma's hand trembled as she carefully pressed the photo to the black pages of a scrapbook. She had been careful not to apply too much glue. First she made sure to scan the photo—a perk of being in her parents' home office—in case it got damaged, because this one was special. They all were, if they featured a tall man with blonde hair. And amazing cheekbones that she had also inherited, although hers weren't nearly as prevalent. She blamed her father for that. Emma could have been skinny like her mother or uncle, rather than beefy like her dad. She didn't really mind though. People's tiresome comments about her weight could be annoying, but screw them. Their opinion didn't matter. That's what Jace had taught her.

Emma wiped her hands on the cotton dress she wore, wanting them to be clean before she gingerly pressed her fingertips to the photo, sealing it to the page forever. Then she leaned back to consider her work, pleased that the corners were even with the top of the scrapbook. That was important, especially considering this was the first page of the memory album, as she preferred to call it. She had created a few before and always found them helpful. Thoughts were easier to organize once outside her head. She could rearrange them as required, and right now, she needed all the help she could get.

Her attention flitted back to the content of the photo. Uncle Jace was standing next to a horse and holding the reins while smiling up at her in the saddle. Back when Emma took the photo, she had done so because she didn't want to forget the horse—the first she had ever ridden, and come to think of it, the last too. These days, whenever she saw the photo, she barely lingered on the mare. Jace was more important, and this was the only way she could see him, although her memories didn't quite match up. He had seemed so tall back then. No doubt he would still tower over her if alive today, but she was five foot nine and wouldn't have to crane her neck as much. Jace didn't look as old to her now either. He must have been in his late twenties when the photo was taken. Emma was on the verge of turning twenty herself. Eventually she would overtake him and become the older one. That was an odd thought, and not the rabbit hole that she was supposed to be tumbling into. She'd had years to come to terms with his passing, and while it still hurt, it wasn't a problem that needed to be solved. Not like the ache in her chest. Her present predicament was a more insistent pain, but the past did hold an important piece of the puzzle. Returning her attention to the memory album, Emma picked up a marker with silver ink, took off the cap, and wrote: *The day I began to figure it out*. Then she leaned back, reliving the memory while hoping to find answers there.

"How's your tush?"

Emma needed every ounce of willpower before she could tear her eyes away from the horse to consider her uncle. Jace was smiling up at her, holding the reins as he led them along the practice track, a boring oval loop. She couldn't wait to leave the ranch behind and go galloping off into the horizon. First they had to learn the basics. Or so the riding instructor kept telling them.

"My what?" she asked.

"Your tush," Jace repeated. When she shook her head he added, "Your backside. You know, the thing your father is always threatening to spank?"

"Fine, I guess," she said, making a face. "Why?"

"Because I remember how bad mine hurt. Your dad was always trying to get me to join the Boy Scouts. I was never interested until horse-riding week. I signed up just for that. All I remember is the horse not doing what I wanted and how bad my butt hurt afterwards." Jace's eyes went wide. "But it was great!" he said hurriedly. "You're going to love it!"

Emma had no doubt of that. She leaned forward to stroke the ivory mane of the mare she rode. She would tumble into that hair and lose herself in it, if that were possible.

"Are you enjoying yourself?" Jace asked.

Of course! This was her birthday wish. Emma had wanted to spend the day with her uncle and go horseback riding. The only other things she could ask for were lots of presents and a cake, which would happen later, so it really couldn't get better than this.

"I'm really happy," she answered.

Jace's smile got bigger. "So am I."

"Can we go faster though?"

"I don't see why not."

Her uncle picked up the pace, his long legs stretching out in front of him. The horse began trotting faster, Emma bouncing along atop as she giggled. They were going so fast that they passed the horse in front of them, the boy in the saddle complaining to his parents.

"When do we get to run?" he grumped.

"When you get faster parents," Jace whispered, shooting her a wink. Then he really started moving, working himself up into a jog so they could pass more horses.

"Aunt Sandra, look out!" cried a little girl. She was small and didn't seem comfortable on her horse.

That's probably why Jace gave such a wide berth when blowing past them. The instructor noticed these antics, expression stern, so they eased back into a walking pace.

"That was fun," Emma said, still laughing.

"Now it's my turn," Jace said. "We'll trade places and *you'll* run around the track."

"No way!" Emma enjoyed being so high up. Not only did she feel like royalty, but she could see more. She glanced around, still wanting to gallop into the wilderness. Emma was ready for that. Maybe the others weren't, especially the little ones. They weren't nearly as grown up as she was. Eight years old! That should be the minimum age for riding horses. She was sure they would be done practicing by now if it was. Her eyes lingered on the littlest girl, something bothering her until she figured it out.

"Hey," Emma said, turning her attention to Jace again. "How come I don't have an aunt?"

Jace seemed distracted. The instructor was waving them toward the gate. Finally! Jace led the horse there, making them first in line as they waited. Then he looked up at her and answered the question at last.

"Because your dad doesn't have a sister. If he did, she would have been your aunt. Your mom doesn't have any sisters either, and I won't be marrying a woman, so you're out of luck."

"Oh," Emma said, feeling disappointed. It didn't seem fair that everyone else got to have one and she didn't.

"The good news is," Jace said, "when I marry Ben— I mean if! *If* I marry Ben, ha ha, then you'll have a brand new uncle. Would you like that?"

"I guess so," Emma said.

"Then maybe you should drop a few hints to Ben. Start putting pressure on him now. That way he's primed when I pop the question."

She scrunched up her face. "Huh?"

Jace seemed distracted for a moment before looking sharply at her. "Can you keep a secret?"

"Yes." That's how she always answered, even though it wasn't necessarily the truth.

"I'm going to ask Ben to marry me. Soon. This summer, in fact."

Emma thought about this. "Does *he* have a sister?"

"Sure does."

"Will that make her my aunt?"

Jace seemed puzzled. "I'm not sure. Either way, once you meet Karen, you won't want her to be your aunt."

"Oh." Emma began to pout.

"If it means that much to you," Jace said. "I can be your aunt. Or maybe Ben. I bet he'd be up for it."

"That's not how it works."

"Why not?"

Emma struggled to get the words out. Wasn't it obvious? "Because you're boys!"

Jace shrugged. "So what? There's no law about it. I can be an aunt if I want. It's up to me. Aunt Jace sounds nice, don't you think?"

Emma laughed. "But you're not a girl!"

"True, but I love you, and if you want an aunt that badly, I'll be a boy aunt, just for you. I bet none of your friends have one of those."

Emma shook her head. "You're silly."

Jace raised his chin, eyes shining up at her. "Probably. But I learned long ago not to let others decide what I'll be. No limits. A lot of people don't think that Ben and I should be together. Did you know that? They don't like it when two boys love each other."

Emma frowned. As much as she wanted an aunt, she wouldn't trade Ben for one. She liked him too much. "That's dumb," she said.

"I agree. You'll run into that too, especially as you get older. You'll meet people who think girls can only work certain jobs, or can't play the same sports that boys do, but you shouldn't listen to them. You can be whatever you want. It's entirely up to you. Just promise me one thing, okay? Be true to yourself, but also be kind. It's easy to forget that other people have feelings too, especially when you're angry, but they do. So you don't need to yell at them and say how stupid they're being when they try to hold you back. Prove them wrong instead. Ignore them if you have to and do whatever it is they said you couldn't. Does that make sense?"

She wasn't sure. Emma could tell that this was important to Jace, but he could be hard to understand. Did this mean she no longer had to listen to her teachers at school?

"Become the person you dream of being," Jace tried again. "And be good to everyone along the way."

That was easier to grasp. Who did she want to be though? Emma looked at the other riders. In particular, the only other girl her age. She was pale and gangly with bright red braids and a cowboy hat perched atop the ginger hair. Emma felt a strange sort of admiration for her. Why? Because she wanted to be a cowgirl? That wasn't quite right. She didn't want to *be* the girl with red hair either. Emma wanted to know her. That was closer.

"No matter who you become," Jace said, pulling her attention away. "I'll be proud of you. Remember that."

Emma nodded. Then she perked up, having noticed the instructor approaching with another horse. It had to be for Jace. They were finally going to ride together! This would be the best birthday ever!

As the door to the home office opened, Emma quickly wiped the tears from her cheeks. Her mother noticed anyway, Michelle pausing before she approached.

"Are you okay, hon?"

"Yeah," Emma said. "I just got a little…" She gestured at the open memory album, which still only had the one photo in it. She wanted to say more but her lip wouldn't stop trembling.

"Oh," Michelle said, now close enough to see. She got down on the floor with her, eyeing the spread of photos that Emma had taken out of storage. All were from her eighth birthday, Jace present in most of them.

"Oh my goodness," Michelle said, her laughter tinged with sorrow. "Look how young everyone is." She picked up a photo. In it, Emma's cheeks were puffed up. So were Jace's as he helped blow out her birthday candles.

"I still miss him sometimes," Emma managed to croak out.

"Good!" Michelle said. "I don't want you to ever forget your uncle. He loved being part of your life."

Emma nodded. "He still is. But I wish I could talk to him. I need his help. Especially now."

Michelle set down the photo and reached over to stroke her hair. "I'm here for you. Talk to me."

Emma resisted the urge to shake her head. Her mother couldn't possibly understand. Not about this. Still, she didn't want to hurt her feelings. "Maybe later, okay? I need to keep working on this."

"Will it be about Jace? If so, I know where we have plenty more photos."

"I already did a memory album about him. Remember?"

"Of course!" Michelle said. "I thought you might want to do another. I wouldn't mind."

Emma managed a smile. "You sure loved him."

"Always did, always will. I'm glad to see I'm not alone."

Emma nodded but didn't say anything in response.

"You want your privacy," Michelle said, able to read her without effort. That was the comfort of a mother—never needing to explain. "I was just checking to see if you were getting hungry."

"Not really," Emma said. "Hey, do you remember those boxes I left behind when I moved out? I thought they were up here too."

"Your father moved them to the guest room closet. He wanted more space in here."

"For the endless shirts and coffee mugs with his company logo on them?" Emma asked.

Michelle snorted. "Basically, yes."

"I don't want strangers going through my personal things," Emma complained. "Can't he store his swag in the guest room?"

"Sure. Want to help me move it all?"

Emma decided she wasn't *that* concerned about her privacy. She stood, and when her mother did too, they hugged. Then she went to the guest room, only needing to pull out one box to find what she needed. She refused to be distracted as she tipped the contents onto the carpet. Cute photos of her and Jason hanging out together? Forget them. For now, at least. The clay ashtray that her youngest brother had made her for Christmas one year, even though she never smoked? It still made her laugh, but this wasn't the time. Emma was after one thing and one thing only. When she spotted a letter, the envelope still sealed with a sticker, she snatched it up and moved to the bed. There she sat, intending to rip at the paper flap, but she hesitated. How long had the letter waited to be read? More than five years. She had never bothered reopening it before, knowing that it would remind her of an embarrassing moment, but as she thought back, the circumstances surrounding the letter's creation weren't so bad.

"Movin' right along!" Ben sang into a wooden spoon.

Emma was right there with him, adding a "dug-a-dung, dug-a-dung" before letting her uncle take the next line, since Kermit's voice was too high for her.

"Hey LA, where've you gone?"

Emma grinned, gripping her spatula tighter. "Send someone to fetch us we're in Saskatchewan!"

"Movin' right along," Ben sang.

Emma followed this up with another "dug-a-dung, dug-a-dung," but Ben didn't chime in with the next line. When she opened her eyes, she saw why. They were no longer alone, and perhaps like her, Ben was embarrassed to be so into the soundtrack of *The Muppet Movie*, a film intended for children. She was thirteen and he was an adult, but so what? It was still an absolute classic.

"Don't stop on my behalf," Tim said, setting groceries on the kitchen counter. "Keep going."

"I lost my place," Ben said, turning to her for guidance. "Were we on the 'birds of a feather' verse?"

"Not yet."

"Hm. Maybe we should start over. After I help Tim unload the car."

"No need," Tim said, strutting toward his boyfriend while making his muscles bounce. "I can handle it."

"Yeah, but maybe—" Ben held out a hand, which connected with Tim's chest and held him at bay. "—I want to get some fresh air. With you."

"Oh." Tim seemed confused. Then his eyebrows shot up before he glanced in Emma's direction. "Got it. I could use your help actually."

"I'll help too," Emma offered.

"No!" The two men said in unison.

Ben was the first to laugh. "We'll be right back. Grab yourself a drink, Emma. Gotta keep that beautiful voice of yours smooth."

He was the only person in the world to describe her singing in that way. Just one of the many reasons she loved her uncle. Emma watched them leave the room before she wandered over to the counter and opened one of the twelve-packs of soda Tim had just placed there. Then she casually moved to the window that faced the front of the house. She could see Tim's car parked nearby rather than at the separate garage. That made sense for carrying in groceries, although neither man seemed intent on doing so, even though their arms were filled. With each other. Emma stared as she watched them kiss. This wasn't a casual peck. The last time she saw anything like it was when Jennette Dixon had started dating Steven Booker and wanted to mark her territory, right there in the cafeteria. Emma hadn't realized adults made out like that too.

The kiss broke off suddenly, Ben's head turning toward the house, so she stepped away from the window, cheeks burning. Emma wasn't sure why until she thought of Hannah. No surprise there. She couldn't get Hannah out of her mind lately. That was probably normal. Why shouldn't she think about her best friend?

Emma risked another peek out the window. They were hugging now, Ben standing on his tippy toes so he could wrap his arms around Tim's neck. This time, when Ben checked the window, she wasn't fast enough. She was pretty sure he caught her spying. Feeling ashamed, she sat at the table and grabbed a catalog that had come in the mail, pretending to browse it when Ben and Tim returned to the kitchen lugging heavy plastic bags.

The pair was oddly quiet. She did her best to ignore them, even when she heard whispering.

"Wanna help me put these things away?" Ben eventually said at a normal volume.

Emma looked up and noticed that Tim had left the room. When she glanced out the window, she saw his car pulling into the garage.

"Okay," she mumbled.

She wasn't much help. Unlike at her own home, she didn't know where everything was supposed to go. She tried to guess rather than have to ask. They were halfway through this task when Ben sighed.

"Sorry about that," he said.

"About what?" she replied. "I didn't see anything."

Ben was silent. When she looked over at him, he wore a knowing expression, a can of soup in each hand. "Let's be honest with each other. Okay?"

Emma's shoulders slumped. Then she nodded. "Sorry."

"It's fine." Ben put the cans away. "I didn't want you to see that, but it's hard to hide it all the time, especially when—"

"Why not?"

"Hm?" Ben seemed surprised by the interruption.

"How come you don't want me to see you guys kissing? Do you have to hide it because of homophobes?"

Ben stared at her. Then he shook his head, seeming to laugh at himself. "No! Not at all. Sometimes we have to be a little careful, but that's not why we... You know I loved Jace, right?"

Emma nodded. "Obviously. You were married to him."

"That's right. Just because he's gone doesn't mean I don't love him anymore. I still do, but I worry that it might upset you to see Tim and me being affectionate. I know this has been an adjustment for everyone. Your father especially, so we've tried to tone it down while you're staying with us. Which is dumb, because you aren't a kid anymore. You get it, right?"

"Get what?" Emma said defensively. She glowered and looked away. She wasn't upset at them. She was mad at herself. For some reason. "You don't need to hide anything from me," Emma added, attempting to sound more civil. "I don't mind."

"Okay." Ben looked anything but certain. "Well, if you have any questions, just let me know."

"Why were you kissing him like that?" she asked. "Did he buy you a present?"

"No," Ben said sheepishly. He turned to the nearest cabinet, shifting around the contents. "Although he did remember to get orange juice despite it not being on the list. That's pretty good. Honestly though, sometimes it just hits me."

"What does?"

Ben turned to face her. "How much I love him."

She thought of Hannah again, even though she didn't want to. Was obsessing over someone the same as being in love with them? "Were you that way with Jace too?"

Ben chuckled. "Uh, yeah! You don't remember?"

Emma shook her head. She couldn't recall seeing them kiss, aside from the wedding, but she did remember that she rarely saw Jace without Ben at his side.

"I guess you were a lot younger then," Ben said. "Jace and I were just as affectionate, although maybe we were more subtle about it. We tended to snuggle up on the couch together. Things like that. Tim brings out the teenager in me so we… Sorry. I'm guessing you don't want to hear any of this."

"I do!" Emma said, surprising even herself. "It's important."

"Important?" Ben said, shutting the cabinet. "What do you mean?"

"There's something I need to tell you."

"Okay. I'm listening."

Emma couldn't get the words out. They waited on her tongue, wanting to be spoken, but they felt too huge. "Can we sit down?"

"Sure."

This bought her time, but not much, so she decided to describe how she was feeling instead of saying it outright. "My best friend, Hannah, we had a sleepover recently and were giving each other makeovers."

"Sounds fun," Ben said patiently.

"It was. I did her makeup, and while putting gloss on her lips, I couldn't stop thinking about how much I wanted to kiss them."

"You wanted to kiss Hannah?" Ben asked.

Emma studied the surface of the table and nodded. "Yes."

"Was that the first and last time you had that urge?"

Emma shook her head. "Huh-uh. I can't stop thinking about it. Or her."

"Oh. Okay. There's nothing wrong with that. It's perfectly normal. In fact, it's great!"

"But how do I know if I'm..." Emma bit her bottom lip. "Shouldn't I try kissing guys first? Doesn't that make sense?"

"It's okay to experiment." Ben shrugged. "Then again, why bother if you already know what you want?"

"To be sure," Emma answered. "There's a difference, right? Kissing a guy isn't the same as kissing a girl. Is it?"

Ben squirmed in his seat and seemed unable to find an answer.

"Have you ever tried with a girl?" Emma pressed. "Did it creep you out? Is that how you knew?"

"Um... You know who can answer that?"

Before she could guess, Ben started hollering for Tim, seeming relieved when he finally walked into the kitchen.

"There you are!" he said. "Emma has a question for you. She keeps thinking about kissing her best friend, who is a girl, and she's wondering if she should kiss a boy first."

"How come?" Tim asked, sitting next to Ben.

"To see if I think it's gross," Emma said. "That way I would know for sure."

"There's not much difference really," Tim said, looking to Ben. "Don't you think?"

Ben shrugged, his mouth clamped shut.

Tim stared at him. "You've never kissed a girl?"

Another shrug, except now Ben's face was bright red.

"You must have," Tim pressed. "You're telling me you and Allison never got desperate enough to try? Or just wanted the practice?"

"If we ever did anything like that," Ben shot back, "it would be the sort of thing we'd take to our graves."

Tim barked laughter. "Oh man... You're so busted!"

"*Anyway*," Ben said, nodding violently toward the other side of the table.

"Oh! Right." Tim looked at her. "I made out with a lot of girls before I ever kissed this fool, and no, it didn't make me realize that I'm gay. I liked it. But when I got infatuated with someone—when I couldn't stop thinking about kissing them or whatever—it was always a guy. *That's* when I knew."

"In that case..." Emma looked back and forth between

two sets of sympathetic eyes. She found no suspense there. Or judgement. The only person at this table she needed to admit the truth to was herself. "I'm gay."

"Awesome!" Tim said, grinning broadly.

"Super awesome," Ben said, standing up and walking around the other side of the table to hug her. "We love you, Emma. And if it turns out that you're actually straight, or bi, or anything else, we'll love you just the same."

"Thanks, Uncle Ben," Emma said, hugging him back. "I'm pretty sure though. Do you mind if I ask you both some questions?"

"Please do!"

"Yeah, go for it," Tim chimed in.

They sat there for an hour, maybe longer, and talked. Emma had so many feelings she needed to validate, so many fears that they were able to dismiss. Hearing about how much doubt they'd experienced, and what a struggle it had been for them, albeit in two very different ways, made her feel much less alone. By the time they rose to get dinner ready, she was elated instead of weighed down. She wanted to call Hannah and tell her everything, but that was an intimidating prospect.

"Try writing her a letter instead," Ben suggested. "Even if you end up calling her, at least you'll have it all written down. That always helps me organize my thoughts."

She did as he suggested and found it to be true. Once her thoughts and feelings were all written down, the picture became surprisingly clear. She loved Hannah. All she needed to do was find out if Hannah loved her back.

*

Emma stood outside the door of a house, wearing an outfit which made her feel pretty, her mother's perfume a reassuring fragrance on her skin. She was doing her best not to sweat despite the heat, a letter gripped in both hands so it couldn't be dropped or whipped away by a sudden gust of wind. Before she could change her mind, Emma knocked.

Hannah opened the door, blonde hair spilling over her shoulders like a waterfall that Emma wanted to bathe in. She imagined it surrounding her face like a curtain, Hannah staring down at her, their bodies pressed together as their mouths neared for a kiss.

"Emma!" Hannah said, sounding surprised. "I thought you wouldn't be back until next week!"

"I came home early," Emma said. "I missed you. And you said you had a surprise for me. I have one too."

"Really?" Hannah glanced over her shoulder, speaking to someone in the shadowy interior. "It's my best friend," she explained.

Emma leaned to the side, expecting to see Hannah's mother or little sister. Instead she saw a skinny guy with tan skin and spiked blond hair that was almost bleached white from the sun. Clive Bryant was one of the cool kids. Not the popular jerks, but one of the aloof outcasts who refused to associate with any clique, like he was above anything so petty as status. She and Hannah often talked about him. Other boys at school too, although Emma mostly chose her favorites based on personality, and yeah, sometimes looks, because gay or not, she knew who the attractive guys were. Clive certainly fell under that category.

"Emma," Hannah said, turning forward again and practically squealing with excitement, "may I introduce Clive Bryant... my boyfriend."

Her grin became manic, like this was the best possible news, and Emma knew she had been the only one pretending. She couldn't fake that sort of enthusiasm for boys if she tried.

Clive gave an upward nod and a very chill, "Hey."

"Hey," Emma replied, balling her hands into fists.

She heard the crinkling of paper. So did the others. As a group, they looked down at the letter clutched in her hand.

"What's that?" Hannah asked.

"A letter," Emma said. "From my boyfriend. I met a guy in Austin. I'll tell you all about it later. I don't want to bother you."

Hannah mouthed the words "thank you" before nodding.

Emma shot Clive a withering glare before she turned away. She was pretty sure she could take him in a fight, the skinny little twerp. She would beat him up, be sent to juvenile hall, and meet some hot dyke behind bars who made her forget about Hannah entirely. Or she could go home, throw herself on the bed, and cry, which is exactly what she did.

Emma stared at a letter that had once seemed like the most important confession of her life. As her eyes moved across the lines, she couldn't help but laugh, no matter how earnest she'd been at the time.

I know I'm probably not your type. I don't look like any of the Jonas brothers. Then again, I was only pretending to like them. They definitely aren't my type. But you are.

Embarrassing, but also kind of sweet, in a naive sort of way. Hanna never did learn the truth. They remained friends, although Emma tended to make herself scarce whenever a new boyfriend appeared. Eventually they outgrew each other, and when Emma looked back on what she'd been sure was the greatest love of her life, she now knew it was little more than a crush. Nothing compared to the feelings she experienced later. Hell, since then she'd had friends she cared about more. Loved deeply, in fact.

Emma put the letter back into the envelope and glued the back of it to a page in the memory album. That way she could still take it out and read it when need be. Beneath this, in silver ink, she wrote, *You can't learn to walk without stumbling.*

Then she set aside the book and reached for the photos of her and Jason. She wished there were some from the first day they'd met. Emma hadn't known then what an important part of each other's lives they would become. She had only agreed to tag along during the ride to Austin so she could meet the person who reminded her mother so much of Jace.

Emma selected a photo of a guy with messy bangs that usually hid an intense gaze. Not in this one. Jason had his arms spread wide, like he was pretending to be an airplane while rushing toward the camera. She glued this into the book, and beneath it wrote: *My wingman.* Emma didn't see any resemblance to her uncle, physical or otherwise. Jason was nothing like him, although she hadn't known Jace when he was still a teenager. Maybe he was different then. Regardless of the reason, Jason had become her mother's pet project, and very quickly, Emma's best friend. That had been tricky at first. Emma only got to see him when she visited Austin, but they texted and called each other every day. Hanging out with him in person was the most fun. Especially when they went to the gay youth group together…

The girl had a small tight frame, which was the exact opposite of Emma's lush curves. Her hair was different too. Emma's was long and honey brown. This person had short dark hair gelled into spikes, the very tips dyed blood red. She looked kind of tough, maybe because of the lip and eyebrow piercings, or the clothing and jewelry that were varying shades of black. She wasn't hardened by the world though, her spirit dulled by too much adversity. Whenever their eyes met, all Emma saw was fire.

As for the gay youth group, it wasn't what she had expected. Emma had imagined herself overwhelmed by choices, too many pretty faces to focus on for long. Sort of how Jason was behaving, although he seemed to have whittled the selection down to two choices: a slender black guy and a beefy dude who was pasty white. Both were attractive in different ways, but eventually, Jason made his decision, elbowing Emma while the pale one was talking. She had done the same, which was good, because when the group leader made them pair up with someone of the opposite gender, they both knew who to go after.

Emma approached the gentle giant, William, who turned out to be in a relationship with the gorgeous black guy, Kelly. Too bad. Jason would be disappointed. As they sat together in a church classroom and talked through their assignment, Emma kept wondering if she would be disappointed too. She couldn't stop looking in the girl's direction, wanting to absorb every detail.

"Do you know her?" William asked.

"Not yet," Emma said, forcing her gaze away to focus on her partner. "Do you?"

"Sort of. That's Bonnie. She's friends with Kelly."

"Bonnie," Emma repeated. Then, in a Scottish accent she said, "I've never seen such a bonnie lass! Is she single?"

"That depends. What time is it?"

Emma grimaced. "She gets around a lot?"

"No." William's cheeks turned pink. "Well, kind of. She dates a lot of people, but none of them seem to last."

"Because she's difficult to be around or…"

"Kelly says that none of them are good enough for her. I'm not sure if that means Bonnie is really picky, or if that's just him being supportive of his best friend."

Emma bit her bottom lip and looked across the classroom again to where Bonnie and Jason were chatting together. Did she really think she'd make the cut if no one else had? A lot of the girls here were pretty, in the traditional sense. And skinny. Emma was neither of these things. She felt despair pulling on her leg, trying to drag her down, and mentally kicked it off while flipping the bird, because that attitude wouldn't do at all. Emma had inherited a lot from her father, including salesmanship. Greg Trout's name and face were on advertisements all over Houston. He was one of the most successful real estate agents in the city, and as he had once told her, "When you feel something, it usually shows on your face. That works in reverse too. So no matter how nervous I get when meeting an important client, on the outside I'm all smiles. By the time I'm done, I usually feel whatever I was pretending to." In other words, fake it until you make it.

With that in mind, she turned back to William and said with a smirk, "Yeah, well she hasn't met me yet."

Literally. Emma intended to change that at the first opportunity. Everyone was called back to their original seats so the lecture could continue. Emma kept her attention on the group leader, but the moment he turned around to write on the marker board, she leaned toward Jason and murmured, "Single?"

"Yup," Jason said. "Mine's not."

"Sorry," she said, despite feeling elated about her own good news. The second they were set loose to socialize, Emma was on her feet. Jason stopped her before she could get away.

"She's interested," he whispered. "But she thinks you're sixteen."

"No problem," Emma said. She'd always felt mature for her age. Maybe because she was smart—according to her test scores anyway—or perhaps, as her mother had once told her, "You're an old soul, just like your uncle." If only the government would recognize that and issue her a driver's license and updated birth certificate. That would be great. For now, she was very used to lying about her age. And besides, sixteen wasn't so far from the truth. Technically she was only fourteen, but her birthday was just around the corner.

Emma imagined herself striding over to Bonnie, who would be overwhelmed by suitors, rejecting one after the other. Emma would shove them away, sweep Bonnie off her feet, and rush her off to somewhere safe. And private. Instead, as everyone clustered into social groups, Bonnie stayed where she was, alone but still facing Emma as if expecting her. That was intimidating. Emma refused to show it, placing one foot in front of the other until they were near enough to talk.

"Hey," Emma said, doing her best to sound cool.

It must have worked, because Bonnie smiled and echoed her with a, "Hey."

"So," Emma said. "Should we set a date? Or should we tell everyone first?"

Bonnie shook her head. "Tell them what?"

"That we're getting married."

Bonnie stared. Then she laughed. "Nice line. How many people have you tried that on?"

"Just one. I don't think it worked. She thought I was kidding."

Bonnie's eyes twinkled. They were a deep blue that begged to be stared into. "Could you imagine?"

Emma nodded. "Yes. Wouldn't it be a beautiful beginning if we got married right away? We'd only ever know each other as wives. That's how it should be when meeting your soulmate."

"Maybe," Bonnie said. "I'd at least like to know your name before we commit to anything."

"I already know yours," Emma said. "I woke up with it on my lips this morning." She learned close and whispered dramatically, "Bonnie."

"William must have told you."

"Are you kidding?'" Emma retorted. "He asked *me*. Said he couldn't remember your name and was too embarrassed to admit it to you."

This earned her a laugh. "Okay. In that case, what's my last name?"

"Doesn't matter," Emma said. "We'll take mine. Or better yet, choose a new one together."

"Again," Bonnie said, "it's hard to weigh my options when I don't even know them."

Emma held out her hand and said her name.

"Emma Trout?" Bonnie repeated with a subtle smile. Their palms touched briefly before separating again. "How appropriate."

"Why's that?"

"Because my last name is Rivers. Want to go swimming, little fishy?"

Emma was so surprised that she was speechless. Then she chuckled. "I'm an awfully big fish. You'll find that out when you try to catch me."

Bonnie pantomimed like she was reeling Emma in. Then she dropped the act and shook her head. "Who *are* you?"

Emma never felt like anyone but herself. Until now. Her need to impress Bonnie, the insistent desire to win her heart, made Emma feel like a more powerful version of herself, like she had woken up not just with a name on her lips, but a previously undiscovered identity. She would become whatever was necessary to impress Bonnie. A pirate captain who would plunder ships of their treasure to give as a gift. A warrior on the field of battle, slaying anyone who dared speak ill of her queen. Or a slave to a corporation, working overtime to provide Bonnie with a home and anything else she desired. At the moment, all Emma had to offer were words, so she spoke again.

"All I know is that I was nothing before I met you."

Bonnie grinned. "Damn. You've got *all* the lines!"

"I try," Emma said.

"But do you have substance?"

"Oh, we don't want to bother with any of that boring reality stuff."

"I mean it," Bonnie challenged. "Get real or go home."

Emma sighed. "You're not actually going to make me do this, are you?"

Bonnie answered by crossing her arms over her chest.

"Fine," Emma said. "I'm just a girl from Houston who, despite having three gay uncles, is scared to tell my parents that I'm a lesbian. I keep coming to Austin so I can be myself, but there's always something missing, because more than anything I want a girlfriend. Simple as that. I'm one of those sad people who doesn't feel complete outside of a relationship. That's my theory anyway. I don't actually know because I've never even kissed a girl. Or dated one."

"Wow," Bonnie said, seeming stunned. "I think I like this version of you better."

"So will you?"

"What?"

"Marry me." Emma waited just long enough for Bonnie to look panicked before she laughed. "You don't have to answer now. Give it a few years, maybe even a decade. The offer stands."

"I'll keep it in mind," Bonnie said ruefully. "Three gay uncles, huh? Most people have one, but three sounds like a lot."

"One of them is blood," Emma explained, "another is by marriage, and the third one, well, it's more of an honorary title. What about you? Who is Bonnie Rivers when she's not out fishing?"

"Oh. I actually *am* one of those sad people who don't feel complete outside of a relationship. Although I can also be happy when I'm single. I never stay with someone if they're a bad match. Being lonely is better than that. But I always have this nagging feeling everything would be more fun—that I would be a better person—if I found the right girl. You know what I mean?"

"Yes," Emma answered instantly. "Tell me more. I want to know everything about you."

Bonnie studied her before replying. "I like your intensity. Um… Let's see. I'm perpetually broke, so if that matters to you, run away now."

"I have rich parents," Emma said. "They don't shower me in cash or anything. They want me to learn the value of money, but eventually, when they both croak, I'm going to be loaded. How's that sound?"

Bonnie's eyes went wide. "Terrible!"

"Good. I was just testing you. I don't intend to mooch off my parents. Much. What else?"

"Um… I play the cello. That's a big part of my life. I have a big recital coming up soon."

"I love recitals!"

"Really? Have you been to many?"

"None. But there's one coming up that I'm excited about."

Bonnie laughed and shook her head. "Okay. I'm giving you my number, whether you want it or not."

Score! Emma exchanged information with her, and while doing so, she said, "I need a photo of you. All the entries in my contacts list have one. That way they pop up on the screen when someone calls." While that was true, she mostly just wanted an image of her to drool over.

Bonnie agreed, but only if Emma allowed her to do the same. After they were finished snapping photos of each other, she said, "My shift starts soon. Unfortunately. I have to go."

"Where to?"

"A bookstore. Isn't that where all lesbians work?"

Emma laughed. "We can't all be truck drivers."

"Or security guards."

"Love the uniforms though," Emma said wistfully.

Bonnie was biting her bottom lip while smiling. "I need you to walk away now. Otherwise I'll never convince myself to leave."

Swoon! "Only on the condition that you call me after work."

"Consider it done."

They stood there grinning at each other until Emma fulfilled her end of the bargain and turned away, excited to tell Jason the big news. She finally had a chance. No matter where this led, or how short-lived it turned out to be, at least she had met someone who liked her back.

Emma sifted through the photos and trinkets on the floor until she found what she was looking for. After meeting Bonnie, she had used Ben and Tim's home office to print a photo—the same one she had taken during that first encounter. At first it lived in a math textbook, taped to the inside cover so she could look at it during school. As promised, they had spoken on the phone later that day and most that followed. The chemistry was always there, even with one hundred and sixty miles separating them. They were desperate to see each other again and, before long, had managed to.

After gluing Bonnie's photo in the book, Emma grabbed something else that had caught her eye: a ticket stub for the Bates Recital Hall. That had been one of the best nights of her life, even though it nearly ended in disaster. Bonnie had driven out early that day to pick her up, which was crazy, because it meant six hours on the road round trip. They took a nice long break in between, Emma showing Bonnie around Houston and blowing through most of her meager savings to take her out to lunch. Where else could they eat? At home? Her mother would realize. The second she saw them together, it would be obvious to her that Emma had feelings for Bonnie, and she wasn't ready for that. She lied instead, claiming that she was staying the night with Hannah, when really, they had a big night in Austin planned.

Emma brought along her best dress—the one she had bought for a junior high dance before deciding that she would be miserable going alone. So she hadn't, but ended up keeping the dress, which she finally found an excuse to wear. Emma had wanted to be elegant for Bonnie. Sophisticated. This didn't come naturally to her, so she did as her father taught and started from the outside. She locked herself in Bonnie's bathroom once they were back in Austin and didn't come out again until she looked the part.

Stunning.

That's how Bonnie had described her. It was the first compliment about her appearance that hadn't come from a relative or friend. Best of all, when Bonnie said it, she wasn't looking at the dress, or staring at the newly styled hair that Emma had practiced for days to get right. Instead she was looking at *her*, Emma's face and sometimes her body. That had been such a thrill. As much as she pretended to be confident, she used to fear that romance wouldn't be a part of her future.

She was just as giddy later that evening when, sitting in a concert hall on the University of Texas campus, she watched Bonnie coax sorrowful music from her cello. Emma had always enjoyed music, and often tried making it herself, even though she had a terrible singing voice. The music Bonnie created was pure artistry. Emma still remembered the way she had glowed on stage that night, like a goddess in the spotlight.

What had happened afterwards was complicated and messy. Kelly was also in the audience, wanting to support his friend, and in the name of filling empty seats, had brought along his boyfriend, William, and another young couple... Jason and Tim.

Emma snorted at the memory. What a weird night! Jason had been caught lying for reasons of his own, and over dinner, one of Emma's stories had fallen apart too. Bonnie found out the truth about her age, but even that wasn't enough to come between them.

Emma busied herself with gluing mementos into the scrapbook—the receipt from the lunch in Houston, the recital ticket, a matchbook from the restaurant they'd gone to for dinner—all while thinking fondly of how the night had ended.

"Your uncle seems nice," Bonnie said as she drove them toward the western edge of Austin. "So explain it to me one more time, and I swear I won't ask again. He's not related to you?"

Emma shook her head, conflicting emotions swirling inside of her. She was busted. No matter how cool Tim was, he would tell her parents where she really was tonight. That meant getting grounded. For now, she intended to revel in what freedom she had left. Currently she was being driven back to Ben and Tim's house—by her freaking girlfriend!—after an amazing concert and dinner. It didn't get much better than that, and was unlikely to ever again, once she returned to Houston. "Ben was married to my biological uncle, Jace, before he died, but now he's with Tim instead. So technically Tim isn't my uncle, but I'm sure it'll happen eventually. You should see them together. They're repulsive in the best way possible."

"Think they'll invite me in?"

"Not tonight. Ben is a lot more responsible than Tim is. I bet he'll have my mother on the phone when he opens the door." Emma's own phone had been powered off since the recital. She was intentionally forgetting to turn it on again. What was one more deception after so many? "Thanks for not being mad at me."

"Because you lied?" Bonnie shifted in her seat. "It's not a big deal. You're right that I probably would have backed off had I known how young you are."

"I'll be—"

"Fifteen soon. I know." Bonnie glanced over at her. "I dated a twenty-year-old once who would literally throw tantrums if she didn't get what she wanted, so personally, I don't judge maturity by a superficial number. And I understand if there are things you aren't ready to tell me. We just met. A lot of people demand absolute truth, but that takes trust, and trust takes time. So I can forgive the occasional fib. Besides, most people keep secrets from themselves, so how can anyone expect us to be completely honest with each other?"

Emma looked over at her girlfriend. The artificial light was growing dimmer as they left the city, deepening the shadows on her face. It's true that she didn't know Bonnie very well, but they were working on that every day. Still, so far from home, she had to ask herself just how much trust they had built, and how deep those mysterious depths of hers went. Maybe it was a good thing that she was staying with Ben and Tim tonight, instead of the original plan of sharing a bed with Bonnie. After all, they hadn't even kissed yet.

"Do you have a lot of secrets?" Emma asked.

Bonnie was quiet before she answered. "I don't know. Remember what it was like before you accepted yourself, how you were able to deny a part of your identity that you knew was true?"

"Yeah," Emma said, waiting for her to continue.

Bonnie didn't. The next time she spoke, it was to ask for directions. Once they had turned down the correct road, she changed subjects. "Explain to me why a girl with three gay uncles is still in the closet."

"I'm mostly out. Okay, nobody at school knows yet. I get enough crap for being unabashedly fat, and some of the guys still haven't forgiven me from the grade school days when I whooped their asses at football."

"So hot!" Bonnie said approvingly.

"Thanks," Emma said, catching sight of herself in the side mirror. She didn't look like a tomboy tonight. She often felt more feminine than masculine, and the older she got, she saw no reason to shy away from either side of herself. But when it came to her life in Houston, that was more complicated, especially in regard to her parents. "My dad is always trying to give me advice about boys." She made her voice deeper to imitate him. 'I am a boy, so you don't have to wonder what they're thinking. Just ask me. And maybe you can shed some light on how I keep getting myself into trouble with your mother.'"

"No!" Bonnie's mouth fell open. "He didn't really say that!"

"He did, and before you start picturing some macho jerk, he's actually very sweet. Often clueless, but a total sweetheart."

"Then why not tell him?"

"Because I know that's not how he sees me. He always interrogates any guy friends I make, like I'm boy-crazy and he needs to keep me safe. You know how dads are. Oh. I'm sorry! I didn't mean—"

"It's totally fine," Bonnie said. She had already told Emma during a late-night phone call how she lost contact with her father when she was little and didn't have many memories of him. "I know what you mean anyway. I've seen it happen to my friends."

"Yeah, so it's dumb but fairly typical. What bothers me about it is the assumption. There's no question in his mind that his daughter is straight, and to me, that reveals what he actually wants me to be. He was best friends with my uncle when growing up, so it's not like he hasn't been exposed to this sort of thing. He should know better than to assume."

"Sure," Bonnie said, "but that doesn't mean he won't accept you. He was fine with Jace being gay, right?"

Emma sighed. "Yeah. Don't you think people treat us different though? There was this girl in my drama class. Her best friend was flamboyantly gay. I don't think he owned a single T-shirt that didn't have a rainbow on it. We talked sometimes, but I never confided in him. When he moved away, I thought his friend seemed lonely, so we would pair up during class. And I told her, thinking she'd be safe. When she asked if I had a boyfriend, I said, 'No, I'm a lesbian.' Do you know what her response was? 'Ew! Are you serious?' I chickened out and said I was only joking. Lame, I know, but can you believe that? She's best friends with a gay guy but she thinks lesbians are gross?"

Bonnie grimaced. "That goes both ways. Straight dudes will hate on gay guys but jerk off while looking at lesbian porn."

"People are such turds," Emma complained.

"Not all of them," Bonnie said. "But yeah, there are some major assholes out there. What about your mom? Any idea how she'd react?"

Emma sighed. "She's weird. Whenever the subject of me dating anyone comes up, like when I bought this dress, she gets really quiet. As if she doesn't want to talk about it. I think she suspects and it makes her uncomfortable."

"Or maybe she doesn't want to assume the wrong thing. You know, like your dad does."

Emma thought about it. Then she laughed. "I'm making it impossible for them, aren't I?"

"Kind of. What would you prefer them to do? Ask you directly?"

"No way! Well, maybe I do now. I wasn't ready to talk about it before."

"Sounds like the kind of thing a mom would pick up on, if she had a gay brother. Maybe she's waiting for a sign that you're ready."

Emma leaned back in her seat and exhaled. "Oh my god. I've been an idiot."

"Nah. I think everyone is scared of telling their parents,

whether they have a reason to be or not. It's never easy until the second it's over. Then you'll wonder why you waited so long."

"Turn up ahead," Emma said. "See the mailbox with the reflectors on it? That's the driveway to their house. It's easy to miss. Anyway, I'm kind of relieved. I've been trying to figure out what I'm going to tell my parents when I'm home again. Like how I could possibly explain what I'm doing way out here, but I haven't come up with a good cover story."

"So you're going to tell them the truth?"

Emma nodded. "I think so. Yeah."

"Good. I'm proud of you." Bonnie whistled under her breath. "Are your uncles rich too? Because I've never seen a driveway this long."

"I don't really know."

The house that came into view could have belonged to any middle-class suburb. Sure it was two stories tall and had three or four bedrooms, depending on what each space was used for, but it wasn't excessive in any way. Only the land surrounding the house made it special, offering an unusual amount of privacy. She supposed it *was* a lot of house for just two people, but that's what had made it possible for Jason to move in.

"Nice place," Bonnie said as the car slowed to a stop.

"I wish you could come inside," Emma said, eyeing the house uneasily. "I'm pretty sure there's a lecture waiting for me. Especially since we took the scenic route to get here."

"Tell them that it's my fault. I wasn't ready to drop you off yet."

Emma wasn't ready to part ways either. "Wanna walk me to the door?" she asked.

"Hell yeah!"

They both got out of the car. Bonnie had a saunter in her step, taking Emma's hand as they strolled toward the house. Emma knew what was coming, and it made her nervous. If only she could dart inside, floss, brush her teeth, and maybe use mouthwash. She'd made sure not to eat anything too smelly during dinner and chewed gum after. Why hadn't she practiced this before, even if that meant kissing a boy? Bonnie had so much more experience and would surely notice that Emma did not. Had that ever come up in conversation? She knew that Emma hadn't dated anyone but—

Too late. They reached the porch and turned to face each other. Bugs were dancing around the lightbulbs on either side of the door, insects chattering from the shadows that surrounded them. She could see why Ben and Tim liked it out here. Endless privacy.

"I'm not hung up on your age," Bonnie said. "I promise. But I don't think I should make any moves. Not until I'm sure that you're absolutely ready, so you need to either tell me or—"

Show her. Emma lunged forward, like she intended to headbutt someone, but she was careful enough that the resulting peck wasn't too much of an impact. And it was fine but...

"There has to be a better way of doing that," Emma said, not hiding her uncertainty. She had expected her first kiss to be a monumental experience. Explosive! Instead it was a mushy fizzle.

"Want me to show you?" Bonnie asked.

Emma nodded.

Bonnie took both of her hands, grin cocky as she stared into Emma's eyes. She grew increasingly serious as they contemplated each other, the intensity of their feelings building, which didn't leave room for doubt or nerves. The more they prolonged their potential, the greater the need became. Bonnie moved a hand to Emma's neck, sliding it around to the back and making her skin tingle. Then their lips met, tenderly at first, as they readjusted and explored what the best position would be. Emma had never expected to be able to kiss for so long without losing her breath, but it worked. They were calm and careful in their motions, but inside, the fire was building into an inferno.

"Better?" Bonnie asked when she pulled away.

"More," Emma pleaded.

"Some other time," Bonnie said, looking happy. "I want that too. For now, I better let you go before you get into any more trouble."

"I'm already grounded," Emma retorted. "Maybe if I go missing for a few days, they'll worry so much that I won't be in trouble at all."

"You have a devious mind," Bonnie said with a smile. "That should be rewarded."

They kissed again. This time it was shorter, but it promised what mattered most.

More.

* * * * *

These memories usually filled her with warm nostalgia. Not anymore. All Emma felt now was heartache. Everything had become so complicated since then. She wished she could travel into the past, just to relive those simpler times. She supposed that's what she was here to do. Filling the empty pages of the memory album was easy now. She and Bonnie had squeezed so much into every visit, and Emma had saved mementos from each: a photo of Bonnie hunched over a coffee mug at a diner, her half-lidded eyes seductive. A homemade bracelet, the threads worn out and frayed. A birthday card, the imprint of Bonnie's lipstick next to the words *Love you, girl*.

That was a day to remember. Emma had invited Bonnie to Houston and introduced her to the entire family as, "my girlfriend." Her youngest brother had laughed, her mother bursting into tears while still wearing a smile. As for Emma's father, he was confused at first, but once she assured him that she had no interest in boys, he seemed relieved. Ultimately, they were fine with her being a lesbian. That seemed obvious in retrospect. Emma knew from conversations she'd had with others that this was often the case. Bonnie had put it best: Coming out was the scariest thing in the world, until the second it was over. Not everyone was lucky enough to have supportive parents, but she hoped those who didn't felt some sort of relief anyway. Suspense could be torture. And as Tim had once told her, it's better to be disliked for who you are, than to be loved for living a lie.

The thought made her pause. Then she swallowed and continued her work, blowing through nearly a year of happiness until she reached a single page that had been torn out of a book. A poem. She could still remember when it had been read to her...

"Twisted up inside, unable to find comfort in my own skin,
Your touch reaches through the noise, helping me relax again.
A world filled with deception, pierced by a solitary truth,
Your love, warm and soothing, a cupid's sweet vermouth."

Emma was stretched out on the bed in Bonnie's room, a small space that was perpetually cluttered. Clothes sat in piles on the floor, were draped over armchairs, or in one instance, hung off a lampshade. The walls were covered with everything from posters to newspaper articles to handwritten scribbles. Garage sale furniture crammed what little space remained, leaving only a narrow walkway, and yet, there was something undeniably cozy about this space. Maybe because Bonnie felt like home. Not the one Emma knew, filled with over-concerned parents and annoying little brothers, but a future home, where their lives would finally intertwine instead of being constantly interrupted by distance.

"What do you think?" Bonnie asked, sitting cross-legged on the bed. She looked up from the book, eyebrows raised and awaiting feedback.

"I think you're beautiful," Emma replied.

Bonnie smiled. "Did you hear a single word I read?"

"Yes. I was captivated, but I'm also certain that poem has never sounded better, even when read by the author."

"I'd love to hear them read it," Bonnie said, considering the cover. "They're my favorite. I devour a lot of poetry, but this is the author I keep coming back to."

"I liked it."

"Really?" Bonnie set the book on her lap. Then she tore a page free.

"What are you doing?" Emma protested.

"I want you to have it," Bonnie said, holding out the poem.

"But it's your favorite!"

"I have it memorized." Bonnie smirked. "You can give it back once you do too."

Emma took the poem and carefully stowed it away in the backpack she lugged around with her. Her pulse started racing as she zipped it up. Emma licked her lips, returned her attention to her girlfriend, and said, "What now?"

Bonnie stared at her. Then she laughed. "You're so transparent."

"What?" she said innocently.

"You tell me."

Emma sighed. "It's been three weeks! That's nearly a month."

Bonnie stretched out, resting the back of her head on Emma's thigh. "I know. I missed you too."

"I researched emancipation the other day. You know, legally divorcing your parents? Technically you have to be seventeen, but if you're sixteen and living on your own, it's possible. I haven't figured out if it'll count if I'm living with Uncle Ben."

"What are you talking about?" Bonnie said. "You love your parents!"

"I know, but they won't let me move here. I asked. I want us to go to the same high school. I want to see you every day."

"Same here," Bonnie said, reaching for her hand. "Maybe after I graduate, I'll move to Houston instead. How's that sound?"

"Not as good," Emma admitted. "I love Austin."

"Me too. There's no sense in you coming here now, even though I like the idea. By the time you're a sophomore, I'll be done with high school."

"Stop being reasonable," Emma pouted. "Give me something I can dream about."

"No problem." Bonnie sat up, slid out of bed, and stood. When she turned around, she was wearing a smile. *The* smile, which only made an appearance when she was feeling particularly naughty.

Emma sat up too, not wanting to miss a single detail. Bonnie began to sway, singing a generic stripper tune under her breath. "Bah dah bah dah boooom, chucka boom chucka." Emma would have laughed if she wasn't getting so turned on. Bonnie slowly shimmied her T-shirt up an inch at a time, revealing her bra before the shirt went over her head. Hair covered her armpits. That was new. Emma only saw a flash of them and was soon distracted again as Bonnie turned around, shaking her shoulders and walking backwards. Emma moved closer to help her unfasten her bra, and when Bonnie spun around to reveal two perky breasts, she nearly applauded. Instead she pantomimed like she was sending a stack of dollar bills flying in Bonnie's direction, one at a time.

"Hey!" her girlfriend said, putting on a stern expression. "I don't do this for money."

"What do you do it for then?" Emma breathed.

"Love."

Bonnie tumbled into bed, Emma opening her arms to catch her. They kissed while fumbling with each other's clothes, tossing each piece away. In this mess, Emma would be lucky to find her outfit again. Maybe that would be her excuse. She'd call home and say she couldn't leave here, ever again, because she didn't have any clothes.

"You're so handsome," Bonnie whispered in her ear, just before nipping at it.

"Thanks," Emma said. "But for you, I want to be pretty."

"You're that too," Bonnie said, pulling back to consider her. Then she slid a hand down while biting her bottom lip.

Emma gasped and pulled her closer so they could kiss. Everything felt wonderful, like it always did. Except…

"Something's scratching me," Emma said, craning her neck to look downward. She saw the familiar naked body that filled her every fantasy, although something was off. "When's the last time you shaved your legs?"

"Not since I saw you last," Bonnie said, coming in for another kiss.

Emma dodged. "Did you forget?"

Bonnie pushed herself up, locking her elbows. "No, I didn't forget. Any other questions?"

Emma studied her, not understanding why she sounded so irritated, but yes, she still had questions. "Are they always going to be hairy from now on? I feel like I'm with a boy."

"So?"

"Uh, I'm a lesbian? I like women. Remember?"

Bonnie glared. "That's such a stupid thing to say." She rolled off to the side. "Women have hairy bodies too. It's natural."

"I know that," Emma said. "I hate shaving. But I do it anyway. For you."

"I never asked you to," Bonnie shot back. She was sitting up now, her back turned, legs pulled up to her chest.

"Are you saying that you want me to be hairy too?"

"No. Ugh. I don't care. If that's what you want, I won't make a big deal out of it."

"I'm not making it a big deal! I just don't get why you wouldn't at least try."

"Try what?"

"To look nice for me!" They were the wrong words. Emma knew it the second they slipped free, but it was too late now. Bonnie looked great! She always did, but sometimes it felt like she wasn't making the effort anymore. She didn't always wear makeup, for instance. That wouldn't be a problem if they saw each other more often, but days like these were so limited that they should be treated as a special occasion. Emma preened herself to an obsessive degree before each trip. She did so out of love.

"I should have known you wouldn't get it," Bonnie said,

shaking her head. "You can keep buying into society's twisted ideals all you want, but I won't."

"When did you get so political?" Emma asked, genuinely confused.

"It's not political," Bonnie growled. "This is who I am! You'd get that if you weren't so young."

Emma tensed. She *hated* when Bonnie brought up her age. They were supposed to be equals, and usually it felt that way, but anytime they got into an argument, Emma was always wrong by default because she happened to be born a few years later. "Gosh, I'm so sorry," she spat. "Maybe when I'm your age, I'll realize how sexy hairy legs are. For now, you'll have to forgive me for being so immature."

"Never mind," Bonnie said, rising and reaching for her shirt.

Emma sighed. "Don't! I'm sorry. Please come back to bed so we can talk."

"I can do that with my clothes on."

"I want to hold you."

"No you don't. I might scratch your thin skin."

Emma clenched her jaw. "Now which one of us is being immature?"

"I am," Bonnie said as she stood. "I've needed to grow up this entire time, because it was dumb of me to believe I could have a serious relationship with a freshman." She snorted while shaking her head. "You were in junior high when we met. What was I thinking?"

"Screw you!" Emma snarled.

"No thanks," Bonnie retorted. "That boat has sailed."

Emma stared. "Is that how it's going to be? I guess I'm just another of Bonnie's girls, huh?"

"Meaning what?"

"That I'm one in a long line. This is what you do, isn't it? You never stick around for long."

Bonnie swiped at the clothes out of Emma's reach and tossed them to her. "I dated you longer than anyone else. Think whatever you want, but that's not what this was."

"Was?" Emma repeated.

Bonnie nodded. "You heard me."

Emma stood so she could finish dressing, her hands shaking. With anger or hurt, she didn't know. Too many emotions were competing for her attention, her thoughts jumbled as she tried to figure out what to say. She was supposed to be smart, but this was a puzzle she couldn't solve. All she managed was to grunt a single word. "Bitch!"

Bonnie pointed to the bedroom door. "That way."

The fight went out of her as quickly as it came. "Wait. Bonnie…"

"Leave!"

Emma grabbed her backpack, digging for her phone on the way down the hall, barely able to see the text she sent through her tears. She made it outside, the day calm and clear. Couldn't the world give her a fucking thunderstorm? Her heart was breaking! She didn't want to hear birds singing, or wave back at the neighbor mowing his lawn. Thank goodness Jason wasn't far. He showed up in a blue polo, still wearing a pet-store name tag.

Jason leapt out of the car after parking, attempting to give her a hug, but Emma knew she would break down entirely if she let him. Instead she gently pushed him toward the vehicle. "Get me out of here," she pleaded. "Please."

They were cruising down the road when he reached over to place his hand over hers. "Whatever happened," he said, "it's going to be okay."

Emma wanted that to be true, but how could it be when her entire world was falling apart, and she still didn't understand why?

In retrospect, Emma viewed the argument in a completely different light. It set the tone for what came later, the cracks never disappearing completely. Nor did their feelings for each other, but for whatever reason, each time she got especially close to Bonnie, something would happen to push them apart. She used to wonder if it was a sign that they weren't meant to be together, like they were ninety percent compatible and the missing ten percent was what kept tripping them up. Those doubts were never enough to keep her away. Not for long, as she discovered a few days after that first breakup…

Emma once considered the gay youth group to be the best place on Earth. At first she had only wanted to meet someone, but even after Bonnie became her girlfriend, she still enjoyed going there. Back home in Houston, people were either overly considerate of her feelings or they condemned her lifestyle. Only in this group was she treated like a normal person. Nobody cared that she was gay, their apathy an odd sort of comfort.

At the moment, she was anything but comfortable. Whenever someone entered the church classroom, Emma's head would whip around to face the door, but it was never who she both hoped and dreaded it would be. Three days. That's how long she and Bonnie had gone without contacting each other, and it felt terrible, but so did that final argument. Of all the fears she once entertained, never had she imagined that grooming habits would be what broke them up.

The door opened again. It was Lisa, a mousy girl who had caught her eye before. Emma smiled at her. With intent. She made sure it was transparently flirtatious. Lisa blushed and rushed to her usual seat. As for Emma, she felt dreadful. Putting the moves on another woman obviously wasn't going to soothe her broken heart. She was beginning to think that nothing could.

"Are you doing okay?" Jason asked from the chair next to hers.

He had been of tremendous help the past few days, having experienced similar emotions when William left for the Coast Guard. He not only knew the pain of a breakup, but also the strain of a long-distance relationship—no matter how much he insisted that he and William were no longer together. That was only a technicality. Each time William returned home, he and Jason would pick up where they'd left off, and when the Coast Guard claimed him again, Jason would be heartbroken. Emma was always there for her friend, helping him pick up the pieces, so these roles were familiar to them, even when reversed.

"I'm okay," Emma answered. "I guess. I was hoping she'd be here."

"She's outside."

The voice was a squeak. Emma wasn't sure where it had come from, until she saw Lisa staring at her. "Bonnie is outside?"

Lisa nodded.

"Okay," the group leader said. "Should we get started?"

"No thanks!" Emma hopped to her feet. She didn't bother explaining herself as she rushed from the room, nor did she worry about what she'd do once outside. All she knew is that they had to see each other, because it couldn't end this way. That conviction doubled when she saw Bonnie standing next to her beat-up old car, and tripled when they both broke into a sprint at the same time.

"I'm sorry," Emma said, gathering Bonnie into her arms. "You never have to shave your legs again. You can grow a beard! I don't care."

"I'm the one who's sorry," Bonnie said, taking her hand and pressing it to her lips. "I shouldn't have flipped out like that. I don't know what's wrong with me."

"Nothing," Emma said. "I could have found a different way of asking you, or waited until a better time."

"You were only being open with me," Bonnie stressed. "That's real maturity. Relationships don't work without communication."

"Do we still have one?" Emma asked.

"Is that what you want?"

"Yes!"

Bonnie looked so relieved that she was on the verge of tears. "Can we pretend that argument never happened?"

Emma grinned. "Better yet, let's rewind back to that moment. I want to do it over again."

Bonnie tilted her head. "What are you saying?"

"That I want to go home with you."

Bonnie shook her head like she couldn't believe her luck. Then she walked around to the other side of the car and opened the door so that Emma could climb in.

Emma didn't have any keepsakes from that day. Just memories, all of them good. Breaking up had only made her realize just how much she loved Bonnie. That old saying about not knowing what you have until it's gone was true. They had nearly lost each other, but the aftermath felt like a second honeymoon.

Emma reached for a white box small enough to fit in the palm of her hand. She opened it, revealing a dried corsage, thinking back to when she had first seen it, the petals still flush with life.

Her plan was to walk down the stairs of Ben and Tim's house to the living room, where she would then present herself. That's how it always worked in the movies. Instead, after checking herself in the mirror once more, she left the bathroom to find four adults blocking the hallway.

"Look at my little girl!" Michelle enthused.

"Mom!" Emma complained.

"Fine, fine," Michelle said, still rosy cheeked. "Look at my young woman. She's beautiful."

"Stunning," Ben said.

"Gorgeous," Tim agreed. "I love the dress. Maybe I should get you one of those."

"Ha ha," Ben deadpanned.

"Hey, I'm not kidding!"

Emma ignored their antics, turning to her best friend. She could count on him for an honest opinion.

"Smoking hot," Jason confirmed with a nod. "You know I had my doubts about the sparkly fabric, but if it looks this good in a dim hallway, then you'll light up the dance floor."

"Thanks." Emma felt a vibration from the small clutch purse she was holding. There was only enough room inside for her phone and a few other necessities. She had thought it would be elegant, but the miniature purse was already becoming a burden, since it didn't have a strap she could put over her shoulder. After some finagling, she managed to slip her phone free so she could read the text.

"Bonnie's almost here!" she said.

That was the signal for the others to get out of her way. Jason had the decency to retreat down the hall, but he stopped when noticing he was the only one.

"You aren't going anywhere until I get some photos," Michelle said.

"Fine. At least wait until Bonnie shows up so we can take them together."

"I want you to have fun tonight," her mother continued, "but I also want you to be safe. I'll still be up when you get back. If you need anything before then, just text or call."

Ben cleared his throat. "Do you remember your own prom, Michelle?"

"Of course. I went with Danny Hildebrandt. Everyone used to make fun of his big nose, but he was the sweetest guy. Even though he did step on my feet all night."

"What did you do after the dance?" Ben asked.

"We went out to eat with friends, and afterwards he drove me to the lake so we could—" Her mouth snapped shut. "It was a nice night."

"Was your mom there too?" Tim chimed in, having picked up on his boyfriend's point. "Did she help make it extra special?"

Michelle clenched her teeth, not willing to give up so easily. "I was seventeen!"

"I'm sixteen," Emma said. "And it's not like Bonnie and I haven't—"

"Okay!" Michelle said, holding up a hand. "On second thought, I'm getting a headache and will be going to bed early. But when I wake up, you'd better be here and in good condition. No drinking! No drugs either. Don't make me regret driving you all the way out here."

"I'll be good."

They heard the doorbell. Emma rushed down the hall, the others pressing themselves against the wall to let her through. Their own fault for not moving out of the way sooner. Emma remembered how expensive the dress was and forced herself to slow down so nothing would tear, when really she wanted to run. She hadn't seen Bonnie this month and was desperate to. When reaching the front of the house, she took a deep breath to steady her nerves. Then she opened the door.

"Hey, babe," Bonnie said, shooting her a crooked grin.

Emma stared. Bonnie was wearing a black tuxedo, her hair slicked back. She looked cool, but this isn't what they had agreed on.

"I thought you were going to get the red dress to go with my blue one. Fire and ice, remember?"

Bonnie held open her suit jacket, revealing a crimson cummerbund. "I didn't forget." She stood back and spread her arms wide. "What do you think?"

"You look amazing!" Emma was still surprised, but not in a bad way. "Very dashing."

Bonnie's grin grew wider. "And you look like a movie star. Here. I got this for you."

She held out a plastic clamshell, white roses bound together with lace inside. Emma extended an arm, blushing as Bonnie tied the corsage to her wrist. It felt like getting married. Including the guests. She glanced over her shoulder and saw four people clustered in the doorway, watching it all.

Emma groaned. "I hope you're in the mood for photos."

Bonnie didn't seem to mind as they were fawned over and moved from one location to another, their photo taken at a tedious number of angles. Emma had to admit that she was eager to see the results. Some other time. Right now, she only wanted to be alone with her girlfriend.

"You sure you don't want a limo?" Tim asked as they were leaving. "I bet I can still find one. I know a guy. Or if you don't want to wait, I can drive you there in the Bentley. I'll be your personal chauffeur."

"Thanks," Bonnie said, "but that's not our style."

"It's almost like they want to spend time alone," Jason said sardonically. He began waving the others away from the door. "I got this," he said to Emma. "Have fun."

"Thanks."

Her friends and family were soon forgotten as she was escorted to a junky old car. It might as well have been a fairytale carriage, as far as she was concerned. Everything about this night was enchanted by default, because not so long ago, it seemed an impossible dream that she would ever have a girlfriend, let alone go to prom with one.

Bonnie was in high spirits as they drove to the venue at a downtown hotel. Once inside, they took yet another photo before hitting the dance floor. They attracted a few stares, but if anyone had something bad to say, neither of them heard it. Bonnie occupied her full attention. She seemed to vibrate with energy, which was weird, because in the weeks leading up to prom, she hadn't expressed much excitement. In fact, she had repeatedly asked Emma if she really wanted to go, as if she was unsure.

"I need to cool down," Emma said, fanning herself. She didn't mind being a big girl, although it did mean struggling to stay cool in situations like these. Especially when Bonnie wouldn't let her leave the dance floor. She did so now, leading her outside and around the building to a pool. A few others had the same idea, quietly making out next to the glowing water.

"Let's show them how it's done," Bonnie said, leaning against a table and pulling her near.

Emma was more than happy to kiss her back, although she was more in the mood to talk. "You're really enjoying yourself!"

Bonnie bit her bottom lip, eyes sparkling. "Don't I always when I'm with you?"

"I guess I didn't expect you to be this excited."

"I feel good," Bonnie admitted. "I'm almost done with high school, I got that scholarship I was after, and best of all, I have the most gorgeous girlfriend imaginable."

"Stop," Emma said, hoping that she wouldn't listen.

"Are you still happy?" Bonnie asked. "I know you wanted me to enroll at the University of Houston so we could be closer, but the music program here is exactly what I need."

"I'm fine with it," Emma said. "Did I ever tell you how Uncle Jace moved here to be with Ben? He used to live in Houston before they met. So once I graduate, I'll be following in his footsteps, which I like."

Bonnie's expression grew serious. "I love you, Emma. I never expected to find someone like you. Not in a million years. And yet, here you are."

"Here I am," Emma said, moving closer. "And I know you've heard this a million times tonight—"

Bonnie didn't let her finish. Emma didn't need to. Why bother, when it was obvious to anyone who happened to look in their direction. Even the twinkling stars above must see it, despite being millions of miles away.

They loved each other.

The happiness they felt that night was unforgettable. There was no need to fix the dried flower to the page, or glue their prom photo next to it. Emma did so anyway, because the happiness of that evening was not only unforgettable. It was significant. For one of them anyway. She sorted through more photos and souvenirs, adding them to the album and creating a timeline of a relationship that was sometimes harmonious, and at others nonexistent. Their tempers had been more volatile when they were younger. Some arguments lasted more than a few days, and some reunions were months apart. They always found each other again though. All it took was a glance from across the room, or hearing the other person's voice over the phone, to summon up those old feelings.

I miss you.

Emma wrote this next to a photo after gluing it in. The university campus was the backdrop, where they were both enrolled now. Bonnie was hanging from the low branch of a tree while making an ape face. Emma stood next to her, laughing. The scene appeared so carefree, and yet, she still managed to interpret it in a new way. Emma was wearing a football jersey. Her father had bought it for her as a gift, and Bonnie had gone wild the first time Emma put it on, making her wonder if her girlfriend was bisexual and attracted to men. Why else would she keep telling Emma that she was handsome with such admiration in her voice? That was an easy question to answer now. She stood, returning to the home office where she had left a DVD brought from home. All she needed was the paper cover. She slid this free from the plastic case, walking back down the hall and through memories so fresh that they shook her still.

"Why did you make me watch that movie?" Emma wailed.

The credits were rolling on *Boys Don't Cry*, and while Hilary Swank had given one hell of a performance, Emma felt like someone had ripped the heart from her chest and stomped on it. She usually loved the ridiculously large television hanging on the wall of the apartment she shared with Jason, but all it had done was pull her into the story that much more, so she could really suffer.

"Did you not like it?" Bonnie asked, turning her head away to blow her nose.

"I loved it," Emma managed as another bout of tears wracked her body, "but it was so sa-a-ad!"

Bonnie joined her after saying, "And it's all true."

Even worse! Tear jerkers were difficult enough, but when real-life people had suffered as much—no, even more—than the characters on the screen. Ugh! They were going to need another box of tissues.

"It's horrible what trans people have to go through," Emma said, wiping at her eyes.

"That's like saying it must be horrible to be gay," Bonnie replied.

"It can be. I'm glad it's not *that* bad for most trans people—" She nodded at the screen. "—but it's definitely harder than what we go through. We only have to tell people how we really feel. They have to change their bodies or always feel like they're in the wrong one."

Bonnie's shoulder shook with sobs. She didn't seem capable of responding yet, so Emma kept talking.

"We should do something. We keep saying we're going to

join that pride alliance on campus. I bet they know a way we can get involved. We have to raise awareness or... Are you okay?"

Bonnie was still crying. Sure, it was a sad movie, and a tragic turn of real-world events, but she was really weeping. The way you do when someone has died.

"Bonnie?"

"It's the truth," her girlfriend mumbled, gesturing at the television. "That's why I wanted you to see it."

Emma looked at the screen. Then back at her girlfriend again. They had been on rocky ground lately, Bonnie distant and distracted. She even looked different, having lost weight, which was alarming because she wasn't very big to begin with. Her face seemed gaunt, but that could have been due to her wearing less makeup and...

Oh.

"It's your truth," Emma said, her throat growing tight. "Is that what you're trying to say?"

Bonnie sobbed harder and toppled over into her lap. Emma stroked her hair, which was shorter than ever, and tried not to panic. She wasn't ready for this. What was she supposed to say? That she was sorry? Emma didn't want anyone pitying her for being gay. She could reassure Bonnie that everything was fine, but if that was true, why was dread slowly creeping over her?

"I need you to talk to me," Emma said, voice shaking. "You're freaking me out."

"This isn't who I'm supposed to be," Bonnie squeaked.

Emma fought against tears and failed. She wasn't sure why. Mostly because she hated to see her girlfriend in such pain, and maybe because she was scared of what she might lose. As in everything.

"It's okay," Emma said, rubbing her back. "We'll figure this out together."

She kept whispering soothing words, even if she didn't believe them. Bonnie's breathing eventually slowed until she was able to sit upright again. They took turns blowing their noses, Emma unsure how to continue the conversation, because Bonnie now seemed incapable of looking at her.

Emma waited as long as she could, not wanting to overwhelm her, but she needed answers. "You think you might be trans? Is that right?"

Bonnie shook her head. "I *know* I am. I'm not crazy. I thought I was until I started talking to Allison."

"The counselling sessions?" Emma asked. "I thought you were going there to talk about your father."

"I don't care about my dad," Bonnie spat. "I don't even remember him. I was going so I could figure out why my own body disgusts me."

They hadn't been sleeping together much lately. The last few times had been one-sided, Bonnie keeping her clothes on. Emma had wondered if she was hiding an illness. Anorexia maybe. That's not what this was though. Not by far.

"Tell me everything," Emma said. "From the very beginning. Don't hold back because this is important."

Bonnie finally made eye contact. Then she nodded. "The earliest sign was not liking the clothes my mother dressed me in. I don't recall doing this, but my mom told me she'd leave the room and come back to find that I'd taken off my dress. I only wanted to be in my underwear. I do remember playing with my sister and having her call me big brother. We didn't have any men in the family, so that's how I justified it, like I was fulfilling a role."

Emma opened her mouth to ask a question. Then she shut it again, not wanting to offend.

Bonnie noticed. "I need you to be open with me too," she said, voice shaking. "If you make me imagine what you're thinking…" She took a shuddering breath. "It won't be good."

"I'm not thinking anything bad," Emma said, grabbing her hand. "I'm embarrassed to ask, that's all. But I will anyway. Do you think your dad not being around is the reason why you're trans?" She grimaced. "I hate those bullshit theories that gay people are raised that way, so I'm sorry. But I honestly don't know what makes someone trans."

"It's biological," Bonnie said. "Like being gay, it's the way our brains are formed. Upbringing has nothing to do with it. Plenty of women without men in their family still feel comfortable in their own skin. I don't, because my mind doesn't match the rest of me. I've always felt that way. I remember in grade school, when they split up the boys and girls for PE, how unfair that seemed. I felt like I should be given a choice. And when I got older." Bonnie shook her head. "Puberty made it worse. I didn't like the way my body was changing. I wanted to stop it, no matter what it took. When my friend Kelly got into an accident and lost his leg… It's hard to say this out loud, but I started fantasizing about getting into an accident too, like being thrown from a car and skidding face down along the street so my chest would be damaged. Or when we were taught how to do breast cancer screenings, I didn't. For years I ignored that, because I thought cancer would be worth having my breasts being removed."

"Jesus," Emma breathed. She could only imagine how tormented Bonnie must have been to entertain such thoughts. "I don't want you to feel that way."

Bonnie's lip trembled. "Me neither. I'm so tired of it."

"I wish you would have told me sooner. Or anyone else."

"I tried. I was in the third grade and some girls had been bullying me because I wasn't like them. When I told my mom about it after school, I remember saying 'I think I was supposed to be a boy.' She told me I was being silly, and that there were all kinds of girls out there. She explained that I was a tomboy, and that there was nothing wrong with that. She meant well. I felt better too, because I liked the sound of it. I was a boy. Of sorts."

"All those times you got depressed," Emma said, thinking back on their relationship. "You told me it was a chemical imbalance that ran in your family. But it wasn't. Was it?"

Bonnie shook her head. "No. It helped if I avoided looking in the mirror too much. When I decided that I was a lesbian, that made a tremendous difference because it gave me permission to be a dyke. I could make myself more like a boy without needing to explain why, even to myself. But it never lasted. I would always get depressed again because this isn't who I'm meant to be."

That was hard for Emma to hear. She loved the person she was sitting next to. She didn't want them to disappear and be replaced by someone else, but… "I want you to be happy," she said.

"Thanks." Bonnie breathed out. "I'm trying. Allison says I'm ready to start T soon which should help. And it'll get my weight up again. She thinks I starve myself to make my body less curvy."

"Testosterone," Emma said. "You want to transition? All the way?"

Bonnie nodded, expression concerned. "This is the hardest part. But we have to talk about it."

Emma squeezed her hand. She wanted to do more than that. They should strip off their clothes, make love, hold each other, and not let go until they absolutely had to because a huge unasked question now hung in the air: What did this mean for their relationship?

Bobby.

Emma wrote the name at the bottom of an empty page. She didn't have a photo to glue into the album. Not yet. She drew a question mark where one would be someday, but it had nothing to do with how she... *he* might one day appear. For now it asked a bigger question: Would she still be able to love Bonnie when she was in the body of a man? Emma had been struggling for days to find the answer. The memory album was supposed to help, but she had reached the present day and felt no closer to the answer. She stood on stiff legs and stretched. Then she went downstairs, her stomach rumbling.

"Hungry?" her mother asked as Emma passed through the living room.

"Starving."

Soon they were standing in the kitchen together, a freshly made sandwich on the breakfast bar. Emma sat on a stool. Her mother, appropriately enough, stood on the other side like a bartender, attempting to decipher Emma's inner thoughts by studying her features.

"Did you finish your project?" Michelle asked.

Emma nodded and swallowed her first bite, shocked that her mother let her get so far before the interrogation began.

"Do I get to see it?" Michelle pressed.

Emma took another bite and shook her head.

"It must be a surprise then," Michelle said. "Ben and Tim's wedding! You made something for them."

Emma felt a surge of guilt. If only she had done something so considerate. "I still need to get them a present."

"Let your father and me take care of that. No one expects a college student to have money." Michelle tilted her head. "I was surprised when you showed up here. We'll all be in Austin in a few days. We could have brought your things to you."

"I needed to get away," Emma said, her appetite vanishing. "Can I ask you something?" Her mother's expression was pleading for her to be open, so she didn't wait for an answer. "Would you still love Dad if he became a woman?"

Michelle snorted at the thought. Then she grew serious when she saw Emma's face. "Your father as a woman? He wouldn't make a very pretty one."

"Imagine that he did though. He would still be Dad, and kind of look like him, but he'd be an attractive woman."

Michelle pondered this. "I know I'd still love him. But I don't know if we could be together intimately. I'd still want to live with him and continue raising you children together. As for the rest... I don't know. That's a tough one, honey."

"What if Dad couldn't get it up anymore? Would that make you love him any less?"

"You certainly get your directness from him," Michelle said, sounding exasperated. "No darling, that wouldn't make me love him less. We'd simply have to get creative."

"What if he was a woman and you got creative?"

Michelle blushed. "What's this about?"

Emma decided to tell her. Everything came pouring out, along with more tears, as she tried to explain the situation. Her mother was sympathetic, but disappointingly, she didn't have the answer either.

"I'm sure you want to be supportive," Michelle said, "and I know you won't stop loving her..." She shook her head. "I wish your uncle was still alive. He'd know what to do."

Emma thought of him again, and the photo on the first page of the memory album. Then she sat upright. "He'd tell me to be true to myself. And to be kind."

"Good advice," Michelle said. "You still have a hard decision to make though."

That was for sure. But at least now Emma had a course of action. She would be honest about her own needs, while treating the person she loved with the utmost respect.

"You're the best!" Emma said, grabbing the sandwich and taking another bite.

Michelle blinked. "So glad I could be of help. You can return the favor by cleaning up the mess you made upstairs."

"You were spying on me?" Emma asked incredulously.

"No. I don't need to spy on you because you're my daughter, and you've always been messy." Michelle placed a hand over her chest. "And darling, whatever you need to be happy, no matter how much change that involves, please know that nothing can change my love for you. Ever."

Emma swallowed again, but this time because of emotion. "Thanks, Mom. I love you too."

The house slowly filled with guests. Jason was seated on the couch while tuning his guitar. Marcello occasionally glided through the room, instructing the waiters and staff. Or if he wasn't around, Nathaniel would show up and bark orders at them. There was still much to do before the two grooms returned from their romantic getaway. Wouldn't they be surprised to discover that a full-scale wedding had invaded their home? Ben and Tim were the stars of the day, and yet, Emma struggled to focus on any of that right now. She kept watching the door, waiting for a different arrival.

"She's still not here?" Jason asked,

"Him," Emma said. "He's still not here."

"Oh. Sorry! This is going to take some getting used to."

"You're telling me?" she said, but she grinned to show that she was only kidding. "He's been really patient with me each time I slip up, so don't beat yourself up over it."

"I'll try harder anyway," Jason said. "I've always liked him. Speaking of which, have you made any decisions?"

Emma was distracted by her phone before she could answer. The text was from Bonnie. *Bobby*. She needed to get that through her head. Emma didn't want to make any mistakes today, no matter how natural they might be.

I'm outside, the text read. *Would you mind coming to meet me?*

"He's here," Emma said, rushing for the door. She felt the same swell of emotion that accompanied each reunion, although this time, she was more nervous than usual.

Emma opened the front door, and when she didn't see anyone on the porch, she closed it behind her and walked out into the yard. She spotted Bonnie's car first, parked off to the side among all the other vehicles. The person standing next to it wasn't Bonnie. He could have been her brother, enough resemblance remaining to be mistaken for family. He wore a gray suit, his shoulders appearing broader than usual. The black pressed shirt beneath the jacket was flatter than Emma was used to, giving the impression of a beefy chest rather than breasts. A brace instead of a bra. The dark hair was buzzed short and brushed forward, no longer needing styling product.

Bobby seemed nervous. He fidgeted with his car keys, as if he might need them soon.

Emma wanted to cry. Not because she was disappointed or heartbroken. In many ways, the differences in appearance were subtle, but even these small changes must have made him feel better. These were only the first steps too. She wanted Bobby to be happy, the tears gathering in her eyes joyful, but she didn't set them free, too worried they would be misinterpreted.

"You're so handsome," Emma said softly as she neared.

The uncertainty on Bobby's face wavered. "Really?"

"Really," Emma said.

She stopped in front of him. This is usually when they would kiss. They could at the very least hug, but she felt they needed to talk first. That would be fairest.

"I'm nervous about what everyone will think," Bobby said, eyes darting to the house.

"Don't be," Emma said. "We don't have to go in right away. I wouldn't mind a little time alone, just for us." She didn't say this flirtatiously.

Bobby didn't take it that way, but his eyes did move over her affectionately. "I like the tuxedo. You look very debonair."

"I wanted to be supportive," Emma explained.

He nodded his understanding. "I always admired how handsome you can be. Beautiful too. You've got a little of everything." He looked away, as if wanting to reassure her that they didn't have to get romantic if she wasn't willing. Instead he nodded to the side of the house, where a path outside the backyard fence had been worn down over the years. One of Tim's jogging routes. "Wanna go for a walk?"

She nodded and turned. As they strolled side by side, she was aware that they still hadn't touched.

"I've been thinking," she began.

"I bet," Bobby replied.

They both laughed, the release welcome.

"All I've done lately is think," Bobby continued. "I don't mean to put it all on your shoulders, but I figure this is your decision to make. My feelings for you haven't changed, and they won't, even when I'm done transitioning, because I like women. I'm sure of that. But I also get why this might be a deal breaker."

Emma nodded. "I don't know if my feelings will change," she admitted. "I fell in love with who you are as a person, but now it turns out that you weren't able to be yourself. So maybe I need to get to know him and decide. I have to be honest though. I've never been attracted to men. I wish I was bisexual. That would make this so much easier."

Bobby seemed to take this well. "I'm glad you're being honest. I was scared you would say everything is fine. That would feel like you shutting me out—telling me what I want to hear." He stopped and turned to face her. "I won't be mad if you can't do this. Promise me you won't feel guilty either. None of this is your fault."

"There's no one to blame," Emma said. "I'm not trans, but I know how it feels to deny who I am, and I really *really* don't want you to do that anymore."

"Thanks," Bobby said.

He was staring at the ground, which was a shame, because the day was beautiful. Beyond the wooden privacy fence, they could hear people chatting and laughing. On this side, the sun was beating down on the lush green grass that Tim kept trimmed. The woods began just ahead, shadowy and cool. There were so many directions they could go, if they chose.

"I'm only certain about one thing," Emma said, gently touching his chin so he would raise it and meet her eye. "I want you in my life. No matter what form that takes. You're too important for me to ever let go of. That's all I can promise right now. Okay?"

"Yeah," Bobby croaked.

He held out a trembling hand, which grew steady when Emma took it again. "Which way?" he asked, nodding to their options.

"No idea," Emma admitted. "I guess we'll find out when we get there."

Bobby started to walk, but she pulled on his arm, needing that hug after all. They grinned at each other bashfully afterwards, and then, hand in hand, they continued their journey together.

Something Like Bones

by Jay Bell

Acapulco, Mexico
2014

William stood in a hallway between two hotel doors, trying to decide which called to him more. Behind one was his heart's desire, the man he hoped to marry. Jason wasn't much of a morning person and took forever to get ready. All he needed to do today was put on a swimsuit, a simple task he still managed to drag out. That left William free to consider the other door, behind which was the adorable and huggable Ben and his freshly married husband, smoking-hot Tim Wyman. Were they getting ready for plans of their own? Or were they still in bed, expressing their love for each other? And what exactly would such an expression sound like? Sweet murmured words? Moans of pleasure? Shrieks of ecstasy?

He supposed it wouldn't be difficult to find out. William crept forward and was just about to press his ear to the door when a voice made him jump.

"What are you doing?"

He turned around in time to see Jason shaking his head.

"Never mind," his boyfriend continued. "I don't want to know."

"I just thought we should invite them," William said quietly, hoping that Ben and Tim weren't sitting upright in bed and listening to the voices beyond their door. Then again, if they decided to come investigate...

"Invite them to what, exactly?" Jason said with a knowing expression.

William looked him over, his libido reorienting on a new subject. Jason wore forest green swim trunks that cruelly failed to cup a bulge, although the white tank top showed off his broad shoulders nicely, the bare skin begging for a kiss. The sunglasses that held back his messy hair made it easier to see the intense eyes William loved staring into, especially while in bed together. The guitar slung across Jason's back reminded him of other talents that he appreciated too.

"Ready to go?" his boyfriend prompted.

"Yeah," William said breathlessly. He should have waited for Jason before taking a shower this morning, so they could have had some fun together. Maybe it wasn't too late.

"Come on," Jason said, taking his arm and guiding him down the hallway. "You can be so weird sometimes."

Not weird. Horny. With so many yummy guys around, who could blame him? William felt the need to defend himself regardless. "Ben and Tim invited us on their honeymoon. It's only polite to do the same."

"This isn't our honeymoon."

"No, but we can give them the option of joining us."

They reached the elevators, Jason jabbing the button and turning to face him. "We agreed last night to make separate plans, and I intend to spend the day with the greatest love of my life."

William was flattered until Jason adjusted the strap of his guitar and began stroking it affectionately with a thumb. "I can't wait to get my hands all over you, baby," he murmured.

"Then I'll give you enough privacy to make that happen," William said, feigning offense. He started marching back down the hall at a slow enough pace that Jason easily caught him and pulled him back.

"*Both* of the greatest loves of my life," Jason amended. "Don't judge. You're the one who can't stop checking out my parents."

"Am I that obvious?" William said, feeling embarrassed.

"A little. You just need some extra TLC today."

That sounded promising. He was about to suggest they head back to their room when a ding sounded and the elevator doors opened. Jason stepped inside. William followed. He would have to work off his sexual frustration some other way. He put cute guys out of mind and thought about azure waters instead. Acapulco was gorgeous. He had enjoyed visiting Mexico so far, but few things held as much allure as diving into warm water and letting his body propel him beneath the waves. He would still long to do so even if the bay was frigid, like Cape Cod had been, or Astoria would be.

Jason made them stop in the resort gift shop for a cooler filled with ice, drinks, and snacks. Then he ran back upstairs for a blanket and towels. William didn't mind the delay. He walked to the window and eyed the surf, his attention moving to each swimmer to assess if anyone was in danger. No need for a rescue today, it would seem. Jason returned, panting but smiling, and together they walked to the beach to choose a spot on the sand.

"You can go for a swim," Jason said as he laid out the blanket.

"I'll help first," William said, but only out of politeness. The second Jason declined the offer, William stripped down to his scuba panties—as Kelly had once called them—and ran for the water. He wasn't sure how much time passed. Being in Austin for so long had made him feel landlocked. Now he was back in his element. Good thing there wasn't a Coast Guard air station in Acapulco, or he would be tempted to relocate here. When his muscles were hot and humming from exertion, he left the water again and returned to Jason, the upcoming move still on his mind.

"We have a lot of planning to do," William said as he toweled off.

"Sunbathing, lunch, and shopping," Jason said. He sat cross-legged on the blanket while tuning his guitar, although he paused to look William up and down, settling on his face. "Or did you have another idea in mind?"

"No, I still like all of that. I meant Astoria."

"Ah." Jason scowled with concentration as he played a chord experimentally. Then he resumed adjusting.

Jason didn't say anything else, so William took the initiative. He settled down on the blanket and stretched out in the sun to finish drying off. "I was thinking we should get a two-bedroom apartment. Yes, it will cost more, but the extra space might be useful."

"For what?" Jason asked. "Don't tell me you want separate rooms. Or worse, a roommate."

"You don't like living with Emma?"

"I do," Jason murmured, "but I also like the idea of having complete privacy. With you."

"Me too," William said. "I'm fine with small places. That's all I've had since enlisting. I thought you might want, I don't know, a home office."

Jason snorted. "I'm a pet store manager, not an entrepreneur. What do you picture me doing in this office?"

"Who knows what kind of job you'll have there. You aren't limited to pet stores. You might become a corporate big shot.

Besides, an office would help with the job hunt, if you don't find one before then. How's that going?"

Jason was quiet. William looked over his shoulder when he didn't get a response, which finally prompted one.

"I'm fine with my laptop. I can use it on the couch, the kitchen table, or even the toilet. No need for a special room. It would be a waste."

"Are you sure? With two of us living there, it might come in handy."

Jason nodded to their surroundings. "Vacation. Remember?"

"Sorry," William said, closing his eyes and turning his face to the sun. "But we have to start planning eventually."

"Now though? This might be the only chance we get to visit Acapulco. Try living in the moment, just this once."

"Fine, fine," William said with a chuckle. "No more talk about work. Let's keep figuring out our future home though. That's okay, isn't it?"

Jason sighed. Then he started strumming the guitar, and when he sang, it was a song about paradise being paved over for a parking lot and the trees being shoved into a museum for people to see. William laughed, getting the point that was being made. They were in a beautiful paradise and he shouldn't take it for granted. His amusement faded as a certain line caught his attention though. *You don't know what you've got until it's gone.* That was a feeling he knew well. When they had first met, William's life had been a complete mess. Despite this, he had managed to fall deeply in love with Jason, but he hadn't truly realized how much that relationship meant to him until they were separated by distance and time. That's exactly why he wanted to discuss their future together. Why was he alone in this?

"Joni Mitchell," Jason said in reverence when the song came to an end. "I love that one, but I never understood why it's called *Big Yellow Taxi.*"

William sat up and turned to face him. "Is there something you need to tell me?"

Jason looked surprised. Then he started fussing with his guitar again, even though he had just proven that it was perfectly tuned. William remained silent. He kept staring, his stomach sinking. Everything was okay. Wasn't it?

Jason's eyes finally met his again. Then he lifted the guitar and ducked beneath the strap so he could set it aside. "Okay," he said. "There's something I need to say, and it's pretty important."

William's mouth went dry. He forced himself to swallow and nodded. "I'm listening."

Jason sighed heavily. "I think it's time— Well, I don't know how to tell you this but... You're looking a little pink."

"Pink?" William repeated. Then he groaned and swiped at the sand, intentionally missing Jason but coming awfully close.

Jason laughed and reached into the cooler. "Let me put sunblock on you."

"You left it in there?" William asked as he recoiled. "It'll be freezing! Besides, I put some on before we left the hotel."

"Gotta be washed off by now," Jason said, opening the bottle and squeezing lotion into his hand. He winced. "And yeah, leaving this in the cooler was a bad idea. I'll warm it up first. Can we start with your front?"

William watched him rub his hands together with a gleeful expression. How could he resist? He flopped down on the blanket, the sun soon blocked by a body instead of a chemical compound. Jason, leaning over him, went straight for his pecs. No surprise. Jason often started there, but normally when they weren't in public. His touches felt good regardless, palms greasing up not only his chest but his shoulders, stomach, hips...

"Better get my back," William said hurriedly, flipping over without explanation. He glanced around and noticed a woman walking by while talking on her phone, an old couple reclining beneath an umbrella not far away, and kids in the distance building a sandcastle. All potential witnesses to the growing slab of meat between his legs. A public boner? Really? He hadn't dealt with that sort of embarrassment since he'd been a sexually frustrated teenager. He tried to will the erection away, but without success. Jason was rubbing his back and inadvertently shifting William's body from side to side, which made him feel like he was humping the blanket. And it felt kind of good. He stifled a groan. Jason noticed, his hands paused in their work. When they resumed, they focused on his thighs.

"I should probably get the front of your legs," Jason said.

"Maybe later," William mumbled.

"I didn't get all of your arms either."

"Can't you do that without me turning over?"

Jason slid a hand up William's leg. "Are you—"

"I don't want to talk about it."

Jason laughed. "So… What are we dealing with here? Completely hard or just a semi?"

"If I wasn't wearing Speedos, I'd be plowing a hole in the sand."

"Nice," Jason said. Then he hissed a cussword and flopped forward onto his belly, partially draping himself over William.

He didn't need to ask why. William felt something hard pressing against his leg. He also heard female voices giggling as they shook out towels and settled down not far away. If he or Jason rolled over now, those women would be in for a breathtaking view of twin sundials. Speedos didn't offer much cover, and the swim trunks Jason wore might not be form fitting, but they would still tent.

"Stop moving," Jason said.

"I'm only breathing!" William shot back. "You need to make yours go away. That way mine will too."

"Maybe mine will go away if you stop talking about yours," Jason retorted. "God this is awkward."

"Yeah. We're basically stuck here."

"Yup. Trapped by our boners."

William had been horny even before they left the resort. Jason was always in the mood. This didn't bode well. Unless… "We could call Ben and Tim for help."

Jason groaned, and not in pleasure. "I'm officially divorcing you."

"We aren't even married yet!"

"I know. I'm skipping all the way to the end." Jason slid to the right so they were side by side instead of rubbing against each other. "Irreconcilable differences."

William laughed. "Right now we've got a couple of big things in common. I'll tell the judge that I have hard evidence to prove my case. Just wait until he makes me show the jury. Exhibit D."

"Stop talking about it," Jason said, hissing laughter. "This is ridiculous."

"We could try discussing our plans again."

Jason turned his head to face him, eyes squinty and wet. "Here's what we're going to do. I'm going to think about work, in particular the weird customer who insists on opening cans of cat food to taste-test them. Then I'm going to walk back to our hotel room, *with* the guitar in front of me, just in case. When you feel capable of meeting me there…"

"Yes?" William said, already liking this plan.

Jason smiled. "Then we'll see if we can't reconcile our similarities."

Something Like Spirits

by Jay Bell

Austin, Texas
~~1974~~
~~2008~~
~~1999~~
????

Marcello peered at the calendar on his refrigerator door, trying to extract any useful information from it. October. That was a good start. He was pretty sure the month was nearing its end. Of course it was! Halloween was here. How could he forget? That just left the year in question. Marcello's eyes moved upward, but during their quest for four simple digits, they were waylaid by a photo of greasy muscles and strong hands that gripped a fat hose, liquid dribbling from the tip.

"Oh my," Marcello breathed.

"I've seen bigger," a voice said.

Marcello didn't need to pry his eyes away from the tensed biceps and narrow waist. He knew that voice too well, since it belonged to one of his closest companions. "Had you laid eyes on a hose that lengthy, dearest Eric, without sharing the details with me until now... Well, that would put a severe strain on our friendship."

"I dated a volunteer fireman," Eric replied. "Briefly. He wasn't quite that blessed though. Where are these boys from?"

Marcello squinted, his vision blurry. He patted himself down for his glasses before remembering that he didn't wear any. His vision was nearly perfect when not impaired by certain mind-altering substances. "Canada," he guessed. "Why am I standing here again?"

"You wanted to get us a drink," Eric said.

"No," Marcello said. "That's not it. Well, it is, but my primary goal was to see if this dreadful day had come to an end yet."

"The night is still young, I'm afraid."

Marcello looked over at his friend. Eric was paler than

normal. He also didn't usually wear a black collared cape, a charcoal grey vest, or ruffled ruby fabric around his neck. "Have you been getting enough sun?" Marcello teased.

"I'm not getting enough something," Eric said, raising an empty wine glass. In a hokey imitation of Dracula he added, "Count Conroy is parched!"

"My apologies," Marcello said, opening the refrigerator door. He saw a number of options, but none of them felt right until his friend nudged him with a helpful reminder.

"Considering what day it is, we should pair our wine by costume rather than by food."

"Of course," Marcello said, shutting the door again. "Communion wine for me, virgin's blood for you."

He went to a nearby wine rack and selected one of his finest bottles. To be fair, they were *all* fine, so this meant choosing randomly. He only concerned himself with the color. He had the bottle open with practiced skill and two fresh glasses filled with red liquid in under a minute. Then he smiled and proposed a toast. "May tomorrow come sooner rather than later."

"You're not having fun?" Eric asked after taking a sip. The plastic fangs weren't in at the moment, thankfully, or Marcello would be wiping wine off the floor again.

"I'm having the time of my life," he replied, although not convincingly. He took an extra swig, hoping to make this statement come true. "What a joyous celebration."

"I'm sure we'll get more trick-or-treaters soon," Eric said reassuringly.

"I can scarcely wait. In fact, why wait at all? Let's hit the streets and take the candy to them! And may I suggest a more efficient method of delivery? A slingshot perhaps. That way they receive a scare along with their treat."

Eric studied him, seeing straight through his humor. "You're unhappy."

Marcello sighed. "I regret that neither of us threw a party this year. What were we thinking?"

"That we wanted to have a traditional Halloween. For children that means going door to door. For us it means passing out candy."

Marcello snorted. "Is that what you recall from the Halloweens of your youth?"

Eric seemed puzzled. "Am I forgetting something?"

"The pranks!" Marcello said. "Poor sweet Eric. Perhaps you should be dressed as a priest instead of I. Then again, it would hardly be much of a costume, would it?"

"I'm no saint," Eric said defensively.

"Aren't you? Enlighten me with a story! What's the most trouble you've gotten into during this holiday?"

"Well..." Eric frowned in concentration, which was adorable, especially since they both already knew the answer.

"None at all. I suspected as much. Did you never throw eggs at a house? Toss toilet paper into trees? Smear shaving cream on a car? You're missing out. The tricks are always more satisfying than the treats. And speaking of tricks, I'm reminded of a hustler I picked up during a previous All Hallows' Eve. At least I assumed that was his occupation. As it turned out, he was merely dressed as John Travolta from *Welcome Back, Kotter*, but he still earned his share of college tuition that night."

The doorbell chimed.

Eric perked up. Then he looked concerned. "Please restrain yourself this time."

"Naturally! I'm the very picture of restraint!"

Marcello grabbed the Bible where he had left it on the counter. Eric went for the bowl of candy instead. They raced each other to the door, Eric stopping to collect a few candy bars that sloshed over the edge. This gave Marcello the needed edge. He threw open the door, raised the Bible above his head, and started shouting, "SINNERS! SINNERS! EACH AND EVERY ONE OF YOU SHALL ROAST IN THE BLAZING INFERNOS OF HELL!"

The children didn't seem to appreciate this performance, judging from the way they shrieked and ran for their lives. Marcello, caught up in the joy of the moment, chased them halfway down the drive before he returned to the front door.

Eric didn't share in his amusement. "Can't you let me give them the candy first?"

"I take back what I said earlier. This *is* fun!"

"You're doing it wrong."

"From my perspective, I'm the only one who is doing it right." They reentered the house, Eric still shaking his head in disapproval. Marcello expressed his frustration too. "It's Halloween! Give in to your dark side. Surely there is someone upon whom you would like to exact revenge? An inconsiderate buffoon who slighted you previously, earning a flaming bag of feces on their doorstep."

Eric set down the candy bowl and moved deeper into the house. "*It's the Great Pumpkin, Charlie Brown* is about to start. Let's watch that. And please try to behave while we do. For me."

"Very well," Marcello said.

They settled down in the living room, where Marcello yawned his way through the first ten minutes of a cartoon that—yes, he too enjoyed *but*—made him feel old and nostalgic for his youth. He didn't miss being clustered around an old black and white television with the other children of the group home. What he longed for were the days that followed his awakening, the realization that life was for the living, and that rules were made by those who never followed them.

He was about to switch off the television and insist they do something to push them both closer to a heart attack when fate intervened. A commercial break, which began with a political ad for a would-be lieutenant governor. The hopeful campaigner was handsome enough to be eye-catching, his message delivered with practiced care.

"You've been told the choice is between paying higher taxes or having more programs cut—services that affect you and your family—but I intend to curb wasteful spending and reroute that money back to the community." On the screen, the speaker walked along a line of people. All colors, ages, and creeds were represented. Each conveyed their discontent with upset expressions as the message continued. "Too many lawmakers are lining their pockets at your expense, but no more. If you help elect me, Zachary Nelson, as Lieutenant Governor, I'll be fighting to protect your interests, not my own. That's what our forefathers intended elected officials to do. Let's embrace the values of the past and use them to move us toward a better future."

Marcello slowly turned his head toward Eric, who was glaring at the screen while clenching his jaw. When the cartoon resumed, Eric stared at it unseeing until he finally shook his head, grabbed the remote, and turned the television off. "Amazing how he manages to ruin everything. Even all these years later."

The 'he' no doubt referred to Gabriel, who had once been Eric's greatest love… until a young man with political aspirations got in the way. Zachary. If only Gabriel had possessed the decency to end his relationship with Eric first. That might have helped matters. Or not. Eric still would have ended up angry and hurt, but perhaps he would have felt less betrayed. Marcello hadn't been completely blindsided by these events. Gabriel had always given priority to his aspirations. Even the vicarious ones. Enough time had passed that they were all friends again, but it was never truly the same. Not like before.

"Will you be voting for him?" Marcello asked, gambling on humor to defuse the tension. "I'm tempted, but something in my gut tells me that Zachary Nelson is a cheater."

Eric's scowl deepened. Then he laughed. "He's not a cheater. He's a homewrecker. And he's not to blame. Gabriel on the other hand…"

"Deserves that flaming bag of poo?"

Eric smiled and began to shake his head. Then he looked over sharply. "I'm not interested in squatting over a bag, or carrying around your best effort but…"

Marcello leaned forward eagerly. "Yes?"

"Maybe we could throw a roll of toilet paper through his trees. Just one though! That's it!"

"Excellent!" Marcello said, intending to leap to his feet, but it was more of a stumble that ended with him grabbing a standing lamp for support. "Into the car, my friend. Vengeance is calling our names!"

Eric grinned as he stood. Then another concern chased the happiness from his features. "You aren't planning to drive."

"One of us needs to," Marcello said, "and you've been guzzling my best wine all night."

"So have you."

"Yes, yes," he said, attempting to wave a hand dismissively and meeting resistance, "but I have a higher tolerance than you."

"Says the man who just knocked over the lamp."

"Did I?" Marcello said, refusing to acknowledge it. "I don't see a lamp here." He looked left and right. Anywhere but down.

Eric didn't feed into this, choosing instead to peer at him suspiciously. "Have you done more than drink tonight?"

"Certainly not. Aside from some mushrooms, but that was hours ago and I still don't feel a thing. I'm guessing they were of the grocery store variety. Realizing that I had been ripped off put me in an agitated state, so I calmed my nerves with a tranquilizer. Or two. Having achieved a placid state again, I decided to reward myself with a glass of champagne—"

"And by glass, you mean bottle," Eric interjected helpfully.

"Bottles are made of glass, you are correct. That's all I had. Aside from the wine we drank together. Oh, and one of those brownies on the counter. Have we given out any of those to trick-or-treaters?"

"No," Eric said.

Marcello smacked his mouth, which felt a little dry. Like cotton. "Probably best not to. Just in case."

Eric sighed and shook his head. "Call the limo service. Please."

"As you wish," Marcello said, phone already in hand as he tapped at the screen.

Before long, they were seated in the back of a car and zooming toward their destination, a sealed eight-pack of toilet paper between them.

"You really need to take better care of yourself," Eric said.

Marcello had been braced for a lecture and already had a reply locked and loaded. "At our ripe old age, what's the point? I'll never fit into my prom dress again, and if a cocktail of drugs kills me, isn't that better than heart failure, cancer, or whatever miserable fate the grim reaper has in store for me?"

"I've had similar thoughts," Eric said.

This wasn't the response he was expecting. The merest suggestion of Eric giving up made him unhappy, but why? They were both healthy. It's not like either of them had been diagnosed with cancer. Marcello felt his stomach lurch, which was strange, because his was usually made of iron. Countless illicit substances had been tossed into it over the years and his body had processed each with no intent of giving them back. Not until they passed the normal way.

"Are you okay, sir?" the driver said, eyes watching him in the rearview mirror.

"Fine, fine," he said, wishing he had ordered a stretch limo instead, for the privacy. "We're nearly there, aren't we? Make sure to drop us off a few houses down."

The driver's brow furrowed at this request but he nodded and complied. Gabriel had moved across the country and back again in his attempt to launch Zachary's political career. Now he had returned to Austin, but at least he'd had the decency not to live in West Lake Hills where he and Eric had once shared a home. Instead he chose Barton Creek, a neighborhood that wasn't far away and not quite as illustrious, although the houses were still of a price and size that most Americans would never be able to afford. So much for representing the community.

"I don't know if I can do this," Eric said when they were standing outside of the car.

"Just follow my lead," Marcello said, wishing they had donned night-vision goggles and covered their skin in camouflage paint, if only for fun. Then again, their current costumes weren't without merit. "Wrap that cape around yourself. That way you're less likely to be seen."

"What about you?"

"The priesthood grants me immunity," he replied. "Especially where God's work is concerned."

"And that's what we're here to do?"

"Close enough."

"We left the toilet paper in the car."

"I'll text the driver and have him circle back around," Marcello said. "Let's assess the scene of the crime until he gets here."

They had no trouble locating the house. Marcello had been there before. Just a few times for dinner and such. He was delighted by the number of trees dotting the front yard, and noted the lack of any gates or surveillance equipment. That would have to change if Zachary's campaign was successful.

"This is where they live?" Eric asked.

"You haven't been here before?" Marcello asked in surprise. The former lovers weren't estranged. They remained civil and could even be called friends, but that didn't mean they felt comfortable in each other's presence. Especially when Zachary was around. That's why Marcello made sure to be there for Eric during those occasions, although the last such party had been some time ago. Was there a reason why? Had old wounds reopened?

"It's a nice house," Eric said, staring at tall windows glowing with light.

"It's a prison," Marcello countered. "They've locked

themselves inside on Halloween night with no sign of festivities. What sort of a fool would do that?"

Eric smiled his appreciation. "Me. I always made sure to pass out candy to kids, even during my parties. I loved being home."

"I remember." Another pang of sorrow, but he quickly shoved it aside. This was no time for melancholy thoughts! They were here to get even!

"Oh no," Eric breathed, his eyes on the house again. "They really are home!"

Marcello followed his gaze and saw two figures passing from window to window, their attention on each other. Gabriel was gesticulating. Zachary turned around to shout something in return, the words almost loud enough to be understood, even from outside. As the animated conversation continued, Zachary passed by two more windows before he and Gabriel were lost to sight.

"Maybe this isn't such a good idea," Eric said. "They seem like they're arguing. That's already bad enough without their house getting toilet papered."

"I can think of something even worse," Marcello said. "Just imagine your ex-boyfriend showing up in the middle of such an argument."

"No!"

"Oh yes!" Marcello said, already walking toward the front door.

Eric caught up with him to pull on his arm. "No no no! I can't do this!"

"You can, and you will." Marcello stopped with his index finger just inches from the doorbell. "You'll thank me later."

"I sincerely doubt that!"

"If I didn't adore you so much, I'd make it a bet and add profit to my personal satisfaction." He focused on the door and, with some effort, managed to push the buzzer with only a few failed attempts. Then he put on a pleasant smile and waited. When the door swung open, Gabriel's expression strained, Marcello said to him, "Have you accepted Jesus Christ as your personal trainer? Because he has the most delectable abs, don't you think?"

"Marcello!" Gabriel said, relaxing somewhat. "What are you doing here?"

"We were just in the neighborhood for a little trick-or-treating," he said innocently. "Although I would prefer a drink to any—" He noticed the bowl that Gabriel was holding. "Scratch that. Reese's Peanut Butter Cups are undeniably delicious. We'll take some of those and whatever you have on tap."

"We?" Gabriel said, looking past him to the yard.

Marcello turned and found himself alone. Eric must have run off before the door was answered. No sense in embarrassing him. Marcello would go inside, snoop, and report back with any unflattering tidbits he could pick up. That should raise Eric's spirits. "We, as in myself and the holy spirit that walks alongside me at all times. Do you not see him? Do you not feel his calling, even now?"

"This isn't the best time for—"

"SINNER!" Marcello cried. "I can smell your need for confession. That *is* whisky on your breath, isn't it?"

Gabriel rolled his eyes. "All right. *One drink*. Then you're back on the streets."

"Make it a tall one," Marcello said happily.

He followed Gabriel through the house, small talk accompanying them to the kitchen. Gabriel poured another whisky for himself and one for Marcello. Then they went to the living room, Gabriel stopping as soon as they passed the threshold. He glanced around, sighed, and said, "Now where did Zachary get to?"

"He's probably powdering his nose," Marcello said. "Such a nasty habit."

"He's off the coke," Gabriel snapped. "Are you?"

"Never my forte. I seem to have struck a nerve. Is everything all right?"

"No," Gabriel said, pausing to listen once more. When they didn't hear anyone nearby, he sighed again and led the way to the couch. "What really brings you here?"

"I was having the dullest evening, when to my delight, guess who appeared on my television screen?"

"The commercial," Gabriel said, mustering a smile. "What did you think?"

"Very impressive. Total nonsense though. Politicians only ever serve their own needs, especially when deciding what is best for the masses. Without asking them directly, of course. Still, should Zachary be successful, I'm comforted that he will have you as a moral compass."

Gabriel averted his eyes. "I hope you're right. He never listens to me anymore."

"But the commercial was your idea. It must have been. You've always excelled at gaining the public's attention. Remember the protest you staged where everyone showed up naked at the capitol?"

"The Nixon masks were my idea," Gabriel said with a warm chuckle. "The nudity was yours. And we wouldn't have gotten arrested for public indecency had we been wearing more."

"Nor would it have been front page news the next day," Marcello replied. "We were a good team. It's a shame that we let events—and people—come between us."

Gabriel's grin faltered, picking up on the slight. It was a petty one. Marcello was kicking a man who was already down, but he was merely human. While he had long ago bridled his emotions, they still bucked rebelliously on occasion.

"Maybe you're right."

Marcello stared. "Do I misunderstand what I'm hearing? You feel regret? Not about Zachary, surely!"

Gabriel broke eye contact again. "I'm tired."

"Of?"

The air that escaped Gabriel's lungs sounded weary. "Everything. I can't keep up with him anymore. Zachary is in his forties. Do you remember how good that felt? Our bodies were still holding up, our minds were sharper than ever, and most of all, we had the energy to get things done. Whatever we wanted. I felt like a conqueror back then. Now I feel like an ailing king. We're not young anymore. Do you realize that? I'm in my seventies and you're—"

"On the cusp of turning fifty," Marcello said. "It strikes me that your age isn't the issue, but rather the company you keep."

"The price of loving a younger man," Gabriel said. "You don't need to tell me that. I've thought about how it could have been. Eric and I enjoying our retirement and maybe traveling the world together. Not the major destinations. We covered all of those. I was reading about this little village in Africa recently, and the fresh water initiative which— None of that matters. I just wanted to go there and see it all for myself. And I wanted someone with me who wouldn't complain that we could be in Moscow or Geneva instead."

"Someone who has already seen as much as you have," Marcello said. There was no sense in rubbing salt in the wound. Gabriel did indeed look tired. His short hair was white, his dark skin wrinkled and sagging. He was still handsome though. For his age. Marcello enjoyed the company of younger men, but there were times when he didn't want to be reminded of how smooth and flawless a body could be. On occasion, he wanted someone to commiserate with, and only an older man understood what aches and pains were really about, or how it felt that the world kept changing, a new generation of malcontents taking up causes that felt increasingly alien and strange.

"I thought he would be a senator by now," Gabriel said. "So did Zachary. You can guess who he blames for his lack of progress. I believe he's going to leave me."

Marcello didn't want that. As angry as he sometimes felt over Gabriel's infidelity, they were still friends, and he hated the idea of Gabriel ending up alone so late in the game. Did he deserve that? Perhaps. But it would also be a shame if all of Eric's suffering had been for naught. At least a relationship and political career had sprung from the wreckage. "I'll speak with Zachary. On a day when my head is clearer. I'm sure he'll see sense. And if not?"

Gabriel shook his head. "I can't bear to think of it."

"You'll still have me. And Eric."

Gabriel considered him. Then he took a sip of his whisky. "What's that supposed to mean?"

"You don't think he would welcome you back with open arms?"

Gabriel laughed humorlessly and shook his head. "You're got a mean streak tonight. We both know that's never going to happen, but even if it could... Never mind."

"Oh, I *always* mind," Marcello said, "and my intent isn't cruel. Finish your thought."

Gabriel took another sip. "I wouldn't go back to Eric. Even if I could. Mostly for the same reasons I left. It's hard enough looking in the mirror these days."

Seeing how much older Eric was, and knowing how much

time had passed since they were last together, would be a constant reminder. Gabriel still had a fear of aging, and of death, which was ridiculous considering how late in the game it was. They were already old. They would die soon enough. How sad then that, for all his talent and intellect, Gabriel was still in denial.

Marcello made short work of his whisky. Then he set the glass aside. "I'll have a word with Zachary on your behalf, but don't worry. Even if my words can't penetrate that crockpot he calls a brain, I'm sure you'll find some other project to take on. One young enough that they'll mistake your obstinance for wisdom. A piece of advice before I go: You might want to consider powdering your own nose, if you plan on keeping up with a twenty-year-old."

He rose and walked himself to the front door, although he wasn't unaccompanied.

Gabriel opened the door for him, expression stony. "You always took Eric's side, but I didn't realize until now that you cared about him more than you did me."

"I just reached a similar conclusion," Marcello replied, "because it's become clear that I must have loved him more than you were ever capable of."

He left the house regretting his clumsy choice of words. Loved? Nothing past tense about it. His love for Eric was ongoing. It grew every day! Gabriel's seemed to fade, but Marcello was happy to take up the slack. When he didn't see his friend lurking in the shadows, he went to the car and found him waiting in the back seat.

"How did it go?"

"He's miserable," Marcello murmured. "I think he finally realizes that he would have been happier with you instead."

Eric didn't take any joy in this. Of course not. Marcello wished he would, but then, Eric wouldn't be the generous soul who he adored more with each act of kindness.

"Is he going to be okay?" Eric asked, voice laced with concern.

"I'll make sure of it," Marcello answered. *For you*, he thought without letting himself say it. Eric often misinterpreted the intensity of his affection and dedication, when Marcello didn't want anything more from him than his companionship.

"Where to, sir?" the driver asked.

"Away from here," he answered. "That's a good enough

start." He turned his attention back to Eric. Vampires weren't meant to look so downtrodden. "What we need is good company to bolster our spirits. Why don't we stop by Nathaniel's house and see how he and Kelly are doing?"

Eric shook his head. "Who?"

"Nathaniel! My protégé. I've told you about him. You must have met before." Except he couldn't remember seeing Eric and Nathaniel in the same room. Ever. How could that be?

"Nathaniel Courtney?" the driver interrupted. "His home address? Or is he at the office?"

Marcello ignored him, attention still on Eric. "Gabriel isn't the only one feeling old. You'll have to forgive me. This is a shocking oversight. You simply must meet Nathaniel! He means so much to me."

"I don't know if I'm up for that tonight," Eric said. The creases on his forehead easing as a smile tried to edge its way in. "What if we visit Tim instead?"

"But of course!" If anyone could chase away unhappy thoughts of Gabriel, it was Tim. "The only man to stake a claim on your heart since those trying times."

Eric covered his chest with his hands and hissed theatrically. "Let's keep stakes away from my heart!"

Marcello wasn't dissuaded. "Something tells me you wouldn't mind being penetrated by this one." Louder he said, "Driver, please take us to the Wyman residence."

"How has he been?" Eric asked once the vehicle did a U-turn and they were on their way.

"Tim? Don't tell me he's been too busy for you lately."

"He has his own life now," Eric said. "Away from this old fart. That's how it should be."

"Nonsense," Marcello said. "He talks about you all the time. You've very much a part of his life."

"Really?"

"Yes! Why, earlier in the year he was asking me how you feel about him."

Eric smiled, perking up a little. "How I feel about him?"

"He seemed uncertain, which is silly, because I thought you of all people would have told him. Have you not?"

"I tried to show him instead," Eric said. The white makeup was likely disguising a blush. "His parents never did, from what

I can tell. I worried that it wouldn't be enough to say those same empty words, so I attempted to demonstrate my love for him as best I could."

"By giving him a home?" Marcello said.

"By giving him what he needed most."

Love. Guidance. Respect. Security. All that Tim had been lacking, and everything good that Eric had to offer, even though he had been ill. Deathly so.

"And yes," Eric added with a chuckle, "I gave him a home, and later a house. Maybe that was a bit much."

"Not to mention the money," Marcello added, but he couldn't share in Eric's mirth because he was confused. If Eric had given Tim his house, then where were they driving to now? The driver had missed his turn. He was about to say as much, until he remembered a long winding road through undeveloped land, and at the end of it, a humble home that was bursting with love.

"Have you spoken to Ben much since they moved in together?" Marcello asked. "You should. He's an astute young man. He doesn't wear his heart on his sleeve. No, I picture it instead on his head, like a crown. Good King Ben. All he demands from his subjects is that they love too. Themselves especially, because when you are at peace within yourself, it makes it so much easier to be at peace with the world. Don't you agree?"

Eric's smile was serene. "I am at peace. I hope you are too."

"Never. It's not my style. Ah! We're nearly there."

He turned his attention to the outside. Luminaries lined the drive—simple paper bags that had been filled with sand and a candle. When the house came into view, he saw two jack o' lanterns on the porch along with projector lights, which were casting revolving images of witches and ghosts on the facade. If Ben and Tim were having a party, it wasn't a successful one, because there weren't any cars in the driveway.

"Won't they be surprised," Marcello said as he exited the car, grabbing his Bible on the way.

"Please don't," Eric groaned.

"I have no choice," Marcello said as he knocked. "I'm a man of the cloth now. It's my sacred duty to save their immortal souls."

"Maybe you should start with your own," Eric murmured.

No time for a snappy comeback. The door was opening. Ben

and Tim were standing there! Two for the price of one! Marcello brandished the Bible above his head and shouted, "SINNERS! BOTH OF YOU! REPENT!"

Ben started laughing. Tim grabbed candy from the bowl he held and began pelting him with it.

"Stop!" Marcello cried, swiping his Bible just in time to deflect a miniature Twix bar. "I call upon the demons of Hell to rescue me. Count Conroy, answer my summons!" He glanced over, surprised to find the space next to him empty. "Eric?"

"Eric?" Tim asked, stopping his assault.

"He was here just a moment ago," Marcello said, spinning around. "Where has he gotten to? Eric? Eric?!" He spun the other way, searching the yard. The light from one of the projectors blinded him, so he raised an arm to shield himself from it. He turned, wanting to get away, but too much was happening at once and he fell, the ground unforgiving as it slammed into him. Or the reverse. He wasn't sure, nor was he able to make sense of anything, so he shut his eyes, in full agreement with his brain that it was time for a much needed break.

"I'm not dead!" Marcello gasped while sitting upright.

The scenery had changed. Gone was the comfort of the night—tranquil, silent, and forgiving of sin. Day had returned, full of brightness, the sound of bustling activity, and worst of all, judgement. He was in a hospital, which he liked waking up in even less than a jail cell, although the latter was a much more common occurrence. Thank goodness.

"Although I should probably be put under arrest," he added hopefully. "Take me away and lock me up. Anywhere but here."

No such luck. Nathaniel stood up from a chair in one corner, glared at him (in concern, Marcello chose to believe), and left the room. Who he came back with was worse than a police officer.

"I'm Dr. Piper," the physician said as she entered the room. "How are you feeling?"

Marcello groaned. "I have the most terrible pain on my everywhere. Nathaniel tried giving me over-the-counter medications a few hours back, but they had no effect. You'll have to prescribe me something stronger."

Dr. Piper turned to Nathaniel. "I thought you said he had just woken up?"

"That's correct," Nathaniel grumbled. "Must have been a dream."

"The pain!" Marcello cried. "Let's begin with Percocet. Although I'm willing to settle for Darvocet, if they still make it. Not my favorite, but when paired in the right combination—"

"He has pain medication that he takes for his back," Nathaniel said, reaching for Marcello's hand, but only to squeeze it in warning. "His physician switched them recently, which might explain some of the confusion. That, and the Halloween prank we discussed."

"Prank?" Marcello repeated, attempting to sound pathetic before instinct—and another hand squeeze—told him to go along with it.

"Remember the brownies the neighborhood kids gave you?" Nathaniel prompted. "The trick-or-treaters?"

"Oh yes!" Marcello said. "Such sweet children. I never expected anything in return. It's true that I give out the most candy each year, but it's not supposed to work the other way around." In reality, he usually put a bucket of single dollar bills outside his door with a sign that asked each person to only take one. He loved reviewing the surveillance footage to see how long it was before someone stole all the money. Three visitors was the unbroken record, bless their ambitious little hearts.

"We're afraid you've been the victim of a prank," Dr. Piper said. "You've heard of marijuana brownies?"

"Mari-wha?" he said theatrically. "I think so," he added when Nathaniel squeezed his hand painfully tight. "Oh dear. Will I be addicted?"

"Unlikely," Dr. Piper said, already patronizing in tone, as if he were nothing more than a silly old man. "Cannabis—that is, marijuana—isn't habit forming. I am concerned, however, that there might have been other substances involved. We drew blood but the results aren't back from the lab yet."

The results would never come back from the lab. Marcello would see to that. He ignored the rest of the doctor's lecture and tolerated his vitals being taken. When she left and they were finally alone again, he turned to Nathaniel.

"I'm sorry," he began.

"I don't want to hear it," Nathaniel said, his chin trembling. He clenched his jaw to stop it. "Just don't. Okay? Whatever happened, never again. For me."

"You have my word," Marcello said.

Nathaniel nodded, pulled out his phone, and glared at it. "Tim's here. He wants to talk to you."

And with that, Nathaniel stormed out of the room.

Marcello listened to his footsteps until they were distant. Then he leaned back in bed and sighed. "I love you too, darling boy. And I really am sorry."

He thought back on the evening: how the mushrooms had kicked in stronger than expected, and how he had tried to balance that out by taking a tranquilizer. This had lowered his inhibitions enough that he began putting more into his body than he normally would have dared. He refused to consider any other detail of the evening. Especially since he knew he would be forced to confront the truth soon enough.

Tim entered the room. Unlike Nathaniel, he didn't try to disguise his emotions. He took one look at Marcello, rushed over, and threw himself across the bed. "Don't you ever fucking die, you stupid asshole!"

"Go easy or I will," Marcello chuckled, grinning as he was hugged all over. Normally he would find it titillating. At the moment, he felt more like returning the gesture, which he did. "I'm perfectly fine. I simply needed a nap."

"You need a babysitter," Tim said, pulling away.

"I'll make sure to hire one as soon as I'm home. A man with a strong firm hand, just in case I misbehave. I only hope he'll look as fiercely handsome as you do when angry."

"Whatever it takes," Tim said, flopping down into the chair that Nathaniel had previously occupied. "Are you really okay?"

"Yes."

"Good. It's just that..." Tim's face crumpled before he pulled himself together again. He still barely managed to get the name out. "Eric."

"Ah. I see." Time to face the music. "I may have been hallucinating. Just a bit."

"Oh." Tim said. "You saw him though?"

"I did."

Tim needed to work up the courage to speak again, and when he did, his expression was pleading with Marcello not to laugh. "Because some people say that on Halloween, the barrier between the spirit world and ours is at its thinnest. I don't know how that works, or if it's true, but do you think…"

"Was it more than just a hallucination?" Marcello considered the idea. "He did make sure to tell me how much he loves you. The real Eric would have done the same. For what that is worth."

Tim swallowed and nodded. "I love him too. And you."

Marcello smiled. "I suppose that's all that matters."

"Screw that," Tim said, propping his feet up on the edge of the bed. "Tell me everything. I want details! I don't care if it was real or not. You made new memories with Eric!"

Marcello laughed and humored him. He made sure to embellish the story, just to make it that much more exciting, and by the end of it, they were both filled with warm nostalgia.

"What exactly did you take last night?" Tim asked, clearly tempted to do the same.

"If I shared the recipe," Marcello said, "Ben would never forgive me. I already need to apologize to him for collapsing in front of your home."

"Naw," Tim said. "You made his night. He was desperate for trick-or-treaters. You're the only one we got."

Marcello made a show of patting himself down. "Then where is my hard-earned candy?"

"The driver left your things," Tim said, jerking his thumb.

Marcello looked in the indicated direction and saw eight rolls of toilet paper, still wrapped. "How thoughtful of him. And my Bible? It's a family heirloom, you know."

"It's a book of obscene drawings!" Tim shot back. "Only the cover is from the actual Bible. Found that out the hard way. I wanted to say the Lord's Prayer for you. Instead I found a ridiculously huge—" His face turned red.

"Tom of Finland's art can be a religious experience, if one is in the correct mindset. Would you care to borrow the book?"

Tim squirmed uncomfortably. "Uh… Yeah. I should at least get Ben's opinion on it."

"That's the spirit!"

"Is there something else you need?" Tim said. "Clothes from home?"

"Oh, I don't know," Marcello said. "I rather enjoyed my time as a priest. Is the costume still here?"

"Nathaniel said something about burning it," Tim said, "so

you wouldn't start your own cult. I'll be back with... what? A suit? Something more comfortable?"

Marcello gave him a list of items. Then he was left alone again. As unpleasant as the evening had ended, the sleep had been welcome. He closed his eyes, trying to recapture the feeling, and didn't have to search far. They remained shut when he felt the mattress sink with someone else's weight, because he wasn't completely sober yet, and he saw nothing wrong with wish fulfillment.

"Those mushrooms were truly exceptional," Marcello said.

"You need to stop this," Eric replied. "I mean it."

"Concerned that I'll be joining you soon?" Marcello retorted. "Or worried that I'll cramp your style. How many deceased celebrities are you dating these days? Anyone I would know?"

"Rock Hudson can't keep his hands off of me," Eric replied.

"Ah, now I know that you are a hallucination. Eric always preferred Gregory Peck. But I don't mind. Better a make-believe Eric than none at all."

For a figment of his imagination, the laugh sure sounded accurate. "I'm going to leave before you get yourself committed. I meant what I said though. Slow down. If not for your own sake, then for them. Tim. Nathaniel. All the others who depend on you too. You might not want to take care of yourself, but you need to take care of them, and you can't do that if you're dead."

"Speaking of dead, I thought I killed you off a long time ago."

"Sorry?"

"My conscience. The angel on my shoulder. That's who you really are, isn't it?"

He opened his eyes, not expecting to see much of anything. For a second, he thought he saw Eric sitting on the corner of his bed. Not dressed as a vampire, or as old as he would have been had he never died. Eric looked just the way Marcello remembered him, young, pensive, concerned, and most of all, sweet. Then he blinked, and all that rested on the mattress was a beam of light from the window.

"Exceptional mushrooms," he repeated. Then, after allowing himself to consider the impossible, he added, "Very well. I'll slow down. Just don't expect me to stop living. That would kill me too. Both figuratively *and* literally."

* * * * *

Marcello stood outside a home that wasn't his own. It was late on a Sunday morning, which meant the neighborhood was attempting to cover its head with a pillow and resist waking up. A few motivated souls were out walking their dogs or mowing lawns, but none of them were nearby at the moment. That suited him just fine. Marcello stood there, considering long windows that he had peeped through the night before. He wasn't sure how many things he had said out loud, or how much had occurred solely in his head, but he knew the conversation with Gabriel had been real. The unpleasant details weren't lost on him. Even so, the poor man already had enough troubles of his own. Did he really need one more? Marcello weighed the roll of toilet paper in his hand. Then he considered the house again.

I wouldn't go back to Eric. Even if I could.

Madness came in many forms. Some were self-induced. Others must stem from blindness, because Eric had been one of the most wonderful men imaginable. Not the perfect kind that he found so unengaging, but rather the flawed sort who could fulfill everyone else's needs while still being incapable of tending to his own. Selfless. That was Eric. Only a fool would turn his back on a man like that, and such people weren't worth his time.

Marcello dropped the roll of toilet paper on the ground and headed toward the car. He stopped a few paces later, knowing that Eric would want him to help regardless. And he would. Marcello would do what was necessary to smooth things out between Gabriel and Zachary. But at a price. Marcello turned, hurried back to the toilet paper roll, and picked it up again. Then he tossed it into the air and over a branch, already laughing gleefully, because there were many ways to live, and this was quickly becoming one of his favorites. A trick, and a treat, rolled up into one.

Something Like Stories: Volume Three

Something Like Snow

by Jay Bell

Austin, Texas
December 23rd, 2016

—harrumph!—
—harrumph!—
—harrumph!—

Each huffing noise was accompanied by a jiggling of the mattress. Ben kept his eyes squeezed shut in an attempt to find sleep again. After another round of grumbling canine impatience, he realized that cleaning dog poo off the carpet would be worse than waking up early. Ben sat up in bed and glanced over at Tim, who was snoozing peacefully. How he was able to sleep through absolutely anything, Ben didn't know, but he did envy the ability. Especially on a cold morning like this one.

"Hold your horses," he mumbled to Chinchilla, who had her front paws on the mattress. If she was taller, or spry enough, Ben had no doubt that she would hop onto the bed and tap dance all over him every morning, leaving her precious master undisturbed. "Why me?" Ben whispered to himself dramatically.

Chinchilla wiggled her rump as if to say, "Because I love you!"

At least that's how Ben chose to interpret it. The heavy down comforters they used at this time of year made it possible to sleep naked, but mere steps away from the bed and a multitude of layers was required: flannel pajama bottoms, a long sleeve T-shirt, and thick socks. Ben kept these in the nightstand next to the bed, and with them on, he was able to make the trek to the bathroom, adding slippers and a robe before making use of the facilities, even if it wasn't the most practical order. Tim's ritual was much simpler. He would strut nude from the bed to the bathroom, throwing on a bathrobe after using the toilet like the cold couldn't touch him. Sometimes he even tied that bathrobe shut. Although with Jason now living elsewhere, Ben preferred the mornings when the bathrobe hung open.

Such thoughts were the furthest—well, not the furthest from his mind, but letting Chinchilla out to potty and then crawling back into bed sounded the most appealing at the moment. Ben followed the dog downstairs and was heading for the back door when a smile broke out over his face.

"Just one second!" he said, rushing to the front of the house. To the closet in particular. While out shopping with Allison, he had recently discovered a winter coat that he'd been dying to wear. The coat was long, reaching almost to his knees. The fabric was green from the very bottom all the way up to the high collar, but the sleeves were black. He loved how that looked, and how the coat hugged his body so tightly. Finding such a stylish and colorful coat in the men's department was nearly impossible, and this one was no exception, because he had found it in the women's department instead. Ben had bought it regardless, but only after swearing Allison to secrecy.

Now he had a legitimate excuse to put on winter gear, since there was actual frost on the windows. That didn't happen often. Not in Austin. Ben let his bathrobe drop to the ground, trading it for the green coat. Then he pranced his way across the house, even twirling once, because he felt so dang pretty! Laughing happily, he opened the sliding glass door and stepped outside, Chinchilla blowing past him and racing to one of her favorite potty spots. The sun was shining, so Ben walked out into the yard and heard crunching beneath his slippers. The ground was glistening, each blade of grass encased in a delicate layer of ice. Winter had come to South Texas!

Ben could see his breath in the air, so he pretended each puff was smoke as he used two fingers to pantomime holding a cigarette. Even Chinchilla seemed thrilled, tearing around the yard and snapping at the ground. Ben spun toward the house, wanting to share this frozen surprise. He thought he saw motion, and when he opened the sliding door to check, sure enough, Tim was standing there yawning in his bathrobe. Which was tied shut, unfortunately.

"Are you ready for a winter wonderland?" Ben asked with a grin.

Tim was instantly awake, hope shining in his eyes as he hurried over. He was always complaining about the winters in Texas, and how Christmas just didn't feel the same. Now, with only two days remaining until the big holiday, he was likely to get his wish. If the weather remained cold enough.

"Coming through!" Tim said, practically knocking Ben over

on his way out the door. His pace slowed as he reached the edge of the patio, but not in awe. When he turned around, his expression was pure disappointment. "I was expecting snow."

"Oh," Ben said. "This is close. Everything is frozen."

"Seriously? This is nothing. It'll all melt by the time the sun finishes rising."

Ben rolled his eyes. "Okay, Kansas boy. I know the winters we get down here can't compete with those you grew up with, but you have to admit, this is magical weather."

Tim frowned and turned around to consider the yard. Then he shrugged. "It's all right."

Ben snorted. "You know that movie about the kid who's sad because all he wants is a BB gun for Christmas?"

"Yeah."

"That's who you look like right now."

Tim didn't respond. No teasing barb about how the holidays weren't as good in the South, or jokes about how he used to walk through blizzards to reach school. Come to think of it, one of the best parts of that movie was when the kid woke up to see his neighborhood covered in snow. That scene made it all seem so enchanting. Aside from fleeting moments like those, Ben never felt like he was missing anything. Snow simply wasn't part of his life when he was growing up. An occasional happy surprise, yes, but not something he hoped for each year. If it had been, maybe he would be upset now too. "Sorry," he said. "I didn't mean to get your hopes up."

"It's fine," Tim said, squatting to pet Chinchilla, who was still excited. "It's not like there's anything either of us can do."

"No," Ben said. "Although maybe Marcello could. He's a miracle worker."

"Yeah!" Tim said, standing again. "I'll call him and ask. Maybe he can—I don't know—seed the clouds or something."

Ben laughed, thinking it was a joke, but his husband returned indoors. Chinchilla ran in the opposite direction. Ben wasn't quite ready to go back in, but when his ears started to ache from the cold, he whistled for the dog to follow and sought the warm comfort of his kitchen. He entered just in time to see Tim setting down his phone.

"Did you really call Marcello?"

"Yeah," Tim said, looking a little pale. "I don't think he understood. I asked him to make it snow and he started talking about... Listen, if a Columbian man shows up at the front door with a bag of white powder, don't answer!"

Ben laughed and set about making himself some tea. He wondered how the conversation had really gone. If he had called Marcello and requested any sort of weather, the man probably would've had them on a flight somewhere that same day. Ben stopped pouring hot water in his mug, a thought having occurred to him. He couldn't afford to fly them anywhere, but surely there was snow within driving distance.

He looked over at Tim, who was morosely jabbing at a bowl of cereal. Ben joined him at the table, not giving anything away but desperate to research the idea. He waited until Tim went to take a shower before grabbing his laptop. Kansas was his first thought. Tim would love showing him around while they slowly froze to death. The things Ben did for love! Sadly, the weather forecast suggested that snow was unlikely there. Texas was a big place. He'd heard that the Panhandle got its fair share of snow. Not this week, it would seem, but that search led to a hot tip.

New Mexico. Not the first place Ben would think to look for winter weather, but when he checked the forecast for a town in the mountains named Ruidoso... Bingo! Snow, and lots of it! The nine-hour drive was shorter than a trip to Kansas. And they wouldn't have to fly. That was too expensive, especially at this time of year. He could hear Tim's voice in his head, reminding him that everything in the bank account belonged to them both. Ben was coming to accept that, but never for the holidays. Tim shouldn't receive a present bought with his own money.

Ben could manage this expense on his own. All they needed was a hotel. Ruidoso attracted a lot of skiing enthusiasts. Finding a cheap room wasn't easy. Ben considered and quickly dismissed the ski lodges as too expensive. He eliminated any sort of resort for the same reason, but he did find a barely affordable motel on the edge of town. It was barebones and dated, but they wouldn't be spending much time in their room anyway. After booking it, Ben was reminded of one final concern when Chinchilla padded into the kitchen in search of food. She did okay on car trips, but for a true romantic getaway, Ben wanted to be alone with Tim. And to sleep in for once.

"Hey, little gal," he said. "How would you like to stay with Santa Claus for Christmas?"

Chinchilla looked up at him with concern.

"You're going to love it," Ben said. "He's got a great big mansion and everything."

Once he had eaten breakfast and taken a shower, he would call Santa Claus to ask. Ben only hoped he was feeling jovial at such an early hour.

"Leave everything to me," Marcello said from the other end of the line. "I've already instructed my travel agent to book a vacation package to Denver for you both. How could I not when poor Timothy sounded so sad?"

"Oh!" Ben said, struggling with this news. "That's very um... Very generous of you."

"Oh dear," Marcello said, astute as ever. "Have I overstepped my bounds? You can always be honest with me."

Ben exhaled. "It's just that I wanted to do this myself. I don't really have a good Christmas present for Tim this year, and lately he's been so..." He thought back to the summer, when Tim had not only done detective work to figure out their true anniversary, but had grown out his hair, making it feel like they were teenagers again. He had even surprised Ben with a date night to one of Houston's haunted houses, which had resulted in lots of nostalgic memories, along with kissing and groping in the pitch-dark maze. "Considerate?" he said at last. "It's hard to put into words."

"Where do you intend to go?"

"Ruidoso."

"Ah! I can already imagine how—what is that, a ten-hour drive?"

"With pee breaks and lunch factored in, yeah."

"—how being trapped in the car for any length of time with the man you love would be preferable to a crowded airport. I'll inform my travel agent that his assistance is no longer needed." Marcello cleared his throat, not sounding offended at all. "Now then, you'd like me to provide lodgings for Chinchilla while you are away? I'd be happy to."

"Yes," Ben said in relief. "Thank you."

"I rather enjoy her company," Marcello replied. "Where will you be staying? The phone number will suffice, just in case there are any questions or concerns."

Ben relayed the information to him, and after chatting for a few more minutes, hung up. Then he looked around, feeling energized with anticipation. He had a trip to prepare for!

Ben loved Tim. Dearly. But even the intoxicating power of that emotion was stretched thin in such a barren environment. He was beginning to despair. West Texas offered little in the way of breathtaking scenery, unless empty horizons and hard cracked soil counted. The scenery wasn't unexpected, but when they crossed the state line into New Mexico, he had hoped for some sort of transformation. Instead it was more of the same. Desert. Not the kind with rolling dunes of glistening sand. Just the desolate variety where life struggled to take hold.

There was nothing to see and even less to do. A spontaneous pit stop in Roswell, of all places, didn't help alleviate their boredom. They visited the International UFO Museum and Research Center, which despite its impressive name, had very little to show except for framed newspaper clippings and printed-out internet articles. Currently they were stopped at a gas station an hour outside of Ruidoso, which felt like being in a movie about the end of the world. Two sunbaked pumps sat in front of a rusty convenience store, the shelves only partially stocked as if food supplies were scarce way out here.

Nowhere. That's where Ben had brought them, he realized while standing next to the gas pump and staring at the bleak landscape. Tim had even allowed him to drive the Mitsubishi Challenger—or whatever it was—for a stretch, as if getting in a wreck would be preferable to suffering one more second of boredom.

"I realize I'm not the easiest person to live with," Tim said as he squeezed the pump handle to refuel his car. "I'm always leaving dirty laundry around, or sometimes I promise to do the dishes and then forget. And I know I can be demanding..." He reached for Ben's butt, fingers already making a pinching motion.

His hand was slapped away, but only because Ben was enjoying this confession too much. "Go on."

"Just don't give up on me yet. I'll try harder, I swear. I don't want to die!"

Ben laughed. "What are you talking about?"

"That's the only reason I can think of for you driving me way out here. You're going to kill me and bury me in the desert, *Breaking Bad* style."

"Don't be ridiculous," Ben said. "I decided a long time ago to chop you up and bury you somewhere on our land. But not while you're still so handsome."

Tim grinned. "Thanks, hon! I get that you wanted to surprise me, but maybe it would make the trip more bearable if I knew *where* we were going."

"We're almost there."

Tim looked around. So did Ben. Scorched earth and little else. Big surprise. The gas pump handle clicked and went silent before Tim put it back in the holster.

"We're almost there," he repeated.

Ben's shoulders sagged. "I know, I know. This is a disaster. I think I might have been conned."

"By who?"

"The internet. This was supposed to be a winter wonderland. I wanted you to have your snow."

Tim blinked. Then turned, as if getting his bearings. "We've been travelling west all day."

"Yeah. So?"

"I'm just trying to think. On the other side of New Mexico there's Nevada. As in Las Vegas. And past that there's California—"

"You forgot Arizona."

"Okay, but are any of those places known for snow? Shouldn't we be driving north?"

"Probably," Ben admitted. "The motel isn't far away. Let's just get there, check in, and then decide what we want to do for Christmas."

"It'll be fine," Tim said as they climbed back into the car. "We've got presents in the trunk. And each other. What more do we need?"

A miracle. Ben kept hoping for one until they reached their destination on the outskirts of town. That's when he gave up hope. Aside from hills on the horizon, there was little else to see. Their motel was even worse than the photos online had implied. Everything seemed to be rundown, maybe because the intense sun made it impossible to keep things looking new.

"Wait here," Ben said. "I'll be right back."

He would return with the key and then they would park in front of their room... and hopefully not get stabbed to death by the owner while showering. He was relieved to see that the person behind the counter was an old woman, which at least increased their chances of fighting her off. Ben gave his name, the woman looking surprised.

"But your reservation has been canceled!"

Ben stared in disbelief. "Why would you do that?"

"I didn't," the woman replied. "You did!"

"I did no such thing," Ben said. "There must be a mistake. Could you please check again?"

She clicked the mouse of her computer a few times before she seemed to remember something. "Oh! Here's the fax you requested."

"Fax?" he repeated, surprised such things still existed.

She peered at him like he might be drunk or worse and handed him an envelope. Ben pulled out a folded piece of paper. At the top, in familiar handwriting, was a note.

Please do forgive me. I simply can't resist meddling, if even a tiny bit, but let's make this a secret that remains between us.

Marcello. Ben glanced down at what was clearly a room reservation, but not for this place. Marcello had booked them into a proper resort!

"Never mind," he said. "I think I understand now. When I called earlier, did my voice sound different? Huskier?"

"You know, I think it did," the woman said.

"That was my fairy godfather," he said. "I have to go. Thanks anyway!"

He skipped on the way back to the car, Tim laughing as he neared.

"Let me guess," he said. "Free upgrade to the honeymoon suite."

"Something like that," Ben said. "Here. Plug this address into the map app."

"We're not staying here?"

"Nope! I only needed directions."

Soon they were on the road again, and better yet, travelling upward. The road continued to wind and curve, but surely that wouldn't get them high enough for— Ben pressed his hand to the window. It felt cold! And now he felt silly. Winter resorts needed hills for people to ski down. It just seemed impossible for there to be a snowy mountain in the middle of a barren desert. In his own defense, he *had* booked this trip in a hurry, doing very little research. Marcello was right. They should keep this a secret. That way he could pretend his confusion was all a clever ruse.

"Dude!" Tim said, turning on the wipers, because a scattering of flakes had created melted droplets on the windshield. "Snow!"

He was right! Snow was not only in the air, but stubborn patches of it were clinging to the ground. Not bad, although Ben had hoped for more… and he got it! As they continued to ascend, the snow became a flurry. They even had to slow down.

"Happy?" Ben asked.

Tim answered by laughing joyfully, and when they reached the resort, he parked the car and ran straight for the sparkling drifts beyond the pavement, flopping down on his back and spreading his arms wide to create a snow angel. "Try doing this in Texas!" he exclaimed.

"You did last year," Ben reminded him. "You got mud everywhere."

"This is more comfortable." Tim made a face. "And colder! We aren't dressed for this."

No, they weren't. Ben was already shivering, so they gathered up their luggage and made a beeline for the lodge entrance. He glanced back wistfully as they entered. The sun had nearly set, and he worried it would soon be too dark for either of them to see the winter weather.

Tim seemed to have similar thoughts, chatting on the way to their room about how they needed to get back out there. "We'll build a snowman!" he raved. "Have you ever done that?"

"No," Ben admitted. "We did get some snow in Houston a few times, and I tried, but I could barely manage a snowball."

Tim was already shaking his head. "If our snowman isn't taller than us both, then we've done something wrong. Did you pack hats and gloves?"

"I've got everything we need," Ben said. Including his awesome green coat, which he intended to practically live in while here.

Any plans were forgotten when they entered their room. *Rooms.* Despite being in a large complex, they seemed to have stepped into a log cabin, complete with a separate living room and fireplace, a full kitchen, a luxurious bedroom, and a bathroom that included a hot tub.

"This must have cost you a fortune," Tim breathed. Then he looked over. "Or did you use my— It's okay if you did! I'd be happy, actually!"

"I didn't pay for it," Ben admitted. "The hotel we stopped at wasn't for directions. That's where I booked us to stay until Santa Claus intervened."

"Marcello?" Tim guessed, looking thrilled by this news. "Wow! This is going to be incredible! The motel would have been fine too but—"

"I'm with you one hundred percent," Ben said. "I'd much rather stay here. I just wish there was a way of repaying him."

"If I were as rich as him, it would be fun spreading money around like that. Besides—" Tim stripped off his shirt, puffing up his chest. "—I'm told those old modelling photos of mine still rake in a lot of cash."

"I bet they do. Mind showing me the rest of the goods?"

"Just a flash," Tim said. "I want to tuck my long john into some long johns and go back outside. We can hit the hot tub afterwards. Okay?"

"Sure!" Ben was happy to wait, because if Tim was turning down sex, it proved just how excited he was about this trip.

After bundling up, they went outside, both of them pausing to breathe out a chorus of "oohs" and "ahhs." The resort had switched on charming old-fashioned post lamps and strands of lights, making it truly appear like a scene from a Christmas card. Tim grabbed Ben's hand and pulled him toward a blanket of perfectly undisturbed snow. The pristine appearance didn't last long. Tim dived right in, demonstrating how a small ball of snow could be rolled into the size of a boulder. He did this twice more, Ben taking off his gloves to help. Before long they had three balls stacked on top of each other. Tim managed to find stones for the eyes and mouth, and Ben donated his scarf and hat, but it was still missing something.

"We need a carrot for the nose," Tim said. "Be right back."

He took off for the lodge while Ben waited. Past the initial shock of cold, his body had adjusted somewhat. He stood there, glancing around and finally understanding what Tim had missed.

Everything was silent and still, like time had stopped so the world could be dressed in white for the holidays.

He heard Tim's footsteps returning from behind, smiling when arms wrapped around his shoulders.

"Did you find a carrot?" Ben asked.

"Yup," Tim said, nuzzling his nose against Ben's cheek. "Twenty-four of them."

Ben's confusion was compounded when he saw the gift in one of Tim's hands. The small box sparkled red, a white ribbon holding the lid down.

"Go ahead," Tim said, passing it to him. "Open it up."

"You shouldn't have," Ben said, ripping into the present to prove that the opposite was true. He gasped when the lid came off. He saw gold, two wings, curved antennae, and sparkling stones that he hoped weren't real diamonds. But only because of the expense. "A butterfly?" he asked.

"Yup," Tim said. "You know why."

Ben turned to face him and saw a big grin. He wasn't the only one feeling nostalgic! "It's beautiful."

"Just like my man," Tim said, reaching for it. "Here, let me put it on you."

As much as Ben liked the butterfly, he still wasn't sure what it was for.

Tim pulled it free, pinning it to the lapel of Ben's coat. "There. What do you think?"

"I love it!" Ben enthused. "Although… A broach? Aren't those for women?"

Tim rolled his eyes. "Then it's a perfect match for your girl coat."

Ben's mouth dropped open. "Allison told you!"

"She didn't tell me anything! I liked your coat enough that I checked the label, wanting to see if the brand had something for me. When I did a search online…"

Ben laughed. "The men's department is so boring. Can you blame me?"

"Not when you look so handsome." Tim pulled him near. "Thanks for giving me back a piece of my childhood. This was a great idea."

"Thanks for giving me…" Ben trailed off while shaking his head. There was too much to consider, much less express in words. Tim had made him happier than Ben thought he could ever be again. "Everything. I love you."

Tim touched his cold nose to Ben's own. "I love you too. Merry Christmas, Benjamin."

"Merry Christmas," Ben said while he was still able to use his mouth for talking.

Tim kissed him. And didn't stop. They were making out like teenagers, and as hot as that was, it was still freezing outside. "Hot tub?" Ben murmured against Tim's lips.

His husband pulled away, his grin wild. "You wanna see my carrot?"

"If that's what you're calling it now, sure."

Tim pulled it from his pants. It was long, hard, and... orange. "Oh."

"First we take care of the snowman," Tim said, already turning away. "Then you take care of me."

Merry Christmas, indeed! Just so his husband didn't get too cocky, Ben squatted, rolled a quick snowball, and pelted Tim in the back of the head with it. Then he spent the next five minutes bobbing and weaving while running, because Tim didn't find his prank nearly as amusing as Ben did. But they did eventually backtrack to give the snowman his nose. They made it to the hot tub too, where they did things guaranteed to put them on Santa's naughty list. Or considering who had booked their room, the nice list, because they couldn't imagine him wanting it any other way.

Something Like Pride

by Jay Bell

Austin, Texas
2017

"Underwear," Marcello repeated. "In case anyone forgets their own."

Nathaniel Courtney looked up from the laptop he was using to take notes for the next event he was helping to organize. Few things fazed him anymore. Not after a decade of working for Marcello, although his boss still managed to find ways of surprising him.

"Why would anyone forget their underwear?" Nathaniel asked, already dreading the answer.

From behind his massive desk on the top floor of Studio Maltese, Marcello tilted his head and gave the question serious thought. "We should be prepared for any occurrence. Take those who free-ball, for instance. Have you never tried that? I found it rather liberating, at least until chafing became an issue. I don't know if uncircumcised men share that problem, but I'll endeavor to find out and report back to you. Oh, and some people might prefer to change into more festive underwear, or opt for a jockstrap, thong, or the sort of boxers that allow body parts to flop out, either by accident or design. Come to think of it, we'll need quite the wardrobe on hand. We should find a fashion label to sponsor the event."

Nathaniel held up a hand, wishing for one of those stop signs that crossing guards used. "Back up. Just what sort of party is this?"

Marcello blinked. "Did you forget already? Our yearly soirée to celebrate Pride."

He hadn't forgotten. The festivities seem to grow in number each year. Pride now included multiple festivals—some for movies, others for shopping and drinking—a parade, historical lectures, and more events than he could keep track of. Marcello always made sure to host a philanthropic party of some sort. That made it easier to tolerate his strange requests, but this one was throwing Nathaniel for a loop. Although he felt he was starting to get the picture.

"Will this be a pajama party?"

Marcello shook his head. "Heavens no! I've never understood pajamas, personally. Too much fabric. One might as well be wearing normal clothes. No, underwear will create a much more jubilant atmosphere."

Nathaniel tried to imagine the usual charity balls, except with all the donors stripped down to their skivvies. "We're going to need one hell of a coat check," he murmured.

"Yes! An apt observation. We had better hire extra staff solely for that purpose, and to help anyone who needs assistance dressing—and undressing—themselves."

Hiring manpower was an ongoing issue. The staffing agency that used to provide them with shirtless waiters was no longer willing to do so, and Marcello had been struggling to find a replacement ever since. "So instead of waiters who are half-naked, you want everyone else to be shirtless, and now pantless, instead?"

Marcello leaned forward, a wicked gleam in his eye. "That's the clever bit. The agency has agreed to staff this particular event on my terms. They don't consider it exploitation when the guests are stripped down too."

Nathaniel sighed. "Please tell me this is a temporary solution. I don't want every charity ball in the future to be full of mostly-naked people. The waiters are usually college age. Our benefactors…"

"Don't possess the effortless beauty of youth, I know." Marcello said, waving away his concern. "Fear not! I promise this is a solitary incident. In the future, I'll likely have my own waiters to rely on. I intend to found a catering service."

Nathaniel didn't hide his alarm. "You're supposed to be easing into retirement, not starting a new business! What's the point of handing over the GAC if you're going to replace it with more work?"

Marcello raised an eyebrow. "I thought your concerns were limited to the legal liability of an escort service, not my workload."

Nathaniel furrowed his brow and focused on the laptop,

pretending to take notes. He knew a lot about Marcello, including his true age. Considering the man's lifestyle, it was a miracle that he hadn't keeled over years ago. Nathaniel didn't want to lose him. He knew it was inevitable, but he planned to do everything possible to stave off that day. "It would be a waste of time," he said, trying to think quicker than his boss, which required the mental equivalent of rocket fuel. "And unfair."

"Unfair?" Marcello repeated. "How so?"

"Noah is trying to legitimize the Gentlemen's Agreement Club. He has an entire staff of good-looking guys who are comfortable with nudity. Asking them to go shirtless won't even register. They'll just do it, and while the charity auction proved that they still need training, it wouldn't take much to make them into real waiters."

Marcello didn't gasp in surprise, or pause to think this over, proving to Nathaniel that he wouldn't win any cerebral races today. His boss was already waiting for him at the finish line. "That seems dangerously close to a handout. Mr. Westwood has always preferred opportunity to charity. He's eager to prove himself. Making that easy would cheapen his accomplishments."

"Then we offer him less than we did the previous agency. We'll pay enough that he has a base income to calculate with, but not one so generous that he has to work less to make the GAC sustainable. He'll get an increased sense of security out of the deal, and the studio will save money."

"How uncharacteristically cutthroat of you!" Marcello said approvingly. "Quick, call your husband and let him see you like this. I'm sure it will act as a natural aphrodisiac. Speaking of which, I hope Kelly will not only attend, but also participate. He does make an impression."

Nathaniel shook his head instantly. Not out of jealousy. He was doing better with such things. But with so much nudity involved, he could already imagine Kelly's irritated expression when people made the wrong assumptions about his amputated leg, or stared at his prosthetic like he was some sort of novelty. "I don't think so."

Marcello leaned back and rested his hands on his belly. "Why not?"

"It's not his scene. Or mine. I'm sitting this one out too."

There. That should take the focus off Kelly. *Should.*

"You could at least ask him," Marcello said.

"I will. I know him though. He won't want to do this. We haven't had much time together lately, so I'll organize the event, but I won't be there that night to manage."

"Then it will be trial by fire for young Noah," Marcello said.

"I'll help prep him," Nathaniel said, relieved that the topic had been glossed over so easily.

"You *will* ask him," Marcello said, gaze penetrating. "Won't you? Just in case he finds the idea amusing."

Nathaniel focused on his laptop. "Can we set personal matters aside? We have a lot of details to plan."

"By all means," Marcello said easily. "I've identified a few potential dates, but I prefer the night before the pride parade. What do you think?"

That sounded good to him. Feeling as though he had avoided a potentially heated situation at home, he turned his attention back to his work, mentally categorizing the matter as settled.

Nathaniel watched as Kelly slowly chewed, moving the food from one cheek to the other before he grimaced and swallowed. "It still tastes like tofu," he complained.

"That's because it *is* tofu," Nathaniel said, looking past him to the stir fry pan. Currently it contained a rainbow of sliced vegetables along with goopy white cubes. The clouds, he supposed. "Maybe add more curry paste. Or sriracha."

"I like the rest of it," Kelly said, poking at the stir fry with a wooden spatula. "Maybe we can get our protein from another source."

"We don't have to do this," Nathaniel said. A documentary had convinced Kelly to attempt a vegetarian diet, but he suspected it wouldn't last. Especially since they still had to cook homemade meals for Zero, which contained chicken and other meats. Unless... "I wonder what the mutt would think of it?"

"Why do you think I've avoided making it too spicy?" Kelly asked. "Someone has to eat this mess."

Together they fished out a few cubes of tofu, placed them on a small plate, and set it on the kitchen floor. The Siberian Husky waiting there wasted no time shoving his nose in and scarfing them down. Or he started to. After spitting out a bite of mangled tofu, Zero looked up at them like he had been betrayed.

"Maybe I should have gotten the firm kind instead," Kelly said. "It was good when we had it at that restaurant, remember?"

"Add more spices." Nathaniel's phone dinged, so he pulled it out. "Stop holding back. If it becomes inedible, we'll go back to the Thai place."

Kelly smiled. "To eat, or to steal their recipe?"

"Both."

Nathaniel glanced at the text message, not surprised when he saw it was from Marcello. The underwear party was officially underway. Nathaniel had already fielded a number of questions from nervous staff members before the event began. Being there in person would make it easier to oversee things, but spending the evening with Kelly was his top priority.

No need to be concerned, Marcello wrote. *I simply thought you would like to know that Noah has risen to the occasion.*

That was good news! *The real test will be the second half of the night,* Nathaniel texted back. *That's when the waiters slack off.*

We'll see how he does then, Marcello replied.

Noah would be fine. Nathanial had already advised him about this potential pitfall, but he didn't want to let on. *If anyone spills a drink, at least you don't have to worry about a dry-cleaning bill.*

Always the silver lining! Marcello texted. *I do wish you were here. No change of heart from your spouse?*

None. This one little word made him uncomfortable, since it was edging close to a lie. Kelly hadn't had a change of heart because he had never been told about the party. Why should he be when Nathaniel knew it wasn't a good fit for either of them?

"Hey, this is starting to taste like actual food!" Kelly said, turning away from the stovetop to offer him a spoonful. "I'd still rather have meat, but I think it's passable."

Nathaniel took a bite and was impressed. "Did you add pineapple?"

"Yes. What do you think?"

He nodded in approval, his appetite increasing. They would have a nice meal, cuddle up on the couch together, and maybe afterwards—

Kelly set down the spoon and wiped his hands on the apron. Then he took his phone from the front pocket. He read the screen, scrunched up his face, and laughed. "Marcello isn't making sense. He's probably drunk."

"Probably," Nathaniel said, although it was no longer the certainty it had once been. After pleading with him and repeatedly pointing out that alcohol wasn't likely to extend his lifespan, Marcello was finally making the effort to pace himself. Daytime drinking had all but ceased as Nathaniel encouraged him to slow down in the evenings as well, which he did. Sometimes.

"He says I could get myself an underwear contract if I show up tonight," Kelly said, reading the text again. "I have no idea what that means."

"Probably best to ignore it," Nathaniel said, watching with unease as Kelly sent a response. "Should I set the table?"

"Uh-huh," Kelly said distractedly, expression becoming more confused as his eyes moved back and forth across the screen. "There's a party tonight. And apparently I don't want to go, which is a shame, because I'm missing out on an opportunity." He looked up. "As a photographer."

The fashion sponsor. Not only had Marcello managed to find one willing to provide them with free undergarments, but they were also a potential client for future photoshoots. "Whatever it is, I'm sure it can wait."

Kelly studied him. "You don't know?"

"Know what?"

Kelly held up the phone. "What this is about. Marcello doesn't plan anything without you these days. It's part of him handing over the business."

Nathaniel sighed. "There's a party tonight to celebrate Pride. An underwear party, which doesn't sound like our style."

Kelly's eyes narrowed. "Okay, but Marcello seems to think that I don't want to be there."

"I'm the one who didn't want to go. I turned down the invitation for both of us."

"Oh." Kelly pocketed the phone and turned around to face the stove, his posture tense.

Nathaniel opened a drawer to take out cutlery. He set these on the table before returning to the kitchen. Kelly hadn't moved. "Is it ready?" he prompted.

Kelly tapped the spatula against the pan, set it down, and turned around. "If you're feeling jealous, we need to talk about this before it turns serious."

"I'm not jealous," Nathaniel said. Although he was tempted to lie and say he was, just so the party would no longer be a subject, but he knew how much that would worry Kelly. Jealousy had cost them years that could have been spent together. He had learned an important lesson from that painful experience. It was better to be open, no matter the issue. "I knew that you wouldn't be into the idea, so I didn't bring it up."

"I like his parties," Kelly said. "Especially the charity balls, since that's how we met. Each one is like a little anniversary."

Nathaniel smiled. "I like them for the same reason, but this one sounded annoying."

"How so? The dress code?"

"No." Nathaniel sighed and pinched the bridge of his nose. "Sort of. Everyone would see your leg and either stare or ask you the same tiresome questions."

Kelly opened a cabinet and took out two plates. After he set these on the counter, he turned to face Nathaniel again. That's when he knew he was in trouble. Kelly's eyes were narrowed again, which was a surefire indication that his temper was rising. Once it got started, there was no stopping it. "So basically, you decided that neither one of us should go. Because of my leg."

"That's not why," Nathaniel said, crossing his arms over his chest. "How many times have people assumed that you're a war veteran? That irritates both of us. And if people are going to be staring at you—which I'm fine with, by the way—it should be for the right reason."

"Because you think I'm attractive."

"Yeah."

"As long as my prosthetic leg is hidden away in shame."

"That's not what I said!" Nathaniel snarled. "I was trying to protect you from people's stupidity!"

He braced himself for the inevitable backlash. Kelly would tear into him with cutting words, and they would likely have to go their separate ways until they both calmed down. Except that didn't happen. Kelly was tense and clenching his jaw, but he didn't shout back. Instead he busied himself with scooping rice onto the plates. The stir-fry went on top of this. Kelly walked toward the table, his voice neutral when he said, "Ready?"

"Yeah." Nathaniel felt relieved, but it didn't last. They sat down at the table, Kelly attempting a smile before taking a bite.

"It's not as good as the Thai place," Kelly said, "but it's also not bad. What do you think?"

"I love it," Nathaniel said without even picking up a fork, and it was true. Kelly had cooked for him, which was nurturing and thoughtful and… God damn it all to hell! Nathaniel had messed up. He knew that now. Kelly losing his temper would have been indication enough. That he had managed to keep himself in check said so much more. Kelly was hurt, and despite that, he loved Nathaniel enough to try to hide it so they could enjoy a meal together. "Talk to me. What did I do wrong?"

Kelly shook his head, as if it didn't matter. Then he set down his fork. "It's fine. You're a human being."

"I'm starting to wish I wasn't."

"Really," Kelly said. "It's okay. I was only taken off guard because you've always gotten it right before."

"I'm not ashamed of your disability," he said. "Your prosthetic," he corrected, knowing that Kelly didn't consider himself handicapped or impaired in any way.

"I didn't think you were," Kelly replied. "But you also never treated me differently because of it. Not until now. A boyfriend with two legs would have been told about the party and asked if he wanted to go."

Nathaniel thought about it and groaned. "You're right. I fucked up. I'm an idiot."

"You're wonderful," Kelly said, trying another smile, this one more genuine. "I wouldn't have my awesome bionic leg if not for you. No one has supported or empowered me like you have, so you deserve a free pass. And I'm happy to give it to you. I'm not angry."

"Just hurt," Nathaniel said, his gut twisting up.

"I'm okay," Kelly said. "Although I'd feel a lot better if you would eat what I worked so hard on."

"Of course!" He was happy to shovel food into his mouth, then do the dishes, and afterwards show Kelly just how much he loved him. But he already worried it wasn't enough. The damage had been done.

Austin's annual pride parade started at the Capitol building. Such parades usually took place during the day, but with the Texas heat so unrelenting, this one began at night. A good thing too, because even though the sun had set, the air was still stifling hot. T-shirt and shorts weather. Despite this, Nathaniel was dressed in one of the suits he usually wore to work. That was important to him. So often these parades were full of colorful characters: ostentatious drag queens, or muscled guys who were all but naked. Bears, leather daddies, slaves, masters, and shrieking twinks. Nothing wrong with any of those things, but Nathaniel wanted people to see that one of the many colors on display was gray. Everyday people who worked long hours in an office or elsewhere to earn a living. Maybe that would give the parade's dissenters something they could relate to.

Kelly teased him that this was a boring choice, but he supported the idea by doing the same and wearing what he would during a photoshoot, dark pants and a casual T-shirt. Nathaniel still thought Kelly looked stunning. At the moment his husband's eyes were twinkling at all the flamboyancy on display like he wouldn't mind taking part. Instead he was stuck holding on to Zero's leash while standing next to someone who dressed like a banker.

"Gentlemen!" a familiar voice declared. "It's so good to see you here. You were missed last night."

Marcello seemed to magically appear in a glowing ball of light. No, he *was* the glowing ball of light. His arms and legs were wrapped in illuminated bracelets of varying colors, as if he had robbed an army of ravers of their glow sticks and jewelry. Nathaniel was momentarily concerned that was *all* Marcello wore, until he noticed a skin-tight shirt and pants laced with hundreds of LED lights. A glowing crown atop his head completed the look. "I see you dressed for the occasion, Nathaniel. As always."

Kelly snorted and hid his mouth behind a hand. Nathaniel wasn't sure which of them his husband found more ridiculous, considering that they were two sides of an extreme: the stuffy suit and the glowing geezer.

Marcello placed a hand on Nathaniel's arm affectionately and even kissed his cheek, which he only did when feeling especially sentimental. "Handsome as always," he murmured before turning his attention on Kelly. "And you, my vicious little recluse, owe me a debt of gratitude. I invited the new client to my home last night, just to expose them to your work, and they're interested. They would have been convinced sooner had they seen you in action at the party. Next time, set aside your reservations and take part."

"It's not his fault," Nathaniel said hurriedly, eager to make amends. "I didn't invite him. I was being stupid. Again."

"Ah," Marcello said. "And here I am, shooting off unfair assumptions… and no doubt a few poorly timed texts last night. I hope you'll both forgive me. I didn't intend to cause domestic tension."

"There's nothing to apologize for," Kelly said generously, but his jaw clenched tellingly. He doubted Marcello noticed, although Nathaniel knew him too well not to. Even if he got it wrong sometimes.

"No harm done then," Marcello said. "The underwear party was successful enough that there will be another opportunity to attend next year. Now if you'll excuse me, I'm the centerpiece of a float this year. Most of them actually, or at least as many as I can climb onto. I've never been the sort of person to await an invitation. Now then, where is that Swedish man I hired to help lift me? He's magnificently tall. I wonder if his entire body is gifted with length? Hmm. I shall not allow this mystery to remain unsolved!"

They said goodbye and watched him spring away, Kelly with longing in his eyes. He was biting his bottom lip now, and not because he wanted Marcello as his husband instead. But he probably did wish he was with someone a little more exciting. Or with someone who spent less time worrying. Nathaniel looked around. Then he reached a decision.

"Come here," he said.

Kelly eyed him and stepped closer, face tilted upward for a kiss, but he had misunderstood. Nathaniel complied anyway. Then he reached down for the hem of Kelly's T-shirt and pulled it up and off.

"What's this all about?" Kelly asked with a laugh.

"I'm not jealous," Nathaniel answered, loosening his tie before shrugging off his jacket and letting it fall to the ground. "When guys stare at you, I understand why. But it should be for the right reasons. I want them to see how strong you are."

"Oh," Kelly said, his smile faltering. He flexed an arm halfheartedly. "Thanks. I've been doing push-ups lately."

"That's not what I meant." Nathaniel quickly unbuttoned his shirt and took it off. "I also want them to understand how proud I am of you."

Kelly's expression softened when looking him over, his affection transparent. "I feel the same way."

"Good, because we're not finished yet." Nathaniel reached for the waist of Kelly's pants. His fingers were on the top button when Kelly attempted to pull away.

"What are you doing?"

"What I should have done last night. Letting everyone see how accomplished you are."

Kelly's eyes searched his. "You mean my leg?"

"Yup. The pants gotta go."

Fine eyebrows arched in surprise. "Are you sure about that? I'm wearing the purple underwear you bought me."

The pair that left very little to the imagination, but there was no backing down now. "I'll go first." Nathaniel let his pants drop. Luckily he was wearing boxers, but this wasn't about him stepping outside his comfort zone. This was about proving how he truly felt. "And now you."

He moved close to Kelly, unfastened his pants, and then stooped to help him out of his shoes so it could all come off. Zero was hopping around him and licking his face like this was a game. A few people were staring, and one or two made good-humored comments, but there was so much going on around them that they were mostly left alone. Before long they were both facing each other, naked except for a relatively small amount of fabric.

"What I am," Nathaniel said, "is proud. Of everything you've overcome, but that's not how I see you. You've always been an entire person to me, complete and perfect. That I wanted to protect you from getting your feelings hurt was foolish because I know how resilient you are. That I ended up hurting you instead—"

Kelly didn't let him get any further. He pressed his lips to Nathaniel's, which was enough to chase away any lingering doubts. Kelly had forgiven him.

"I love you," Kelly said, pulling away ever so slightly. "And I couldn't be prouder to be married to someone who wanted to do the impossible for me. People will always stare and make ignorant comments, but I don't let that bother me, because I know one man out there sees me for who I truly am."

"I love you too," Nathaniel said, going in for another kiss. Then he thought better. "Erm."

"You also have a lot to be proud of," Kelly said, glancing downward, "but I'm not sure I want anyone staring at it."

Nathaniel laughed. "Now that I've made my big gesture, can I put my clothes back on?"

"Not a chance," Kelly said. "Although we should wear shoes, because we're going to walk this entire parade together. Right?"

Zero barked. He was staring at a poodle whose hair had been dyed rainbow colors, but it sounded like a "yes" anyway.

"Okay," Nathaniel said, offering his arm. "Let's show this city what love looks like."

They walked together down the streets of Austin, Marcello screeching in delight when he spotted them, and although they were surrounded by like-minded people, Nathaniel only had eyes for one person. His proudest achievement. The love of his life.

Something Like Stories: Volume Three

Something Like Her

by Jay Bell

Astoria, Oregon
November 22nd, 2017

"Heart attack."

William heard the words, body and mind urging him to leap into action. All his years of training as a rescue swimmer were to blame for that. He took a deep breath, switched the phone from one ear to the other, and reminded himself that this wasn't a search and rescue.

"Is he okay now?" William asked.

Lily, one of his oldest friends and the mother of his child, sighed heavily. "He's weak. That's how Mom keeps describing him. I tried talking to Dad on the phone but he's…" Her voice squeaked and faltered.

"I'm sorry." William felt helpless as he listened to her blow her nose. "If there's anything I can do, just say the word."

"I'm flying down to Austin tomorrow."

"On Thanksgiving?"

"Nothing gets past you," Lily teased, but her heart didn't seem in it. "The thing is, I don't want to take Daisy with me."

Was this finally… No. He would be excited later, if it was true. First and foremost, he needed to be there for his friend. "Why not? I'm sure your mom would love to see Daisy. That might cheer her up. Your dad too if he's—"

"In and out of consciousness," Lily said. "I had the same thought, but she's so smart. Daisy soaks up information like a sponge, and I'm not ready to have a talk with her about what it means to be seriously ill or—god forbid—why grandpa won't ever come home from the hospital."

"Is it that bad?"

Jason strolled into the kitchen, looking concerned at these words. William tried to signal that things were okay. For them, at least.

"My grandpa passed the same way," Lily said. "A series of heart attacks. That was on my father's side, so yeah, I'm worried. I don't want Daisy to see me if… You know. I'm not sure I'll be able to hold it together. For anyone. I need you to watch her. Is that okay? You were going to drive down here tomorrow anyway. I'll be back on Sunday."

"Yes," William said with hesitation, but only for practical reasons. "She'll need to come back with us to stay here. Tomorrow is clear for me, but I'm on call after that. Jason is off work though. He's great with her."

"I trust him almost as much as I trust you," Lily said. "So it's settled. Do you want to be the one to tell her?"

"Sure!"

"Just a sec."

He listened as Lily walked through her apartment, the sound of cartoons growing louder. Then he heard grumbling before Lily spoke again.

"She spilled milk on herself. Let me get her cleaned up and I'll call you back. Are you sure you're up for this?"

"Yes," William said, clamping down on his enthusiasm. If the circumstances were better, he would be leaping around the room! "Absolutely."

"Okay. Thanks. Call you in a bit."

William lowered the phone. Then he smiled. And grimaced. And chewed his bottom lip.

"I can't tell if you're happy or upset," Jason said, plopping down in one of the kitchen chairs.

William joined him at the small square table. "Lily's dad had a heart attack."

"Whoa! Is he okay?"

"He's in the hospital, so we'll see. Lily wants to fly there tomorrow."

"So no Thanksgiving plans. That's understandable. Did I hear right though? Are we getting a little visitor?"

William grinned. He couldn't help it. "Daisy is coming. For three nights!"

"About time," Jason said, smiling back at him. "This is a first, right? She never stayed the night with you, even before I moved here?"

"That's right," William said. "I've been waiting for this, but

Lily is so protective of her. I appreciate why, and I know she trusts me. I just hope…" He looked around the room, bogged down by a number of concerns.

"It'll be fine," Jason said. "We've got the space. At least we're not living at the motel anymore."

Their previous home was a *former* motel, but William tended to think of it that way too. Not only had the place been worn down and small, but some of their neighbors were truly strange. That had likely been the source of many of Lily's reservations. Although they'd had the new apartment for a while, which included two separate bedrooms—pure luxury after sharing a sofa bed in a narrow living room.

"We need to make the office nice for her," William said. "Like a real bedroom. For my baby girl!"

Jason laughed and shrugged easily. "No problem."

"What are we going to do with her?"

"Put her to work," Jason said without missing a beat. "I bet those little hands of hers can clean all sorts of hard-to-reach places. Like behind the toilet."

"Oh god!" William said, leaping to his feet. "We need to clean the entire apartment! And shop. Not just for groceries but—"

"Sit," Jason said, pulling out his phone. "And breathe. I don't want you having a heart attack too. We'll make a list, divide it up, and be done in no time."

"Good plan," William said. "Let's start with groceries. She likes bananas. And peaches."

"Are we going to do a traditional Thanksgiving meal?"

"I don't know. Do you think she'd enjoy that? I remember Thanksgiving being boring when I was a kid. I wasn't into the food, and there's nothing fun like an Easter basket or a stocking to dig through. And what about the other days? I love Astoria, but how can we possibly compete with Portland?"

Jason made a gun with the fingers of his right hand and pointed it at William. "Pew! That was an elephant-grade tranquilizer dart. You'll feel a lot calmer starting right about… now."

"I mean it. This will be Daisy's first night away from her mom. I want to keep her happy. She's almost three. Is that old enough for a kid's museum?"

"No idea," Jason said. "Why don't we ask her what she wants to do?"

"Simple as that?"

"Yeah. I had a couple of foster families do the same for me. That always made it easier to adjust. I had something to look forward to instead of worrying about being somewhere strange and new."

William stood again, this time so he could lean across the table to kiss his boyfriend. "You're a genius."

"Thanks," Jason said, straining to reach his lips again as if wanting more.

William's phone rang before that could happen. "Sorry."

"It's cool," Jason said. "I'll work on the grocery list."

William flashed him an appreciative smile as he answered his phone. His teeth remained on display, thanks to the voice he heard.

"Hi, Daddy."

"My little daisy petal!" he enthused. "How are you doing today?"

"We saw kittens at the pet store."

"Pet store? What were you doing there?"

"She's not getting a cat!" Lily said from somewhere in the background.

"I'm only allowed to look at them," Daisy informed him glumly.

"Jason works with cats," William said. "Dogs and birds and bats too."

"Bats?" Daisy asked, sounding more interested than repulsed.

"All sorts of animals," William said. "Wild ones especially. When they get hurt, he helps make them better." Jason had begun volunteering at a wildlife rehabilitation center, having missed his work with the animal shelter in Austin. "Right now he's taking care of a fox with a broken leg."

Daisy gasped. "A for-real fox?"

William relaxed a little. This was going well. "Yeah! Do you want to meet the fox? You can come stay with us for a few days. We'll have a sleepover."

"Mama, can I go meet the fox?"

Lily caught on quickly. "Yes, but no touching. They bite!"

"Mama says I can," Daisy informed him. "Come get me."

"Soon," William said. "We're going to have a lot of fun together. What do you want to do while you're here?" He looked to Jason, who nodded encouragingly. "Anything you want. Just name it."

"Can we have a tea party?" Daisy asked. "A real one."

"Sure!" He'd already had a few pretend tea parties in her bedroom. Adding real food and beverages to the mix wouldn't be so hard.

"In a garden?" Daisy asked.

"You want a tea party in a garden?"

Jason looked a little concerned at this.

"Yeah," Daisy said. "Please, Daddy?"

"Sure. We can do that!"

"And a castle."

"Huh?"

"Can it be in a castle?"

William looked to Jason for help. He should have put her on speakerphone. "I thought you wanted it in a garden?"

"Yeah. Inside a castle."

"Like a courtyard?"

The line was silent until… "Can we?"

"Okay, baby. If that's what you want."

"Yay! When are you coming?"

"Tomorrow morning, I think. I'll need to ask your mom."

"I'm going to pack now."

He heard a *thunk* as the phone must have been set down, then an excited voice that said, "Mama, we're having a tea party at a castle!"

"That's great, honey. Did you hang up?"

Lily checked the phone, confirmed that he was still on the line, and together they discussed times. William jotted the information down on the back of some junk mail, talked to her a little longer, and hung up.

"I'll have to leave early tomorrow," William said to Jason, who was anything but a morning person.

"How early?"

"I'll need to be on the road by five. You can stay in bed if you want."

"I love you," Jason said, looking relieved. "What was that about a tea party?"

"That's what she wants to do. It needs to be in a garden."

"In this weather?" They looked as one toward the window above the kitchen sink. It was gray and wet outside. At this time of year, it was always raining in Astoria.

"We'll get a big umbrella," William said. "Oh, and we need a castle."

Jason stared in response.

"You said I should give her whatever she wants!"

"Within reason! Where are you going to find a castle? Let's take her to Burger King. They have those paper crowns there and— Don't cross your arms over your chest. It scares me. You only do that when you're determined."

"I promised her a garden tea party inside a castle, and that's what she's going to get. Can we build one out of cardboard?"

"A castle?" Jason said. "It'll melt in the rain."

William uncrossed his arms so he could bury his face in his hands. "You're right. I messed up. I'll call again and have her choose something different."

"No," Jason said. "We'll make it work. Somehow. Just leave it to me."

William dropped his hands to see Jason already searching on his phone. "Really?"

"Really," Jason said. "I got you into this mess, I'll get you out. Anything for my little princess."

"Do you mean her or me?"

Jason grinned. "I love that you need to ask. Now let's get to work. We've got a few miracles to pull off."

William kept his attention on the road. Only when he saw zero potential hazards did he allow himself to look in the rearview mirror, checking the back where Daisy slumbered in her car seat. She had spent the first hour of the drive asking him questions and babbling on about whatever passed through her mind. He adored every single word. Even the ones he didn't understand, like Shopkins or Equestria. She could start reading from a boring old dictionary and still capture William's complete attention. Now she was all tuckered out, which was fine. He was content to safely ferry her home. *His* home, although he loved the idea that it was hers as well. Why shouldn't she have two?

Their apartment building was a converted house with four units. The biggest benefit was living in a proper neighborhood now, and not on the edge of a commercial district like their old place. Daisy was still asleep after he parked along the street, so he picked her up and walked to the communal front door. Jason met him there, no doubt having tracked their progress with his phone. He led the way upstairs to their apartment. They spoke in whispers until Daisy was tucked into the child's bed they had set up in the office and music room. That sounded fancier than it was—the space consisted of a desk for their laptops, a corner where Jason kept his guitar, and a cushy chair where he often played it. Now the far end had been cleared and turned into a temporary bedroom, complete with colorful posters and other decorations that they couldn't keep themselves from buying.

They retreated to the kitchen, where they could speak at a normal volume.

"Is everything set up?" William asked.

"Yeah. How's the weather out there?"

William walked to the window. Half the sky was blue, the rest gray. He focused on the clouds and glared. "Don't you dare! Not today! Some other time. For now, let's call a truce."

"Okay," Jason said, still yawning himself awake. "We'll get you some mental help as soon as Daisy is gone."

"I fight those skies every single week," William said, pointing at the window accusingly. "I've been soaked to the bone from rain, nearly frozen to death from wind chill, and don't get me started on hail. All I'm asking for is clear skies. Just this once."

"You might get your wish," Jason said, ducking into the refrigerator for canned caffeine. "The forecast looks good."

"It better," William said. "Otherwise we're driving south until we find sun."

"I love this side of you." Jason looked him up and down between chugs of soda. "So, uh, how does it work when there's a kid in the house?"

"How's what work?"

Jason answered him with a crooked grin.

William shook his head. "Well, with my parents, they always told me and my brothers that they were going to scrub the bathtub together."

"They only did it in the shower or something?"

"That was just their excuse." William rolled his eyes. "I guess they thought it was a good explanation in case we heard a repetitive noise. They didn't even run the water, or clean the tub, which is something Errol pointed out to me once. When he told me what they were actually doing, I was mortified."

Jason laughed. "Do you want to 'scrub the tub' with me?"

"Now?" William said incredulously.

Jason shrugged. "I have a thing for dads, maybe because I didn't have one of my own."

"You're terrible," William said.

"And you love it," Jason said, moving closer.

They kissed, and yeah, more sounded good, but it was all too new. Jason understood this and didn't need to be told. They hung out in the living room, enjoying the downtime, until their little guest made an appearance an hour later.

She didn't waste time. Daisy was rubbing her eyes, still half-asleep when she said, "Are we gonna have a tea party now?"

"Sure!" William said, rising to scoop her up into his arms. "But first we have to get dressed."

"I'm already dressed," Jason said, joining them. "I made sure to wear my special tea party hoodie." Which was just a normal hoodie, but this made Daisy smile bashfully. She tucked her head into the crook between William's shoulder and neck.

"Did you remember to bring formal attire?" he asked her. "We can't have tea without an extra special dress."

Daisy pulled her head away, looking at him with concern.

"Let's go see," he said, equally amused by Jason's puzzled expression. Hopefully it would remain friendly. He led them back to the office and set Daisy on the bed before digging beneath it. "Let's see. I think I have a spare dress around here somewhere."

Jason snorted. "But will it fit her? That's the question."

"I have a feeling this one will." He pulled out a flat white box and set it next to Daisy, who was already excited, no stranger to presents. William spoiled her. Lots of people did, but hey, he only had one kid, and she only had one childhood. If she started turning into a brat, they would tackle the issue then, but for now...

"Is that for me?" she asked.

The lid had come off the box, revealing a sleeveless yellow dress with a sunflower pattern. It hadn't been cheap, but when a coworker had shown him a photo of her daughter and told him of a local seamstress, he hadn't been able to resist.

"I thought Santa wanted to give that to her?" Jason said, voice terse. He knew how much it cost.

"Santa heard about the tea party and thought it would be the perfect occasion," William said.

Jason shook his head and smiled.

Daisy ignored all of this, her attention focused solely on yellow fabric that frilled out at the waist, her tiny hand stroking the material lovingly. "Now I can be a queen!"

So much for their little princess. The girl didn't mess around! "The flower queen," Jason said, getting down on his knees next to her, "and you know what every queen needs, don't you?"

Daisy turned to him, eyes alight with interest. "A castle?"

"That's right. Get dressed and we'll take you there."

William watched all of this with worry, hoping against hope that she wouldn't be disappointed.

Tapiola Park was nice. That wasn't the issue. The park was large, situated just on the edge of Youngs Bay, and boasted its own baseball diamond, softball fields, and picnic shelters. It had other less-typical amenities too, such as a concrete bowl sunk into the ground that William mistook as an empty swimming pool, until he saw a skateboarder make use of it. That was special. As was the playground, which was partially hidden behind the facades of colorfully painted buildings—miniature recreations of historic locations in the area. Past these pint-sized buildings were a series of wooden walkways and steps. Lots of places to climb up and down. The community had come together to build the playground. William appreciated the concept, but would it be enough? Tapiola Park was nice, but it was no castle.

"The power of imagination," Jason murmured when noticing his doubtful expression.

They had just pulled up and parked. William wasn't sure how to proceed, but as promised, Jason had it covered.

"Close your eyes," he said, twisting around to address Daisy in the backseat. "You're about to see your castle."

Daisy smiled and did as requested. Jason got out of the car. William followed, opening the back door and picking her up. She kept her eyes covered as they walked closer, although he could tell that she was starting to peek from between her fingers.

"Your Majesty," Jason announced grandly, "may I present to you, your very own, Castle Tapioca!"

That wasn't quite the park's name, but William didn't have time to correct him. He was too focused on what his daughter's reaction would be. Her hands fell away, green eyes the same color as his own moving over it all. Then she gasped and started clapping. She liked it!

"Over there," Jason said, pointing to a squarish entrance that was supposed to represent Fort Clatsop, "that's the drawbridge. If any invaders come, they'll never get past it. And over there—" This time he pointed to an ornate tower resembling the Flavel House, "—that's where Rapunzel used to live. She was the previous owner before she moved in with her prince."

"*Tangled!*" Daisy shouted gleefully.

He was pretty sure that was a Disney movie. No matter what, she was happy and excited. William shot Jason a grateful smile.

"Can we go play?" Daisy asked.

Jason looked to him for instruction.

"You guys go ahead," William said. "I'll get our tea party set up."

"Yay!" Jason and Daisy cried in unison.

William set her down and they both took off. Jason's enthusiasm didn't seem faked as he chased her down one of the pathways while talking about a dragon he had seen nearby and how they should make friends with it. William went to the back of his Range Rover where he had the picnic gear stowed. Before unloading it, he turned to reconsider the park. The sky was blue, the sun shining over Youngs Bay. The view from Castle Tapioca must be spectacular. He could hear Jason roaring as Daisy squealed with delight, which helped him relax. She was happy. He was too. Time for a tea party!

William spread out a blanket near the playground and decorated it with plastic tea cups that appeared elegant despite the cheap material. He filled the teapot with apple juice and set out plates and forks. Then he returned to the car for the final touch—a fancy cake of miniature proportions. It was four slices at best, but that would be more than enough for the three of them. After surveying his work and deciding he was satisfied, he cupped his hands over his mouth and shouted, "The kettle is boiling!"

Jason was the first to appear, Daisy right behind him, both running fast enough that William was forced to spread his arms wide. "Don't trample the cake!" he warned.

Jason came to a halt, laughing as he stripped off his hoodie. "She's already wearing me out, and it's still day one."

"Just wait until she gets all this sugar into her," William said, picking Daisy up and swinging her around to where she should sit. "Who wants cake?"

"No no no," Jason said. "That's not how it's done." He cleared his throat, put an arm across his waist, and bowed. "Your Majesty, tea is served. Does it meet your expectations?"

"Do you like it?" William whispered helpfully when Daisy looked confused.

"Yes!" she said.

Jason held up an instructional finger. "I believe what you mean to say is, 'quite so.'"

"What's that mean?" Daisy said, scrunching up her petite little nose.

"It's like saying yes," Jason explained, "but way fancier."

"Can I pour the tea?" Daisy asked.

"Quite so," Jason responded.

They both watched Daisy take the pot, which was already swinging around dangerously. Luckily he hadn't filled it completely. Juice sloshed over the blanket as she filled three cups, but it wouldn't be polite to acknowledge that. William had to admit he was getting into this too. "Would Your Majesty like me to serve the cake?" he asked.

"Quite so," Daisy said.

This made them both laugh, which they quickly had to stifle when she looked at them sternly. A natural monarch! William focused on quickly cutting three slices, lest he be sent to the guillotine.

"Now we just need minstrels," Jason said, snapping his fingers. "Man! I should have brought my guitar."

"You can sing," William said.

Jason scoffed. "No way! I'm not Ben."

"It's better than no music," William said. "What does Her Royal Highness think? Would you enjoy some music while we drink tea?"

"Quite so," Daisy said again, eyes slightly narrowed, but this time they managed not to laugh, and she seemed satisfied.

Jason didn't sing, choosing instead to whistle. Mozart, probably. Music wasn't William's area of expertise, but the song was used in almost every generic royalty scene on screen. He noticed the way that Daisy sat so prim and proper on her knees, tiny teacup in her hand, eyes filled with unbridled joy, and he nearly cried. This was perfection, and he had one person to thank for it. He looked over at Jason, stretched out casually while whistling, and felt more in love than ever. If only every day could be like this!

The thought remained on his mind that evening, when he was tucking Daisy into bed. Her new dress was on a chair nearby, her eyelids too heavy to stay open. She seemed so small and fragile, and yet, was always brimming with life. William was kissing her on the forehead when her eyes fluttered open again.

"I love you, Daddy."

"I love you too," he said. "Sleep tight, my sweet little flower queen."

She smiled at this, sleep soon overtaking her. William watched her for a moment, wishing he could be there every night, before he quietly slipped out of the room.

He found Jason at the kitchen table, a glass of wine in front of him. "Grown-up time," he explained. "Even with the cake, I think I burned enough calories to get away with drinking a whole bottle. Want a glass?"

William shook his head and sat down. "That was fun."

"Yeah!" Jason said. "I loved it. In fact, I want more."

"More days like these?"

Jason nodded. "And more kids."

He was smiling but didn't seem to be kidding.

"How many?" William asked.

Jason exhaled and gave the question serious thought. "We should start with one and take it from there. When we have enough money saved up for a house, we should buy the biggest we can. Or at least make sure it has lots of bedrooms."

William waited for him to scoff, wink, or anything else to show he was joking. But he didn't. "I'd like that too. How though? Should we ask Lily to be our surrogate or—"

"Foster care," Jason said. "I want to be on the other side of the system and see if I can do a better job than some of the families I stayed with. It won't always be easy. A lot of kids will be damaged like me. That can be challenging."

William reached across the table to take his hand. "You're

perfect. I'd love to invite more people like you into our lives."

"Good," Jason said. "Let's plan on it."

"Speaking of which, before we buy a house or adopt anyone, we should probably get married."

Jason pulled his hand free and leaned back, but he had a sparkle in his eye. "Maybe."

"Seriously?" William said. "You're willing to do everything else, but you still can't give me an answer?"

"Four years," Jason said with a shake of his head. "That's when you'll get my answer. Not now, and not here. But you don't have much longer to wait. We'll need to book a flight soon."

To Austin, because Jason had promised to give his answer in the same place William had proposed. In the backyard of Ben and Tim's house. "Do you miss them?"

"Always," Jason said.

"Because you could see them a lot sooner. We could get this over with next month."

"So tempting," Jason said, "but I think I'll play it safe. What if I get tired of you before then?"

"Please don't," William said, rising from the table.

"Why not?"

"Because it would break my heart, and then I'd be forced to follow you around wherever you go, howling like a heartbroken hound." He couldn't be loud at the moment, so he kept his voice down as he did just that, bringing his mouth close to Jason's ear. "Arooooooo! Arooooooo! Arooooooo!"

"I've got a soft spot for animals in need," Jason said, turning his head for a kiss.

William scooped him up into his arms while their lips were still locked.

Jason pulled back as they left the room. "Where are you taking me?"

"Isn't that obvious?" William asked. "It's time to scrub the bathtub."

———

Something Like Stories: Volume Three

Something Like Stars

by Jay Bell

Austin, Texas
2017

Ben hit the button to close the garage door, the electronic rumble loud as the afternoon light was slowly blocked out and replaced by the cold energy-saving bulb above. He went to the door that led outside, glancing back once to confirm that Tim's car wasn't there. That was fine. Ben adored his husband, but he preferred to unwind in solitude after school.

He grinned to himself, amused by how that sounded as he walked toward the front of the house. He wasn't a fulltime student. Ben still worked at the hospital. Only his theater performances had been waylaid while he earned his master's degree. The rest of his time was taken up by other obligations. Such as chores. Tim wasn't the greatest at cleaning. Organizing, maintaining, and repairing… yes. But cleaning was something he only did if Ben asked him to. The same with cooking. So an hour of peace before the circus of his life resumed was very much welcome.

Ben had his house key out and was aiming it for the lock when the door swung open.

"Here you are at last!" a husky voice declared.

Ben had experienced this particular surprise often enough that he barely reacted. Marcello didn't normally answer the front door though. More often he would be lurking in one of their rooms, sipping champagne and waiting to be discovered, but usually he provided some warning sign.

"Where's your car?" Ben asked, glancing back to see if he had missed it. He hadn't. The driveway was empty.

"I took an Uber." Marcello put a hand over his mouth and tittered. "Isn't that quaint?"

"That depends," Ben said. "Did you choose one of the luxury options?"

"No, and I intend to shun such things in the future," Marcello said. "The experience was too positive. A man picked me up in a Ford Bronco. Can you imagine? And he was a construction worker with the most intriguing hands. They were callused all over, from what I could observe. Sadly, his hands never made the leap from the wheel to my body, but this *has* given me an idea for a new cruising app that incorporates ridesharing. I plan to call it Bumpr."

"Sorry," Ben said, nodding toward the interior of the house. "Do you mind?"

"Not at all!" Marcello said, stepping aside. "Come in, come in! Make yourself at home!"

"I'll try," Ben said, shaking his head ruefully. As much as he had been looking forward to being alone, he always enjoyed Marcello's visits, and truly wasn't bothered that the man was there.

"I could hardly wait for either of you to arrive," Marcello was saying. "I have exciting news about the movie."

"What movie?" Ben asked.

Marcello spun around. "Why, *your* movie of course."

"Really?" Ben said, leading the way to the kitchen. "I was hoping you had forgotten about that."

"How could you say such a thing?" Marcello cried. "I thought you were as enamored with the idea as I."

"It seems vain." Ben began filling the electric kettle with water. "Did you already open a bottle?"

"Not yet," Marcello said. "In fact, I probably shouldn't."

Ben raised an eyebrow in concern. "Everything okay?"

"Excessively. I feel like a man who is jogging on a treadmill while clenching his cheeks shut to hold in a kale enema. That's how robust my health is these days. No, I only refrain because of Nathaniel. He does worry so, and I promised not to drink quite as early in the day."

Except it was now late afternoon. Ben was impressed. "Tea for two?" he offered.

"That would be lovely," Marcello said. "Getting back to your point, there's nothing vain about feeling enthusiasm for this project. Sharing your story with the world will have a positive impact on many lives, I'm sure of it. Why, you allowing this to happen is a noble deed."

"If you say so," Ben replied. "What's the big news? Did we sign Neil Patrick Harris to play me?"

"Oh, wouldn't he be a delight on the casting couch!"

"Your life is a lawsuit waiting to happen," Ben murmured as he poured steaming water into two mugs.

"But no," Marcello continued. "I'm afraid auditions are still a mile away. All I can offer you today is the first portion of the script."

"Really?" Ben asked, his interest piqued. He had read his fair share of scripts for theater productions he participated in. Never a movie script, but he couldn't imagine them being much different.

"Yes indeed!" Marcello gestured to the kitchen table where a short stack of papers awaited them. "Please. Have a seat."

"You're such a gracious host," Ben teased.

"I do try my utmost. Am I wrong, or do you now seem keener?"

"Of course," Ben admitted as he sat. "It's not every day that you get to read about your own life."

"I'm so pleased to hear it," Marcello said. "Pretend I'm not here. Just relax and allow yourself to be carried away by the story."

Ben pulled the papers toward him, reading aloud the text on the topmost page. *"Ben Loves Tim?"*

"A working title," Marcello said with a dismissive wave of his hand. "Although it does have a certain ring to it."

"Hmm," Ben said. "I was thinking more along the lines of…"

Marcello leaned forward. "Yes?"

"I don't know. Something like…" Ben shook his head. "I almost had it, but now I'm drawing a blank."

"I'm sure it will come to you," Marcello said, but he wagged a finger. "Let this be your first lesson. The muse cannot be summoned. She must be coaxed to the table. Uncorked bottles are the most effective bait, I've found, but even my noblest of efforts have resulted only in the paltry number of pages before you."

"You wrote this?"

"Yes, but have no concern. I know the limits of my creative abilities. Once we have the skeleton in place, my script doctors will gussy it up for a glamorous night on the red carpet. Please! Go right ahead."

Ben turned the title page over and set it aside. Then he began to read.

BEN LOVES TIM
Screenplay by Marcello Maltese

INT. BEN'S BEDROOM - NIGHT

FADE IN:
A teenager's room is dimly lit by a computer monitor, a hint of clutter visible as we pan past this to a window. There sits BEN BENTLEY, 16, who rests his arms and head on the window sill. The camera moves so we can share his view of the world outside. Below, strolling along the city streets of HOUSTON, TEXAS, we see a number of beautiful gay couples walking arm in arm.

BEN: Just look at them all! And yet, here I am, painfully alone. Why not me? When will I find my other half?

Ben sighs wistfully as he raises his head. Then he opens his mouth and begins to sing.

"Wait a minute," Ben said, looking up from the script. "Is this a musical?"

"Not at all!" Marcello said. "What makes you think so?"

He looked down and scanned the text. "Because you have me singing more exposition than a Disney princess. Hey, maybe we should animate this instead!"

Marcello tsked. "Everyone's a critic. Perhaps because it's the easiest thing to be."

"And some of these lyrics," Ben continued, unable to stop himself. "*I don't understand this feeling in my heart, but getting into your pants would be a start.*"

"Merely the skeleton," Marcello reminded him. "Someone with more romantic sensibilities will correct all of that."

"It's good that you're open to corrections," Ben said carefully. "You know I grew up in The Woodlands, right? The only things I ever saw out my bedroom window were trees. And I definitely don't remember openly gay people being around. That would have made me feel less alone."

"Ah, a sense of isolation," Marcello said, pulling a pen out of his jacket pocket. He took the page Ben was reading and started scribbling notes. "Small town boy feels he's the only of his kind."

"Yeah," Ben said. "That's a lot closer." He looked down at the next page. "Is this when Tim and I first met?" he asked, but he didn't wait for an answer, too eager to relive the moment.

```
EXT. NATURE TRAIL - NIGHT

Ben waits in the boughs of a tree,
dressed only in black so as not to be
detected. The camera moves to capture
what he sees: a paved path.

BEN: Come on, come on! You can run
all you want, Mr. Blue Shorts, but
you can't hide. Not from me.

Ben licks a finger and holds it up, as
if testing the wind, before his eyes
narrow in satisfaction.

BEN: No, you can't hide from me.

CLOSE-UP
Ben's face is the very picture of
elation as we cut to TIM WYMAN,
17, a shirtless young man of
Mexican descent. The camera remains
stationary as we watch Tim jog toward
the screen. Once he passes, we remain
focused on the path as Ben drops
down from the tree. With a look of
determination, he gives chase.
```

```
DISSOLVE TO:
A montage of Ben running from bush
to bush, tree to tree, attempting to
remain hidden from his prey. This
continues until we reach a lake. Tim
squats next to the water, moonlight
illuminating taut muscles as he
scoops handfuls of water into his
mouth. Ben is drawn out of hiding by
this spectacle, unable to resist an
alluring antidote to his unquenchable
desire. Tim hears him coming and
turns his head, silver eyes seductive
as they consider the newcomer.

TIM: What a hot night. I don't know
about you, but this weather makes
me so... thirsty. What about you,
Benjamin?

BEN: So thirsty that I'm burning up!

Tim holds out cupped palms filled with
water. Ben swoops in obediently to
sip from his hands.
```

"O-kay," Ben said, tearing his eyes away from the script. "Where to begin?"

"It's good," Marcello said with a wide smile and an eager nod. "Isn't it?"

"Sure," Ben forced himself to say. "But it's not accurate. First of all, how does he even know my name at this point? Tim and I didn't interact until the school year started." He scrunched up his face. "In fact, I don't think we said a single word to each other until the day I sprained his ankle."

"That part turned out particularly well," Marcello said, reaching across the table to turn more pages. He tapped one of them. "Right here. Take a look!"

EXT. SCHOOL - DAY

A bell rings as students swarm outside a school building, all eager to flee the public institution. Ben is standing next to a bicycle some distance away, watching this spectacle with disdain.

BEN, VOICEOVER: Those bullies can call me Butterfly Boy all they want. I'll never stop being me. My heart is too strong. And yet, one of those bullies always makes me feel weak. In the knees.

Ben loads his textbooks into the basket attached to the handlebars of his bike. Then he mounts the saddle, wanting to be whisked away from his troubles. He looks down at the bicycle and pats it affectionately.

BEN: At least I've got you, old friend. You've always carried me to where I most need to be. We'll never part!

EXT. NATURE PATH - DAY

Ben is singing to himself as he rides his bicycle, his troubles forgotten until neon blue jogging shorts attract his attention like a hummingbird drawn to nectar. Young Timothy is on the path ahead, the sweat beads on his bare skin catching the light and making him glow. The clenching thighs and taut muscles of his back all beckon the eye to his sensationally pert buttocks. Ben notices this and becomes mesmerized, unable to tear his attention away. He's so taken that he forgets to brake as he nears. The bicycle knocks Tim down, the camera cutting to...

CLOSE UP
A bicycle tire runs over one of Tim's ankles as we hear him cry out.

BEN: What have I done? Stay there! Help is on the way!

Ben hops off the bicycle while it is still in motion, letting it roll away into the woods, never to be seen again. He has outgrown such childish interests. Today he begins his journey on the path toward manhood, a voyage that must be navigated on foot. Ben kneels next to Tim to better inspect the damage he caused.

TIM: Get away from me, you creep!

BEN: Is that how you see me? Because when I look at you I see...

TIM: What?

BEN: It's not important. We need to get you home so you can rest. Can you walk?

Ben helps him to his feet, his hands moving over Tim's body as if unsure where to settle.

TIM: I think so. What about you? You seem shaky.

```
BEN: It's the accident. It upset me
more than I realized. I think I'm
going into shock.

TIM: You're shivering. Here. Let me
carry you.

Tim lifts Ben into his arms, and
together, they begin the long ~~walk~~
hop home.
```

Ben raised his head from the script, eyes already narrowed in suspicion. "Is this for real? You aren't kidding?"

"I did warn you that it's an early draft," Marcello said, looking wounded.

"And it's very entertaining. Really. I'm just struggling with accuracy."

"Again?" Marcello said, pen poised to make changes. "You have my undivided attention."

"For starters, I wasn't on a bike when I ran into Tim."

"A shame," Marcello said disapprovingly. "I envisioned the bicycle as its own character. A sort-of inanimate friend that kept you company until you and Tim could meet."

"I had Allison, and she's very animate. Use her instead."

"Surely you're not suggesting that you ride her into battle. How would that even work? Would you be on Allison's back as she charges at Tim?"

"No," Ben said with a chuckle. "Although that's definitely something I would pay money to see. I was on Rollerblades that day. I was never very good with them, which is why I messed up when braking and knocked him into the ditch."

"*Into* the ditch," Marcello said. "Now I'm getting the complete picture. That must have been a steep incline."

"It was, yes."

"Then how did Tim carry you out? Especially with his injury."

"That's the other thing," Ben said. "He couldn't put weight on the sprained ankle. It hurt too much. Even if we hadn't ended up in the ditch, how would that have worked with him carrying me?"

"I raised the same concern. Tim insisted he had to hop the entire way home. That's why I made the revision."

Ben's eyebrows shot up. "*Tim* told you this is how it happened?"

"Yes." Marcello frowned. "Although now that I think about it—and being considerably more sober—I am having difficulty imagining the logistics."

"Because he's full of it!"

"Then tell me what really happened."

Ben remembered needing to pull Tim up the incline, since he had been (and still was) too weak to carry anyone. Once they were supporting each other and hobbling along, Ben had struggled to contain his excitement at being so close to a guy he had previously only admired from afar. Their bare skin had touched in places, their sweat intermingling and, well... It was all much easier to forgive now that he wasn't an awkward teenager. He'd been young. That was nothing to feel ashamed of. Then he imagined seeing these events portrayed on a big screen while surrounded by absolute strangers. Just the thought made his cheeks turn red. "I carried Tim home."

Marcello looked surprised. "You did? As in you lifted him up or—"

"Yeah," Ben said, holding out his arms to demonstrate. "I just scooped him up and away we went!"

"I see," Marcello said, the pen nearing paper but not yet writing. "It's just that Tim isn't exactly small, and you *are* rather petite."

"He wasn't nearly as beefy back then," Ben said. "That, and I had one of those emergency adrenaline rushes. You've heard about those? Mothers can fight off grizzly bears to defend their children and all sorts of crazy things."

"I have indeed heard such stories." Marcello pursed his lips. "I wonder why Tim felt the need to tell me otherwise."

"He finds it emasculating," Ben said. "Little old me carrying him all the way home. It wasn't easy, believe me!"

"I imagine it wasn't," Marcello said, jotting down notes at last. "I wonder what other details Tim felt the need to embellish."

Ben pulled out his phone and checked it, noticing a text. "He's running late, but if you want, I'd be happy to go over the rest."

"Most of it is very straightforward," Marcello said. "You two fall for each other, he struggles with his sexuality, you clash with his parents. Sparks fly and love is made. It's only when we reach that initial parting of ways that I'm lacking in details."

"You want to hear about the first time we broke up?" Ben asked.

"I'm afraid so. I would have asked Tim about it, but as I said, we were drinking and I was concerned he—"

"You don't want to ask him about that," Ben said quickly. "He gets too emotional. I, on the other hand, will tell you everything you need to know."

Marcello perked up at this news. "The unadulterated truth?"

Ben felt his smile tighten. "Of course!"

```
EXT. PARK - NIGHT

Voices can be heard, giggling and
murmuring to each other. The camera
moves across a playground at night,
following these sounds until we
discover two young men standing
intimately close to one another.

BEN: I can't believe we've been
together for a year already!

TIM: And I know just the way to
celebrate.

Tim strips off his shirt.

TIM: Let's get it on, baby!

BEN: Here?

TIM: Yeah! You've heard of a jungle
gym? Well I'm a jungle Tim!

Tim pounds on his bare chest in an
imitation of Tarzan.
```

BEN: One year of me pretending to be impressed. I don't know how much more I can take.

TIM: I bet you can take all of this.

We see the neon blue jogging shorts drop to the ground. What follows depends on to what degree the MPAA censors us. Note to self: Inquire if the boys would be comfortable with an NC-17 rating.

After an as-of-yet undetermined amount of passion…

BEN: Hey, did you hear something?

VOICE, OFF-SCREEN: Stop! Police!

Flashlights cut through the darkness, giving us tantalizing glimpses of bare skin, but it's only Tim who is completely undressed.

BEN: It's the fuzz! Run, honey! Save yourself!

TIM: What about you?

BEN: I'll take care of this. Now go!

Tim runs naked for the nearest line of trees. Ben pulls from his backpack two Rollerblades and starts to put them on.

BEN: My old friends, I need you now more than ever!

```
Ben gets to his feet, a police officer
running down the path toward him, but
Ben isn't scared. He lowers his body
to pick up speed as he rolls toward
the officer, determined to knock him off
the path and buy his man more time
to flee.

BEN: This is what I'm good at. Just
one more accident in the name of
love!
```

Tim did his best not to laugh, which involved holding back a snort and nearly choking.

"Are you okay?" Marcello inquired from the couch across from him. "If you need to cry, don't hold it in. This part of the script *is* rather emotional."

"Not for the guy running home naked," Tim said.

"Ah yes! What could be more invigorating?"

"Except it never happened," Tim said.

Marcello sighed, checked his watch, and must have decided it was a suitable time to drink, because he rose and went to the nearby kitchen. "Would you care for anything?" he called.

"The usual," Tim said, adding, "Whatever you've got on tap." He wasn't being colorful. Marcello had installed a tap in his own kitchen, just for Tim's benefit. And other guests too, he supposed. How many guys had sat on this very couch and been plied with alcohol and overwhelmed by charm?

"So you didn't streak naked across The Woodlands to reach home?" Marcello asked when he returned. He set down a mug of frothy beer and sat across from him again while pinching the stem of a champagne flute. "Next you'll probably tell me you didn't have sex on the playground at all."

"Oh we did," Tim said. "Or started to anyway. It took us another five years before we finished."

"A new world record in edging," Marcello said drolly. Then he shook his head. "I shouldn't joke. All those years of separation… I'm looking forward to penning that part of the story. Such a bittersweet tragedy. Then again, there are plenty of tears in the high school portion too. Yours in particular."

"Huh?"

"Surely you haven't forgotten." Marcello nodded to the script. "If so, it's all there in black and white."

Not understanding, Tim turned the page to see what he meant.

```
INT. SCHOOL GYMNASIUM

A talent show is in progress, a stage
set up at one end of the hall. A
floor normally used as a basketball
court is now filled with rambunctious
teenagers. We catch the tail-end
of an act just before it is booed
off stage. This is a tough crowd,
unlikely to give fair treatment to
any performance. We see Ben take the
stage with his loyal friend Allison,
who is nearly as dear to him as his
faithful Rollerblades. A handful of
bandmates are setting up instruments
behind them.

BEN: This won't end well.

ALLISON: Are they still booing the
last act, or is this all for us?

BEN: I don't know. Do you think he's
out there?

ALLISON: Tim? Only one way to find
out.

The duo begin to sing a rousing
rendition of I Would Do Anything For
Love by Meat Loaf. During the middle
of this song, Ben points to the
audience. The crowd parts down the
middle, revealing Tim Wyman and his
```

```
circle of friends. Tim's enchanting
eyes are fixed on Ben. Then they fill
with tears, as there is no containing
the overwhelming cocktail of emotion.
Unfortunately for Tim, his friends
soon notice.

BRYCE: What the hell, Tim. Are you
crying?

DARRYL: Holy shit, he is! From now on
we'll call him Whiney Wyman!

KRISTA: I never deserved to be with
you, Whiney Wyman!

TIM: That's one hundred percent true,
Krista. Now leave me alone. All of
you! I don't need friends. Not when
I've got so many tears to keep me
company.
```

"Okay," Tim said, dropping the script on the coffee table. "Fuck this. You know I love you, but are you trying to make me look bad?"

"Certainly not!" Marcello said, pressing a hand to his chest. "I know it can be difficult to revisit the past, but—"

"None of that happened!" Tim shot back. "The talent show, sure, but this..." He gestured at the script. "I'm surprised you didn't have me wet my pants too. Or is that on the next page?"

"I merely wrote down events as they were described to me," Marcello said haughtily. "If you dispute their authenticity, take that up with your husband."

Tim stared. Then he started laughing. "Ben told you all of this?"

"Yes, and I'm starting to feel taken advantage of. I'm attempting to create a movie based on truth. Now I feel as though I've been spoon-fed fairy tales."

"The script isn't completely wrong," Tim said. "It's pretty close, actually. Ben didn't point me out in the crowd. He kept staring at me while singing, and yeah, I was really sad, but I never would have let my friends see that. They would have torn me apart."

"So only a slight adjustment is needed," Marcello said, seeming appeased. "And the rest?"

Tim took a deep breath. "Let's find out."

INT. TIM'S BEDROOM - NIGHT

Tim is asleep in his bed (Shirtless! Always shirtless.) as Ben creeps in through the bedroom door. He doesn't announce his presence or slide beneath the sheets. Instead he seems content to stand there and watch Tim sleep. After enough of this, Ben sighs heavily and, with a somber expression, takes the key from around his neck and sets it on the nightstand next to Tim. He has decided that they must part ways, but he can't without giving into temptation one final time. Ben bends over Tim to place a kiss on his lips. Then he turns to leave, until a hand reaches out to grab his wrist.

TIM: Don't go.

BEN: I have to. I'm sick of having my heart broken. I won't let you do that to me again. And I won't do it to myself anymore.

TIM: I can't change. I wish I could. I tried, Benjamin. I really did.

BEN: I know.

TIM: You can do anything though. I

know you want us to be open but… What if you changed instead?

BEN (shaking his head): Maybe changing isn't as easy I thought. If it was… I think I would, because I know how badly this is going to hurt. I'll probably never stop looking back and wondering what we could have been if I'd stayed. But this is the way it has to be.

TIM: Please don't do this to us.

BEN: I'm sorry. Goodbye.

Ben reaches the door, pausing to look back and offer a sad smile. Then he walks out into the hallway and away from Tim forever. Almost.

TIM: I can't live without you!

Ben's progress is halted when Tim tumbles from the bedroom and latches himself on to Ben's ankle.

BEN: Be quiet! You'll wake your parents.

TIM: They're out of town. They're *always* out of town!

BEN: Let go! You only have yourself to blame.

TIM: I regret everything!

Tim is dragged down the stairs as Ben refuses to stop marching toward the

```
front door. When he gets there, he
sits on the front step to pry Tim's
fingers off his ankle.

BEN: This is goodbye, you rogue!

TIM: That's what you think. I've
spent my entire life running. I'm
good at it. You'll never escape me.

BEN: I will… with a little help from
my friends.

Ben holds up his Rollerblades, and
while Tim continues to beg and plead,
he puts them on. Ben stands, and with
a kick of his leg, launches himself
into the night. Tim runs after him
(still shirtless) but to no avail.
Ben has finally rolled his way to
freedom.
```

"Well?" Marcello inquired wearily. "No doubt this segment is inaccurate as well."

"Ben told you this too?" Tim asked.

"With a few embellishments from my own pen. Mostly the Rollerblades. They don't have as much personality as the bicycle, but I think they have spinoff potential."

"You're so weird." Tim took a swig of his beer. "And since you asked, that *is* how it really happened. Every single word."

Marcello raised an eyebrow. "For someone who spent so much of his youth lying, you're not very skilled at it."

Tim averted his gaze. "Does the movie have to stick to the facts? Because this is how it should have happened. The truth is, I pretended to be asleep until Ben left. That's it. I just laid there and wished he would fix everything. We didn't kiss. Maybe he wanted to, and that's why he made it happen in the script. And I *should* have begged him to stay. I wanted to, but I also knew I couldn't change. I wasn't ready to. I never realized he felt like he couldn't change either. That line about him always looking back and wondering what could have been... Was that you?"

"No," Marcello said. "That was your husband's suggestion. Does it surprise you? Did you truly believe after he walked out of your room, that he never looked back?"

Tim shrugged. "He was always the strong one. I figured he got over me pretty quick, yeah."

"The ring on your finger would suggest otherwise." Marcello leaned back and sighed. "I'm pleased the two of you are learning how it must have been for each other, but I no longer feel I'm making progress on this enterprise. You've both proven yourselves to be unreliable narrators."

"It's hard to resist changing things," Tim admitted. "I'd rather be the hero than the villain. Better yet, I'd rather Ben and I never broke up at all. We can do that in the movie version, can't we?" He sat up, excited by the idea. "Yeah! Why not?"

"Certainly," Marcello said. "Shall I be the one to tell Ben that we've erased Jace from history, or would you rather have that privilege?"

"Point taken," Tim said. "In that case, you should ask a neutral party. Someone who knows all the details without being directly involved. Allison is close enough. She's probably on Ben's side more than my own, but that's okay."

Marcello pursed his lips thoughtfully. "It's a shame Jace is no longer with us. For all the obvious reasons, of course, but I also would have liked to get his take on events."

"You can ask his sister Michelle," Tim suggested. "Or her husband. Greg was his best friend."

"Greg," Marcello repeated. "The meaty temptation that I occasionally see during the larger gatherings at your house?"

"Yeah. He's my friend now too, and he's always looked out for Ben."

"Meaning he cares equally for all three of you."

"I don't know about equally," Tim said. "He and Jace knew each other since they were kids and—"

"He's perfect for my needs," Marcello said. "Oh yes. I'm sure I'll find talking to him very inspirational. You simply must put me in touch with him immediately."

"Okay," Tim said, pulling out his phone. "Just promise to keep your hands to yourself. He's married. With kids."

"Aren't they all?" Marcello purred.

Tim rolled his eyes, listened to the phone ring, and wished he was calling Ben instead. Not only to remind him of all the lost years they had made up for, but also to promise that a lifetime still awaited them.

"Is this for real?" Greg looked up from the script at the strange man sitting in the booth across from him, confused about who exactly he was. Tim had tried to explain. Marcello owned some sort of modelling agency, which wasn't so hard to come to terms with, but then why did he also officiate weddings, hold charity balls, and now this? How did making a movie factor into any of the other things?

"I assure you—" Marcello replied, sparing a disdainful glare for the TV in the bar corner. "—this is very much for real." He raised his hand to get the attention of the waiter. "Excuse me, would it be possible to lower the volume slightly? Even the television closest to us would help. My friend and I have important business to discuss. Thank you." Marcello smiled at him pleasantly. "My goodness! With so much noise, I'm surprised you were able to read the script at all."

Greg shrugged. "When you've got a wife and three kids, this place is quiet by comparison."

Marcello batted his eyelashes in a way that was surprisingly feminine. "I find that incredibly hot."

"Uh... what?"

"It's incredibly hot in here," Marcello said, eyes glazing over slightly. "Before too long we'll have to strip off our shirts, just to stay cool."

"That's something you really nailed in the script," Greg said with a cackle. "Tim is always finding excuses to take his shirt off."

"You like it then?" Marcello said, snapping to attention.

"I love it!" Greg said. "If this happens, I want to be a part of it."

"A role in the movie perhaps? That would lend it an air of authenticity. I don't suppose you and Jace spent much time at the beach together. Or at the pool?"

"No. Why?"

"I'm trying to envision the particular assets you could bring to the film."

"There was a lake where we grew up, but it was usually too

cold for swimming." Greg shook his head. "Anyway, I don't want to be *in* the movie, but uh... When I was younger, I used to write my own scripts."

"Oh really?" Marcello rested his elbows on the table, his considerable chins supported by both hands. "Do tell."

"Mostly action movies," Greg said. "Jace and I watched a lot of those together, and I was always complaining about what I'd do differently, so one day he told me I should write my own. And I did!"

"Then we have much in common. Perhaps you can help. I've been struggling with the very script you hold. It's one thing to dream up a story and write it down. Attempting to catalog real-life events is proving more challenging than I anticipated."

"That's what you wanted to talk to me about, isn't it?"

"Yes. I want to know about those early days that Ben and Jace shared together. Where did they meet? And how did things progress from there?"

Greg made a face, still confused about why he was the right man for the job. "You'd be better off talking to Ben since—"

"He's too close to the subject to provide true objectivity. That's what makes you the ideal choice. Loyal friend, brother-in-law, best man at the wedding... You either witnessed the most important moments or heard about them directly, which means you're invaluable. I can't express my gratitude enough. Would you care for another beer?"

"Sounds good," Greg said, and before he could chicken out, he said, "What if I wrote part of the script?"

"I'm open to it," Marcello said. "Ben and Tim have both made contributions, albeit less directly. If you want to save me an extra step, then I say the more the merrier."

"Awesome! Do you have a pen?"

"Do you mean..." Marcello blinked a few times. "Surely you don't intend to write your portion of the script now?"

Greg shrugged. "Why not? It's easy."

"Very well." Marcello reached into his coat pocket, pulled out a shockingly ornate pen and removed the cap. "At least I'll have plenty to look at while you work." He nodded to the nearest television screen, but his eyes never left Greg.

He knew what was behind that stare. It's the same kind Ben sometimes gave him, and that Jace used to, before he would catch himself and turn bright red. "Knock yourself out," he said with an easy grin. "Hey, where should I start?"

"At the point where their two stories first intersect. How exactly *did* Harry meet Sally?"

"Got it." Greg reached for the fancy looking pen, and with his tongue sticking out one corner of his mouth, he went to work.

> INT - An Airplane. Make it a really big one, like an A380. Yeah!
>
> All the passengers are getting on the plane, doing that thing where they're totally in the way of each other. People are shoving carry-ons into the overhead bins, others are arguing about who the armrest belongs to, and there's probably a baby crying. One man watches all of this in silence. A flight attendant. He looks incredibly cool. None of the chaos seems to bother him. He just watches until another flight attendant comes up to him. She's a total babe.
>
> BABE: That's the last of them, Jace Holden. All the passengers are aboard and accounted for.
>
> JACE: Okay everyone. Time to settle down.
>
> The baby stops crying and everyone hurries to take their seats. They know not to mess with this man!
>
> BABE: The captain is requesting permission to depart.
>
> Jace shakes his head.

JACE: Just a moment. Something's not right here.

He walks up and down the aisle, looking at each passenger. He stops when he notices a good-looking guy, BEN, but Jace is too professional to let his hormones distract him. He keeps searching until he spots an old lady who is busy knitting. Then he knows. He *knows*. But he's not allowed to act without proof. That's the flight attendant code. Jace walks down the aisle to where the old lady is sitting.

JACE: You've settled in nicely, ma'am. Are you okay with that middle seat?

OLD LADY: Yes, thank you very much.

Jace looks at the other two passengers sitting next to her and notices that they don't seem annoyed.

JACE: You've got these fine gentlemen to keep you company, I see. Have you shown them photos of your grandchildren yet?

OLD LADY: No.

JACE: Uh huh. Could I see those photos?

The old lady's eyes dart back and forth. She's starting to sweat.

OLD LADY: I must have left them at home.

JACE: I see.

He turns, catches the eye of the nearest air marshal, and gives the signal. Within seconds, two plain-clothes officers rush over and pull the old lady from her seat. She's kicking and screaming as she's dragged down the aisle.

OLD LADY: You'll never stop me! I'll be back, and when I am, I'll blow you all to kingdom come!

JACE: Not on my watch!

Then the old lady says a bunch of crazy stuff in a foreign language. We better not make it any of the obvious ones, or it wouldn't be politically sensitive. Use something neutral, like whatever they speak in Switzerland.

Once she's thrown off the plane, one of the air marshals returns, his expression full of awe.

AIR MARSHAL: We found a bomb hidden in the ball of yarn. How did you know?

JACE: Because I don't just work this job. I *live* it. Tell the captain he has my permission to take off.

He looks over and notices the good-looking guy from before, who is practically shitting himself in

```
admiration. Jace removes one of the
barf bags and writes something on it.
Then he hands it to Ben.

JACE: And here's something for you.
That's my phone number. My name is
Jace, by the way. I'm the man you're
going to marry.

BEN: Not only that. You're the man!

All the passengers burst into
applause. Jace puts his hands on his
hips, and the camera zooms in on his
badass smile.
```

"Goodness me," Marcello commented. "You're certainly making steady progress."

Greg set down the pen so he could clench and unclench his hand, working out the tension. "It's going really well. I've already finished the story about how they met. I guess next would be their first date which uh…" He shrugged. "I'm not super motivated to write that part. They went ice skating and stuff. That might be too boring for a movie. Not enough action."

"Conflict drives every plot," Marcello said, nodding in agreement. "I can fill in the blanks for the romantic scenes myself. Or perhaps you and I could brainstorm those together in a quieter, and more secluded, environ."

Greg snorted. "Sure."

"For now," Marcello said, "what would the next conflict for our young lovers be?"

"Everything was cruising along after that," Greg explained. "Jace moved to Austin to be closer to Ben. If you want to keep the budget down and avoid an extra filming location, we can have Jace stay in Houston instead. Ben could move back there to be with him. That would have been better."

Marcello raised an eyebrow. "Would have been?"

Greg laughed while scratching the back of his head. "It wasn't easy for me when Jace moved away. Especially considering that

I moved all the way from freaking Warrensburg just to be with him." Greg cleared his throat. "I mean uh, I mostly came to Houston to further my career. It was pure luck that Jace already lived down here."

"Was it?" Marcello asked.

Greg laughed. "Not at all. I missed him! He was my best friend."

"How sweet!" Marcello clapped his hands together. "I didn't realize that you two had such a bromance. Perhaps I'm chasing down the wrong plot. Maybe the movie should be entitled *Greg Loves Jace* instead."

"I wouldn't mind." He felt a familiar warmth in his chest. One that he still missed. "I loved the hell out of that man. Nothing gay ever happened between us, but if I could have been that for anyone, it would have been him."

"Very endearing," Marcello said, sounding wistful. "And what a loss his passing was for all who knew him, and those who never would."

"Yeah," Greg said. "I'm glad he's going to be in the movie. It's the next best thing to actually getting him back."

"Let's return to work then," Marcello said, sounding determined. "What brought Ben and Jace's happy days to an end?"

"*Him*," Greg said. Then he sighed. "Tim. All of this was less confusing when I still hated his guts. These days we're friends. Never thought that would happen."

"I know precisely what you mean," Marcello replied. "Go on."

"I'm not sure what went down when Ben and Tim ran into each other again. Jace was out of town when it happened, and it wasn't something he liked talking about much. I do know that Tim kept hanging around until—" Greg snapped his fingers. "Splashtown!"

"Ah! My birthday party," Marcello said happily. "To be forty again. Or was I thirty? Yes, that seems more likely. Unfortunately I was too busy playing host to keep up with the dramatic events that unfolded. Perhaps you could fill in any… holes."

"If I can't manage, we can still cuddle," Greg said, picking up the pen. "Don't worry, I've totally got this."

EXT - SPLASHTOWN - DAY

Jace, Ben, and Tim are all swimming and having a great time. We'll do a montage of all the fun they're having, but the happy music turns sinister while they're eating hotdogs together. Or better make it hamburgers to avoid the obvious sorts of jokes. We cut to a closeup of Jace taking a bite of his hamburger, and then another closeup of Tim narrowing his eyes sinisterly. Maybe we can do some CGI to make them glow red.

JACE: That was delicious, but now I feel unusually tired.

BEN: Take a nap, darling. I'm sure you'll feel better soon.

Jace seems unable to keep his eyes open. With Ben and Tim's help, he's led to a nearby sundeck. As soon as he lays down there, Jace starts snoring.

TIM: What a bore! Let's go swimming!

BEN: I better keep watch over him like the good and faithful significant other that I am.

TIM: Fine. Have it your way. I'm going swimming.

Ben sits down next to Jace, stroking his hair lovingly until we hear A SCREAM!

TIM: Help! Leg cramp! I might possibly drown!

Ben leaps to his feet, clearly torn between leaving his husband defenseless and wanting to play the hero. Another scream makes his decision easy. He runs toward the sound, having to climb up treacherously wet rocks to reach the cave entrance. Ben drags himself into this and we cut to…

INT - GROTTO

Inside the cave is a pool. Tim is standing in the middle of this, wearing a shit-eating grin.

BEN: What's going on? Are you okay?

TIM: I am now. Come closer.

BEN: Wh-wh-why?

TIM: Don't be scared, my pet. I merely want to show you something.

Ben looks terrified as he complies. He creeps closer like he's trying to sneak up on a deadly crocodile.

BEN: N-n-n-now what?

TIM: Kiss me!

BEN: What? I couldn't! What about Jace?

TIM: He's fine. Mwa-ha-ha-ha! Who am I

kidding? Your lover has been poisoned, and only I have the antidote. If you want to save his life, you'll have to prove your loyalty to me. Pucker up!

Ben looks really *really* sad.

BEN: I guess I have no choice.

Tim grabs him and forces the issue. Ben is struggling to pull away when we hear a new voice.

JACE: Did somebody call for a lifeguard?

The camera cuts to Jace, who is standing in the entrance and looking victorious.

JACE: Yellow frog poison, Tim? Ha! I can't tell you how many Swiss terrorists have tried killing me with that. I've built up an immunity.

TIM: And I never leave home without a backup plan!

Tim pulls out a detonator from his swim trunks and pushes a button. An explosion rocks the grotto, the entrance starting to cave in. Jace dives for the water to avoid falling boulders. When he surfaces again, all three guys notice that the entrance is blocked. Jace turns to Tim and cracks his knuckles.

JACE: I guess we finish this today.

TIM: Yes. We shall fight to the death.

BEN: And the victor shall win my heart!

JACE (looking haunted by his past): Victor… This one is for you!

Jace pulls back and punches, sending Tim flying across the grotto. They don't call him Tim the Terminator for nothing though! He's soon back on his feet and doing all sorts of crazy martial arts stuff. We should get Jackie Chan to choreograph this part, and maybe Michael Bay to direct. Christopher Nolan would be good too. Anyway, at the end of an epic fucking battle, it's clear that Tim is about to lose.

TIM (wiping blood from his mouth): You may have won the battle, Jace, but the war is just beginning. Ben will be mine.

JACE: Not on my watch!

TIM: Another day then, sucker.

Tim plunges beneath the surface. Jace waves his arms through the water, but can't find anything, so he dives to seek his prey. When he returns, he delivers the grim news to Ben.

JACE: I found a subterranean entrance down there. I'm afraid Tim got away. I've failed you.

```
BEN: No. You're my hero!

Ben runs to him and the music swells
as Jace takes him into his arms and
delivers a big-screen kiss. Because
this movie is TOTALLY going to take
Hollywood by storm!
```

"Are you looking for investors?" Greg said, trading the pen for a mug of beer. "This is going to make a shitload of money."

"Financing isn't the most pressing issue," Marcello said. "The scene you were working on just now... You were grunting quite a bit. Was it a scene of passion?"

"You bet it was!" Greg said, smiling down at what he had managed to write. Or scribble. "I hope you can read it all."

"Your handwriting can't be any worse than Nathaniel's."

"I hope there's enough material," Greg said, experiencing a pang of doubt. "The wedding is next, but I'm not sure the audience will be into that."

Marcello didn't seem concerned. "I'll find some way of making it appeal to them."

"Oh. Right. I guess they'll be more into the mushy stuff than I am, huh?" Greg nodded. "Cool. So that just leaves—" His mouth snapped shut. When he opened it again, it was to chug more of his beer.

"Ah," Marcello said, seeming to understand. "Yes. I don't think any of us are eager to revisit that moment in history."

"Maybe he doesn't have to—"

Marcello raised a hand. "I've already consulted with Ben on this very subject. He feels it would be acceptable, just this once, to retell events slightly, but only to keep the more intimate details private. The outcome must remain the same. Jace's death *will* be a part of this movie."

"I can't do it," Greg said, shaking his head. There were times, like now, that the pain hurt nearly as bad as when he had first found out. He had been showing a house to some newlyweds when Michelle called. She couldn't speak at first. She just cried, like the world was coming to an end, and he had croaked out a guess, but it was the wrong one.

"The kids?"

"They're fine. Come home. Just… come home."

Greg swallowed and shook his head. "I can't."

"I understand," Marcello said. "Ben expressed similar sentiments. I don't intend to press either of you on the matter. Still, this leaves me in a difficult situation. Who shall I turn to for the truth?"

"Michelle," Greg said. "She's better at handling this sort of thing. Let me take the script home with me, and I'll have her write that part."

"I imagine such an undertaking will require peace and quiet," Marcello said. "No doubt she'll be up until the crack of dawn, burning the midnight oil, digging deep, etcetera. This is no easy task that she faces. Why don't we get a hotel room together, in order to provide her with sufficient solitude?"

Greg snorted. "I'll let you feel my bicep while I'm flexing, and I'm willing to give you a hug at the end of this date, but that's as far as you'll get with me."

Marcello reached across the table, offering his hand. Greg laughed and shook it.

"You sir, have a deal!" Marcello said. "Now then, tell me more about your past with Jace. Not for the script, but rather my own benefit. I'm eager to hear more about the man who was a legend even before his untimely passing."

"You really want to know?" Greg said.

Marcello settled back in the booth, as if making himself comfortable. "I can't think of any other way I'd rather spend my time."

Greg began to talk, digging up old memories and dusting them off, the pain in his heart soon replaced by a special kind of love. One that could never be replaced.

"This script is insane." Michelle leaned closer to the bedside lamp, trying to decipher Greg's handwriting, which only became worse the further along she read. Next to her, buried beneath the sheets, was her lump of a husband.

"Insanely awesome," Greg countered.

Even though she had heard him brush his teeth before getting into bed, she could still smell the beer fumes. She shook her head and returned her attention to the pages. "I'm really struggling with the notes here at the end."

"The handwriting or the content?"

"Both! It says that Ben gives Tim a dog, which actually happened, but that Jace also put a spy camera in her collar to keep track of Tim's movements."

"That's right." Greg's grin was dopey. "So awesome! You're awesome. Do you want to do awesome things together?"

"Are you feeling brave?" Michelle asked. "The last time you were this drunk, you weren't the only thing that had trouble standing."

"Oh shit. Why'd you have to go there?"

"It's the truth."

"No it's not! I'll prove it." Greg rolled onto his back, an arm moving rhythmically beneath the comforter.

Michelle raised her eyebrows and waited.

Greg scrunched up his face in concentration. "Five more minutes. I can do this."

"Try closing your eyes," she suggested. "You need sleep."

"Sorry, babe. A quick cat nap and I'll be your tiger again. A tiger that's stalking through your jungle. Hey, that's a good line! Think we can work it into the script?"

"I'll try to find an appropriate place. Now close your eyes."

She soon heard snoring. Michelle hoped he wouldn't be too hung over. Especially since he never had performance issues in the morning, and she really did like having him stalk through her jungle. She snorted, shook her head, and returned her attention to the script, which was just as cheesy as her train of thought. That worried her. She saw nothing wrong with finding humor in one's past. She had never expected Ben and Tim's story to be portrayed as a comedy—intentional or otherwise—but when it came to Jace's death… That was no laughing matter. If done right, this could be a beautiful tribute to her brother's life. But only if the depiction of his death was handled with finesse. Easier said than done. How could anyone possibly write that scene and do the truth justice? Michelle appreciated her husband's faith in her, but she was no writer.

She set the script on the nightstand, prepared to let it remain there. Then she shut off the light. A few minutes later, she turned it on again, grabbed a pencil, and gave it her best.

INT - BEN AND JACE'S HOME - KITCHEN

The morning light is soft and gentle, filling a quaint but charming kitchen with a golden glow. Ben is seated at the table, wearing a pair of pajamas. He gets to his feet in excitement when Jace enters in a bathrobe, hair sticking up even more than it usually did. He's still handsome despite this. Jace was *always* handsome, even when he didn't realize it.

BEN: Good morning!

JACE (wincing): Someone had too much sugar in their cereal.

BEN: Either that, or you're so sweet that you've got me buzzing.

JACE (still making a face): Nice line. Ugh. I slept rough.

BEN: You don't look so good. Hey! I've got just the thing!

Ben rushes over to the kitchen counter to a filled coffee pot. He takes out a mug from the cabinet and pours a cup.

BEN: They were giving out samples of a new brand of coffee at the grocery store. The salesman talked me into it. I hope you think it's good.

JACE: It must be to convince you. You hate coffee.

BEN: Oh. I haven't actually tried it.

JACE (with a knowing expression): And this guy handing out samples, was he good-looking by chance?

BEN: Maaaybe. Here. Tell me what you think.

Jace takes a sip of the coffee and nods. Not bad! He takes another sip and starts walking toward the table when something goes wrong. The camera's point-of-view is now from Jace's perspective as the room loses focus and starts to spin. We cut back to Ben, who reacts with shock when Jace hits the floor.

BEN: Jace! Oh god, oh god, oh god! Honey? Are you okay?

Jace springs to his feet, healthy and whole.

JACE: Fine! I'm perfectly fine. Boy… That was weird!

BEN (looking relieved): You're okay?

JACE: Yeah. I must have stood up too quickly.

BEN: You weren't sitting.

JACE: No. That's true. Hmm. Maybe we should go to the hospital, just to make sure I don't have any underlying medical conditions that should be attended to immediately.

BEN: That sounds like a very good idea. Let's have a nice breakfast and enjoy spending time together. Then we'll go.

JACE: That sounds perfect. We should always stay this way, you and me.

Ben bounds over for a hug, Jace's arms wrapping around him tightly as the screen fades to black.

INT - HOSPITAL EXAM ROOM

Jace is sitting on an exam table. Ben is clutching his hand, expression concerned as the doctor opens the door. Let's make her female. Older too. No one too pretty, although it's okay if she has an elegant appearance.

DR. SERENA: I've just gotten your results from the lab.

BEN (sounding panicked): Is it good news or bad?

DR. SERENA: We ran every test we could. Blood analysis, CT scans, X-rays, ear scope, urine in a cup, and the knee reflex test that uses a hammer. (Note: We should consult with a medical professional to make this part sound more, well, professional.)

BEN: I can't take the suspense!

JACE: Easy now. I'm sure everything is fine.

> DR. SERENA: That's where you're mistaken. Everything *isn't* fine. [pause for effect] Everything is great! In fact… Jace Holden, I'm pleased to announce that you are the healthiest man in the world!
>
> The doctor presents him with a very official-looking certificate as balloons and confetti fall from the ceiling.

Michelle groaned as quietly as possible. She was out of paper. Just as well, because she was making a mess of the script. Or doing as bad as the others had. This was harder than it looked! Mostly because she couldn't bring herself to pull the trigger. That's how it felt, as if she was holding a gun and pointing it at Jace. Logically she knew that she should be using his untimely death to raise awareness about aneurysms and the importance of preventative screenings. That's what made sense. It was just too darn hard.

She looked over at Greg, who was sleeping peacefully. He had already briefed her that the movie wouldn't depict events exactly as they happened. She had leeway, but that didn't make it any easier. Dream up a new way for her brother to die? How could she even entertain the thought?

Then again, she *could* make his death a noble sacrifice, one so grand that audiences would forever remember Jace Holden as a hero. And he had been, in his own subtle way: the pep talks that always left her feeling better, the kindness and patience he had treated everyone with, and the love he both inspired and gave so freely. Jace had been her hero. Ben's too. All she needed to do was show that in a more dramatic fashion. She got out of bed, went to the master bathroom for her robe, and tied it around herself as she padded to the office. There she booted up her laptop and opened the word processor, determined to set things right. No matter how difficult that would be.

EXT - HOSPITAL PARKING LOT

BEN: I can't believe I'm married to the healthiest man alive. That's so cool!

JACE: Think they'll give me a raise at work?

BEN: I don't know, but we should celebrate.

JACE: Let's go out to eat.

BEN: Great! There's a new Chinese place I've been wanting to try.

Ben grabs his hand and starts yanking Jace toward the car. Jace shakes his head, pulling Ben close instead.

JACE: It's a beautiful day. Let's walk. Is it far?

BEN: Not at all. Just across the street, in fact.

Together they amble through the parking lot. We can't hear what they say to each other over the touching foreground music, but it's clear that they are more in love than ever. They reach a crosswalk and push the button for the signal. A close-up shot of Jace's face shows it turn from a happy smile to an expression of concern.

```
We cut to the street, where a little
girl is skipping along, oblivious
to the car roaring down the street
toward her.

BEN: Oh no! She'll be a flat little
pancake in no time!

JACE: Not on my watch!

Jace shoves Ben behind himself
protectively. Then he lunges into
the street, picking up the little
girl and cradling her in his arms,
but there isn't time to continue
crossing. The car is too close now,
the driver not slowing. Maybe he's
texting, which would make a good PSA.
Anyway, all Jace can do is spin around
and place the girl out of harm's way,
even if that means sacrificing his
own… Sacrificing his… favorite shirt
as it gets caught on the driver side
mirror, the car narrowly missing him.
```

Michelle hissed in frustration. She could do this! Jace was already gone. This was a character, not her actual brother. She was dealing with letters on a screen, not real-world events.

"Stop being a wimp and get it done," she grumbled to herself, pulling the laptop closer.

```
EXT - PEDESTRIAN CROSSWALK

Jace sets the little girl down. She's
safe, but a little shaken.

LITTLE GIRL: You saved my life!

JACE: It's important to look both
ways before crossing the street.
```

BEN (staring into the camera): Remember that, boys and girls.

LITTLE GIRL: I usually do. I only ran into the street because of my puppy.

JACE AND BEN (simultaneously): Your puppy?!

We cut to the street where a dumb looking dog is still bounding back and forth like he's playing a game. He doesn't realize that two more cars are roaring toward him from opposite directions. The situation looks hopeless.

JACE: I'll be right back.

BEN: No! I can't lose you!

JACE: I'll always be with you. Right here.

Jace places a palm on Ben's chest. Directly over his heart. Then he turns and runs back into traffic. The dog sees him and stops in the middle of the street, his tail wagging. The oncoming cars are mere seconds away! Jace's long legs bring him to the dog, which he picks up and clutches protectively. Tires screech and horns blare, but it's too late. This is the end.

For the cars! Jace leaps into the air, the two vehicles colliding. When he lands again, he has a foot on each

> hood, the dog licking his face in gratitude. The little girl and Ben run over to join this happy scene.
>
> LITTLE GIRL: You're my hero! I'm going to name my dog after you. Jace the dog!
>
> JACE: Do me a favor. Name him after the love of my life instead. Ben.
>
> LITTLE GIRL: I know! I'll combine your names. Ben and Jace. Benji!
>
> NARRATOR: And that's how Benji got his name.

Michelle leaned back in the office chair. She used to love *Benji* movies when she was a kid. Did they still make those? She opened a web browser to check. Then she closed it again, recognizing what she was doing. Distracting herself from the cold hard reality. She had failed. Again. She wouldn't give up though. After rereading what she had written, Michelle decided it could still be salvaged. She had already established that Jace had everything to live for: a loving husband and ideal health. The audience had seen what a heroic and self-sacrificing person he was. Now they were primed to really have their hearts broken when he finally died. For real this time.

> INT - CHINESE RESTAURANT
>
> Ben and Jace sit at a round table filled with mostly empty plates. They're both smiling and content, thanks not only to the meal they had enjoyed, but the thoughtful and attentive conversation as well.
>
> BEN: Now that was a feast! I ate so fast that I nearly choked a few

times. Wouldn't that be ironic? Dying while eating some of my favorite food?

JACE: That would be heartbreakingly tragic. Speaking of which, we're not quite done with this meal. We still have these.

Jace passes Ben a fortune cookie.

JACE: You go first.

Ben opens his, and after chewing, he reads the fortune out loud.

BEN: "Love will never abandon you, even when you seem to be alone. Remember that." Huh. That's a strange one! What's yours say?

Jace unwraps his, the fortune already poking out, which he takes and reads without breaking the cookie.

JACE: "A new adventure awaits you. But don't worry. Time reunites all estranged lovers." I like that. And now for the best part.

Jace opens his mouth, intending to toss the entire cookie in, despite the potential choking hazard. And then… And then… Just then, before he can eat it, a dart zips across the restaurant, lodging itself into the fortune cookie! Jace turns the cookie to better examine the dart, which is dripping with a vile looking poison. If he hadn't been holding up the cookie at that very moment, he would have died.

BEN: What the…

Jace scans the restaurant and easily spots the assassin, who has a tube to his mouth, about to blow another poisonous dart.

JACE: Get down!

Jace leaps to his feet, grabs a plate, and uses it like a shield, the dart bouncing off it harmlessly. Jace has little time to react, but he comes up with a plan. Grabbing a piece of sweet and sour chicken, he shoves one of the poisonous darts into it. He throws this into the air, performing a roundhouse kick which connects with the chicken and sends it flying across the room. The assassin's mouth opens in shock, just in time for the poisonous chicken to get lodged in his throat. Jace slowly approaches as the man gasps and writhes.

JACE: How ironic indeed, choking on your favorite food. I see that you also ordered the sweet and sour chicken, which is why my comment makes sense. You won't be needing this anymore.

Jace takes a fortune cookie from the assassin's table and opens it, popping half the cookie in his mouth.

                    After chewing and swallowing, he
                    reads the fortune aloud.

                    JACE: "Don't even try it." You should
                    have listened!

                    BEN (from across the restaurant): My
                    hero!

Michelle had managed to kill someone at last. That was progress. Greg was bound to love this part of the script as well. Two pros. The rest was all cons. Wasn't it? The script was already wacky. What if she used that to her advantage? Michelle laughed madly, quite possibly due to sleep deprivation, and put the finishing touches on her masterpiece.

                    EXT - DOWNTOWN AT NIGHT - THE HARBOR

                    The scene is shadowy, the lights
                    of the city distant, as MICHELLE
                    HOLDEN creeps along an old wooden
                    dock. This is where a mysterious
                    message instructed her to be. She
                    clutches the note to her chest,
                    like a talisman to ward off fear.
                    The familiar handwriting provides
                    her with reassurance in an otherwise
                    frightening situation. Michelle
                    approaches a worn-down fishing boat
                    but is too scared to board. She is
                    peering at it and searching for signs
                    of life when she hears something
                    right behind her. Michelle spins
                    around with a shriek. One that is
                    still dignified. Somehow.

                    JACE: Sorry, sis. I had to be sure it
                    was really you.

MICHELLE: What's going on? Why didn't you just call? Or come to my house?

JACE (shaking his head): Too dangerous. Someone is trying to kill me.

MICHELLE: What? How? And why? And also who?

JACE: It all started yesterday.

The screen does that squiggly thing that indicates a flashback. It takes us back to Ben and Jace's kitchen in the morning. Ben is making coffee, the camera focusing on an open package with coffee grains spilling out. In particular, the small print, which reads: *Packaged in Switzerland. Ingredients: Coffee and yellow frog poison.*

MICHELLE (voice over): The Swiss?

JACE (voice over): I'm afraid so.

Next we see a busy street, the little girl and her dog crossing the road. The camera flies around to focus on the car barreling toward her. In particular, the license plate which isn't American at all. It's Swiss!

JACE (voice over): As a flight attendant, I've thwarted one too many of their terrorist attacks. They've realized that to get at this country, they'll have to go through me first.

The only problem? Their agents are everywhere.

We see the Chinese restaurant again, before the assassin made his move. He's eating sweet and sour chicken, but not by using chopsticks. Instead the assassin spears each bite with a fondue fork.

The squiggly lines bring us back to the present.

JACE: You just have to know where to look.

MICHELLE: This is terrible! Your life is in danger.

JACE: It's not *my* life I'm worried about. I don't want you or anyone else I love to get caught in the crossfire. That's why I have to do the unthinkable. I need to fake my own death.

MICHELLE: But if you do that, who will keep the terrorists at bay?

JACE: I'll continue thwarting them. I'll just be invisible while doing so. Like a ghost… for justice.

MICHELLE: What about Ben?

JACE: He can't know the truth. If he did, it would put him in too much danger. This is the way it has to be.

MICHELLE: How though? How can we convince Ben that you're dead?

JACE: He'll have to see it with his own eyes. This won't be easy. For either of us.

CUT TO - EXT - PUBLIC PARK - DAY

The camera slowly approaches a baseball diamond. A figure can be seen standing on the home base, but the person is unusually still. As we near, we see it's actually a mannequin wearing clothes that we've previously established as belonging to Jace. And a wig made from his actual hair. This decoy doesn't stand up to scrutiny, but that won't be necessary. After circling the mannequin, the camera zips over to where a young man has just parked and is now taking in the bright cheerful day.

BEN: How romantic! The first place Jace and I kissed. I bet he packed us a picnic for today.

MICHELLE: You know, I think he did!

Michelle gets out from the passenger side of the car. She smiles at Ben, but as soon as his back is turned, her eyes look elsewhere and narrow knowingly. She spots a man watching from far away. He looks like Jace but with a freshly shaved head. He nods to her, also knowingly, then moves backwards until he's absorbed by the trees.

> MICHELLE: This is going to be a picnic to remember.
>
> We cut back to the mannequin, which has a picnic basket at its feet. The camera angle tilts, allowing us to see a bomb inside, the timer counting down.
>
> BEN: There he is! Hi, Jace! You look good!
>
> The timer reaches zero. We rejoin Ben, who stops in his tracks as flames explode and engulf the Jace mannequin. Ben's eyes go wide in shock and he rushes forward, wanting to help, but Michelle restrains him.
>
> MICHELLE: Stop! I've seen this before. It runs in the family and there's no cure. It's... spontaneous combustion!
>
> BEN: NOOOOOOOOOOOOOO!!!!

With her elbows resting on the edge of the desk, Michelle covered her face with her palms and slowly shook her head. Then she let her hands drop and reread the last few lines.

"This is horrendous. Really and truly horrendous." She checked the clock in one corner of the screen. Halfway through the night, and all she had accomplished was convincing herself that she was not, and would never be, a writer. She still wanted to pay tribute to her brother, but not like this. Greg wasn't willing to do it either, and she couldn't imagine asking Ben and Tim. It would be too painful for one of them, and too awkward for the other. She needed help.

That made her think of one person in particular. After mulling it over, she rose and went to the bedroom. She returned with the hand-written portions of the script. She fed these and the rest of the script into the scanner. Then she bundled the scans up into a single file and attached them to an email. The subject simply read: *Advice?*

The problem with her line of work, was that she spent most of her day trying to help people. Her personal life was much the same. She didn't regret either choice, although she did occasionally take it too far and obsess over finding a solution, no matter how exhausted and desperate she became. Allison Cross shared the same inclination, so they had agreed to be there for each other—a friend to turn to when pride needed to be abandoned for outside assistance. Even so, Michelle had her doubts. A fresh perspective could work wonders, but to transform this script into something that wasn't an embarrassment, Allison would need to work miracles.

```
EXT - THE ERIC CONROY GALLERY - NIGHT

A black stretch limousine pulls up
alongside the gallery and parks. The
red carpet is empty, the roped-off
spectators searching for a thrill and
finding nothing. Then the door of the
limo opens, and out steps a woman of
indescribable beauty. To her friends,
she's Allison Cross. As far as the
rest of the world is concerned, she's
the triple platinum international pop
star, ALLI. (In all caps. This isn't
a script formatting thing. She's a
living brand!) The red carpet comes
alive with flashing cameras and voices
calling out, hoping to attract her
attention. Allison stops on the
carpet and waves, addressing everyone
there.

ALLISON: Hello, my adoring fans! It's
wonderful to see so many of you here.
```

Although please don't forget that, for tonight only, I'm *not* the main attraction. No, that honor goes to the art on display. I hope you enjoy it as much as I plan to.

Ben leaves the limousine, sheepishly trailing along behind Allison.

BEN (in a hissing whisper): Art? What's going on here? I thought this was the premier party for your new single.

ALLISON: That's tomorrow. Or is that when I have dinner with Drake? I can't keep up. Did I tell you that Bruno Mars wants to sing a duet together? I don't know if I have time. Justin Timberlake keeps nagging me to show him some new dance moves before—

BEN: Could you please stop name-dropping for two seconds and tell me what's going on.

Allison takes her best friend's arm, pauses so more photos can be snapped, and then guides him forward.

ALLISON: I'll tell you what we're doing here, but first, I need to drop one more name.

She nods to a poster in the window, advertising the art gallery opening. Ben sees this and stops to stare.

BEN: Tim Wyman? This is *his* show?

ALLISON: Honey, this is *my* show. It's always my show, no matter where I go or when. Now come on. The entire world is watching. Don't make me drag you in there kicking and screaming.

Ben finally relents. Once they are inside the gallery, bouncers have to block the doors to stop fans and paparazzi alike from following.

BEN: He's not here. Is he?

ALLISON: Of course he is.

BEN: What do you expect to happen? That I'll just forgive him for everything?

ALLISON: Let me ask you a question, and it's not rhetorical. How many times have I had to forgive you?

BEN: More than I can count.

ALLISON: And did you forgive me on your birthday because I had to be at the GRAMMYs to accept all those awards?

BEN: Yes.

ALLISON: Just a second.

Allison stops to sign autographs for a bunch of people and poses for more photos. Her best friend watches all of this with shining eyes.

BEN: You're so awesome.

ALLISON: Thank you. My point is, I've forgiven you, and you've forgiven me. Why is that?

BEN: Because we love each other.

ALLISON: Are you telling me that you don't love Tim? Even after all these years?

Ben thinks about it and swallows.

BEN: I do love him.

ALLISON: And I love you enough that I want you to be happy. I think he's about to give his big speech. Go on now.

Allison gently pushes her friend toward the right direction. She watches long enough to make sure he won't chicken out, and after signing many *many* more autographs, she slips into the back room of the gallery and out the exit to the alleyway. Her limousine awaits her there (better make it gold instead of black), just as she had instructed. Allison slips gracefully into the backseat, and after a single nod, the driver starts the journey to the next destination.

The night is neither hot nor humid, so Allison rolls down the window, and thinking about all the success she's had in her long illustrious career, she begins to sing a slow but soulful version of *Fame* by Irene Cara.

This stunning performance comes to an end just as the limo pulls up in front of Ben's house. We see her exit the vehicle and approach the driver's window, a one-hundred-dollar bill in her hand, which she gives to him.

ALLISON: Take the night off, Ronnie Adams. No no! Don't give me those sad eyes. You know I'm too famous to be with you anymore. Besides, I'm madly in love with my manager, Brian Milton. Just drive on and never look back. Otherwise, your heart might break.

After watching the limousine pull away, Allison approaches the front door, pulls a pin from her hair and picks the lock. We cut to:

INT - BEN'S HOUSE - NIGHT

Allison stands in the dark interior of a living room. The furniture is draped in dusty sheets, and the windows have been boarded up against the light, even though Ben still lives there. A mouse squeaks and runs by, chased by Samson, who resembles a mangy stray cat. Allison surveys all of this and shakes her head.

ALLISON: Things sure haven't been the same since you left, Jace.

JACE (stepping out from the shadows): I know, but until I can bring down the Swiss government, this is the way it has to be. I don't want him to be alone anymore.

ALLISON: Then we have a lot of work to do.

Through a montage set to music (*We Found Love in a Hopeless Place* by Rihanna), Allison and Jace transform the gray and shabby living room into one that is clean, tastefully decorated, and aglow with candlelight. Samson now sits on a silk pillow, his fur fluffy and clean, a bow on his head. Allison and Jace smile proudly at what they have accomplished as the music comes to an end. Then a noise attracts Allison's attention. She looks out the window. A black sports car is parked outside.

ALLISON: They're here. You better go.

JACE: Just one thing before I do. There's something I've been meaning to ask you for a long time.

ALLISON: Yes?

JACE: Can I have your autograph?

Allison smiles and signs an 8x10 photo for him.

JACE: How will you get home without your limo?

ALLISON: Let me worry about that.

She turns to the front door with

worry when she hears voices behind it.

ALLISON: How will you—

She looks over her shoulder, but Jace is already gone.

ALLISON: Wow! He's good!

She hurries across the room and into the kitchen. We see her hide before the camera cuts to Ben and Tim, who are still outside as Ben struggles with getting the door unlocked.

BEN: I don't know about this, Tim. As good as it is to see you again, I'm just not sure the magic is there anymore.

TIM: I'm also not sure. Was this all a mistake?

The front door swings open. Ben and Tim enter while wearing expressions of awe. They take in their surroundings, the camera focusing on a variety of beautiful details while cutting multiple times back to Allison, who looks fabulous, even with her face half-hidden in shadow.

BEN: Never mind. I was wrong. The magic was here all along.

Tim turns to Ben and takes his hands.

TIM: I love you, Benjamin.

BEN: I love you too. Now what?

TIM: What does your heart tell you?

BEN: That we should dance. Have you heard ALLI's new single?

TIM: No. I've been dying to!

Ben goes to a stereo and puts on the single, which I will have written and recorded before the movie goes to post, I swear. Then he and Tim begin to dance, their expressions joyful. The *entire* song plays until the very end, when they kiss.

We cut back to Allison, who nods in satisfaction. She walks toward the back door, stopping only to take a duffle bag from the closet. Once she's safely outside, she sits on the back stoop and pulls out a pair of Rollerblades.

ALLISON: Well, old friends, we finally did it. We helped Ben find love after all these years. I guess we're not needed anymore.

Allison puts on the Rollerblades and rises. She glances back at the house once more with a satisfied smile before she skates off into the sunset.

"Roll credits," Allison said, lowering the script. She was standing in Marcello's living room, the couches rearranged so that five people could face her. A captive audience. Not because they were captivated, but rather they looked like actual captives who wanted nothing more than to escape. She had read aloud the entire script from the first page, including the ending that she herself had penned. "What do you think?"

Ben was the first to raise his hand. "It was already nighttime in the final scenes. How can you skate away into the sunset?"

"We'll make it the moonrise then," Allison said, pretending to jot down a note. "Any other feedback, or do we all agree that the script is perfect?"

Ben's hand shot up again. "The GRAMMYs are at the beginning of the year. My birthday is in October. You couldn't have missed it because of them."

"Another easy fix," Allison said. She was beginning to wonder if her actual fix would work at all. "Anyone else?"

Michelle raised her hand. Then she pressed her lips together before gathering the courage to speak her mind. "Does anyone else think that it's not very good?"

"My part is great!" Greg said from next to her. "Yours isn't bad either. Especially the Chinese restaurant. I think we should pad out the battle with the assassin. Maybe have a bunch of ninja henchmen come in."

"More ninjas," Allison said, pretending to write again. She moved to sit on the coffee table. "What about you two? This movie is about your lives. Any other feedback?"

"I like that Jace only faked his death," Ben said, but his brow was furrowed up in the way that meant he was struggling internally.

"Can't I win just one fight?" Tim asked. "We skipped over the part where I beat Bryce's ass. That needs to be in there."

"Totally!" Greg said.

Tim leaned over to address him. "And maybe he's got back-up. The whole football team! And it seems like we're doomed until Ben and I start doing these amazing coordinated moves. Like I swing him around while he's got his Rollerblades on and he takes down a bunch of guys that way."

"Yes!"

Marcello cleared his throat theatrically. "I'd rather like to return to the point Michelle was making. Would you mind expounding, my dear?"

"The script isn't very good," she said. "In fact, it's terrible."

"Why is that?" Marcello asked innocently.

Michelle exhaled. "Because it isn't real. It starts out that way, but the plot always gets sidetracked by how we each wished it would have been. There's so much fiction that we might as well make a movie about talking dinosaurs who enter a baking competition instead."

"Dinosaurs *would* make it cooler," Greg said. "But uh… my wife has a point. This doesn't feel very much like our lives."

"No," Ben said at last. "It doesn't." He turned to Marcello. "Maybe this was a bad idea. I'd rather the movie not get made at all than for it to be untrue."

"It's our fault," Tim said. "Sorry, Marcello. We shouldn't have gotten involved. We meant well. The road to Hell and all that."

"There's nothing to apologize for," Marcello said, his eyes meeting Allison's. The nod of his head was so subtle that no one else was likely to have noticed. "I must admit though, that I am heartbroken. Is there no way of salvaging this project?"

"We didn't do so well individually," Allison said, "but now that we're all here, maybe we could try again. If we keep each other in check… We have the basics down. We just need to revise."

"No ninjas," Greg said helpfully.

"Or assassins," Michelle chimed in. "Or Swiss terrorists."

"Aww," Greg whined. After a sigh, he nodded. "Jace was cool enough, even without all of that."

"I agree," Ben said, placing a hand over Tim's. "Both my men are awesome. There's no need to exaggerate. The same goes for all of you. Let's try again. This time we'll get it right."

Allison nodded her agreement. "Okay. Starting over. Page one…"

"That went exceedingly well," Marcello said.

Allison looked up. She was stretched out on one of the couches and yawning, tempted to crash there for the night. Everyone else had gone home, and she knew she needed to also, but the glasses of champagne Marcello held convinced her to delay those plans.

"Thanks," she said, accepting one. "What are we toasting to?"

"Why, you, my dear!" Marcello said. "Your insight into human behavior has been invaluable."

Allison pulled her legs close so he could sit. "I was only trying to help."

"That you did." Marcello clinked glasses with her and took a sip. "I must admit, when I first asked for your assistance, that this is not the form I expected it to take."

Marcello had contacted her when first beginning work on the script. He'd had concerns about some of the details Tim told him and wanted someone to fact-check his version of events. Allison had quickly pointed out how fruitless that would be. "Even if you and I had written the script without outside assistance, as soon as we showed it to everyone, they would have argued over every detail. Especially the small ones. I've seen Ben and Tim do that often enough. Everyone makes revisions to their own history. Sometimes that's a conscious decision. Other times it's not. Either way, the memory doesn't cheat. We do."

"And thanks to your quick thinking," Marcello said, "you helped everyone realize just how flawed their own narration was *and* made it possible for us to work together in harmony."

"Once people can admit that they were wrong, they're usually more open to finding a solution."

"I'm very pleased with the end result." Marcello nodded at the freshly revised script. "Are you?"

"Yes," Allison said after some hesitation. "It's still not completely true. I know Ben didn't want some of the details of Jace's death made public, but there are other little things…"

"One must allow for artistic interpretation. Although I think it's a shame that the world will never experience ALLI's rising star. Why did you feel compelled to participate in this experiment? So the others wouldn't recognize the game we were playing?"

"No, because I'm a human being, and I had a few fantasies I needed to get out of my system too." Allison took a sip of champagne and frowned. "We weren't playing a game, were we? I don't like how that sounds."

"I prefer to call it the gentle art of persuasion." Marcello tilted his head. "Some of us practice it on a daily basis."

She supposed her work as a counselor involved a lot of that. Getting someone to recognize their personal shortcomings wasn't difficult. Getting them to actually do anything about it was the real struggle.

Marcello wasn't finished. "Such a skill could be useful in a variety of career fields. Business, most certainly, but also politics."

Allison drained her glass and stood. "I'm perfectly content to go back to being a wife, a mother, and a best friend. And when I get paid, a therapist." She gathered up her things and paused. "Although... There *will* be a premiere for this movie, right? One with a red carpet?"

Marcello smiled. "I guarantee it."

"Good. Just make sure every photographer who works for you will be there that night."

"To try in vain to capture the beauty of stars both known and those yet undiscovered? Yes. I look forward to seeing you there, my dear." Marcello stood. "The pleasure was all mine. Shall I accompany you to the door?"

"I know the way," Allison said, giving him a peck on the cheek. As she went, she threw one last wish over her shoulder. "And don't forget the limo!"

"Gold, not black," Marcello called in return. "Wait! I forgot to get your autograph!"

Allison heard a drumroll of footsteps. When she looked back, she saw a heavyset man catching up to her with impressive speed. Another desperate fan! She ran for the door, laughing the entire way. During the drive home, she spent a good deal of it singing a song about fame, and when she adjusted the angle of the rearview mirror, all she saw were ALLI's eyes staring back at her.

```
                    THE END?
```

Something Like Us

by Jay Bell

Something Like Stories: Volume Three

Austin, Texas
2018

Dear Diary,

I know, I know. It's been a long time. Sorry. I haven't written in you since I broke up with— Nope. I won't sully another of your pages with his name. He no longer matters enough to mention. I guess I've written those same words before, especially when I was so hurt in the aftermath, but now they're actually true. A short unhappy relationship in high school can't compare to what I have now.

Felix Ramos looked up from the small red volume spread out on the kitchen table, his cheeks attempting to match the color of a book that had once been his only confidant. The past seemed so destitute compared to the richness of his current life, although he would gladly say goodbye to every object in this apartment— even the shelves filled with his collectibles—if that's what it took to keep the greatest treasure of them all. Noah. The name sent Felix racing down the hall to the home office where his boyfriend was.

Even with his back to the door, Noah inspired his lips to open so a gentle sigh could escape. A shock of red hair was tinged blue by the surrounding computer monitors—spreadsheets and legal texts open on the dual-screen setup. Felix was tempted to rush across the room and spin the chair around, just to see those green eyes go wide with surprise. Or maybe he would kiss skin that was tan from the frequent walks Noah took to clear his head. Or so he claimed.

Felix often wondered if all that pavement pounding was a habit left over from his life on the streets. Not that long ago, Noah had known the true meaning of destitute. Felix might have had only a few friends in high school, and just one forgettable lover, but he had never known life without a family or a home. The world Noah grew up in for most of his young adult life consisted of a homeless shelter, visits to the public library, and endless hours on aimless walks. No wonder he had leapt at the opportunity to improve his situation, even if that meant—

Felix swallowed, fighting against the urge to judge. He was coming around on the issue. It had been over a year since he learned the truth, and while the sting was gone, he still struggled to imagine the reality of it all. Noah—the smartest, most caring guy he had ever known—working as an escort! The job title didn't encompass the full truth, intentionally vague while leaving room for doubt. Noah had done more than just accompany other men. He had slept with them. For money.

And after it was back to life on the streets. Felix didn't enjoy thinking of that either, but he did so as an antidote to his own prejudices. Cause and effect. A problem resolved by a reasonable solution. It all made sense, even without imagining his boyfriend hungry and exposed to the elements, because Felix still saw the aftershocks of that life each day: the way Noah cleared both their plates during meals, eating every last crumb like it might be his last. The rare leftovers that landed in their fridge were never forgotten or thrown away. Then there were those endless walks, and the way bad weather made Noah anxious and unhappy, as if he feared he would be caught out in extreme conditions again. He *still* smiled goofily when turning on the air conditioner, like it was God's greatest gift.

Perhaps the greatest evidence of the shadow hanging over Noah was his work ethic. Money mattered to him more than it did to others. Most people worried about paying their rent and bills, or having extra to put into savings or spend on fun. Noah treated money like a dwindling supply of firewood in the heart of Siberia. He stockpiled whatever he could get, spent only what was necessary, and ventured out frequently to find more. Everyone was dependent on money, although few were so keenly aware of just how bad things could get without it. That had its upside, since it provided a sense of security. Noah was older, wiser, and more mature by a mile. Felix had no trouble admitting that. That dynamic was part of the attraction for them both. But at times, Noah's compulsion to work could eat into their relationship.

"Are you almost done?" Felix asked, hoping the question wouldn't annoy, but the swelling emotion in his chest had made it impossible not to ask… even if the timing wasn't the best.

Noah turned around in his office chair, expression incredulous. "Done?" he repeated, sounding manic. And adorable, thanks to the faint country twang in his voice. "Are you kidding? There's no end in sight! I have to read through the revised employee contracts and come up with an opinion, because we're meeting with the lawyers in an hour and... I don't even understand what I'm reading. I've been a bookworm my whole life, but this is like a Vulcan version of Dr. Seuss."

"Nice!" Felix said, offering a smile. Pop culture wasn't Noah's strength. A mixture of a strict religious upbringing and living without TV when homeless meant that he didn't speak the same language as most Americans. Felix had taken it upon himself to provide Noah with a crash course on the basics, which was endless fun, and usually began with, *Hey, have you ever seen...*

"There's nothing nice about it," Noah said, glancing over his shoulder at one of the screens. "I can't keep relying on Nathaniel to explain these things to me. It's embarrassing."

"Then ask Harold," Felix said, feeling a jolt of irritation. All too often it seemed like Noah was burdened with the real work, while all Harold did was worry about looking pretty and... Ugh! He didn't want to think about it. The point was, "He's supposed to be the co-owner of this business. *He* should be helping you."

Those emerald eyes opened further, as if Felix had finally made him see the truth. Or not. Noah swore, repeatedly, and grabbed a fat stack of papers to shake them in frustration. "He was supposed to sign these stupid things yesterday!"

Felix reached out, wanting to comfort him, but he wasn't quick enough.

Noah was already on his feet and pacing. "I'm going to look like an idiot," he moaned. "An incompetent moron."

"It'll be fine," Felix said, blocking his path to get his attention. "Just have him drive over here and sign them real quick. Easy peasy."

"I would, if his car wasn't in the shop."

"Then have him take a taxi."

"I can't afford another business expense," Noah said, looking on the verge of tearing his hair out, which would be a shame, because Felix really *really* liked his hair. "And before you suggest it, I won't allow him to pay for it himself."

"Why not?" Felix said through gritted teeth.

"Because he never wanted this." Noah turned and continued pacing. "Harold only agreed to be my partner so Marcello would trust me enough to give us the company. He's done enough already." He spun around when reaching the door. "I could really use your help."

"Anything!" Felix was always eager for a chance to prove his love.

"I need you to drive over to his place and make sure he signs these. Six signatures, three contracts each. Ugh! Reverse that. Come here and I'll show you." Noah rushed over to his desk and began separating the stack into separate piles. "Each of the six contracts need to be signed and initialed here, here and..." He looked up, expression concerned. "Are you listening?"

No. Felix still hadn't moved, overwhelmed by conflicting emotions. He didn't want to go to Harold's house or interact with him, even for a few minutes. He *did*, however, want to help Noah regain his sanity because when not overburdened with work, he was the best. Even better than the imaginary boyfriends Felix had dreamt up for himself in junior high. And parts of high school, if he was honest. Felix loved Noah in a way he never knew possible. So why did such a small request feel like a huge ordeal? He steeled himself, determined not to fail his man.

"I'm listening," he said, approaching the desk. "Show me again."

This time he paid close attention.

Once the contracts were handed over, Noah took a deep breath, exhaled, and for a fleeting moment, returned to his normal self. "I'm really sorry," he said. "I'd do it myself, but I still need to figure out what we're actually signing, and get dressed, and... I love you."

"I love you too," Felix said, leaning in for a quick smooch.

"I know this has eaten up the entire weekend," Noah said after kissing him. "I'll make it up to you next week, okay?"

"Okay." After another kiss, Felix rushed out the door, his heavy heart dragging behind him, because Noah had said the same thing the previous week. And the week before that. He couldn't be blamed though. Noah was trying to provide them with a good life, and not in the easiest way accessible to him. He wasn't sleeping with strangers for large amounts of money. He was managing an escort service and trying to turn it into something more respectable. If only he had an equal partner that he could rely on.

Grabbing the car keys on the way out the door, Felix frowned, determined to give Harold a piece of his mind. Not a very nice piece either. Things needed to change before his sweetheart was lost forever beneath a landslide of paperwork.

Harold lived in a small house in a quiet neighborhood. Few who drove down his street would find much to be offended by, but Felix managed anyway, scowling at the surroundings as he parked Noah's old pickup truck in the driveway and got out. His anger began to falter as he walked to the door. Nervousness assaulted his stomach, but he clung to his indignation as best he could. Felix rang the bell and then knocked immediately afterwards to demonstrate how urgent his mission was. Annoyingly, it still took ages for the door to open.

"Hey," Harold said with an easy drawl. Even though lunch had come and gone, his hair was messy from sleep and he still wore a bathrobe. He'd probably been up late doing who knows what to a client, while in the meantime, Noah had been awake and working since early morning. On a Saturday. "Are those the contracts?"

Felix followed his gaze down to the stack he was gripping so tightly that the paper was crinkling. "Yes. You need to sign these *right away*."

"Noah explained it all to me." Harold jerked his head toward the interior. "Come inside."

Felix didn't move. His muscles were still too tense. He had imagined Harold stepping outside to quickly sign the contracts so he could be on his way again. "I really need to get these back to him."

"I know," Harold said, his smile casual. "But I don't have a pen on me, and I'm feeling kind of exposed." He pulled the robe tighter around himself and yanked the belt so it wasn't as loose. The fabric around his chest still hung open though, revealing an impressive chest.

That was the other issue. As Felix followed him into the house, he couldn't help but feel insecure. Harold was attractive. Even right after rolling out of bed, which come to think of it, he probably did more often than most people. His handsomeness wasn't the only issue. *All* of Noah's employees were hot—a prerequisite of being a male escort—but only one of them was transparently in love with their boss. If that wasn't bad enough, the feeling was mutual. Or had been at one time.

"Just a sec," Harold said, walking around his living room couch to sift through items on the coffee table. "I have a pen around here somewhere."

The television was on, the screen frozen. Felix recognized the image as being from *The Crown*, season two, which was one of his favorite— No! He couldn't let that distract him from his mission. Either of them. He was here to have the contracts signed *and* to tell Harold that he needed to get his act together.

"What were you doing?" Felix asked.

Harold paused his search to look over his shoulder. "I'm looking for a pen."

"No, before I arrived. What were you doing?"

Harold glanced at the TV, and then back at him again. "Just chilling. Why?"

Felix pointed a finger at the front door. "Because Noah is working his butt off right now. Does that seem fair to you?"

Harold abandoned his search completely and turned around. "I was up late working. So what?"

"How come *you* aren't meeting with the lawyers or worrying about the contracts?"

"I'll get them signed! Calm down. I know I have a pen in the kitchen. Be right back."

He had missed the point completely. Felix started to follow him, intent on not letting the subject drop. Then he changed his mind. This was his first time in Harold's home. He didn't feel like he had the right to go wherever he wished. Presently he was standing in the entryway between the living and dining rooms. He could see the kitchen beyond and hear Harold opening and closing drawers. Considering how messy the living room was, they would be better off sitting at the dining room table instead and signing the contracts there.

Or not. If the coffee table was cluttered, the dining room table was positively hidden. Only the legs were visible, the surface covered by fuzzy green hills. A plastic waterfall spilled over these, a motionless river that wound toward a miniature village. At first Felix thought it was part of a train set, but as he moved closer, he noticed there were no railroad tracks. The village had streets and the occasional vehicle, but that was it for transportation.

What really grabbed his attention were the intricate buildings and numerous tiny people.

"Got it!" Harold returned from the kitchen, a pen held up victoriously. Then he saw what Felix was staring at and looked a little sheepish. "Uh. Just ignore that."

"Yeah, right!" Felix said, still bent over the display. "This is amazing!"

Harold seemed confused. "You like it?"

"Yeah! The details are stunning, especially for something so small. Look at the little lamp posts! Oh em gee. Is that a cat?"

"The black one?" Harold said, bending over to see. "Yup. Her name is Buttons. She belongs to the tailor who lives over there, but she comes down to the docks every morning because the fisherman always gives her a freshly caught treat."

"It's all so old-fashioned and quaint," Felix said, resisting the impulse to reach out and touch one of the tiny figures. He was pretty sure they were glued down.

"That's one of my favorite things about it," Harold said. "Simpler times. When I'm stressed, I like to pretend I live there too. I'm usually stoned, which helps, but I don't have to be. There aren't any politics in my village. Or bad news. I don't have any police or emergency crews because nothing ever goes wrong. It's paradise."

"I'd be tempted to make a little figure of myself," Felix said, putting his nose close to a carousel in the center of town. "That way I could really be there."

"I had the same thought." Harold pointed away from the village to the tallest hill. The figure standing there shared his chestnut brown hair and olive skin, although it wore more than a bathrobe.

Felix took a step back to consider it all, his irritation returning. "You made yourself a god."

"Huh?"

"That's why you put yourself way up there on the hill."

"No! That's not why."

"And this guy has red hair," Felix said, bending over again. At the bottom of the hill, farther down from the waterfall, a small figure stood on the bank. It wore nothing but shorts, or maybe swim trunks, and the top of its head had been painted reddish orange. "Is that supposed to be Noah?"

When an answer didn't come, Felix looked over and saw that Harold's face was flushed with embarrassment. Not understanding why, Felix considered the scene again. The figure on the hill in particular. It wasn't hard to imagine that it was watching the swimmer below. Perhaps longingly, which was kind of heartbreaking, and yeah, embarrassing for another person to see.

"I've *always* wanted an action figure of Noah," Felix hurried to say. "You've seen my toys. You know how I am. I want plastic versions of all the things I love, so I totally get it. I think it's awesome!"

"Thanks," Harold said, cheeks still crimson. "I would have put myself in the village, you know. I've tried. I just can't figure out where I belong. So for now..." He cleared his throat. "We better get those contracts signed. The kitchen table is our best bet."

Felix followed Harold into the next room, feeling terrible. As he watched a pen scribble over paper, he tried to find some way to make it all better. He still thought that Harold needed to help manage the business more, but the rest, especially the unresolved feelings... Maybe it was best not to dwell on any of it.

"There you go!" Harold said, leaning back after completing his work.

Felix hurried to gather up the papers, wanting to be helpful.

He must have come across as impatient instead, because Harold stood and said, "Drive safe. If not for your own sake, then for his. If you get into an accident, it'll break Noah's heart."

"I will," Felix said. "I promise." On the way out, he paused in the dining room. "I really do like your train set. Or model village?"

"Who knows?" Harold chuckled in a way that sounded forced. "I'm probably crazy."

"If you are, I am too."

Harold nodded. That only left awkwardness between them, so Felix said a quick goodbye and rushed out the front door. Once safely in the pickup truck, he exhaled. That had gone even worse than Felix had imagined. Or better? He wasn't sure, but hopefully that was the last time he'd have to be alone in the same room with Harold.

* * * * *

Dear Diary,

Today I went over to Harold's house. It wasn't a great experience, which is fine. If I'm honest, I don't want to like him. Does that make me a bad person? It bothers me the way he always looks at Noah, like he's waiting for the right opportunity to steal him away from me. Or maybe he's just sad that it didn't work out. They didn't date exactly. It never went so far. Noah was in love with him, but Harold wasn't ready for a relationship or something. They slept together anyway. Why does that make me hurt inside? I know it's dumb, like if Noah was bothered that my jerk ex-boyfriend and I slept together in high school. I guess the difference is that my ex isn't around anymore. Harold is. All the time. Not just for business reasons either. They're friends. That's a good thing, right? Oh god... I am a bad person. I must be, because I'm the winner in this situation. Noah is already my boyfriend, and yet I'm behaving like a sore loser. It's Harold who lost, and now he has to see us together and feel weird about it. That probably feels horrible for him, and here I am acting jealous, even though I have it all. In the future, I'll try not to flaunt that so much. In fact, it's probably best if I avoid Harold completely. That way he doesn't feel the pain of seeing us together, and I don't have to fight off petty thoughts.

"You're going to kill me."

Felix tilted his chin upward look at his boyfriend, but he didn't lift his face from the pale chest his cheek was pressed against. Noah might appear tan when dressed, but the parts of him that weren't exposed to the sun were white like... Not ivory. The thought of injured elephants and greedy poachers upset Felix, so maybe Noah's skin was more like china. Did that mean it was equally as delicate? Could be, considering what he had just said.

"Am I too heavy?"

"Are you kidding?" Noah smiled, the right corner of his mouth rising higher than the left. Felix was always tempted to kiss him there, wanting to pin the smile in place so he could admire it forever. "You don't weigh a thing."

"Does that mean I can be your backpack? I want you to carry me around all day so I can see what you do and whisper helpful things in your ear."

"We can try that sometime," Noah said. "Not today. It'll

be boring for you. Bethany is coming over soon, and we'll be working on the new website all day. *However—"*

"Here it comes," Felix said. "You're going to owe me so big. I can tell already."

Noah's chest rose as he took a deep breath. "I need you to take the revised contracts over to Harold's place for him to sign."

"Seriously?" Felix lifted his head to see his boyfriend better. "I already did that!"

"Those were the old contracts. We made too many changes during the meeting."

"So it was all a waste of time?"

Noah grimaced. "Sorry. It wasn't a waste of time though because you did it for me, and that made me feel loved. Now I need a little more of that love."

"Stop being charming. I'm trying to be angry at you."

"Don't be." Noah pushed himself up into a sitting position, forcing Felix to sit up too. "Please. I really need your help. Everything we've been planning, all the changes to the Gentlemen's Agreement Club, they're finally coming together."

Felix sighed. "I'm happy for you. Really. But can't you drive the contracts over for Harold to sign right now? He won't care that you're naked. He was in his bathrobe last time I was there. There's not much difference."

"That sounds like him," Noah said with a chuckle.

"I'll go with you and wait in the truck. We can get breakfast on the way back."

Another wince. Uh oh!

"I need an extra favor," Noah said carefully, as if a bomb might go off if he chose the wrong word. "Harold has a dentist appointment."

Felix crossed his arms. "So?"

"Can you drive him there? I was supposed to, but I can't. You don't work until tonight, right?"

Felix was tempted to lie. He knew from experience how the resulting guilt would torment him, so he didn't. "I have a dinner shift. Hey, I know! How about you take Harold to his appointment, and I'll work with Bethany on the website. I'm better at computers than you are anyway." And he really liked Bethany. She was from the same small town as Noah. A pastor's daughter, although he'd never have guessed from her naughty sense of humor and wild appetite for guys. Felix had learned a trick or two in the bedroom from the details she shared with him.

"It's not about computer skills," Noah said. "She's got enough of that for the both of us. She only needs my input on how the site is supposed to work. The changes we made to the old one don't cut it. That's why we had to—"

"Rebuild it from the ground up," Felix finished for him.

"At least I know you pay attention when I drone on and on." Noah offered a smile.

Felix didn't return it.

"I know I'm asking a lot," Noah said. "You have to understand that Harold was there for me at a rough time in my life. When I needed a car so I could visit Ryan, he loaned me his. No questions asked. It's a four-hour round trip to the prison, and he didn't blink an eye or complain about the miles. He even drove me out to see my parents, hoping we would patch things up, and that trip was nearly three times as far."

"I get it," Felix grumbled. "He's the greatest, and that means I have to be his chauffeur."

"*You're* the greatest." Noah hooked an arm around Felix's neck and dragged him in for a kiss. "If you don't want to do this, you don't have to. Would it be so bad though? You guys seem to get along fine when he's here."

Felix shrugged. "It's weird when we're by ourselves."

"Weird how?"

"I don't know. Awkward."

"Oh. If it helps, you don't have to hold his hand while he's getting worked on. You can play on your phone in the waiting room. It'll all be over before you know it. And I'll owe you a favor. A big one."

"Payable in advance," Felix said, swinging a leg over Noah's hips and sitting. "I want a big one now."

Noah reached for his phone to check the time. "It'll have to be quick."

Felix bit his bottom lip, already bouncing up and down playfully. "Quick like rabbits?"

Noah grabbed him under the armpits and swung him over onto his back, causing Felix to squeal. Then he gently lowered his weight until their bodies were pressed together and said, "Brace yourself, little bunny, because Easter is about to come early!"

"Are you sure that's something you want to brag about?" Felix teased.

Noah soon proved that his timing wasn't an issue. Being with him, in this way or any other, was simply perfect.

This time, when Felix pulled into Harold's driveway, he didn't have to knock or wait long for the door to open. He didn't even have to get out of the truck. Harold must have been watching for him because he was outside before the engine could be shut off.

"I owe you," Harold said as he climbed in on the passenger side.

"No need," Felix said, still feeling warm and fuzzy from the morning. "This service has been paid in advance."

"Yeah? How so?"

Oh! He didn't expect a follow up question. "Noah made me a giant breakfast." In truth, they hadn't had time for breakfast, but there were moments when Felix had felt stuffed anyway.

"Nice! Probably for the best. If I cooked for you, well, Noah always complains that I eat too healthy. Says it all tastes like cardboard. What do you like to eat?"

"Deep-fried and spicy," Felix admitted. "Um. What's the address?"

The dentist office was in another part of the city. Not walkable, unless someone was particularly determined and didn't mind the Texas heat. The distance made Felix feel better about the necessity of this errand, although it did little to banish the awkwardness. He tried turning on the radio, so they wouldn't have to talk, but Harold was in a chatty mood.

"Good song. Do you ever listen to ninety-three point three? They have a nice mix on there. I was grooving to some folk music they had on the other day. You into that at all?"

"No," Felix admitted. "I'm more of a top forty guy."

"That can be good too. For me it's all about the mood I want to be in. I can't deal with too much noise in the morning, so I prefer acoustic stuff then. If I'm working out and need energy, the music has to be pumping."

"I've done that," Felix admitted. "Although it's more about matching what I'm already feeling. Sad songs when I'm depressed, or happy music when I'm having a good day."

"Exactly!" Harold said, twisting to face him. "You should try the opposite sometime. If you're down and you want to feel good, the right music can fix you up. How's this one make you feel?"

"Like driving faster," Felix said, pushing down on the gas pedal. The old engine roared as the truck lurched forward, but he eased up again.

Harold laughed. "Every time I've gotten busted for speeding, music was to blame. Maybe we should put on something slower."

Harold messed with the radio for the rest of the drive, never letting an entire song play. Just enough for them both to get an impression. Then he'd ask, "What about this one?"

Felix gave honest answers at first. Then he started getting ridiculous. "This one makes me feel like pruning hedges," or, "This song has me in the mood to brush a senior citizen's hair." Harold seemed to find this funny, adding his own silly answers. "This beat has me wanting to adopt a dog so I can teach it to skydive."

Felix was enjoying himself by the time they reached their destination and took a seat in the waiting room, although without music, they were left without anything to focus on. "Are you nervous?" he asked, not wanting the awkwardness to return.

"Nah," Harold said. "I'm here way too often." He bared his teeth, so they were on full display. Each was white and perfect. Of course. "A pretty smile is good for business."

"Shouldn't you be focusing on the other half of the business?" Felix said. He didn't intend to be cruel. He honestly didn't get it. "Noah isn't doing *that* sort of thing anymore. How come you are?"

"The money," Harold said, his chin jutting out. "And because I like it."

"Yeah, but—"

"Harold Franklin?" A nurse had appeared in the waiting room and was looking expectant.

"Wish me luck, kiddo" Harold said as he stood.

"I'm not a kid," Felix said, right before wondering if he sounded pouty... like a kid.

"Wish me luck anyway."

Felix wasn't sure what Harold would need it for. A root canal? Something worse? Should he even care? He wasn't sure. Harold was likeable, he supposed. Maybe if they had met under different circumstances, they could have been friends. But they hadn't and they weren't. Felix distracted himself by pulling out his phone. The nice thing about being a fan of so many shows and franchises is that he had a long list of websites to check for the latest news. and groups to visit where he could join in on the gossip. He was only partially through his daily routine when Harold's voice pulled him back into the room.

"Ready?"

"That was quick!" Felix said, getting to his feet.

"No cavities. Just a cleaning."

He stared, his mouth dropping open. "That's what you needed a ride for?"

"And a checkup," Harold said, sounding defensive. "It might have turned out to be more."

Felix did his best to hide his frustration. A simple cleaning could have been rescheduled, although he supposed the contracts still needed to be signed. One way or another, they would have been forced to be around each other. He left the music off on the way back to Harold's house, not feeling so chummy anymore. Maybe because it seemed such a frivolous waste of time: A teeth cleaning so Harold could look good when doing... stuff. To people who were paying for it.

"Did you get some bad news on your phone or something?" Harold said.

"No. Why?"

"You seem tense. I thought maybe... I don't know."

"I'm fine. Just eager to get back home."

"I can dig it. I'm a hopeless homebody myself. That's another reason I like the work. It forces me out of the house."

"You're always welcome at our place," Felix said pointedly. "There's plenty of work to do there."

"Thanks," Harold said, sounding clipped himself. "I'll keep that in mind."

The rest of the ride was silent. Felix had no one else to blame but himself. He should have turned on the radio and let it be an easy trip. Ugh! As he pulled into Harold's driveway, he decided a hasty goodbye and an even hastier retreat was in order.

"Guess we should get those contracts signed," Harold said.

Damn it! No big deal. "Okay."

"I actually know where my pen is this time. Ha ha. Are you coming in?"

"Yeah." As Felix left the truck, he promised himself to be on his best behavior. This was his boyfriend's best friend. Was that accurate? In any case, this was someone important to Noah, and that was reason enough to be civil. He obediently followed Harold to the kitchen, sat at the table with him, and watched as he signed each contract.

"I guess that's it," Harold said.

"Yup! I better get these to Noah. I don't know if he needs them right away but—"

"One more thing before you go." Harold's eyes darted away and back again. "I hope you don't think it's stupid. I'll show you on the way out."

Felix had no idea what to expect, especially when he was led to the model village. He couldn't help looking at the figure on the hill, which was still there, but the red-headed guy by the river was gone.

"I was trying to think of some way to thank you for driving me around," Harold said, plucking something out of the town square, "so I whipped these up for you. Hold out your hand."

Felix did so, and in the cup of his palm, he felt two small items being placed there. The first he recognized immediately. The little figure had red hair, except now a shirt and shoes had been painted over the bare skin. Next to it was a shorter figure with brown skin and black hair. Felix looked up in shock. "It's me! And Noah!"

"You said you always wanted an action figure of him," Harold said, expression uncertain. "I know this isn't the same thing, but it's the best I could do. Are you okay with the hair? I was going to do pale green, like you have now, but you never keep it the same color for long."

That was true. Felix often let it return to its natural black state, but when he grew tired of that, he enjoyed trying other colors. "It's perfect!" he enthused. "This is so cool."

"You really think so?"

"Yes!" Felix moved to the model village, peering at it until he found a general store. "I need groceries. I hope Mr. Hooper has cherry tomatoes in stock."

"Actually, that store is owned by two lesbians," Harold said, moving closer to join him.

"Mrs. Hooper then." Felix tried to place himself in front of the store. His little figure wouldn't stand on its own and fell over. "Oh no! Help me, someone. I've fallen and I can't get up!" Then, in a voice with a country twang, he said, "I'll save you." The little Noah figure was made to bound across the street to help Felix stand.

"Heh," Harold said. "I was going to ask you about that. For the figures I like to move around a lot, I put them on stands. Otherwise I just glue them in place. I wasn't sure what you'd want. Either way, I could maybe create a little scene for you and Noah to inhabit. They're harder to lose that way too."

"Did you make all of this?" Felix asked.

"Not really." Harold scratched the back of his head self-consciously. "It's more like assembling, or at the most, customizing existing parts. Some of these buildings are straight from the box, but I wanted the bakery to have a sign hanging outside the door with a pretzel on it, so I took one from another set and—"

"Kitbashing," Felix said.

"Yeah!" Harold sounded surprised. "How do you know that term?"

"Action figure collectors use it too. Sometimes, if they don't make the figure you want, you have to take the head from one figure and the body from another and hope for the best. I can't customize though. I tried making Korra from a Sokka figure and ended up ruining it. Mostly because the hair I sculpted looked like dreadlocks made of poo."

"Bummer," Harold said. "Avatar is an amazing show."

"*You watch it?*" Felix practically shouted in his excitement.

"Yeah! I've seen them all—twice. *Korra* is the better series."

"Uh-uh. The first season is so rushed toward the end. The original show is perfection."

"It starts too slow," Harold said. "And the ending isn't nearly as emotional. But I'll give you the rushed first season. That's true."

Felix grinned. "You have to help me convince Noah to watch it. He's never been into animation, no matter how good it is."

Harold snorted. "I blame his parents. You know he was only allowed to watch TV in their presence, right? Like they wouldn't even leave the room for a second without turning it off."

"I didn't know it was that bad! I figured they told him which shows he could and couldn't see."

"Nope. It was what they wanted to watch or nothing. He probably didn't see many cartoons because of that. His parents were too controlling."

Felix stuck out his tongue. "Yuck. That explains it. What other shows do you watch?"

"When it comes to cartoons? I've been into *Steven Universe* lately."

Felix put a hand over his chest. Then he sighed dramatically. "You have great taste."

Harold laughed. "Thanks. I really like the episodes with songs."

"Yes!" Felix said. Then he sang, "I wanna see a giant womaaaan."

Those weren't the exact lyrics, but Harold got the reference anyway and smiled. "Or how about the one where they go to Empire City?"

"That one is the best." Not many episodes included songs. The one Harold referred to was especially rare, since it was an entire musical, albeit only eleven minutes long. All the episodes were that short. "We could watch it together," Felix said.

Harold looked surprised. "Now?"

"Why not?"

"Don't you have somewhere else you need to be?"

"Not really. Oh. Do you? If so, I totally understand."

Harold shook his head. "I'm free until tonight."

"Cool!"

They grinned at each other. Harold led the way to the living room, and soon they were sitting on the couch, watching the show together. Which was fun, but also a little too meta. The episode dealt with unrequited love. One of the characters harbored resentment toward the other, since she hadn't been chosen and he had, but in the end, they set aside those feelings and became friends.

"That was intense," Harold said as the credits rolled. His voice sounded strained, like he was emotional and didn't want to be. He was still staring at the screen, even after he paused it to stop the next episode from playing automatically.

"Super intense," Felix said. He attempted to lighten the mood by adding, "I actually dressed up as a character from the show a few years back. See if you can guess who."

He pulled out his phone and had no trouble finding the right photo, which he held up.

"Connie?" Harold said with a laugh. "I love it! And who's that with you dressed up as Steven?"

"My sister, Darli. She doesn't usually have curly hair. It's a wig."

"A fairly convincing one. What made you decide to gender swap like that?"

"It's the only way we could figure out how to do—"

"Stevonnie!" Harold said, snapping his fingers.

"Yes! It's so cool that you get it." If he had been talking to Noah, Felix would have needed half an hour and charts to get his point across. Harold was a true fan, making it easy. That raised an interesting question. "I have figures from this show at home. In the office. I'm surprised you haven't noticed them."

"Oh." Harold looked guilty.

"So you have? Why didn't you say anything about them?"

Harold flopped back on the couch and sighed. "Because I didn't want to like you. I've always tried to keep it civil. We always say hello and hug but—" He gestured at the screen. "You're Greg, and I'm Pearl."

In other words, Felix got to be with Noah, while Harold was left feeling hurt and rejected.

"I'm really sorry," Harold continued. "I know how shitty that must sound. I guess it was easier to blame you than to accept that Noah doesn't love me."

"He does love you!" Felix hurried to say. "I just got lucky, I guess."

"It's more than that," Harold said, shaking his head. "You're a sweet guy. You make him happy. I understand what he sees in you. I just need to accept what that means for me."

"For what it's worth," Felix said, "I've tried not to like you too. Or feel so jealous."

"Of me?" Harold said, sounding surprised.

"Uh, yeah! Are you kidding? Noah is crazy about you. He gets this dumb smile on his face whenever he tells stories from your past together. It's so annoying."

"Stop," Harold said. "You're just trying to make me feel better."

"I'm not, but if you want, we could totally cosplay as Greg

and Pearl at a convention. We should own this!"

Harold smiled, but he looked a little confused. "Cosplay?"

"It's when you dress up as characters you like," Felix explained. "Not for Halloween. That's different. Most people save their cosplay for the cons."

"You do that a lot?"

"When I can. It gets expensive quick, so I try to think of cheap costume ideas."

Harold's expression was difficult to read. "I do some cosplay too. I just didn't know it was called that."

"Really? Have any photos?"

Harold got to his feet. "No, but I'll show you. Wait here."

Felix looked around the room, trying to get a better feel for who this person was. The living room was disorganized, but not dirty. The bong didn't surprise him in the slightest, nor did the framed photo that sat on a side table next to a cozy chair. The image was of Harold and Noah together. An older heavyset man stood between them—their former boss—who they each had an arm around, but Harold's hand was resting on Noah's shoulder, the fingers gripping it tight. The words *Memories in Mexico* were superimposed over the image. It was the hokey sort of souvenir that most people would put on their refrigerator or paste in a scrapbook. Harold had framed the photo and had it proudly displayed. He must have really loved Noah. Must love him still. That usually made Felix jealous. Now it only made him sad.

"It's not from a cartoon," Harold said from behind him, "but it *is* a famous character."

Felix turned around and went rigid, because Harold was naked. Or nearly so. He wore a classic sailor's uniform, although much of the outfit was missing. He had the cap, and the large v-shaped collar that was tied together with a bow in the front, but the dangling ribbons rested on bare skin, the muscles beneath sculpted perfection. The navy pants looked like they had shrunk in the wash and were now glorified shorts that hugged his curves and cupped a bulge. Felix quickly turned around again, his face burning.

"What do you think?" Harold asked, not at all dissuaded as he marched into the living room and stood in front of the couch.

"Are you supposed to be a male version of Sailor Moon?" Felix asked, staring at the nearest wall.

"Ha! No. I'm the Cracker Jack boy. You remember those? The boxes of caramel popcorn that come with a prize? It's sort of old-fashioned now. One of my clients is obsessed with him. Sailor Jack. This isn't totally accurate to how he appears on the box, of course. Why aren't you looking at me?"

Felix tried again and made a choking noise. Harold had his hands on his hips and was smiling shamelessly. Wisps of dark armpit hair matched the small tuft just above the shockingly low waist of the shorts, which looked as though they were on the verge of tearing open to reveal—

"Nrrrgh!" Felix managed to say. Then he averted his eyes again and cleared his throat. "Very nice. You can get dressed now."

"I am dressed," Harold said with a chuckle. "I thought you'd be into this."

"Into it?" Felix said incredulously.

"Yeah! I've seen convention photos before. I know what you're talking about, even if I didn't know the term, and some of those costumes are hot. Especially the superheroes in tight spandex. You've got to have a nice body to pull that off. I'm not sure I could."

"I'm not interested in your body," Felix spluttered. "Maybe I was sending the wrong signals or—"

"Whoa whoa whoa!" Harold said, sounding panicked. "I meant you'd be into the costume and character thing. What did you call it? Cosplay? I wasn't suggesting..."

A sudden motion attracted Felix's attention. Harold had snatched a quilt off the cozy chair and was wrapping it around his waist.

"I thought it would be funny!"

"It is," Felix said, relieved to see that he wasn't the only one who was blushing.

"You didn't laugh."

"No, but I get it now. You're just so..." Hot. He couldn't say that though, or think of another way to end the sentence that sounded natural.

"I'll get changed," Harold said, hurrying from the room.

Felix pulled out his phone and started messing around without seeing the screen.

When Harold returned, he was back to wearing a T-shirt and

a pair of loose-fitting shorts. "I thought about returning in my mailman costume instead, just to mess with you."

"Do you really have one?" Felix asked.

"Yeah. And a few others."

"So you... A lot."

Harold made a face as he plopped down on the couch again. "Sorry, the signal is breaking up. I didn't catch that."

Felix rolled his eyes. "You know."

Harold was the picture of innocence as he shook his head. "No idea."

"Dress up. For clients."

"Do I knock on some guy's door and tell him I have a big package to deliver? Hell yeah. All the time." Harold was grinning now. "My job really makes you uncomfortable, doesn't it?"

"A little," Felix admitted.

"That's okay," Harold said easily. "Although I'm surprised. I figured Noah would have told you enough stories by now that you'd know all about this stuff."

Felix resisted the urge to squirm. "We don't really talk about it."

"Really? Not at all?"

"We did a little, when I first found out and was upset."

"Oh. Right."

"But he didn't go into the details. And I never asked." Felix tried to imagine Noah dressed as a sailor and felt a familiar mix of revulsion and intrigue. "I definitely haven't seen any costumes hanging in our closet."

"His whole schtick involved a costume," Harold said. He grimaced and quickly backpedaled. "Sorry. If you don't want to know details then I shouldn't—"

"No! I want to know. I'm curious."

Harold sized him up. Then he nodded. "It was my idea really. You know how he's got that cute West Texas accent? I made him dress country to match it. Checkered shirt, tight Wrangler jeans. That sort of thing. The clients loved it. Noah didn't. He must have changed his mind eventually, because that old truck he bought matched his image perfectly."

Felix tried to picture what he was being told. "Did he ever wear a cowboy hat?"

Harold shook his head. "Never."

"Oh. Do you think he would?"

Harold stared. Then he laughed. "For you, I bet he'd do about anything. You guys should talk about this stuff together! I know he's got hot stories to tell. Funny ones too."

"I'm not sure that's a good idea," Felix said.

"Why not?"

"I don't want to upset him. Or be upset."

"I see." Harold pulled his bare feet up on the couch. "If you don't mind me asking, what do you have against my sort of work?"

"I don't know." Felix searched inside himself. On the surface was more jealousy. Beneath that, if he was truly honest, was curiosity. It wasn't hard to imagine how turned on he would be, opening the front door to find Harold standing there dressed as the UPS man, and then getting to do whatever he wanted. Living out such a fantasy would be epic. If people wanted to pay for that experience, they should be allowed to. But when it involved the person he loved… "I don't think there's anything wrong with that sort of work. I just don't like the idea of Noah doing it."

"How come? If you truly believe there's nothing wrong with being an escort, then why not him?"

Felix chewed his bottom lip. "I don't know. Maybe it's my upbringing. My dad wasn't around much, so it was up to my mom to explain those sorts of things to me. When she did, it was more about feelings and waiting until the right time. I guess it's like Noah and cartoons. He didn't grow up with them, and now he doesn't get it."

"But you want him to try, right?" Harold jabbed him with his big toe. "You should too. Explore this together. I'm not saying you should work for the GAC, or hire an escort, but one of the best parts of being in love is trusting the other person enough to really open up about what you want. Even just talking about it can be a lot of fun."

"You're probably right," Felix said. "I'm too repressed sometimes."

"I'm sure you're fine. I've never heard Noah complain. Just don't be scared to experiment sexually and have fun. If you want, I can loan you a costume or two."

Felix laughed. "I'll think about it. Maybe that will help."

Harold was taken aback. "With what?"

"Oh. Nothing. It's just that sometimes, I worry that Noah is getting bored with me."

"Any reason why?"

"He doesn't have much time for me lately. I know he's busy, but it's hard not to feel like his work matters more to him. Or that he finds it more interesting. That's one reason I haven't asked about all the crazy things he's done. I'm scared that I'll never be able to compete."

Harold was shaking his head. "He's not getting bored with you. Believe me, I would have noticed and celebrated." He blanched. "That sounds terrible. Sorry."

"It's okay. I understand."

"Thanks. From what I can tell, he's fallen *more* in love with you. He tries not to show it when I'm around, but from the outside, it's painfully obvious. Trust me. Noah only wants to make the Gentlemen's Agreement Club a success. That's why he's distracted. He considers this his big chance and doesn't want to mess it up. So he's not tired of you. He's doing it all *for* you. But if you feel ignored, you should let him know."

Felix waved his hands in the air, banishing the idea. "No no no! I don't want to add to his stress."

"You're the opposite of stress to him. When he's finally done working, who does he turn to?"

"Me?" Felix guessed.

"Damn skippy!"

"Can I ask you something? Since we're being so open."

"Sure."

"Why aren't you involved in the business more?" Felix made sure to keep his tone neutral, which wasn't difficult. He didn't feel as much anger as before. "You guys are supposed to be equal partners, but he's the one doing all the hard work while you…"

"I'm making you say it this time," Harold said. "You censor yourself way too much."

"While you sleep with people. For money."

"There you go. And you're right, I leave all the brainy stuff to him because all I'll do is get in the way. Noah's got this. Trust me. I've never met anyone so determined. I'm not that guy. I know a lot about our clients and the other escorts. I always give him that info when he needs it, but I don't have what it takes for the rest."

Now it was Felix's turn to poke Harold, although he did so

with a finger. "Then maybe *you* should experiment. How do you know if you can run a business if you've never tried?"

Harold scrunched up his face. Then he sighed. "My own advice used against me."

"Damn skippy," Felix said, choosing the words on purpose. "I'm stealing all your good stuff and making it my own."

"In that case," Harold said, standing again. "How about trying my cooking after all? I'm starving."

"Me too," Felix said. "I'll help."

"Awesome." Harold held out his hand.

Felix took it and was pulled to his feet.

Harold didn't let go. He continued to grip Felix's palm. "I want us to be friends," he said. "I'm done pretending I don't like you."

Felix smiled. "Okay, but no more cosplay. I nearly caught the vapors!"

Harold laughed. "Don't worry, I think I have some smelling salts in the kitchen."

Felix followed him, pulling out his phone along the way to let Noah know that he might be a while. After all, he had a new friend to get acquainted with.

Felix opened his eyes against the light of morning and rolled over to face what he knew would be an empty bed. Noah seemed to get up earlier each day, just so he could start work sooner. Back when Felix had first moved in, they had always woken up together and would often stay in bed to have sex or talk about their dreams. That still happened on occasion, although it was the exception now, not the rule. Felix allowed himself to lie there and miss what had been. Then he got up and put on pajama bottoms and one of Noah's old T-shirts before he plodded into the kitchen.

The table was set with two bowls, each filled with cinnamon and spice instant oatmeal that was still dry, and two large glasses of orange juice. The offerings were simple, but they were also Felix's favorite breakfast. Noah turned around, the electric kettle in hand. "I was just about to wake you."

"How?" Felix said, surprised to see him still in his robe instead of showered and dressed.

"By whatever means necessary." Noah set the kettle down on the table. "Hungry?"

"Yeah!" Felix took a seat and beamed at the humble spread. "I can't remember the last time we did this."

"Me neither." Noah poured hot water into each bowl before he sat at the table. "Better eat up. We have a big day ahead of us."

"We do?" Felix asked.

"Yup." Noah picked up a spoon to stir the water and oatmeal together. "I thought we'd check out the Austin Toy Museum and see the new location. We can do some window shopping too and find somewhere to eat on Congress. Maybe that Italian place you like. Sound good?"

Felix stared. "Don't you have to work?"

"Nope!"

"Wow. You and Bethany must have gotten a lot done yesterday."

"We did fine," Noah said.

"So the new website is ready to go?"

"I didn't say that. Hey, what do you think of the orange juice? It's freshly squeezed. At the grocery store, at least. I think it tastes different. Do you?"

Felix set his spoon down. "What's going on?"

"I'm taking the day off and spending it with my boyfriend," Noah said with a shrug. "You said last night that you don't have any plans."

"Are you burnt out or something? Is this a nervous breakdown?"

"I'm fine," Noah said with a chuckle. "You're my top priority. That's all. I haven't been doing enough to prove that."

Felix felt his heart flutter. "Harold told you, didn't he?"

"Told me what?" Noah said casually. Then he gave up the ruse. "Yes. He let me know that I've been too wrapped up in my work lately. And the reason why you were reluctant to tell me so yourself."

"I worried it would—"

"I know. You didn't want to cause me stress. That's sweet of you. I'm glad you felt like you could confide in him, because I need to know these things. Now eat before your oatmeal gets cold and slimy. There's nothing worse."

"And then we'll take a shower together?" Felix asked.

"We'll shower and anything else you want. Today is all about you."

"About us," Felix corrected. Then he made short work of his oatmeal, eager for the day to begin.

Felix's favorite Italian place offered open air seating on the second floor that overlooked Congress Avenue. Giant ceiling fans stirred the air to stave off the heat, but the weather was unseasonably cool today, a light breeze blowing across the city and making the discarded napkins on their table quiver. Felix was full, but not overwhelmingly so. A perk of having eaten here so often was knowing precisely what to order that would leave room for dessert. Which they always shared. Today was no exception. When the waiter came to clear away their plates, Noah ordered the chocolate budino with vanilla gelato.

"Sharing it is hard," Felix said, "One of these days we'll each have our own dessert."

Noah smirked. "I'm perfectly content to sit here and watch you eat it all."

"No way! I'll get fat!"

"You always say that. I think it'll take more than one indulgence before you need to buy larger pants."

Felix shook his head. "It's a gateway drug. One budino leads to daily visits to the Golden Corral dessert buffet."

"Oh, that is a good one," Noah said. "Did I ever tell you about the time I went there while still homeless?"

"The Golden Corral?"

"Yeah. You can imagine what an all-you-can-eat buffet means to someone living on the streets. I was there for half a day, I swear. This was shortly after I started working at the… working for Marcello. Harold and I were uh… I was having a rough time and needed to spoil myself."

Harold was right that Felix censored himself too much. He wasn't the only one who did so in this relationship, but it didn't have to stay that way. "It must have been nice when money started rolling in from the Gentlemen's Agreement Club. Were you hungry a lot?"

"Not as much by that point since I was…" Noah trailed off and peered at him.

"Eating out with clients, right?" Felix said encouragingly.

"Yes. Free food and a steady income, but still no home of my own. I wish I had thought to eat at a buffet before then."

"So why did you? Something to do with Harold? Were you still together then?"

Noah angled his head, as if uncertain he had heard right. "We were never in a relationship, but we had finally slept together for the first and final time. Are you *sure* you want to talk about this?"

Felix nodded eagerly. "I was jealous of him before, but hanging out with Harold helped me get past that. I want to know everything that happened. It's an important part of who you are."

"Oh. Well, to be honest, I was a complete mess. This is right after he and I visited my parents, and I found out they were just as crazy as before. So I was already feeling emotionally raw when Harold made it clear that we couldn't be anything more than friends."

"By sleeping with you?"

"There were a lot of mixed signals, and he was still bouncing back from his own bad experience. The timing wasn't right." Noah made a face. "Or it was never meant to be. To be fair, I was the one who threw a fit and refused to see him anymore. I already felt rejected by my parents. I couldn't handle more. So yeah, I saw an advertisement for a buffet and thought it would be a fast way to fill the emptiness I felt inside." Noah laughed.

Felix did too. "Did it work?"

"No, but it felt good anyway. Until the end when I nearly…"

Censorship was okay sometimes, especially considering their dessert had arrived. After thanking the waiter and feeding each other bites, Felix decided he wanted to hear more of what he'd been avoiding for so long.

"Your work must have been a nice distraction. Like going on a bunch of dates after breaking up with someone."

"It helped create distance from him, that's true."

Felix sucked gelato off his spoon and put on a mischievous expression. "Was it ever hot?"

Noah recoiled from the question. "Sex feels good, no matter who it's with, so yes."

"Yeah, but were there times you were really into it? Stuff that still turns you on when you think about it?"

Noah smirked. "This morning obviously wasn't enough. Can't say I'm surprised. Do you want to go home, or do you want to go shopping?"

Felix shrugged. "Maybe all I need right now is a story. Who

was the hottest client you had?"

Noah chewed and swallowed as he thought about it. "It wasn't that the guy was physically hot. That never mattered much. I became good at imagining someone else, even when my eyes were open. Or I was selective about where I looked. Anyway, this particular client wanted me to go out of town with him for a week-long business conference. That wasn't so unusual. I found out the first night that the guy liked to take his time. I had experience with that too, except at a certain point, he made it clear that I wasn't going to finish at all. He wanted me to save it for the next day." Noah looked worried. "Are you sure you're okay with this?"

"I'm fine." Mostly. Felix already felt some possessive pangs, but he also wanted to know how the story ended. "So what happened?"

"The next night was the same thing. I wasn't allowed to finish. When I expressed frustration, the client took out this thing... Do you know what a chastity belt is?"

"Metal panties that have a lock? Aren't those just for women in the Dark Ages?"

Noah smirked. "That's what I thought too. Let's finish up here. It'll be easier to talk about if we're not surrounded by people."

They weren't alone when walking down Congress Avenue either, but while in motion, it was unlikely that more than a snippet would be overheard.

Felix took his boyfriend's hand as they strolled. "I've never understood how a chastity belt would work. Like, if you can't get your underwear off, how do you pee?"

"I'm not sure how it works for women," Noah said. "For a guy, you have to picture a metal ring that clamps around the base of your cock and underneath your balls. It's not too tight, but it's enough to ensure you won't be able to get it off without the key. Attached to this is a cage shaped like a limp dick, so it's airy and possible to pee, but getting hard is a bad idea."

"For you especially. You're a big boy!"

Noah snorted. "Tell me about it. Avoiding that was tricky. Remember what it was like when you were bored and horny in high school and how, once you realized you were getting hard, resisting only made it worse?"

"That *still* happens to me," Felix said. He was taking classes at the community college, and his mind often drifted to impure thoughts about Noah.

"I bet it does. Anyway, the chastity belt wasn't very comfortable. It made a pretty noticeable bulge beneath my clothes too, so I didn't go anywhere if I had a choice. I basically sat around the hotel room for the entire week, horny out of my mind, and hoping that he'd finally let me finish."

"And you liked that?"

Noah tilted his head back and forth. "Kind of. The sensations when he was doing stuff to me were off the charts, and at the end of the trip when I finally came..." Noah laughed and shook his head. "It was a typhoon! I soaked the whole damn bed. I nearly died it felt so good."

"Then maybe we should try that. Together."

Noah looked over at him in surprise. "Really?"

"Why not?"

"I'd be up for it. But I didn't like the chastity belt. I think we can trust each other not to come if the other person isn't around. And maybe we'll start Friday night and finish on Sunday instead of drawing it out for so long. We can spend most of the weekend in bed and keep it going nonstop for two full days. Sound good?"

Felix grabbed Noah's hand and moved it over to his shorts, so he could feel how hard he was.

"Same here," Noah said. "We either need to find some bushes to dive into, or you need to ask me about the gross encounters."

"I'm not ready to hear about that stuff," Felix said.

"Sometimes it was funny," Noah said, shooting him a questioning expression.

"Funny works."

"Cool. The weirdest fetishes were often the most amusing. One of my regulars had a thing for weddings. The first time he slept with another man was at one, and he liked to recreate that as much as possible. He had enough money to stage fake weddings if he wanted, but authenticity was important to him."

"So what did you do?"

"We both dressed up in tuxes and drove around town, week after week, crashing every wedding we could find. It wasn't enough just to slip into the bathroom at one. We had to mingle, separately, and pretend to meet by chance. We got kicked out of a few, and at others, had a little too much success. My favorite was when I was mistaken for a distant cousin—everyone there was *really* drunk—and I was asked to give a speech."

Felix smiled and looked over at Noah, swinging their arms in his elation. "Did you?"

"Of course! I talked about the importance of honesty, which was ironic, although I finished truthfully by saying I was leaving to go screw someone in the bathroom. They thought it was hilarious."

"And did you?"

"Naturally."

"You're so bad!"

"You have no idea," Noah said, grinning shamelessly.

He was right. Felix didn't know, but thanks to Harold's advice, he was finally getting the more colorful details. Noah told him a few more stories, taking breaks when they entered the thrift shops that Felix enjoyed so much. They were walking back to the car when another thought occurred to him.

"If we never met," Felix said, "do you think you'd still be working as an escort?"

"Probably," Noah said. "I only started searching for a Plan B when I realized I wanted to be with you."

"And what if I left tomorrow? Would you go back to it?"

Noah stopped walking and gently pulled on Felix's hand until they were facing each other. "Are you thinking of leaving me?"

"No! Not at all. I just wondered if I got in the way of something that you loved."

"You *are* the thing I love," Noah said, green eyes intense. "If you left, I don't know what I would do. I'd be a mess for a long time. I like to think I'd keep the business going though. I really believe in the changes we're making. A lot of these guys are just lonely. Life is better when you have someone there to listen. Or to lend a hand. This one client told me about the time he bought a new television, and how the box was so long and unwieldy, he had to drag it from the parking lot and up three floors to his apartment. Even worse, it was raining and the box got muddy because he didn't feel that he had anyone he could ask for help. Most of us have someone special, even a friend or roommate, who is there for us. Some of these guys, for whatever reason, can't maintain relationships like that, but they shouldn't have to be alone. I know they can call a plumber or whoever else they need, but we treat them like friends. We'll stick around for a coffee if they want, or more if both parties are agreeable. It sounds cheesy, but I want everyone to feel loved."

"It's not cheesy," Felix said. "It's noble."

"Then maybe you'd like to work for us," Noah said, leading the way again. The truck was in sight now.

"Work for you?" Felix said in disbelief. "I'm trying to be more open, but I don't want to be an escort!"

"Of course not. That's one of the changes I'm making. Not all of our employees will have sex for money. That'll be listed as 'additional services available' on their profile. Anyone can work for us, as long as they're either attractive or personable, and you're both. We only need to figure out—" Noah shook his head. "Sorry. I promised myself I wouldn't talk about work today."

They reached the truck, Felix leaning his back against it and pulling Noah close. "You can talk to me about anything, whenever you want or need to. Let's promise to make it that way from now on. Okay?"

Noah's eyes searched his, looking increasingly watery. Then he nodded and leaned in for a kiss. Felix felt lips press against his, shut his eyes, and thought of Harold. Not like *that*. He simply felt gratitude. Harold had enough reason to want this relationship to fail, but thanks to him, Felix now felt closer to Noah than ever before.

Dear Diary,

So much has changed since I last wrote. Harold and I are friends now! I know I planned on avoiding him, but Noah made us run an errand together, and we had a nice heart-to-heart afterwards. Turns out Harold isn't such a bad guy. In fact, he's pretty great. He even gave me advice that helped Noah and me become closer. Since then, Harold and I have had a lot of fun together. We like cooking new recipes and trying them. And we both want to support Noah, who is still freaking out over the business. He forgets to eat or take breaks, so we drag him away and make him sit at the table with us. Or this one time we peer pressured him into going to Harold's place to watch the first six episodes of Avatar. Noah <u>still</u> isn't into it. He might be hopeless. I don't know. The last couple of months have been good anyway. Lately we've been *shopping together. Harold wants to redecorate his living room, but he doesn't know how exactly, so we mostly go out searching for ideas. We talk so much during these trips that we often forget what we're supposed to be doing. He's kind of my best friend right now, although I haven't told him that. The tragic thing is, we could have been friends sooner if I hadn't been so butthurt about his history with Noah. How dumb of me is that? From now on, I won't be so quick to judge.*

"He's got like—" Felix did a quick mental calculation. "—nine million points of articulation." He was standing in the home office. Noah only needed his desk, the computer on it, and a chair, which left plenty of unclaimed space. Felix had no trouble filling it. He found cheap glass shelves at Ikea, only buying a set of two, since he never had a lot of money. He was content to use his old ones, even if it meant exposing his collection of action figures and other memorabilia to dust. That changed over Christmas, when Noah surprised him with an entire row of the glass shelves. Felix had to admit it added an element of class to the collection, not that any of their visitors gave it more than a cursory glance. Except for Harold. Now that they were buds, Felix often had a captive audience.

"Who's this again?" Harold said, changing the pose of the figure he held.

"Tuxedo Mask," Felix said as if it were obvious. Because it should have been. "You've never watched *Sailor Moon*?"

"That show is for girls."

"No it's not!"

Harold cocked an eyebrow.

"Okay, maybe it is," Felix admitted, "but so what? You said yourself that Korra is your favorite Avatar. She's a girl."

"Yeah, but she's not *girly*. Korra is a badass."

"Sailor Moon can be badass too," Felix countered.

"Where's she hiding?" Harold asked, looking back at the shelf. "Tuxedo Mask wants some love. They're a couple, right?"

"Yeah, but I don't have her. These are imported from Japan, and they're kind of expensive, so I could only get one."

Harold snorted. "And you chose the boy character, not the girl. Gee, I wonder why." He smirked like he'd won the argument.

"I chose him because he was basically my dream guy. Until I met Noah."

"Aw," Harold said. "Did you hear that?"

They turned as one to face Noah, who had his back to them, an elbow on the desk, and a palm on his forehead. "You guys will be the death of me," he grumbled.

"Anything I can do to help?" Harold asked.

Felix gave him a thumbs up, then took the figure when Harold handed it back and carefully returned it to the shelf. When he spun around to face the room, he saw Harold standing next to Noah at the desk, a hand on his shoulder. Envy creeped over Felix. Although this time it was different somehow. He tried to figure out why, and when he couldn't, he made himself recognize what a supportive and harmless gesture it was. They were touching. So what?

"—couldn't get the old profiles to migrate over," Noah was saying. "I'll have to type them all in manually. If you want to help with that when the time comes, I'd appreciate it. I need to make sure I've got all the correct fields first, which means I *really* need to concentrate."

"Got it," Harold said, moving his hand away. He looked over his shoulder. "We're making too much noise, kiddo."

Harold called him that a lot lately. Felix always pretended to hate it, even though he didn't. He rolled his eyes, a smile betraying his true feelings. "We'll go somewhere else. Sorry, hon!"

"I've got a client I need to take care of," Harold said. "I was thinking of bringing Felix along for this one."

"What?" Noah looked up sharply. "Who?"

"Kirkpatrick."

"Russell? Why would you—"

"He's in Boston this week, remember? I thought Felix would get a kick out of his place."

Noah turned in his chair, expression confused, until his eyes moved to the shelves full of figures and collectable merchandise. "Yeah. He might."

"How come?" Felix asked. At one time he would have been happy to let them speak in code. Now he wanted to know everything. "Does he have a collection too?"

"He's got something, all right," Harold said, pulling out his keys and tossing them in the air. With a swipe he caught them in his other hand. "You up for an adventure?"

"It's not *that* interesting," Noah said.

"He'll love it," Harold said with confidence. "You'll see. What do you say, kiddo?"

Felix grinned, having no idea what to expect. "Let's go!"

Harold's convertible pulled into the garage. Using the same app that had granted them access, he made the door rumble closed again. Felix's first impression as he exited the vehicle was how organized it all was. Most garages were at least a little messy. In this one, everything had its place.

"If your client is out of town," he asked, "what are we doing here?"

"I'm house sitting for him," Harold answered. "Turning the lights on and off to scare away burglars, feeding the cat, that sort of thing."

"But why you?"

"Why hire a prostitute instead of someone respectable?" Harold's tones were teasing. "I was surprised too when I first started. You develop a sort of relationship with your regulars. Especially the guys with more complicated needs. That involves trust, which spreads to other aspects of life."

Harold unlocked the door leading into the house and stepped aside so Felix could enter first. The interior was just as tidy as the garage and brightly lit, most of the furnishings white. Including the longhaired cat with a squished face that appeared in the hall and regarded them with transparent suspicion.

"I love her!" Felix cried, dropping to his knees. When this made the cat tense, he said in a quieter voice, "You're so pretty."

"That's Sinatra," Harold said. "As in Frank, rather than Nancy, so it's a boy."

"I love him," Felix amended.

He reached out a hand, and when this still wasn't enough to establish a connection, Harold squatted on the carpet between them like an ambassador of pets. It worked. Felix was soon running his fingers through white hair. "So soft!" he enthused.

"He has to be brushed every day," Harold said. "And there's a fifty-fifty chance we'll find a hairball somewhere around here. Be on the lookout."

Felix glanced up from the cat. "I can't believe you get paid to do this."

"No kidding," Harold said with a chuckle. "You sure you

don't wanna rethink your job as a waiter? A cute guy like you would be popular."

"Stop," Felix said, feeling a blush coming on. "So… What do we do first?"

He was happy to help. That meant scooping the litter box and changing the water in the cat's bowl. What he really wanted to do was brush Sinatra, but Harold insisted the cat wouldn't settle down enough for that until after he'd eaten, so while he fed the cat, Felix went about his own chores. What he saw of the house was minimal and organized. If there were any collections here, he hadn't found them yet.

"Did he eat?" Felix asked as he reentered the kitchen.

Harold was standing at the sink, rinsing off a plate. "Yup. He'll groom himself until he gets groggy. Then we brush."

"Can't wait!"

Harold's expression was hard to read. "Have you seen the bedroom yet?"

"No."

"Follow me."

This must be it. Maybe the owner of the house kept all the good stuff hidden in his most private room. When they reached the door, Harold stepped aside again so he could enter, living up to the first word of his company's name. Felix strolled in, glancing around and not seeing any shelves or collectables. Then he noticed the bed.

"Oh Jesus!"

Felix clapped his hands over his mouth, eyes wide, because the bed was occupied.

"Sorry!" Harold said, hurrying forward. "I didn't know you were still sleeping. It's nearly lunch! Let's get you up."

The sleeper didn't stir. Felix could see dark brown hair and that was about it. Harold pulled the covers back. The occupant still didn't move.

"Is he dead?" Felix asked in horror.

"Just a heavy sleeper," Harold said with a grin as he slid an arm beneath the person. "He weighs a ton too."

Felix struggled to make sense of what he was seeing. The man was dressed in a T-shirt, his frame toned, and while his eyes were open, he wasn't reacting to the situation at all. Like a mannequin. Or a— "Is that a sex doll?"

"Bingo!" Harold grunted and got it into a sitting position with a few audible clicks.

Felix moved closer. "Like one of those Real Dolls?"

"Same concept, different brand. The male Real Dolls are creepy looking. This guy is kind of handsome, don't you think?"

Harold plopped down on the bed next to it and grinned. He had his arm around the doll, which made it easier to see how similar their skin tones were. The hair was nearly the same too. They could have been brothers. Or twins.

"He looks like you."

"Like I said, he's handsome."

"You're so full of yourself." Felix laughed and reached out to wave his hand in front of the doll's eyes. "Who would want something like this in their bed? It's so creepy!"

"Not really," Harold said. "It's not so different than a grown man collecting action figures."

Felix's mouth dropped open. "You're right. This is the ultimate action figure!"

"Nine million points of articulation at least," Harold said with a wink. "And a few hidden features too."

Felix tittered. He couldn't help it. "He's got all the right parts?"

"Yeah. You want to see?"

"No! Well, maybe. I need to get used to it first." He reached out and touched the skin of the doll's cheek. It was soft, but not entirely lifelike. Or was he biased because he knew it wasn't real? Gently pinching the skin revealed a definite difference in thickness. Aside from that, if the room was dark enough, he might not be able to tell right away.

"Does he have a name?" Felix asked.

"How rude of me. Lance, this is Felix. He'll be helping me take care of you today." Out of the corner of his mouth, he whispered, "Shake his hand."

"Oh. Right." Felix moved the covers aside, relieved to see the doll had jeans on. He grasped the hand and did his best to shake it. While it felt realistic—the hand was the correct shape and size—it was strange to interact with someone who was so unresponsive. "Nice to meet you. Do you need a glass of water, or uh, should we brush your hair too?"

"Nothing so complicated today," Harold said, standing and

throwing back the sheets. "Russell likes it when I take photos of Lance around the house. Makes it feel more real to him. It's tricky though, because these dolls can't stand on their own. You can lean them against something if you're careful, but it's safer to make him sit. Any ideas?"

Felix surveyed the room but didn't see many options. A door was open to a private bathroom. "The toilet maybe?"

"Believe it or not, I've done that recently. Same with the obvious stuff like the living room couch."

"Hmm. Think we can get him on one of the breakfast bar stools?"

Harold grimaced. "Hate to keep shooting you down, but I did that yesterday. I staged it with a bowl of cereal and everything." He nudged the doll and addressed it. "Which I had to eat because you're so dang picky."

Felix shook his head. "Bizarre. I love it. How about in the backyard? I saw patio furniture out there. We can put a pair of sunglasses on him like he's tanning."

"That could work. I did something similar once, but that was a few trips back. Yeah! Why not? Let's brush Sinatra first."

Felix was still interested in that, but not as much now. He had met plenty of cats, but he'd never had the chance to interact with a life-sized doll before. He kept thinking of the possibilities while they took care of Sinatra elsewhere in the house. "Are we still getting lunch after this?"

"Yeah," Harold said as he snapped a photo of the cat for Russell to see. "Soon. I'm hungry."

"Can we take Lance with us?"

Harold stopped what he was doing. "To a restaurant?"

"We could go to a drive-thru. We'll put Lance in the backseat of your car. Think how excited Russell will be when he sees those photos! Or will it upset him?"

Harold thought it over. Then his face lit up. He had the cutest dimples when he smiled. "We'll have to be careful, but I bet Russell will love it. I just don't want greasy food."

"So order a salad or something." Harold was fun to cook with, but Noah was more fun to eat with. "Are we really going to do this? Just imagine people's faces if they notice."

"That'll only make it better."

Felix grinned. Harold did too. Soon they were back in the

bedroom. Harold scooped the doll up and Felix led the way, opening and closing doors as they went. Their progress slowed when they reached the car. The door to the backseat was open, but it was hard to find the right angle to get the doll inside.

"This is dumb," Harold said, backing away. "We'll put the top down instead."

That not only made it easier to get the doll inside and buckled up. It also exposed Lance to the world.

"I don't want to put the top back up," Felix said.

"Neither do I," Harold said with a guffaw. "Lance has been cooped up for far too long. I think he deserves a joyride, don't you?"

Ten minutes later, they had left the neighborhood and were cruising down busy streets. Most people didn't notice. Only at stoplights did they get doubletakes or confused faces, each making them howl with laughter. Nobody at the drive-thru noticed, to their disappointment, even when Felix leapt out of the car to take photos. He continued to do so when they drove to a nearby park to consume their food. Lance had to stay in the car. They couldn't risk him getting dirty or damaged, but the lush green trees made a nice backdrop.

"In some of these," Felix said as he reviewed the photos on his phone, "you'd swear he's real." They were driving back to Russell's house and were almost there. "I'm tempted to post a few and see if anyone notices."

"You can show them to your friends, but only on your phone. Please don't send the photos to anyone or post them publicly. This is Russell's private life. We have to respect that. It's part of the escort code of honor."

"Is he nice?" Felix asked.

"Russell?" Harold checked his blind spot before switching lanes. "Yeah. He's all right. He has a lot of issues. We all do, but his trip him up pretty bad. Enough that it's hard for him to get close to anyone. Russell is OCD. Like, for real. With Lance, he can have everything just how he wants it without having to explain or argue."

"Huh. He must get lonely not having anyone to talk to."

Harold glanced at him. "That's when he asks me to come over."

"What about when you're not there?"

"Have you ever seen someone carry on a conversation with their pet?"

Felix laughed. "Many times."

"I think it works like that. I've never asked."

The car slowed as they reached the right house.

"Don't pull in the garage yet," Felix said. "I want to get a photo of you driving him around."

"No!" Harold said, sounding alarmed. "That would upset him. In fact, I need you to delete any photos where I'm in the shot."

"Why?"

Harold chuckled nervously. "You noticed that the doll looks like me, right?"

"Yeah."

"That's no accident. As far as Russell is concerned, I *am* Lance."

Felix didn't get it. He waited until the car was shut off and the garage door was closed again before asking, "How does that work?"

"I step in when Lance needs to be more animated. We're never in the same place. I'm not sure where he goes when I come over. I can't ask without breaking character. The only time I get to see him is when Russell is out of town. So it's Lance who is taking care of the cat right now. The texts I send Russell, saying that everything is okay back home, aren't from me. They're from Lance. I can't be in any of the photos for that reason. I'll have to say it was you and Noah driving him around. I think Russell will like the idea of him having friends."

He watched Harold unbuckle the doll's seatbelt, noticing again the similarities between them. "But he must know that you're a real person and that Lance isn't."

"Of course," Harold said. "He's not crazy, but if you're going to buy a life-size doll and pretend it's your boyfriend, you might as well go for it. This way Russell can have a sex life that's more involved, have a conversation he can't predict, or go out on the town with me. With Lance. It's pretty clever actually. He used to have a different doll before we met, and some poor escort had to put on a wig and pretend to be it. Marcello was the one who suggested reversing the situation and basing the doll on a real person instead."

"Oh." Felix held open the door to the house so Harold could carry the doll in. "That's sad."

"No," Harold said with a grunt as he rounded the corner. "It's good. Russell goes to sleep every night feeling loved. That's more than I can say."

And now he felt sadder. Felix fought against it. The more he learned of this job, the more he realized that there were many different ways to love. People just kept the odder versions hidden so they wouldn't be criticized by those who didn't understand.

"He doesn't usually sleep in his clothes," Harold explained as he lowered the doll into bed. "It's a pain to undress him. I only do it the night before Russell comes back in town. I wouldn't put Lance in bed at all if Sinatra didn't like sleeping on his legs. Man, I've got to pee!"

Harold didn't have a lot of filters. All the crazy stuff his job exposed him to probably made *everything* seem socially acceptable. Felix liked that. He wanted to be that tolerant. Harold rushed off to use the restroom, leaving him alone. Felix sat on the edge of the bed and tried to imagine what it was like to be Russell. Not in a pitying way. Instead he thought of all the times he had wanted someone to hold, or to touch, and how comforting a doll like this would have been. And yeah, kind of sexy too. He reached out and let himself stroke the toned muscles of the chest through the T-shirt. This wasn't enough. He wanted to know how real it could feel, so he slid his hand under the fabric and over the rippling abs. The sensation was erotic. He wouldn't deny that. Felix was skinny, and Noah's build was natural. He had more meat on him than Felix, but he wasn't athletic. Neither was the only other guy Felix had been with. He'd always wondered what a toned body would feel like. With his free hand, he squeezed one of the biceps.

"What do you think?"

Felix shot to his feet, cheeks burning. Harold was leaning against the door frame and smiling. Then he sauntered over and flexed an arm. "I bet they can't compete with the real thing."

"I wouldn't know," Felix said.

"Then find out," Harold said. "Go on. I don't mind."

Why not? It was just an arm, and he *was* curious. Felix placed a palm over Harold's bicep. It was warmer than the doll, of course. Hotter and harder, which also described how Felix was feeling between the legs, because he was getting turned on. His stomach twisted up with guilt as he yanked his hand away. This wasn't okay. He didn't want to cheat on Noah. Felix didn't even want to think about it!

"Better or the same?" Harold asked.

It was difficult to get a read on him. Harold wasn't making bedroom eyes or anything. This was probably one more boundary that had eroded over the years. Being touched and admired was a daily occurrence for him, and not something especially intimate.

That's not how Felix felt. For him the experience was intense. "Yours feel better," he managed to say.

"Thanks." Harold dropped his arm at last. "I try to keep in shape."

"Must be nice," Felix squeaked. Then he cleared his throat. "I always wanted muscles."

"It's a fairly new thing for me. I was never into sports. I just started working out recently."

"Can't be that recent," Felix said. "You've always looked... good."

"Huh. I guess it has been over a year now." Harold's face fell. Then he sighed and sat on the edge of the bed. "I'm embarrassed to admit it, but I actually started working out because I wanted to win Noah back." Concern crossed his features. "Don't worry! This was before you two met. After I shot him down, I realized what a big mistake I had made, and I kept trying to think of the right words to say. At the time, I was kind of messed up. There was this guy before Noah who I loved so much that I..." Harold laughed and shook his head. "I wanted to marry him."

"It must have been serious."

"For me. Not so much for him. That hurt. Really bad. You know the feeling you get when watching fireworks? Love is like that. It's all gasps, excitement, and one boneshaking explosion after the other. Then it stops, and you're left staring up at an empty sky, hoping there's more to come. You stare until your eyes sting and tears run down your cheeks, but eventually you have to admit that the sun has come up, and it's all over."

"Wow." Felix sat next to him. "When I'm not sure if the fireworks are done, I usually just count to twenty."

Harold looked over. Then he laughed and elbowed Felix in the side. "You crack me up. I could have used you back then. I bet you wouldn't have let me get away with any melodramatic bullshit."

"It wasn't melodramatic," Felix said. "I think it's beautiful the way you described it. Why didn't you tell Noah what you just told me?"

"I don't know. I guess I thought I was protecting myself. And him. I chose the wrong time to be cynical."

"So you started working out."

Harold pinched the bridge of his nose. "Ugh. Yes. I was hoping he would notice me again, like he did the first time. The only problem was, whenever we ended up in the same room, Noah wouldn't look at me or stick around. I tried. It just wasn't enough. By the time I finally got his attention again, he had met this annoyingly adorable kid—sorry, young man—and it was too late."

"I don't like the sound of this new guy," Felix suggested, scowling theatrically. "I'd buy that kid a pair of cement shoes and invite him to go swimming."

"Naw. I like him too much to do that." Harold leaned over enough to bump shoulders. Then he stretched and stood. "Let's get out of here. I think Lance needs his beauty sleep."

"Okay." Felix was the last one to leave the room. He looked back as he went and felt a pang of sorrow. The doll was a lonely sight, especially when he realized this was how Harold's nights ended at home. Alone.

Dear Diary,

Last week I had the strangest dream. I thought I had woken up, even though it was actually another dream (so Inception!*) and the bed wasn't empty like it usually is. Lance the doll was with me, so I cuddled up to him. That felt good, which got me in the mood. I went beneath the sheets, curious to discover what he had down there. It was just like a normal guy, although I remember being confused that he was limp. I put his wiener in my mouth anyway, and to my surprise, it got hard! He tasted real and everything. Then I felt his hand on the back of my head and heard him moan. That's when I realized it wasn't Lance. It was Harold. I didn't stop though. I didn't want to. I woke up right before he came. I know a wet dream doesn't sound like news. The funny thing is, it made me realize the truth. Please don't judge me too harshly, but I think I like Harold more than I should. When I saw him* the next day, I was excited. My heart was beating fast, especially when he hugged me. I'm not sure what to do. I haven't felt this way since I met Noah. I still love him, if you're wondering. That hasn't changed. But sometimes I wonder if what I feel for Harold is a harmless crush, or the start of something more. I know it's wrong, but just like in my dream, I don't want it to stop.

"Happy birthday!"

Albert, the owner of Bottoms 1UP, placed a cloth bag on the table with a thud, tokens spilling out and onto the table. Felix clapped with glee. He leapt up to give the man a hug before Albert went back to tending to his business. What an amazing birthday it had been so far. Noah had taken the day off again, which meant a lot since the official relaunch of the GAC was getting close. In the morning they took their time in bed. Once showered and dressed, they went to Denny's for breakfast, because getting a free meal just because it was his special day was too awesome to resist. Every business should make that their policy. Felix started flashing his ID everywhere they went, pretending that he hoped for more freebies, when in truth he only did it to make Noah laugh. After shopping and returning home for a nap, they ate dinner with his mom and sister. That involved cake and presents. After saying goodbye they went to his favorite barcade. He was finally old enough to be here legally! If that wasn't enough, he was currently staring at *another* cake—this one shaped like a pixelated Donkey Kong—and more presents from his friends.

"Open mine first," Bethany said, sliding a big box to him across the table.

She had the same drawl as Noah did. Felix often thought of them as cousins, even though they weren't related. Bethany was the closest thing to family that he had, due to Noah's non-existent relationship with his parents. It helped that she was from the same town. Noah seemed to take comfort in her presence ever since she moved to Austin. He had needed someone he could talk to about things back home. They would mention names no one else knew or—

"Open it!" Bethany insisted.

"Sorry," Felix said, lifting his phone to take a quick photo. "You guys look so cute sitting side-by-side. Like cousins?"

"Don't start that again," Noah groaned.

"My dad *did* want you to marry into the family," Bethany teased. "Seriously now, open that present or I'll do it for you. The suspense is killing me, and I already know what's inside!"

Felix understood. As he tore away the paper, he thought of how tense it could be, waiting to see if someone would appreciate your gift or not. He didn't have to fake his enthusiasm. "A Colecovision Flashback!" Vintage video games made him even happier than action figures. "Thank you so much! I've never played a Colecovision game in my life. I can't wait!"

"I'm not even sure what that is," Bethany said, but she winked to show she was kidding. "You gotta have me over so we can play together."

"Yes!"

"Me next," Harold said from next to him. "Now that you're twenty-one, I thought it was time you finally got your own shaving kit. Oh darn! I let it slip!"

Felix laughed and took the small package from him. It wasn't a shaving kit, and as he peeled away the paper, his pulse quickened when he saw Japanese characters on a cardboard box. Or maybe the increased heartbeat was due to Harold draping his arm over the back of Felix's chair, their bodies touching in the most superficial way. He leaned back, increasing the physical contact, and forced himself to focus on the gift.

"Sailor Moooooon!" Felix sang when the paper fell away to reveal an action figure. The really nice kind imported from Japan. "This is perfect! They've actually made a few different versions of her. I'm glad you didn't get the one from—"

"*Sailor Moon Crystal*?" Harold said. "The newer animation style wouldn't have matched your Tuxedo Mask figure."

"How did you know?"

Harold winked. "I did my research."

Swoon! "Does this mean you'll watch the show with me?"

Harold snorted. "Not a chance. I do like the different faces she comes with, especially the crying one." He leaned closer and pointed through the clear transparent window, heat radiating off his body. He always smelled so good. "Does the cat do anything? I wasn't sure if it's articulated or just PVC."

"That's Luna, and yes, she's a little figure in her own right."

"I have no idea what they're saying," Bethany said. "Do you?"

Noah's answer was a brusque, "Nope."

Felix looked up and noticed the way his boyfriend's arms were crossed. Noah quickly dropped them again and said, "Ready for some games? Or do you want more cake?" He sounded fine actually. It *was* really loud in here—a bar stuffed full of bleeping video game cabinets. He was probably just trying to make himself heard.

"Let's go play, you guys," Felix said. "There's no way I can use all these tokens by myself. Well, I *could*, but I don't want to."

"Someone should watch over our stuff," Noah said. "Harold, do you mind?"

"Not at all!" Harold lifted his arm off the chair and rubbed Felix on the back with a strong hand. "Have fun, kiddo."

"Thanks!"

Bethany was more interested in playing pinball, so Felix poured tokens into her cupped palms. Then he and Noah walked toward the *Street Fighter II* cabinet, one of Felix's least favorite games, but it held special significance since it was the first they had ever played together.

"Are there more of those Sailor Moon figures?" Noah asked.

"Yeah! They make all the Sailor Scouts."

"Just let me know which ones you want and I'll buy them for you."

This confused him. Felix's birthday had already been extravagant, especially considering how tight money was. Noah had given him a big present earlier in the day, the latest iPad. Those weren't cheap. Maybe he was worried that Felix didn't like it. "I *love* the iPad. You know I've always wanted one. That's already enough. Besides, I don't need to start a new collection. I can handle two of anything, but once it's three, I'll lose control and need to buy them all."

"Then I'll watch the show with you," Noah said. "The one Harold doesn't want to see."

"Really?"

"Really."

"Okay!"

That was a better present, since it wouldn't cost them money, and it meant time spent together. Noah was tense as they played *Street Fighter*, slamming the buttons without mercy. He won. This seemed to make him feel a little better, because when the game was over he looked at Felix and smiled.

"Let's go play something else."

He grabbed Felix's hand and dragged him away, matching his appetite for games. An hour went by. And then another. For the first time ever, it was Felix who said he needed a break. And more of that cake.

"Sounds good," Noah said. "I'm sure Harold would like to play some games now."

He didn't seem that interested when they returned to the table, but Noah was insistent.

"Go!" he said. "It's a barcade. You can't just sit there and drink. You have to play too."

"All right, all right," Harold said as he rose. "Either of you want to come with me?"

"Nuh-uh." Noah answered for them both. "Bethany is getting hit on by a creepy guy. He keeps adjusting himself. Maybe you could bail her out. Say you want to play a racing game together or something."

"I'm on it." Harold ambled away, leaving them alone.

"Are you okay?" Felix asked.

"Why wouldn't I be?" Noah replied.

That was a non-answer if he'd ever heard one. Felix was worried. And detected a theme. Noah was feeling competitive about gift-giving and had now sent Harold elsewhere. If he had noticed Felix's crush or whatever it was… His stomach twisted up. He couldn't help how he felt toward Harold, but he could try to do more to hide it.

"I love you," he blurted out.

Noah stopped cutting the cake and looked surprised.

"It's been an amazing birthday," Felix said, wanting the declaration to sound more natural. "Thank you for everything."

"You're welcome," Noah said, his posture relaxing. He resumed his work. "I'm going to regret eating so much tomorrow."

"I'm not," Felix said. "Make it a big slice."

For the rest of the evening, Felix made sure to focus on him. Harold and Bethany seemed to have found common ground anyway, because when they returned to the table, they were having an animated conversation about dating and relationships. Felix tried not to tune in much, but he couldn't help it when he heard her ask a certain question.

"You're not looking for love?"

"I've already found it," Harold answered. "A few times. That doesn't mean I want to date anyone. I consider myself more of an impartial observer."

They blinked at each other before squealing with laughter. Then they went to the bar for more drinks. Felix had barely touched the one beer he had ordered with his new privileges. Age didn't make him a drinker, it would seem. Noah stayed sober too, which was probably for the best.

An hour later, they were standing outside the barcade and saying goodbye. Harold and Bethany had decided to share an Uber, which hadn't arrived yet.

"Text me when you're both home and safe," Felix told them. "Thanks again for my presents!"

"You're welcome," Harold said, stumbling over to him. "I hope you had a good birthday."

He threw his arms around Felix, who tried to pull away. This was a mistake. Harold treated it like a game and wouldn't let him go, no matter how much he tried to wiggle free.

"Let me go," Felix murmured. He didn't want to say it louder and give Noah an excuse to intervene.

"No way," Harold said. "Birthday hugs last extra long. Didn't anyone ever tell you that?"

"Seriously!" he hissed.

"Why?" Harold didn't let go, but he did pull back enough to make eye contact. He seemed to recognize what was there, his mouth starting to twitch with a smile. Then he looked in Noah's direction and grew somber. "Sorry," he said, voice low. "I didn't realize this went both ways."

He finally released Felix and lurched over to where Noah stood.

"Look at this handsome son of a bitch," Harold said, grabbing Noah in a hug that didn't last nearly as long. When it finished, Harold had his arm around Noah and used it to steer him back over to Felix. "Nobody could give you a better present than this," he said, reaching out to take Felix's hand. He made it connect with Noah's. Once Felix was holding hands with his boyfriend, Harold stepped back, looking satisfied. "You're both lucky," he said. Then he became distracted. "And so are we, Bethany, because that's our ride."

Felix watched them pile into a car, waiting for Harold to look at him again. He didn't. Even when Bethany rolled down one of the windows and waved, Harold kept his head turned away.

"Ready to go?" Noah asked, hand squeezing his.

"Yeah," Felix said with a lump in his throat. "Take me home."

Sorry. I didn't realize this went both ways.

As he got ready for bed, Felix played these words over and over in his mind. He was sure they meant that Harold had feelings for him too. He couldn't find any other interpretation, but he tried his best anyway, because this changed everything. A one-way crush he could deal with. Knowing that he had a choice, that someone else was willing to love him back, was tempting. Felix didn't want to be tempted. He didn't want to have an affair. But what if this became more than he could resist?

"Why are you still looking at your phone?" Noah asked when he walked into the room.

"They haven't texted to say they've made it home," Felix said, sitting on the edge of the mattress.

"So? They probably passed out."

"I know Bethany didn't. She texted, and when I asked who was dropped off first, she said Harold."

"So it's Harold you're waiting to hear from, not both of them."

"Huh?" Felix glanced over his shoulder to see that Noah had unbuttoned his shirt and was stripping it off. "Yeah. Sorry."

"Come to bed. I'm sure he's fine."

"Okay." Felix stood and turned around. "Hey, does he share his location with you? Didn't you say all the escorts have to when they're working?"

"He's not with a client."

"But I thought he might always share it with you anyway."

Noah glowered at him. "Can we just drop it and get some sleep?"

"Please? I'll worry."

"Fine!" Noah grabbed his phone from the nightstand and turned his back to him.

When he spun around again, he was brandishing the screen. Felix saw a map and a blue dot that was on the correct street. Harold was home. Now all Felix had to worry about was his boyfriend's grumpy demeanor.

"I'm sorry," Felix said.

Noah scowled. "Are you admitting it?"

"Admitting what?"

"Never mind." Noah pulled down his jeans and kicked them off. He left his underwear on, which was unusual. He always slept nude, ever since the first time Felix had asked him to. "I'm not going to ruin another birthday. We'll talk about it tomorrow."

"I know what you're thinking," Felix said, his voice beginning to tremble, "and there's nothing to discuss."

"Really?" Noah stormed from the room. When he returned, he was holding a little red book. "If there's nothing to talk about, then what's this?"

"My diary," Felix said, rushing over and trying to snatch it away. Noah held the book above his head and out of reach. "You're not supposed to read that!"

"Then you shouldn't leave it lying around!" Noah shouted.

"I trusted you not to read it!" Felix yelled back.

"I needed a gift idea for your birthday!"

Oh. The fight went out of Felix. He was never much for arguing. Besides, he could be as offended as he wanted, but it didn't change the fact that he was the guilty one. He moved close to Noah, not liking when they fought, and grabbed on. Comforting arms wrapped around him as Noah's voice rumbled against his ear.

"I thought you were leaving your diary out because there was a hint in there for me."

"That sounds like something I would do," he admitted. "I'm really sorry. I never meant to hurt you."

Noah was quiet. He didn't respond immediately. Then he gently moved Felix away and sat on the edge of the bed. "I need you to be honest. Even if it hurts me."

"Of course," Felix said, sitting next to him.

"How far has this gone? Are you two..."

"No! We haven't done anything, I swear!"

Noah looked over at him. "You aren't just saying that because he called it off."

Felix stared. "I'm confused. I don't know what you're talking about."

"Tonight. Right before we left. Harold was acting weird. It was like he was giving you back to me."

Felix sighed. "That's not what happened. When he was

hugging me, he finally figured out that I... like him. Right after is when he made us hold hands. I didn't cheat. I'd never do that to you, and Harold would never allow that. I think he likes me back, but it doesn't matter, because nothing will come of it."

"It matters to me," Noah said, voice strained. "I don't want you to love him."

"Why not?" Felix shot back. "You love him. I've put up with it since we first met. How is this any different?"

"Because that happened before we got together. How would you feel if I fell in love with some other guy? Someone new."

"It would hurt," Felix admitted.

"Damn right it would." Noah clenched his jaw and shook his head. "What are we going to do?"

"I'll get over it somehow," Felix said. "I'll stop having feelings for him."

"It doesn't work that way."

"Then I'll stop being his friend." His heart ached at the thought, but he forced himself to press on. "I'll do whatever it takes not to lose you. Do you know what my birthday wish was? When I blew out the candles, I wished that we would always be together."

"You're not supposed to tell anyone what you wished for," Noah said glumly. "Or it won't come true."

"I'm not worried. I'll never leave you. You'll have to be the one to break up with me." Felix crossed his arms over his chest. "I *know* we're supposed to be together. You'll have to physically throw me out before I'll go anywhere. Even that won't work. I'll just wait until you open the door to get your mail or whatever, and when you do, I'll sneak back inside."

Noah laughed. "You're ridiculous."

"I'm not kidding!"

"I know you're not. That's what makes it so funny. Come here."

Noah grabbed his shoulder and flopped backwards, taking Felix with him. Together they stared up at the ceiling, not speaking a word until Noah rolled over to face him. "It's not like I don't get it."

Felix rolled over too. "He's fun to be around."

"He is," Noah said. "Harold used to be my sanctuary. I'd go over to his place, and once I was there with him, nothing else in the world seemed to matter. Do you guys ever get stoned?"

"I don't know how to inhale. He offered to make me edibles sometime, but I'm nervous."

Noah swallowed. "And you've never kissed?"

"I would tell you if we had. Nothing like that has happened. Just hugs." Felix tried a smile. "Why? Is he a good kisser?"

"Terrible," Noah said. "I get complaints from his clients all the time. I'm always having to give them partial refunds. It's a mixture of bad breath and him being careless with his teeth."

"Really?"

"No. Not really. He's not very big though."

"Oh. I thought all escorts had to be."

"It helps, but Harold has everything else going for him."

"He *is* very handsome," Felix said, quickly adding, "but so are you."

"You're sweet," Noah said, then he sighed. "So is he. I shouldn't try to talk trash about him. It doesn't matter that he's not hung. Harold is a good guy. He's down to earth, caring, and adorably goofy. I'm not going to be mad at you for recognizing that, or for finding it attractive, but please *please* don't cheat on me. I had enough of that with Ryan."

"I won't," Felix said. "I promise. I'm sorry that I hurt you at all."

Noah reached out to toy with his hair. "If anything, I hurt myself by making a big deal out of it instead of talking to you. Did you have a good birthday anyway?"

"The best," Felix said, scooting closer. "I got everything I wanted. Except..."

"Except?"

"I wish I had gotten a goodnight kiss."

Noah smiled. Then he rolled over onto Felix and gave him more than just a simple kiss.

Dear Diary,

I love my boyfriend. Let me make that absolutely clear. I'm crazy about Noah and have been from the first time I saw him. I never told you how we met, did I? I was waiting tables at my glorious job, and while I was standing at my station and entering an order, I saw him walk into the restaurant. His thick red hair caught my attention first. That, and how tall he was. I guess most people are tall compared to me, but with the light behind him he looked like... like a torch! Or a majestic candle? Meh. I wish I could describe him without it sounding dumb. Trust me, it was a moment to remember. The breath caught in my throat, and I started praying that he would be seated in my section. And he was! Noah seemed kind of troubled at the time. I'm not sure if we even spoke. His boss was with him and doing all the talking. I didn't have a good reason to write my phone number on his receipt. I just had this feeling, like I knew he was the one. And I really wanted to see him smile. That came later, along with everything else. I've never met anyone so kind or generous. I love him. I love you, Noah, if you're reading this. I always will. Always always always!

What to do about Harold? That became the ongoing predicament. Felix didn't have to debate if they would continue being friends or not. The decision was made for him. By Harold. No matter how many texts Felix sent him, they weren't answered. Calls didn't work either. After two weeks of this, Felix decided to drive over to his house. Harold was either out or he refused to answer the door. He was no longer stopping by their apartment either. Determined nonetheless, Felix tried asking his boyfriend for help.

"Can you locate Harold with your phone again?"

Noah was at his desk, as always. Rather than inquire about the reason behind this request, he simply said, "Maybe we should give him his space. I think that's best for all of us. Don't you?"

"No," Felix said before he left the room.

Noah didn't follow him or argue the point. Probably because he knew he was wrong. Harold was too. They *had* to know this wasn't right. Otherwise it wouldn't feel so terrible. It downright hurt at times. Felix wanted to be around Harold again. Simple as that. He didn't need someone to talk to about his toys or the shows he loved. He could find that online. Felix could cook on his own or not at all. None of that mattered. He *liked* Harold. With some people, being around them was the best part. What happened while in their presence was immaterial. He refused to believe that Noah didn't feel the same way. They had both lost someone special, but only one of them was acknowledging how that felt.

Felix didn't press the point. Aside from his huffy response in the office, there wasn't any tension over the subject. Mostly because he knew that, very soon, they would all be in the same room again. The official launch of the new Gentlemen's Agreement Club was this weekend, and to celebrate, Marcello was throwing a party. He was no longer involved in the business, but as Noah put it: "The GAC is his legacy, and he wants to see it succeed." Every employee was expected to be there. As co-owner of the company, Harold couldn't worm his way out of it.

Although, as the evening neared, Felix thought of a number of viable excuses. Food poisoning, for instance. Harold might even self-induce it by drinking old milk and send them a congratulatory video message in between bouts of puking. If that happened, at least Felix would know that he was home. He would drive over there, mop the sweat off Harold's brow, and make him talk. That would upset Noah, but Felix refused to let matters end this way.

The party was being held at Marcello's house, although not in the ballroom. Felix had thought Noah was kidding about this until they drove to West Lake Hills, where many of the houses were gigantic. The hills were no joke either. By the time they parked, Felix felt like he had just gotten off a rollercoaster, but any motion sickness he experienced was forgotten as he stared in disbelief at a house so huge that he had to turn his head just to take it all in.

"I've seen bigger," Noah said when he noticed Felix's awe.

"Really?"

"No. Not really. Wait until you see the inside."

When he did, Felix wasn't impressed. Before he had moved in with Noah, his mother had been sleeping on the couch so he and his sister could each have a private bedroom. So yes, the immense rooms, many of which seemed to serve little practical purpose, were impressive. But they also seemed excessive.

"If this business takes off," Noah said, "I'll buy you a house like this."

"No thanks," Felix said, shooting him a smile. "I prefer the apartment."

Noah looked surprised before he put an arm around Felix and pulled him close. "Just one of the many reasons why I love you."

"I love you more."

They rounded a corner and entered a living room. This too felt unnecessarily spacious, even when populated by so many people. The far wall consisted mostly of windows, which looked out on a patio, pool, and a stunning view of Austin's skyline. An open kitchen was to their left, filled with mingling bodies.

"Ah, the man of the hour!" A voice boomed. The person it belonged to was just as boisterous. Marcello was large in size and personality. Charming too. He had good reason to focus on Noah, but he generously put on a big show when noticing Felix, gasping as if impressed. "Don't you look handsome?" Marcello said, taking his hand. "My goodness, I could just gobble you up. Maybe I will. The night is still young!"

Before he knew what was happening, Felix was twirled around. He nearly toppled over until Marcello caught him, Felix's back ending up against his chest.

"It's the ears that drive me wild," Marcello purred. "Does your boyfriend ever nibble on them? Would you mind if I do?"

"I'll take him back now," Noah said with a wry grin. "If you don't mind." He held out a hand.

Felix accepted it and was pulled into another set of arms. "A guy could get used to this!" he breathed. Even though it was pure flattery, he had to admit it worked. Felix felt more desirable now. He was trying extra hard tonight too. His hair was back to being black, which matched the dress shirt he wore. As he stepped aside so Marcello and Noah could talk business, he noticed how many handsome faces were in the crowd. Marcello could have any of them—have anything he desired—which made it all the more gratifying that he had paid attention to Felix at all.

Not everyone here was generically attractive, thank goodness. Felix saw plenty of wrinkles, or cheeks that were either chubby or gaunt. Anyone under a certain age he assumed was an escort. The rest must have been clients, and there were plenty of them. The one person he didn't see was Harold, but he had to be here somewhere.

"I'm going to mingle," he said.

"Don't stray too far," Noah replied.

"You'll be fine," Marcello chimed in. "If you get lost, just ask someone to show you to my bedroom."

"And what's he supposed to do there?" Noah asked him, sounding defensive.

"It's simply the room with the most cameras installed," Marcello said innocently. "That way we'll have an easier time spotting him on the security monitors."

Felix laughed and wandered off. He went first to the kitchen. He wasn't thirsty, but he understood that mingling was impossible without a drink. Once he had a glass filled with sparkling water, he began his search. The younger guys ignored him completely, aside from mild curiosity. Some of the older men made extended eye contact. A few even said hello. Felix always said hello back and smiled but never stopped moving. Not until he went outside and noticed Harold. He was to the far right of the pool, at the very edge of the patio where the grass began, speaking to a pair of middle-aged men. He wore a burgundy suit, the first two buttons of his white dress shirt undone. He looked great, of course, but that's not what mattered to Felix. What he wanted more than anything was to hear his voice.

Harold's eyes darted over to him instinctually. No, scratch that, he must have been regularly checking the door to the house, just in case of this very situation, because when he noticed Felix, there was no emotional reaction. All he did was casually angle his body away until his back was mostly turned. Message received.

And ignored. Felix walked toward him, stopping a few times to rethink his strategy.

"*Can we talk? Please?*" would surely be met with, "*I'm busy right now, sorry.*"

"*Marcello sent me for you,*" would get Harold's attention, but it was also a lie. So was, "*I'm pregnant with your child!*" Although that would be a fun line to deliver. No, nothing would do now except for a plea from one heart to another.

"Excuse me, sorry," Felix said as he interrupted the ongoing conversation, directing his apology to the two men. Then he turned to Harold. "I care about you enough not to give up, and I'm hoping you care enough about me to talk. I've been waiting weeks for this chance. Please don't make me wait any longer."

Harold seemed to be searching for an excuse. Then he sighed. "Sorry, guys. I'll catch up with you later, okay?" His attention remained on the two men as they walked away, as if Harold didn't want to look at him at all.

Felix refused to say or do anything until he did. When those brown eyes finally met his, they softened.

"I miss you," Felix said.

"I was drunk on your birthday," Harold replied. "I shouldn't have said what I did."

"Does that make it untrue?"

Harold took a deep breath and looked off into the distance. "We can't do this."

"I don't understand. We haven't done anything."

Harold made eye contact again, expression intense. "Don't you want to?"

Felix wasn't sure how to answer. He wanted a lot of things, but that didn't mean they were going to happen.

Harold moved close until he was standing in Felix's personal space. "Aren't you tempted?"

The cologne, the tan skin of his strong neck, and those perfectly shaped lips... "Yes," Felix admitted.

Harold stepped back, farther away than he had been originally. "That's why. There will come a time when Noah is too busy, or maybe you guys are fighting, or we're too drunk or high. We'll be too weak to resist, and it'll ruin everything. The business, what little respect Noah still has for me, and worst of all, the relationship you two have together. I'm not worth it. Trust me. The fantasy is better than the reality."

"Aren't you tempted sometimes with Noah?" Felix shot back. "Hasn't it always been that way? For both of you. But you were still willing to be friends and business partners. How is this any different?"

"Yes, I've been tempted," Harold said. "You don't know the thoughts that have run through my mind. Or the things I've said to him."

Felix's stomach sank. "What do you mean?"

"When I broke up with Ruben. Do you remember him? He's one of the guys you talked to when Noah was trying to show you the good side of this business."

Felix had just found out that Noah was an escort, which had torn him up inside. They had nearly broken up over it. Noah pleaded with Felix to meet with him one more time, but not so they could talk alone. Two others had been there, an escort and a client. Both explained how they benefited from the arrangement they had together and with others. Those conversations had saved his relationship with Noah. "I remember him."

"After Ruben and I broke up, I went over to your place. You were there, and after you left, I told Noah I was single again. More than that. I made sure he knew that he could have me. I offered myself to him."

Pain and disbelief made it hard to think, but he managed a question anyway. "Did something happen?"

Harold shrugged. "It could have. What do you think Noah would have done if I had kissed him? Think he would have kissed me back? Would you? What if I begged? Or cried?"

Felix didn't know how he would react to these scenarios. Just trying to imagine them had him feeling conflicted.

"That's why we can't do this," Harold said, recognizing his uncertainty. "No matter how strong we are, the other person is always going to wonder. You can't come over to my place on your own now without making Noah suspicious. No matter how much he trusts you, he'll still have his doubts. Do you want to put him through that?"

"No," Felix admitted.

"Good. Neither do I."

"So this is it?" Felix's lip started to tremble.

Harold noticed. "Oh geez. Please don't do that. I can't take it."

"I love you," Felix said. They were the magic words that always fixed problems in stories like this, and right now, they were all he had left.

"That doesn't make it okay," Harold said. "The one thing you and I will always have in common is that we both love Noah. Right?"

Felix sniffed and nodded.

"Then we'll do this for him. You're going to pull yourself together, because this is his day. We're both going to smile and clap when Marcello gives his big speech praising everything Noah has accomplished. That's what he deserves. After all the work he's done, the last thing he needs is for us to ruin it by being selfish. Today will be good practice."

"For what?"

"For how it's going to be from now on. Smile when it hurts. I promise it only gets easier."

Harold's attention moved beyond Felix. He spotted someone, his teeth flashing as he gave an upward nod. Then he walked away, his hand catching Felix's for a brief second as he passed. Harold squeezed his fingers before letting go. Then he was gone.

As the party continued, Felix struggled to figure out where he belonged. Noah was in constant demand from both clients and escorts, who had questions about how the new system worked. Felix couldn't really contribute to those conversations. He felt increasingly awkward, standing silently at his side, so he wandered off again. That wasn't good either. Men kept stopping him to ask what services he offered. They didn't necessarily mean sex, since that was no longer the default. Some wanted to know if he could take care of their lawn, reorganize their home, and all sorts of requests. On one hand, the new business model was clearly a hit, which made him happy for Noah. On the other, Felix was tired of explaining that he wasn't part of the system.

He tried to find empty places to occupy where he wouldn't be disturbed. This meant standing outside the crowds. He liked people-watching, but even this failed to comfort him, since he kept catching glimpses of Harold. Being so close to him, and yet so distant in other ways, became unbearable so Felix decided to actually go and look for Marcello's bedroom. Why not? He found it with relative ease. So he thought. After sitting on the bed and glancing around, he noticed the lack of personal items. The decorations were nice, but the room didn't seem lived in. He tried again and found other bedrooms with the same result.

He was much deeper in the house when he finally discovered a room that he dismissed immediately due to its small size. Although the comforter was slightly crinkled, implying the bed had been used recently, and the narrow desk against one wall held knickknacks that weren't purely decorative. This couldn't be Marcello's bedroom though. Someone who owned a mansion would surely choose a grander space. This room probably belonged to the butler. One who had great taste in art and a preference for male beauty. Felix was staring at the paintings on the walls when he realized he hadn't seen a butler. Or any sort of serving staff, except for a bartender who probably wasn't a live-in employee. Felix decided to check the desk for further clues. Everything on it was old. An inkwell and pen, a locket, a ticking wind-up clock, and a leather portfolio with handwritten notes sticking out of it. He was reaching for this last item when a familiar voice nearly gave him a heart attack.

"Oh, I don't think you're quite ready for that," Marcello said. "Come to think of it, neither am I."

"Sorry," Felix said, yanking his hand away as if he'd been caught stealing. "I was only curious."

"Then it's a good thing you're not a cat," Marcello said. "Otherwise, you know what I'd have to do."

He was smiling, but somehow, that only made him scarier.

"Is this your room?" Felix stammered.

Marcello cocked his head. "What makes you think that?"

"What you said. About the cameras. You weren't kidding, were you?"

"I don't know if I've ever joked about anything in my life," Marcello replied. "Although people do tend to laugh quite a bit in my presence. I assumed it was that way for everyone."

Felix couldn't help laughing. Out of nervousness mostly.

"How kind of you to prove me right," Marcello said. "Would you mind accompanying me on a stroll? Perhaps together we can find our way back to the others."

"Sure," Felix said. He felt relieved when they were back in the hall and he was still alive. For all he knew, Marcello might be some sort of dangerous mobster. Like a gay version of *The Godfather*. "I'm really sorry. I didn't mean to snoop. Okay, I did, but I didn't mean any harm."

"Think nothing of it and I'll endeavor to do the same." Marcello shut the bedroom door firmly behind him. "Our feet can take us strange places when our minds are troubled."

"That's exactly how I was feeling," Felix said. "It's been a strange day."

"A very successful one for Noah, I'm pleased to report. Financially, anyway. The only obstacle I see in his path to success is an unwilling business partner. Perhaps I should offer to buy Harold out, remove him from the equation entirely."

"No!" Felix said, hating the idea. "There has to be another way."

"I fail to recognize what it might be. Mr. Franklin is seemingly immune to my charm, and he seems to have an allergic reaction to my wisdom, whenever I try to share it." Marcello's tones were playful. "I suppose we could attempt to hypnotize Harold into accepting more responsibility. Do you have any experience with brainwashing?"

"No," Felix said with a titter. "I'm willing to try anyway. They need to be together." Felix stumbled before he caught himself, barely noticing, because his head had filled with a revelation so powerful that it made him dizzy. And sad. Harold and Noah...

Together. It was the one solution that felt right. "I'm the one who needs to go."

"I didn't realize you had a stake in this enterprise." Marcello made a grumbling sound. "My old bones need a rest, and if I'm not mistaken, you're not quite ready to return yet either. I believe there is somewhere we can sit nearby, if you are amenable."

"Oh. Okay."

They rounded a corner. Marcello opened a door, and like magic they were outside. The balcony was small, but the view it offered was massive. The city skyline was to their left, if they chose to look that way. Mother Nature was a tough act to beat though. Directly before them were rolling hills illuminated by a half moon and sparkling stars, and this is what captivated his attention.

"Can I move in with you?" Felix asked. Then he sighed. "I shouldn't joke. I'll need to find a new place soon."

"What a lovely idea! Although…." Marcello settled into one of the wooden patio chairs and gestured for Felix to do the same. Together they stared out over the alluring expanse ahead of them. "I don't believe Noah would feel quite as successful without you in his life. Or will he be moving in as well?"

"No." Felix shook his head. "Don't worry. He won't be alone."

"I see. Well. This does sound serious. I'll admit I'm puzzled. The two of you seem to get along so splendidly. What brought about this decision?"

A lack of alternatives. This was the only way he could see it working. Harold and Noah could finally be together, and Felix would… He didn't know yet. He hadn't thought that far ahead. All he knew was that it felt right. Somehow. "They say when you love something, you have to let it go."

"What nonsense," Marcello said, shaking his jowls. "In my experience, when you let something go it falls to the ground and is likely to break. Is that what you want?"

"No, but—"

"Are you happy?" Marcello interrupted. "We all have our moments, but none are more truthful or telling than when we go to bed each evening. When your head touches the pillow, are you filled with warm contentment, no matter how weary you might be from the day? Because if you are happy, I feel it's my duty to inform you of how rare that is."

"I usually am," Felix admitted.

"I see," Marcello said. And he must have, because he revealed Felix's thoughts and feelings with the next words he spoke. "And yet, you feel it's worth sacrificing your happiness because there is someone else Noah could be with instead. Harold, if I'm not mistaken."

"Yes!" he said, not hiding his surprise. "How did you know?"

"By paying attention." Marcello pointed to the distant hills. "The leaves on those trees are green. I didn't need anyone to tell me that. I simply observed."

Felix groaned. "Are we that obvious? Does everyone know?"

"Not necessarily. I can also name the various species of trees that inhabit those hills, but only because I've had the repeated benefit of sitting here while contemplating their nature. The same could be said of Noah, and to a greater extent, Harold. I've been observing him in particular for many years, and I can confirm that his feelings for Noah are anything but superficial. I don't think there's anyone he's loved more, although to my surprise, Noah now has competition. Funny how it used to be the other way around. As far as Harold was concerned, *you* were the competition."

"It's a mess," Felix agreed.

"Love always is."

Felix shook his head. "I don't know if it's true love though. It might be, but I'm not sure. I only know that I care about Harold. A lot. And that I want him to be happy, no matter what it takes."

"If that isn't true love, then it's something better. I fail to see the issue."

"Harold is worried that if we keep being friends, we'll give in to temptation and cheat."

"That does seem likely, yes." Marcello said this matter-of-factly, but not like it was a problem.

"I don't want Noah to get hurt."

"No, definitely not."

Felix slumped into his chair. "Then it's hopeless."

"I wouldn't say that." Marcello shifted his weight to consider him. "Tell me, are you familiar with the legend of Ben and Tim?"

"Is that a TV show?"

"No, but it will be a movie someday. That wouldn't be a bad title actually, although it wouldn't be fair to Jace. No, I was thinking of calling it *The Many Loves of Benjamin Bentley*."

Felix made a face. "Isn't that a movie with Brad Pitt?"

"Is it?"

"I think so. He plays an old dude who ages backward or something like that."

Marcello swore under his breath. "Perhaps it is too similar. The title isn't important. Nor is the movie. Ben is a real person, and while his story is burdened with many tragedies, I feel there is one that goes unrecognized. Ben had two great loves in his life, and rather than embracing that fact, he tortured himself over which man was right for him."

"But you said they were both perfect."

"Indeed, I did. Why then didn't he choose them both?"

Felix shrugged. "I don't know. I guess the two other guys would have to be okay with that."

"A valid point," Marcello said musingly. "For it to work, Tim and Jace would have needed to love each other. But who's to say they wouldn't have learned to, had their hearts been willing?"

Felix's mouth opened. Then it closed again.

"It's like watching a fish swallow delicious bait," Marcello said, sounding amused. "What a shame that epiphanies don't have an accompanying flavor, although perhaps I can manage that too, with enough practice."

Felix barely heard him. His mind was still reeling with possibilities. Noah, Harold, and him. Together. All at once. "Would that work?"

"It stands as much chance as any relationship," Marcello said, "although the answer I'm offering comes with its own questions. I believe you and Noah experienced some strain early on in your relationship, due to the complexities of his work."

Oh. Right. Harold was an escort. A job he enjoyed so much that he might not be willing to give it up.

"Marriage is of great importance to some people," Marcello continued, "and despite the progress that has been made, the law remains strictly binary with little chance of amendment. In this country anyway. Then again, I've always felt that any law which fails to serve the interest of its people deserves to be broken."

A three-way marriage? Felix couldn't imagine that far along. He could barely think at all!

"Forgive me," Marcello said. "I do have the habit of speaking when other people are weary of listening. I brought you out here for peace and quiet, and now I intend to give it to you. When you're ready to return to the party, call Noah. I'll see that he comes to escort you, if you'll pardon the term. He knows the way. We wouldn't want you getting lost again."

"Thank you," Felix managed, meaning more than just the offer.

"Don't thank me yet," Marcello said, rising and patting him on the shoulder. "Your journey has just begun. However, I think you'll find it preferable to the sort of ending you were contemplating."

That was for sure. Felix didn't know what would happen, or if it even could, but he no longer felt sad. Instead, he was filled with a mad sort of hope.

Felix was quiet as he and Noah began the ride home. So many thoughts and concerns were racing through his mind that he was unable to settle on any for long. His opinion changed back and forth, almost without reason. A three-way relationship! Did he know Harold well enough to attempt such a thing? Felix might have thought so previously, but one revelation tonight had cast doubt on that, and he needed to confront it. Gently.

"I talked to Harold."

Noah tensed behind the wheel but kept his attention on the road. "I figured you would."

"I'm surprised you didn't."

"He congratulated me."

"That's it?" Felix frowned. "You used to be inseparable. Don't you miss him?"

Noah shrugged. "We still talk. We're business partners."

"You know what I mean."

"Yes."

"Yes, you miss him, or yes, you know what I mean?"

The truck came to a stop at a red light. They were still outside Austin. All around them were woods and drainage ditches. No cross traffic could be seen, and yet, they were stuck there despite being the only vehicle at the intersection. This seemed to irritate Noah, judging from the way his knuckles turned white on the steering wheel. "I miss him," he said at last.

"Were you ever tempted?" Felix asked. "Never mind. That's not a fair question. Everyone has thoughts. Even I did. Tonight."

Noah looked over at him. "When Marcello wanted to nibble on your ears?" The humor was forced. Noah wasn't smiling. His gaze was hard. "Or did someone else tempt you?"

"Harold thinks we shouldn't be friends because of that temptation," Felix pressed on, "but I told him that you guys did fine. Didn't you? Did you ever feel like he crossed a line?"

"How?"

"I don't know. Maybe he offered to take my place."

Noah's brow knitted together. He returned his attention to the road, but he didn't say anything. Nor did the truck move when the light changed.

"It's green," Felix said.

Noah finally pushed down on the accelerator. They didn't make it far. He pulled the truck over to the side of the road, put it in park, and turned to face Felix. "Did he offer to take *my* place? Is that what you're telling me?"

"No! He kept saying we couldn't even be friends. But he also claimed that, after you and I got together, he made a move or something."

Noah seemed genuinely confused. "Huh?"

"After he broke up with Ruben."

Noah closed his eyes and exhaled in relief. "Oh, that!"

"So it's true," Felix said, his voice warbling. "He tried to steal you away."

Noah shook his head. "I don't think that was his intention. He only wanted me to know that if it didn't work out between you and me, he would be there."

"In a supportive friend kind of way?"

Noah winced. "No. More than that. He seemed heartbroken and wanted to know if he ever stood a chance, no matter how far in the future. That was my impression. At the time, I thought it was sweet."

"It sounds a lot nicer the way you explain it," Felix said. "And besides that? Did it come up again or did he ever try anything?"

"No," Noah said instantly. "He never tried to kiss me or talk me out of loving you. There *are* little moments, like when he catches me checking him out, he might flex or something to show off."

"I felt his biceps," Felix confessed. "Does that count as cheating?"

"No, and he already told me about that. He thought it was funny."

"I thought it was hot." Felix was deliberately testing the waters.

"Are you saying you want me to start working out?"

"No. I like you the way you are. And I like him the way he is."

Noah's eyes searched his. Then he put the car in drive and resumed their trip. "I trust him," he said. "And I trust you. If you want to be his friend, that's fine with me."

Felix wanted more than that. He just didn't know how to say it.

Things didn't go back to the way they used to be. Nor did they move forward. Harold still didn't answer his texts or calls. Noah seemed content to let distance between them grow.

"You can't force these things," he said, when Felix asked him to intervene.

Maybe not, but he also refused to give up. Hope hadn't run its course. Felix had a potential solution, but he dared not voice it yet. The way things stood now, he had too much to lose. He was already in a relationship with Noah. If his boyfriend wasn't open to the idea, then Noah might assume that Felix was no longer happy with him. Wasn't that the truth though? Wasn't he trying to add a second boyfriend to his life because the first was no longer enough?

The thought troubled him. He still loved Noah and cherished the time they got to spend together. He simply saw a way for all of them to be even happier. This wasn't a selfish wish. Harold and Noah stood to benefit just as much as he did, if not more. He couldn't make this happen on his own though. There were many details he couldn't figure out. First and foremost, he wanted to know if Harold was even willing. It seemed safest to ask him first, since he wouldn't find the idea as threatening as Noah might. If only he would pick up the phone! Felix needed to send a message that couldn't be ignored.

That's when he had an idea. He searched online until he found a railway model of a house, and while the shape wasn't a perfect match, he was sure he could bring it closer with a little work. He poured every spare cent of his meager paycheck into the project, buying craft supplies and carefully altering the exterior of the house until it resembled the one Harold lived in. This meant driving down Harold's street not once but twice to take photos of every detail. The first time he forgot to include the rear of the house. The second time he hopped the fence while praying a gun-toting neighbor wouldn't notice and take the law into their own hands. He survived both scouting missions, and with the help of online tutorials, finished the project with a sense of satisfaction. He had successfully turned the model into a decent semblance of Harold's home.

The most important part came next. He had already bought a little figure that shared Harold's athletic build. Painting the tiny hair and clothing to match wasn't easy. Felix experimented on other figures first, messing them up badly until he switched to a finer paint brush. Then, with a trembling hand, he slowly transformed the figure into a man he missed so much that simply looking at the final result made his heart ache. Once the figure's paint job was dry, he took it, along with the two figures Harold had given him, and glued all three to stands. These he arranged by the front door. Harold and Noah were standing side-by-side. Felix was in front of them, like he was their child or something. That was okay. At least they looked like a family. Felix brought this to Harold's house—the real one—and left it in the same spot where their miniature selves were standing, the doorstep. The note he pinned beneath the model was short.

I think I found where we belong. All three of us.

Then he went home and waited. The hour grew late. Noah went to bed, but Felix remained in the living room. He left the TV off as he sat on the couch and waited. And waited. He was starting to despair when a text arrived on his phone.

It's beautiful. I only wish it was true.

Felix sent his reply. *Want to help make it that way?*

He stared at the screen, awaiting a response. Then his phone started to vibrate. Harold was calling. Felix didn't hesitate. Not even for a second. He answered.

The beer garden was a few blocks away from the Colorado River. Even though Felix and Noah were sitting outside, they couldn't see the river, or much of anything beyond a few trees and nearby apartment buildings. In fact, the outdoor space had very little in common with a garden. Felix was mildly disappointed in that. He'd been hoping for patches of flowers or even homegrown fruit and vegetables when choosing this location. Instead the so-called garden was filled with long communal benches and a dirt floor. The ambience might still improve. A band was setting up on a small stage, and once the sun set, the lights strung all around could be turned on. Maybe it was for the best that there were so few distractions right now, because what Felix really wanted was to talk to his boyfriend.

"What exactly are we doing here?" Noah asked him as he took in their surroundings.

"I thought it would be fun to try something new." Wasn't that the truth! "You don't like it?"

"I do," Noah said. "I thought you hated beer."

"Yeah, but it's supposed to be an acquired taste." Felix frowned at the drinks menu and its seemingly infinite options. "Now that I'm twenty-one, beer should start tasting better, right?"

"I don't think that's how it works," Noah said, sounding amused. "Try a radler. Or any kind of shandy. Those are fruity. You'll like them."

"Okay." Felix trusted his advice. Noah had been on a lot of dates. He was good at recognizing what people wanted and giving it to them. If only he could read minds so Felix wouldn't have to find a natural way to broach a very delicate subject. That's why he had chosen, for their date night, a location that involved drinking. He hoped it would loosen them both up. And it forced him to act sooner rather than later. If they got drunk and *then* talked, he wouldn't know if Noah's answers were honest or influenced by alcohol. One drink only. That's what he promised himself. By the end of it, his time was up.

"Do you know what you want to eat?" Noah asked. He always liked to order for them both.

Felix appreciated it. Usually. "I'm not hungry." His stomach was too upset with nerves for him to even consider food.

"Are you sure? I'll just get a salad then. I've been doing way too much stress eating lately."

"You look great," Felix said, experiencing a pang of doubt. Not about his boyfriend's appearance. Noah was gorgeous, as always. Was he really going to risk losing that? Seriously. Was he insane?

The waitress came and took their order, the drinks arriving

with impressive speed. He almost wished they hadn't. The clock was officially ticking.

"What do you think?" Noah asked after they clinked glasses and had taken sips.

"It's good!" Felix said. The beer was light and citrusy, like a creamy lemonade. "I feel so mature."

"You look it," Noah replied with bedroom eyes. "So… What are we doing after this?"

Going over to Harold's house. Or maybe going their separate ways. Please let it be the former and not the latter! "I thought we'd play it by ear."

"Really?" Noah said. "There isn't some movie you want to see? Guardians of the Justice League or another Star Trek prequel that reveals Bumblebee's secret origins?"

Felix stared. "There's so much wrong with that sentence that I don't know where to begin."

"It was a joke," Noah said. "Mostly. The less I know, the more you whisper into my ear while we're watching the movie. Which I like."

Felix's cheeks grew warm. Hot *and* romantic. He really was an idiot for wanting to rock the boat. Then he thought of Harold, who was sitting alone in his living room right now, waiting to hear how this conversation had gone. The same living room where he spent most of his nights alone. Except when he was working, of course. Maybe it was better to imagine him sitting alone during the day instead. That was probably more realistic.

"You sure you don't want something to eat?" Noah asked. "You're not used to drinking. It can hit you hard on an empty stomach."

Felix glanced down at his beer, surprised to find that it was already half empty. He looked up in a panic, which his boyfriend misinterpreted.

"Don't worry," Noah said. "I'll catch up with you." And with that, he chugged his beer until it was *below* the halfway point.

"Ha ha! Wow!" Felix sounded manic even to his own ears. He took another sip, then set aside his glass so he wouldn't succumb to more nervous drinking. "This is nice. I love spending time with you."

"I like it too," Noah said. "Maybe we should do this twice a week instead of once. I know you have school, and the occasional dinner shift, but if you started working for me instead..."

Uh oh! Noah was steering the subject in the wrong direction. Felix wanted to talk about love, not money.

"I'll think about it," he said quickly. "For now, let's just enjoy this moment, because not everyone is so lucky."

"That's true," Noah replied.

"I wish they were. Everyone should have what we do. When I think about certain people in particular, it makes me sad."

Noah raised an eyebrow. "Who?"

"I don't know. Harold, for instance."

"Oh," Noah said, not sounding surprised. "Your favorite subject as of late."

"I worry about him," Felix said. The words came from his heart. No more trying to be clever by staying two steps ahead. He wasn't good at it. Talking about feelings, that he could do! "Does he seem lonely to you?"

"In a way," Noah said. "Then again, he goes on more dates than we do, even though he's single, so..."

"Did you ever feel lonely when you were an escort?"

The waitress set down the salad between them at that very moment, and after an awkward pause, asked if there was anything else they needed. Once she was gone, they both started laughing.

"Nice timing," Noah teased. "The next time a police officer is around, try not to let it slip that I'm basically a pimp now."

Felix grinned at him before his expression grew serious. "Were you though?"

"Lonely?" Noah poked at his salad. "Yeah. Before I met you. If that's how Harold feels, he can find someone to date. In a more traditional sense."

"It's hard for an escort to find love, isn't it? Most people don't understand, or they get jealous."

"Sure, but in a city this size, there has to be someone out there open-minded enough. This is Harold Franklin we're talking about. He could be a convicted serial killer and people would still line up to get his phone number, once they notice those dimples."

"No kidding," Felix said with a titter. "So why doesn't he have someone?"

Noah was quiet. He took a few bites of his salad and chewed, but the only answer he came up with was, "I don't know."

"I have a theory," Felix said, leaning forward. "I think he never dates anyone because he's still hung up on you."

Noah snorted. "That didn't stop him from taking an interest in my boyfriend."

"I guess not. Maybe it helped that I'm so closely associated with you. We're practically extensions of each other now, don't you think?"

Noah smiled. "I've never thought about it that way, but sure. I wouldn't be complete without you."

"That could be how he feels. Maybe Harold isn't complete without you."

Noah set down his fork. Then he leaned back and sighed. "If Harold is lonely, or if he feels incomplete, he has other options. He lives in that house all by himself. He can get a roommate. Or a pet. I don't think the situation is as dramatic as you're making it out to be."

"Why didn't you do those things?" Felix challenged. "You said you were lonely before we met. The office was just an empty room back then. You could have rented it out, or better yet, filled it with cats. Oh my gosh! Could you imagine? Save that thought for later. For now, just answer my question. If you were lonely, why didn't you?"

Noah thought about it. "It wasn't that sort of loneliness. I already had a lot of people in my life. I was working seven days a week, and you know what that means. Most of my clients wanted to socialize before and after. So a roommate or a pet wouldn't have made a difference."

"But I did," Felix said.

Noah nodded. "Yeah. You sure did."

"I think that's what Harold needs. From us."

Noah blinked a few times. "What are you saying?"

"That we should at least consider the idea. We both like him, and he likes us." Felix held up a palm when Noah tried to cut him off. "I don't mean sex! Well, that too, but only as a normal part of a relationship. All I'm saying, is that maybe we should be open to the idea of inviting him in."

Noah shook his head. "To our home?"

"To everything. All of this," he gestured around him. He didn't mean the beer garden, of course. Their surroundings were neutral. For some it was a location to hang out with friends. For others it was a venue to get wasted. For them it was romantic, simply because it was a new environment for them to enjoy together.

"You want us to *date* him?" Noah asked, sounding incredulous.

"Don't you want to?" Felix pressed. "No matter how much you love me, isn't there a part of you that wishes things had gone differently between you? I know it still hurts. I can see the pain on your face when you talk about it. All three of us being together would make that go away. Harold is lonely. We could fix that too."

"And what would you get out of this?" Noah shot back. "What exactly is it that I'm not giving you?"

"Nothing," Felix said. "Believe me, I'm happy, which is why it took me by surprise that I want this. The only thing I'm sure of is that I'm capable of loving you both. I can either try to bury my feelings for him or... We can at least talk about it, right? I know it sounds crazy, but I've thought about this a lot and only came up with benefits. Especially for you. Do you ever feel guilty when you're too busy with work to spend time with me?"

"Of course."

"You wouldn't have to. Not as often, because he'll share that burden."

"It's not a burden," Noah insisted. "It's what I live for."

"Oh. Thanks." Felix swallowed and forced himself to continue. "Sometimes I feel guilty about it anyway. I know you feel obligated to take care of me. I'm younger and less experienced."

"I like the roles we play," Noah said, still sounding defensive. "I thought you did too."

"I do! But from what you've told me, the dynamic was different between you and Harold. He was *your* mentor, at least at first. I guess you're more like equals now. But that's good! You wouldn't always have to be the responsible one. I feel like you could relax more or something."

Noah was no longer looking at him. He was staring at nothing, his head shaking back and forth. Then it got worse, because his lip started to tremble.

"I'm sorry," Felix sputtered. "It was a crazy idea. I shouldn't have brought it up. Let's just forget about the whole—"

"I've thought about it too," Noah said, his voice a croak. He grabbed his beer and finished it off. "For a long time now, but it was always just a fantasy. Of course I want to be with you both. Are you kidding? I love him and I love you. But it's not that simple."

"No," Felix admitted. "It's not. What worries you the most?"

"That you'll love him more." Noah laughed without humor. "That sounds pathetic, but it's true. I'm worried, once you're with him, that you won't need me anymore. He understands your hobbies better than I do, and he only seems to get hotter each year. When Harold realizes how good your love feels, how sweet and thoughtful you are… I'm scared that I'll end up on the outside. You're right that he's lonely. It's easy for me to recognize because I felt the same way not long ago. That's what I fear most. I don't want to end up back there again."

Felix reached across the table to take his hand. "You need to start believing me when I say I'll never abandon you. I understand why you worry. Your parents turned their backs on you, but I never will. Why would I ever leave? You make me feel safe. I don't mean financially or anything replaceable like that. I mean emotionally. You've never been cruel to me. The guy before you was. You've never pushed me away, or let me run off, even when I was upset about your job. I don't get that from Harold. As much as I love him, I know you would always answer my calls, even if it hurt you. You would do it anyway to make me feel better. You're my safe haven. I realize I messed up once, when I thought I needed to leave, but I promised myself to never do that again. Even if you tell me right now that we can't be with Harold or anyone else, it won't change a thing. I'll still be here. And I'll still love you and feel happy."

Noah swallowed. "But it's possible to make him happy too."

"I think so." Felix squeezed his hand. "We could at least talk about it together. All three of us."

Noah stared, the breath coming out his nostrils in huffs. Then he nodded.

"I keep trying to imagine the semantics," Noah said. They were in the truck and nearing Harold's house, both of them jittery. "Little details like how it'll work when we go to bed each night. Who gets to be in the middle?"

"I like it when you hold me," Felix said. "That's my favorite way to fall asleep."

"Right. So is he also going to hold you from the opposite side? That doesn't sound comfortable."

"We could all spoon," Felix said. He imagined Noah's arms around him, and getting to cling to Harold's muscled torso. How would he ever manage to sleep? "I figured you would have experience with this sort of thing."

"Me?"

Felix watched the light from the streetlights move across Noah's face and asked himself a familiar question. Did he really want to know? These days the answer came quickly and was always the same. "Yes. Have you ever been in a threesome?"

"Not a three-way relationship, obviously," Noah said. "You would have heard about that. When it comes to sex, yeah. I have."

"What was it like?"

Noah took a deep breath. "Awkward. The client wanted me and another guy to do stuff in front of him, which I was into, but then he would jump in on occasion and take me out of the moment. It was overwhelming. There were too many body parts everywhere."

"Oh."

"I didn't know the client or the other escort," Noah explained. "That made it weird. Sex is always better when familiarity is involved. Why? Is that something you want to happen tonight?"

"Sex?" Felix gasped. "Do you think it will?"

Noah glanced at him. "That's entirely up to us. We can decide now, or see how it goes."

Felix chewed his bottom lip. The idea sounded hot but... "I'm not sure I'm comfortable enough yet. Is that bad?"

"Absolutely not," Noah said. "I'm right there with you."

"Good."

"Good!"

They looked at each other and laughed, which helped dispel the tension. It came right back again when they pulled into Harold's driveway. He knew they were coming. Felix had texted to let him know. No doubt that's why he met them at the door.

"Hey," Harold said sheepishly. "So..."

"We're not having sex tonight," Felix blurted out.

"Duly noted." Harold's eyes moved to Noah, and even

though they exchanged a look at his expense, it felt affectionate. More important than that, the interaction between the two men had thawed. A welcome sight after the cold indifference of the previous month. "Get in here, you two."

Soon they were all seated in the living room. Felix took the comfy reading chair and angled it toward the couch, where the other two sat. Before they did, Harold grabbed beers from the fridge for him and Noah. Felix only wanted a water. No one drank though. The guys fiddled with the bottles, picking at the labels or wiping a thumb through the condensation. Felix left his water on the side table. His nervousness was gone. Now that they were all here, he simply wanted it to work. This was his one chance to make something good happen, and he didn't plan on messing it up.

"Who wants to go first?" he asked.

"I don't know where to begin," Noah admitted.

Harold raised his hand, like they were in a classroom. "I think we need rules."

This was something they discussed before approaching Noah. They hadn't reached an agreement.

"I think we should treat it like any other relationship," Felix countered. "We should let it happen naturally."

"We will," Harold said. "Within boundaries."

"What sort of rules?" Noah asked.

Harold cleared his throat. "The way I see it, I would be dating you guys. Like, you're a single entity already. We already know that you two work as a couple. What we *don't* know is if you, plural, are compatible with me, singular."

Noah peered at him. "Are you stoned?"

"If I was, I'd probably be making more sense. Let me put it another way. What if you get really busy in the next couple of weeks, Noah? You usually don't have as much free time, so imagine if me and Felix go on a bunch of dates together. How would that make you feel?"

"Like I was being left behind," Noah said. He looked over at Felix apologetically. "Sorry, but I have to be honest."

"That's good," Felix assured him. "I want you to be. But I also feel like you guys have an entire history without me, so if anything, Harold and I would be making up for lost time." He could see that this answer made Noah uncomfortable, but he too was only telling the truth. "I miss hanging out with him," he said in his own defense.

Harold intervened. "Another reason to do this only as a group is that we don't know what kind of problems we'll be facing until they pop up. No matter how long we sit here and discuss it, we're going to get blindsided by stuff. I think it's better to face that together. Sex is a good example. Maybe we'll find out that, even though Noah is fine with us all sleeping together, it makes him feel weird when Felix and I are on our own."

"That makes sense," Felix said. "I can go without sex, but I still want to see you."

"That sounds reasonable," Noah said after a moment's thought. "The rule could be that our interactions stay platonic unless all three of us are there. So no sex, kissing, or cuddling. Flirting is fine. But nothing that would normally count as cheating unless all three of us are present."

"The tension would be hot," Harold said, shooting Felix a wink. "Even hotter than it has been already."

As flattering as this was, it made him nervous. They were flirting right in front of Noah! Felix looked at him to gauge his reaction

"I'm okay," Noah said. "It's a little strange, but I'm fine. Harold is right. All these little steps, they need to happen when we're together. That way we can take a step back and talk, if need be."

Felix groaned in frustration. "And until then, you and I can't even kiss when he's not around?"

"I don't want that," Harold interjected. "Like I was saying before, you're both an established couple who would be dating me. So you have every right to do what you normally do."

"It's only when one of us is alone with him that we take it slow," Noah explained.

"You two are annoyingly grown up." Felix pretended to pout, making them laugh. Then he dropped the act. "You've convinced me. It sounds like a smart plan."

"Good." Noah licked his lips. "My biggest concern is your work, Harold. Are you going to keep escorting? If so, Felix needs to accept that, and we all need to be careful about STDs. I know you have been for years, but there's always some risk, no matter how small."

Felix had asked Harold about this previously, but he dismissed the subject, claiming there was no sense in worrying about it until they knew if Noah was willing or not. Out of excuses, Harold had no choice but to answer.

"I really like my job," he said.

Felix's stomach sank. "Yeah, but Noah needs you to help him run the business."

"I have been!" Harold shot back.

"He really has," Noah said in calmer tones. "I know you haven't seen him around as much because of everything, but he's been taking on more and more. I suppose the next question is yours to answer, Felix. Would you still want this if he didn't stop escorting?"

"Wait," Harold said, holding up a hand. "I have more I need to say first. I've been thinking a lot about this, and what really bothers me about quitting is that I'd be letting certain people down. Russell, for instance. What would happen to him? And Lance?"

"He could get a new doll," Felix said, but he already knew that wasn't a good option. He himself was emotionally attached to his collection, and that didn't involve a fantasy relationship. Russell would probably have to stage a funeral and go through a grieving process before he was able to move on. And yet, hadn't he done so before? "What was it like when he switched to you and Lance? There was a different doll before, right?"

"It took *ages*," Harold moaned. "Lots of dates and buildup. If it were easy for him, I wouldn't think twice. Russell isn't the only one. There are other guys who depend on me emotionally. I care about them too. I could give that up, but it would be hard. For both sides."

"How many clients fit that description?" Noah asked.

"Five," Harold said. "But if I really had to, I could narrow it down to three."

They both looked to Felix for a response. Despite how beneficial he knew those relationships could be, he still felt apprehensive about certain aspects. For him, sex was exclusively reserved for the people he loved. Although maybe these select clients fit that description for Harold, which raised another question. "If the relationships you have with these guys are so emotional," he said, "why do you seem so lonely? Why do you need us?"

Harold sucked in air. "They aren't typical relationships. It's kind of draining on me, because I have to be something that I'm not with those clients. With you guys, I can be myself, but that's also why I don't want to quit. If I throw away everything I believe in, including this job, I won't be myself anymore. So with that in mind, do you think you can deal with it?"

"I don't know," Felix said. "I guess we'll find out."

Harold nodded. "It's not like I don't get it. If you're thinking about those clients when kissing me and get grossed out..." He shrugged, but his expression was already hurt.

"You're not gross," Felix reassured him. "I've dated escorts before, you know." This earned him a smile, but he had another concern, which he spoke to Noah. "If it turns out I'm able to deal with Harold still having clients, is that going to make you return to that work? Because I don't want you to. No matter how tight we get on money. Is that a double standard?"

"Yes," Noah said, "but I'm okay with it, because I'm not interested in being an escort again. I don't see anything wrong with it, or I wouldn't be in this industry, but I like running a company better. Simple as that. It keeps me on my toes."

Harold jerked a thumb at him. "That's his humble way of saying it keeps his big ol' brain occupied."

"He *is* really smart," Felix said dreamily.

"Yup," Harold agreed. "He's also a good teacher. The more of the business he shows me, the more interested I become. Having fewer clients would free up time so I could get deeper into that and help out more. I think it's a fair compromise, if you're willing."

Felix nodded. He wasn't sure how he would react emotionally, but he knew he wanted to try.

"Awesome," Harold said before addressing Noah. "The STD thing is a valid concern. The clients I would keep don't hire anyone aside from me. They don't sleep around either, but we could still get you both on PrEP, like I am, just to be safe."

Now it was Felix who raised his hand. "That's the pill which makes you less likely to get HIV, right?"

Noah nodded. "Yes. As long as he's escorting, safe sex is crucial in the bedroom."

"Absolutely," Harold agreed. "Condoms are a must."

"Does that mean I can't swallow?" Felix asked.

The other two guys laughed.

"We'll go over the statistics," Noah said, "And you can decide once you have all the facts."

"Okay." This wasn't the most romantic conversation, but he supposed it was necessary. "Anything else?"

They exchanged glances.

"I'm happy," Harold said. "What about you guys?"

"Your rule takes care of my concerns," Noah said. "We do this slow, and only together. If we get to the point that we have sex, we take every precaution. I'd only add that if one of us feels uncomfortable for any reason, we talk about it right away instead of letting it fester. I don't care if it's a mood killer or inconvenient. We have to be open and honest. Agreed?"

Harold nodded. "So uh... Now what?"

An awkward silence hung in the air while they each imagined the possibilities. As hot or sweet as these fantasies might be, it also felt forced. They hadn't been together like this for weeks, and never when free to show their true emotions. What they needed was time to adjust. "It's still date night," Felix said. "That includes you now. I'm hungry, so maybe we should all go out to eat. Oh, and there's this new movie I really want to see—"

Noah groaned. Harold laughed. Then they all rose, and after some deliberation, walked out into the night together to discover how their world had changed.

Felix couldn't stop yawning by the time they returned to Harold's house. Their evening out wasn't to blame. They'd had tremendous fun, although the dinner and movie were both forgettable when compared to the endless conversation and laughter. Not only was the magic still there, it was more intoxicating than ever. From the outside, they must have appeared to be nothing more than friends. They didn't touch each other. Not even Felix and Noah. Doing so might make Harold feel left out, and it also raised the question of how exactly they would invite him in. They couldn't kiss him at the same time, for instance, so who would go first? Felix decided not to worry about it. The others seemed to have reached the same conclusion, although Noah still had reservations. Felix wasn't sure why, but he could tell. He might need more time to adjust. If so, that was fine.

"Should we catch up on *Avatar*?" Harold asked as he tossed

his keys on the coffee table. "We haven't watched any episodes since, well, everything."

"Yes!" Felix said, but he barely managed to get this word out before another yawn followed it. "After a cat nap. Is that okay?"

The others went to the kitchen. Felix stretched out on the couch. He heard muted voices and was reminded of when he would fall asleep as a child while listening to the adults continue their night.

Felix only intended to rest his eyes. He hadn't slept well the night before, too concerned about how Noah would react to this crazy scheme. He fought against sleep now, dozing off repeatedly before rallying again. When he opened his eyes after one such occasion, the living room was dimmer. Noah was seated in the big comfy chair, Harold perched on the coffee table across from him. Their voices were low, and Felix was curious, so he quickly shut his eyes and remained still.

"He's all heart," Noah was saying. "I have no doubt that he loves you."

"It feels real to me too," Harold replied. "I just worry that if it's a crush and nothing more... I don't want to damage what you've got together."

"I don't want that either."

"But you think it might?"

Silence. Felix was tempted to peek but didn't in case they were looking at him.

"If there's something you're worried about," Harold said, "this is when you should tell me."

"Do you remember what it was like before you had your heart broken?" Noah asked. "How you were able to experience love in a way that was... I don't know, purer somehow?"

"You don't second-guess your feelings as much, that's for sure."

"Yeah. That's why I think he really means it. Maybe it is just a crush, but that's often where love starts. So I'm not worried about what he feels for you..."

"Oh."

"Yeah." He heard Noah take a sip and set down a glass. "I need you to be completely honest with me. If you're not, I'll never forgive you, no matter how much pain that might cause, because I'm looking out for his best interests. We've both had our hearts put through the ringer. I won't be the person who does that to him, and I sure as hell won't let you be either."

"I can't promise that I won't end up hurting him. That's a normal part of—"

"I know. I'm not asking for the impossible, and I'm sorry for what I'm about to say, but I need to know that you really do have feelings for him. It's not that I can't imagine why you would. It didn't take me long to fall in love with him. But we have a history together."

"And you're worried that I'm only doing this so I can be with you again."

"Jesus, that sounds vain of me, doesn't it?"

Harold chuckled. "No. I've fantasized about breaking you guys up so many times. That includes seducing him, or you, or telling lies along with plenty of other terrible things. But I never could because the result was always the same. You'd get hurt because of me. Again. You have no idea how terrible I felt about that at the time. Or how much I worried about you not having somewhere safe to stay, or a person you could trust. I pleaded with Marcello to check in on you. Did you know that? He'd never say much of anything that he found out. Just that you were okay and that I should see for myself. I couldn't though. I didn't want to do anymore damage, which is stupid because it only made it hurt worse for the both of us. Was I wrong? If I had found you and begged for your forgiveness, would you have given me another chance?"

"Yes," Noah croaked. "I don't think I would have been able to resist."

"But you did. When I finally stopped feeling sorry for myself and tried to get your attention again..."

"I'd given up hope," Noah said. "And convinced myself that I had moved on."

"Had you?"

"If that was true, would I be sitting here now?"

Harold exhaled. "I guess not. I hate knowing that we could have been together then, if I had gotten my act together sooner. I really do love Felix though. Maybe not as much as I love you. Not yet. But I think I could. And if you decide that you can't handle dating both of us at once, I'll go back to waiting. Even if that means we end up old and gray before we can be together. I don't care. I just want a chance to finally love you like I should have done back then. I'm sorry I was so stupid. There's nothing I regret more."

"I wish I hadn't been so proud," Noah admitted, "or let the rejection my parents put me through bleed into what I was feeling for you. We both made mistakes. I'm sorry too."

Felix couldn't resist any longer. He opened his eyes to find both men staring in opposite directions, unable to look at each other. That wouldn't do at all. He pushed himself upright, attracting their attention, and smiled to show that everything was okay.

"Ready to head home?" Noah asked.

Felix shook his head wordlessly. He walked over to Noah and, while still standing, took his hand. Remembering how his birthday party had ended, he took Harold's hand too and brought them all together. Three sets of fingers intertwined, but they didn't remain that way for long. Once he was sure they wouldn't let go of each other, Felix took a step back and released them. "It must have been hard to hold back your feelings for so long. You don't have to anymore."

Noah looked at him, eyes wide with concern.

"It's okay," Felix assured him. "Really."

He sat on the couch again and wished he could get away with pretending to sleep. This was their moment, and he didn't want to ruin it, but Noah was still watching him.

"I promised myself if I ever got another chance, I'd take it," Harold said.

Then he stood, pulling Noah to his feet, which brought their bodies close together. Felix felt his heart swell, and when Noah looked to him once more, he nodded encouragingly while biting his bottom lip.

"I never stopped loving you," Harold murmured. "Not that terrible morning in the motel or a single second that followed."

Noah finally focused on him completely, his chin quivering. Harold placed a thumb there to steady it. Then he leaned close, their foreheads touching. They stared into each other's eyes, a tear sliding down one of Noah's cheeks, but Felix didn't think it was borne of sorrow. He knew it wasn't when their lips finally met, because he had never witnessed such a kiss. He had experienced it a few times—felt the simple act cause love to radiate through his entire being—but never had he seen it from the outside. He wanted to cheer and applaud, but he didn't dare move a muscle in fear that the spell would be broken.

"I love you too," Noah managed to say, his voice hoarse. Harold hugged him, and with his head over his shoulder, Noah met Felix's gaze again, but there was no longer any doubt or hesitation in his eyes. "And I love you too," he said.

"Yay!" Felix said, clapping giddily.

"God damn, you're adorable!" Harold said, turning to consider him. "You need to get in on this."

"I don't mind watching," Felix said, willing to let them interpret that any way they pleased.

"No way," Harold said. "We're bringing this party to you. Right?"

"Absolutely," Noah agreed.

And with that, they jumped on the couch, two sets of arms grabbing him. Then he was kissed—playful smooches all over his face and neck that had him laughing even before the tickling began.

"I've changed my mind," Felix squealed. "I don't want to do this. I'm extremely uncomfortable!"

"Too late," Harold growled, nipping at the air near his face like he intended to bite. "You've opened Pandora's box, kiddo!"

"Where's the lid?" Felix cried. "I want to shut it again!"

He didn't mean this, and they knew it, so the assault continued. The games culminated in a real kiss from Noah, who was reclining in one corner of the couch. Felix rolled over and leaned against him, his back against Noah's chest. That just left Harold, who moved down the couch on his hands and knees, with a predatory grin. His full attention was on Felix. Only when he was close did he look to Noah. "Do you mind?"

"Better ask him," came the rumbled response.

Felix's smile must have said it all. Harold brought his face close, eyes sparkling. Felix was reminded of all the fun they'd had together as friends, and the fantasies that had followed where they were so much more. Then he stretched his neck to meet him. It felt strange to touch another pair of lips after being with Noah for so long. Felix was almost scared. What if he didn't like it? Would that mean he was wrong about his feelings for Harold? His worries subsided as he began to melt. The kiss was everything he'd imagined if not more. His heart went into overdrive, especially when Harold broke off and went for Noah's lips instead, the arms around Felix tightening. Two sets, soon enough, as Harold slowly lowered his weight down on him.

"We're a sandwich," Felix managed to squeak out. It was difficult to breathe when trapped between two hunky slices of bread, but if this was how he died, he couldn't imagine a better way to go.

The next three weeks were absolute bliss. When all three of them got together, it was like magic. Like fusion! As a group, their dynamic changed in a subtle and somewhat confusing way. They were still the same people as before, and yet, they were also better somehow. Maybe because they were free. No more envy or self-imposed distance. No more buried emotions. This made the biggest difference when it came to Noah and Harold. The new business thrived with them finally working as a team, and when they were off work together, they had serious chemistry. Like two people who had fallen in love. Felix wasn't threatened by this. Their feelings for each other weren't new. They had simply been unleashed.

Nothing sexual had happened yet. Not as a group. Felix and Noah were sleeping together more than ever, due to their increasing frustration. The most recent tumble in bed had been spent talking about what they wanted to do to Harold while doing those things to each other instead. Their bodies might be ready, but their minds kept insisting they take it slow, because Harold was right. There were unexpected issues that had to be dealt with.

Some of these were social. Felix had always been open with his family. He wanted it to stay that way, but finding a way to tell them that he was giving polyamory a try felt like coming out all over again. He did it though. Felix didn't want to make this relationship official while still hiding in the dark. That would imply he hadn't accepted it as okay within himself. His mother was confused and had a lot of questions. His sister, Darli, had laughed and teased him mercilessly, but he loved her for remaining true.

Other issues were more logistic. Simple things, like going to the movies, or cuddling on the couch. Felix's impulse was to sit between Harold and Noah, so he could enjoy them both, but he also knew how long they had waited to be together. In a way, he had already been the obstacle keeping them apart, so he tried to avoid perpetuating that. He voiced all of this, just as they had promised to, and they attempted a few different solutions. At first by taking turns. If he sat between Harold and Noah during a movie, Felix made sure not to the next time. The same with the couch at home, although there was debate over if the couch sessions and cinema visits should be counted separately. Like, if Felix was on the outside during a movie, did that mean he got to be in the middle when they piled onto the couch to watch Netflix? Or did he have to wait until the next cinema outing before claiming his middle seat?

After a disagreement over who had been where and when, Felix created a spreadsheet for them to reference. This quickly became annoying, since they had to check it before doing something as simple as sitting. It was Harold who came up with the perfect solution. They were watching the previews before a movie, Felix in the middle again. Noah always ignored these, dismissing them as commercials and preferring to use the time to catch up on his emails. Felix looked forward to the previews, sometimes more than the actual movie, since it was often where a trailer was first revealed. Harold liked them too, so they talked excitedly during each. When the actual movie started, Harold broke out the healthy homemade trail mix he always smuggled in that Noah also liked and said, "Can we switch?" And it simply made sense. He wanted to be next to Noah so they could share a snack, and Felix wanted to focus on the screen.

From then on, they let need decide for them. If they both wanted to sit next to Noah, he could move to the middle seat, and so on. So far, whatever their collective desires had been, they had managed to find an arrangement of bodies that worked. *All* of it was working, in fact. The initial kinks had been ironed out, and after discussing it, he and Noah had agreed that they both felt secure enough for the trial period to end.

"When are we going to tell him?" Felix asked, pacing the living room of the apartment. "Right when he gets here?"

"When it feels right," Noah said, sounding amused. "Haven't we learned not to plan these things too much? What if he has to pee when he gets here?"

"So we wait until he goes, and then we tell him."

Noah shook his head. "You're hopeless. Since you have so much energy, why don't you grab the feather duster? We're behind on our chores. If we keep this up, I'll have to hire my own escorts just to keep this place clean."

"Make them do it for free," Felix retorted, flopping face-down on the couch. "You're the boss. They have to do what you say." When the buzzer rang, he sprang to his feet again.

"No jumping on the guests," Noah shouted after him as he rushed from the room, "or I'll have to take you to the pet store for more training!"

"Don't care," Felix shouted back. "I'll get my muddy paws all over him anyway. It's worth it!"

He reached the front door, buzzed Harold in, and did the equivalent of a pee-pee dance while waiting for him to make it upstairs. This should be the final time he needed to be let in. Harold would probably get his own key today. Did they have a spare? Felix wished he had discussed that with Noah. They could have had a special one made with a fun pattern printed on it.

"Hey," Harold said when he bounded up the last of the stairs and saw Felix sticking his head out the door.

"Hi," he said, closing his eyes and pooching out his lips for a kiss. It never came.

"You know the rules," Harold said.

Ugh. The rules! Felix couldn't wait for them to be tossed out the window. And they would be. Soon. "Come in," he said, opening the door the rest of the way. "Do you have to pee?"

"No," Harold said with a chuckle.

"Good! Noah is in the living room."

He resisted the urge to grab Harold's hand (accursed rules!) and led the way inside. Noah wasn't in the living room. They found him in the kitchen opening a bottle of wine, three glasses set out on the counter.

"Are we telling him?" Felix asked.

"Telling me what?"

Noah shook his head and sighed. "I'm surprised he hasn't let it slip already. Can I at least finish pouring?"

"But you guys haven't greeted each other yet," Felix said casually. He *loved* watching them kiss. It was both the sweetest and simultaneously the most erotic thing he'd ever seen. So far.

"I'll pour." He took the bottle of wine from Noah and ignored the glasses, eager for a show.

Noah noticed. "Do you ever feel like he only wanted this arrangement so he'd have an extra action figure to play with?"

"Yeah," Harold said, pulling him close, "but I don't mind."

"Me—" Noah wasn't able to finish his sentence, cut off by a kiss.

Felix set the bottle on the counter. "I'm next!"

"Of course you are," Harold said.

Felix received the same embrace, but during their kiss, Harold mussed his hair. "Red? You promised me that pink would be the next color. Maybe I can rub some of this out…"

Felix pulled away with a laugh. "Would you stop? It'll wash out and end up pink, you'll see."

"Do I get to be in the shower when that happens?" Harold asked. "I want to see it for myself."

"That's your cue," Noah said, setting down the wine bottle. He had kept himself busy during their kiss. "You can tell him now. Here you go." He handed each of them a glass before leaning against the counter.

"Don't keep me in suspense," Harold said, looking between them.

"We've talked about it," Felix said, "and we've decided that we're ready to make it official."

Harold looked more confused than excited. "Make what official?"

"Our relationship. We want to commit."

"Oh!" Harold raised his glass. Then he lowered it again. "Do you mean sex?"

"We mean everything," Felix said. "We want you to be our boyfriend now."

Harold shook his head. "I thought I already was."

"Not really," Noah said. "We agreed to date first, remember?"

"True," Harold said, "but I thought I still had that status. I've been telling everyone that I have a boyfriends now."

"A boyfriends?" Felix repeated. He loved how it sounded. Like a meme. "I can has cheezburger?"

"Exactly," Harold said. "I've been telling each client that as I say goodbye. Hey, maybe we should photoshop an image of me to send to them." He made a doofy face. "I can has boyfriends?"

"Yes!" Felix said. "I'll take a photo right now and do it for you."

"Before you two go off on one of your tangents," Noah said, holding up his free hand, "maybe we can toast like civilized people? That is, if you're okay with this." He was addressing Harold. "Do you feel the same way?"

"Yeah!" Harold said, his smile faltering. "As long I still get to keep my select few."

His special clients. Over the past three weeks, Felix had learned more about each of them. Through long discussions with Harold and reading the files Noah kept, he had as complete a picture as possible. What he came away with was one undeniable fact: Harold had a large capacity for love, and these people needed him. Felix didn't want to interfere with that. "I'm fine with it, yes. More than fine. I'm proud of you!"

"In that case," Harold said, raising his glass. "Here's to being boyfriends."

They toasted and took a sip, ogling each other as they did so.

Felix was the first to voice what they were all thinking. "Should we wait?"

"That would be the classy thing to do," Noah said.

Harold's head bobbed in agreement. "Totally."

"Then again," Noah said. "We've already been waiting three weeks."

"Longer, if you think about it," Harold said, "And I'm not getting as much action these days so…"

Felix set down his glass. "I'm ready!"

The others followed his example, and with their hands free, it became clear that they were uncertain what to do with them.

"Think we need to talk about rules for this?" Noah said.

"No more rules," Felix pleaded. "I'm sure we can figure it out."

"Since he's so eager to play with action figures," Harold said to Noah. "Maybe we should let him."

"Okay," Noah said, turning to him with a grin. "Tell us what to do."

"For real?" The possibilities were so overwhelming that Felix nearly fainted. "Wow. Okay. Where to begin?" At least that wasn't difficult. He had only seen a glimpse of Harold's body. Just enough to know that he wanted more. "Noah, I think you should take his shirt off."

Technically it was a hoodie, but it was made of the same thin cotton that T-shirts were. The fabric draped nicely against Harold's chest, rolling over the curves, and when the curtain lifted to reveal the muscles beneath…

Felix bit down on a knuckle in an effort not to squeal, but a sound escaped anyway.

"I'd be jealous if I didn't agree," Noah said, tossing aside the hoodie. Then he ran his palm over the toned abs up to the meaty pecs. "This is new."

Harold flexed and grinned cockily. "Remember this the next time you guys make fun of my healthy diet."

"I'm never going to forget this," Felix breathed. The only thing that could make it better was more nudity. "Now take off his shirt too."

"I can't compete," Noah said, face flushing as he pulled away.

"I disagree," Harold said, grabbing him by the waist before he could escape. "Variety is nice. I don't want you to look just like me."

"I love your body, hon," Felix said. "I can't get enough of it."

"Aw, shucks," Noah said, exaggerating his accent.

"And I love freckles," Harold said, pressing his lips to one of the freshly revealed shoulders. "I'm crazy about them."

"Really?" Noah said. "I never knew that."

"I don't have any," Felix said, worried about what he had to offer.

"I'm sure you have plenty that I'll like too," Harold said, taking a step towards him.

"Not yet!" Felix said. "I'm not done playing."

"Then give me some orders," Harold said with a salute.

Felix should have asked him to bring his sailor costume. "I want to see you guys kiss."

"You've seen that plenty of times before," Noah said.

Did that mean he wanted something racier? No problem!

"Kiss while getting each other's pants off."

"Now we're talking," Harold growled.

He pulled on Noah's hips until they were against his, a tongue sliding across the skin of Noah's neck before his mouth covered the same spot. Felix thought his instructions were being ignored until he noticed that Harold's hands had already undone his pants *and* Noah's. Harold splayed his fingers wide and moved them along the sides of their bodies, catching both waistbands and slowly shimmying them down. Their underwear remained on, Noah in his trusty tighty-whities, and Harold in a pair of maroon designer briefs. Both guys were hard as Harold ground against Noah, their packages rubbing together.

Felix was feeling tight in the jeans too. He wasn't expecting this much of a show. Harold had some serious moves! Felix was starting to worry that he'd seem too much like a fumbling amateur in comparison. These insecurities were forgotten when Harold's eyes moved to him, tongue still in Noah's mouth, but he pulled it free to speak.

"I need you to take off my shoes," he said.

Not the sensual command he was expecting. Felix walked closer and got on his knees. From this vantage point, he had a new appreciation for Harold's request. Felix's fingers tore at the laces, but his attention was higher up on underwear that was stretched thin by the flexing cock it contained, mere inches away from his face. Felix finally got both shoes off and looked up for further instructions. Harold lifted one leg, then the other, so Felix could yank his pants free. He was going to do the same for Noah, but Harold had turned toward him again. With his feet, he stepped on both leg openings of Noah's jeans, then resumed kissing him while moving forward. Noah ended up pressed against the counter, forced to step out of his jeans along the way. That was a creative way of doing it!

"Mission accomplished," Harold said, turning to stand at Noah's side, his back against the counter too. "Are you guys still okay?"

"Yeah," Noah said, looking to him. "Are you?"

"Yup," Felix confirmed, nodding eagerly.

"Good." Harold said this with a self-assured grin. "Now what?"

"The rest of it has to go," Felix said, his mouth dry.

"Hm." Harold turned to consider Noah while rubbing his chin thoughtfully. "There's not much left. Just these."

He hooked a finger in the waistband of Noah's underwear and tugged, revealing ginger hair and the base of a cock. He stopped there, looking up at Felix. "No sense in drawing this out. For either of us. We both know what he's packing, right?"

"God yes," Felix breathed. That never stopped it from being exciting.

Harold yanked downward. Noah's cock sprang free and continued to grow. He rarely got completely hard while still dressed, simply because there wasn't enough room. Noah was big. Very big.

"Please tell me you aren't this hung too," Harold said, grabbing the cock and pumping it a few times. "I don't think my self-esteem could handle it."

"Not even close," Felix said with a titter.

"Keep in mind," Harold said, pulling down his own briefs. "The important thing is what you do with it, and in that regard, I promise not to disappoint."

The wind caught in Felix's throat as Harold's briefs hit the kitchen floor. His pubes were the same pitch black as his armpit hair and eyebrows. As for his dick, it was just as perfectly proportioned as its owner, but not terribly long. Felix didn't care. He could barely handle Noah's size at times.

"What do you think?" Harold asked, draping an arm around Noah's shoulders. "Are you happy with your new toys?"

"Mostly," Felix said, holding down a smile. "There's one serious problem. I can't decide which of you I want in my mouth first."

"That's easy," Noah said. "Come here and we'll show you."

Felix walked over, feeling lightheaded. Was this really happening? Noah turned to face Harold, who seemed to know what to do and copied this motion, their cocks brushing together.

"Let's see if he can figure it out," Harold said.

Felix reached down and grabbed two fistfuls of meat. He was giggling like mad, because this was already more fun than he had expected. Both guys were moaning softly, but he was sure he could get them to do more. Felix dropped to his knees. He had a lot to fit into his mouth. The only way he could make that possible was by pressing the undersides of both cocks together.

"He's a natural!" Harold declared.

Encouraged by this, he opened his mouth wide and went to town. At times he didn't have to do much, since the guys were thrusting against each other. He looked up to see them kissing and decided he wanted every single day to begin and end like this from now on. He almost cried out in protest when Harold pulled away.

"I'm starting to feel like I'm being taken advantage of," he said, addressing Noah. "Aren't you? Here we are naked and vulnerable, while he gets to be fully clothed."

"That's not fair at all," Noah agreed. "Let's remedy the situation."

"Somewhere more comfortable?"

"Yeah."

Before Felix knew what was happening, two pairs of hands grabbed him and picked him up. Noah had an arm around his ribcage and Harold took his legs as he was carried from the room.

"Where are we going?" Felix asked.

"To the honeymoon suite, of course," Noah said, leading the way, "where we can really have some fun."

That sounded good. Felix was set down in the bedroom, his clothes taken off him with surprising speed. Once he was naked, he was picked up again and tossed on the bed. Noah and Harold remained standing as they scrutinized him.

"He's a skinny little thing," Harold said. "I'm worried I'll break him."

"He's tougher than he looks," Noah said, shaking his hips and making his cock wag back and forth. "You should see how he handles this."

"He's a bottom?" Harold asked, sounding interested.

"Yup."

Harold nodded approvingly. "Think he can handle double penetration?"

Noah shrugged. "Don't know. Let's try."

"What?" Felix said, kicking his feet to scurry across the mattress away from them. "No! I'm not ready for that!"

"He always puts up a fight," Noah said dismissively. "It's one of our little games."

"It is not!" Felix cried. "I'm serious!"

"Wow," Harold said. "He's really convincing."

"Just makes it hotter," Noah replied. "You ready?"

"No!" Felix answered for him.

Two leering faces turned to him. Felix was pounced on, but he needn't have feared. He was helpless against their combined strength, and he was most certainly abused, but only with kisses and gropes. Mouths and hands went everywhere, no part of his body left unexplored, but it felt incredibly good. He gave back as much as he could, wanting to make them feel just as much pleasure. The next hour was consumed by a frantic hunger, their appetites insatiable, their needs so varied that they kept switching positions and experimenting. A sixty-nine became a daisy chain. Or he shared Noah's impressive length with Harold, their hands and mouths working together in unison. The best was when Felix was taken from both ends, Harold filling his mouth while Noah gently took care of the rest. That did it for him. He couldn't hold back anymore. He finished first and wondered if he should have held out longer, so they could have all done so at the same time.

Felix moved off to the side of the bed to recover, deciding to watch instead. Time seemed to slow to a crawl. Harold was on top of Noah, and they were kissing, their bodies moving together in a gentle wave. Their cocks were rubbing against each other's stomachs, but this seemed of little concern to them. They continued to kiss, pulling back occasionally to look into each other's eyes, or to whisper things, some of them lost on him, but Felix didn't mind. Instead he choked back tears. He had always known that they loved each other. He just never realized how deep those emotions went. He wasn't jealous. Instead he felt honored to be a part of that love. He *was* still a part of it... Wasn't he?

"We could use a hand," Harold said, looking over at him.

"Or a mouth," Noah suggested.

They remained how they were, Felix inserting himself as best he could. Harold arched his back to better accommodate, straining so that he could continue kissing Noah, or whisper more words to him that were easier to hear.

"Are you ready?" Harold asked.

"Yeah," Noah gasped. "On the count of three?"

They weren't that good, were they? Felix quickly made sure his mouth was where it needed to be and was soon overwhelmed. He couldn't possibly swallow it all. Their thrusting intensified as they finished coming together, his head nearly crushed between two writhing bodies, but it was worth the risk. He managed to free himself and sat up. Harold collapsed on top of Noah, both of them laughing.

"And I was worried that domestic life would be too tame for me," Harold said.

"Really?" Noah asked.

"Yeah. It's been a long time since anyone pinned me down. Without paying first, that is." Harold looked over sharply. "Sorry. You probably don't want to hear about that."

"I'm fine," Felix said. "I just have one question."

Noah looked concerned. "What?"

"Can we keep going?"

"He's kidding," Harold said. "Isn't he?"

"I'm afraid not," Noah replied with an exaggerated sigh. "You might have the body, and I might have the inches, but Felix… he's got the stamina."

"Wow," Harold said. "What have I gotten myself into?"

"You can take a ten-minute break if you want," Felix said generously.

They laughed, and Harold rolled off Noah, but only so they could open their arms and invite him in. Soon they were one big pile of sticky love with Felix in the middle, like an egg resting on a nest of tangled body parts. He set aside his appetite for the time being and let himself enjoy the tender kisses and murmured words. He had wondered what this would feel like, back before he even knew it would be allowed. The answer should have been obvious to him. It felt just like love. Except now there was more of it.

Dear Diary,

I have some bad news. That's how it always begins with us, isn't it? When I read through the previous entries, I mostly come to you when I'm upset. Problems at school, arguments with my family, and let's not forget heartbreak. On occasion I've shared good news with you too. I guess I have a little of both today. I'm not waiting tables anymore. I've started working for the Gentlemen's Agreement Club. Not doing that. Tech support is my specialty, but I'm thinking of adding more services. Anything I can do to be useful. So far it's been a good experience. I'm expected to be extra-friendly with the customers and take the time to socialize with them in addition to fixing their problems. I like that. The only time it backfired was when a guy grabbed my butt while I was bent over his router. Noah called him and very sternly explained why that was a problem. My hero! To be honest, I didn't mind that much.

I'll never be an escort, but I do want to make people happy. If anything, this whole situation with Harold has taught me the benefits of being generous. I could have denied my own feelings and encouraged Noah to ignore his, but why bother? All three of us had love to give. I think that could apply to the entire world. If we give freely the best we have to offer—kindness, patience, and charity—then there should be more than enough to go around for everyone. That brings us to the bad news. It's time for you and me to say goodbye again. I want to focus on others rather than myself, but thank you for always being there for me. I know I'll need you again someday. Nobody lives a perfect life, even though mine feels that way now. Eventually there will be drama again. When that happens, I'll come crying to you. For now, enjoy your vacation. I'll make sure to keep you somewhere nice and dry until we meet again.

Your friend,
  Felix

"Ready?" Noah asked.

Felix looked up and saw one of his boyfriends leaning against the doorframe. He seemed amused. Probably because Felix was stretched out on the office floor, his stomach flat against the carpet. The room was completely empty now except for him, the diary, and a partially filled cardboard box. His collection of memorabilia was gone along with the shelves. The computer, desk, and chair were absent too. So many memories had been made here, and now it was all coming to an end.

"What if I don't want to go?" Felix said as he sat up.

"It's a little late to change your mind," Noah said. "Although..."

Harold barged past him, T-shirt soaked with sweat, which made it stick to his body. "You guys ready?" he asked, putting his hands on his hips and grinning.

"Maybe we should do it here one last time," Felix said, trying his best to look adorable.

"We're all disgustingly sweaty," Harold said, shaking his head, "and you said last night was the final time when we cleaned out the refrigerator. Don't act like you don't remember. The things you made us do with food..."

"He's creative," Noah said. "You've gotta give him that."

"Is this the last box?" Harold asked. He didn't wait for an

answer. He plucked the diary out of Felix's hands, along with the pen, and placed them inside. After shutting the lid, he lifted the box. "I'll take this down to the truck and meet you guys there."

"We'll need a minute," Noah said.

Harold looked between them and seemed to understand. "No problem." He stooped to get a kiss from Felix and smooch from Noah on his way out.

They listened until they heard the front door close. Then Noah walked over to Felix, offering his hand and helping him to his feet. He didn't let go. "This is where it all began," he said. "Do you realize that?"

"The office?" Felix asked.

"Yeah. It was just an empty room, like it is now. I shut myself in here and let myself dream." Noah squeezed his hand. "I had your phone number with me. I was so jaded then. I didn't think I could have anything like this, but I tried. One last time. And look what happened. You're my dream come true."

Felix smiled and pressed himself against Noah's chest. "Now I really don't want to go."

"It's not too late," Noah said. "Forget what I said before. Harold and I will move all our stuff back in, if that's what you need. It's been a while since I've asked you how you feel about everything. Are you still okay? Because now's the time to tell me if you're not. It'll be harder to separate our lives from his once we're living in his house."

"Our house," Felix corrected. "He wants us to call it that."

"It's not ours yet. There's still time to change your mind, if you have any doubts."

Felix took a step back. "Remember when I had that study group the other night? I came home late, and when I went to the bedroom, you and Harold were already asleep. You had your arm around him, just like you usually do for me."

"Did that upset you?" Noah asked.

"No! I loved it. I used to worry when you left in the morning that we'd never see each other again. Maybe you'd be in an accident, or maybe there would be a crazy gunman at my school. I could never decide which would be worse: losing you or knowing the pain you would go through if you lost me."

"It would be bad either way," Noah said with a grimace. "The worst."

"Yeah. I don't worry so much now. If one of us goes, the other two won't be left alone. It'll always be that way now. When's the last time you felt lonely, like you did the first night you called me?"

Noah looked around the room, seeming baffled. "I can't even remember."

"Me neither," Felix said. "I don't want that to change. Ever. I know how happy you are. I see it every time you're together with him. I've never seen love like that before. Not on TV or in movies. Not even in anime. If soulmates are real, then you guys are it. So when I was standing there watching you hold him in your sleep, I wondered if you even needed me anymore." He put a finger to Noah's lips when he tried to protest. "And then I realized how much you must want me, because you have this intense relationship with Harold, including *years* of history, and even that's not enough to make you forget about me. It was like, for the first time, I had definitive proof of just how much I'm loved."

Noah took his hand and kissed it. "You're absolutely right. And when it's all three of us together…"

"It's indescribable," Felix said, laughing gleefully.

"I'm glad we had our time though," Noah said. "Back when it was just you and me, because that was beautiful too."

"Yeah," Felix said, feeling melancholy. "It was."

Noah wrapped his arms around him. They held each other in a room that appeared empty but was, in reality, filled with colors and sounds from their past. So many memories. If only they could be packed safely in a box, but Felix would do his best to carry each with him anyway.

Noah took his hand and led him out of the room and down the hall. Felix was the last one out the door. He looked back as he went, already feeling nostalgic. As he flicked off the light, he turned his heart instead toward a house filled with more love than he had ever dreamed possible.

Something Like Stories: Volume Three

Something Like Him

by Jay Bell

The Astral Wilds
2018 (relative mortal time)

The fire crackled and spat, sparks drifting upward on currents of invisible heat. Victor sighed contentedly. Then he tightened his arms around Jace, who even as a teenager was taller than him. They made it work anyway, just as they had when they were still alive. Jace was stretched out on the forest floor, reclining against Victor's stomach and chest, head leaning against his shoulder. Victor moved long blond hair out of the way so he could place a kiss on Jace's neck.

"Remember this night?" he asked.

"Of course," Jace replied. "This is one of our greatest hits."

They kept returning to this memory. The evening had been cool enough to warrant a fire, but not so chilly that they'd singe their eyebrows by huddling desperately close to it. The smoke had spiraled gracefully into the air that night, leaving them free to breathe in the rich decay of autumn, their bellies full of...

"What did we have for dinner?"

Jace glanced around the clearing where they had spent the earliest days of their relationship. "Canned buffet," he said, nodding toward the shelter where Victor had often slept. "This was before the racoon invasion. See? We left the empty cans sitting there, out in the open."

"Kidney beans," Victor said, squinting to make out the label. "I knew there must have been *something* special about this night."

Jace sighed. "You were just using me to get into my mother's pantry, weren't you?"

"Busted. But you weren't such a bad fringe benefit. Or should I say fridge benefit? The lunch meat was nice too."

Jace shifted to look up at him, the blue eyes just as innocent and vulnerable as they had been back then. "What really made this night so special?"

"Everything was just right," Victor said, not needing to think about it. "No drama with Star. No pressuring you to stay in Warrensburg instead of going away to college. You weren't in the closet, and I wasn't falling apart. This was us at our peak."

"Hey," Jace said, his features growing older. "I think we've had a lot of good times since then."

"We have, we have," Victor said with a chuckle. "Stay in the moment with me. I'm not ready to leave it yet."

The afterlife was a funny place. Nothing was physical, meaning there truly were no limits. Victor had long ago created his own version of this special place—the clearing where he had fallen in love, dreamed the impossible, and even cursed his own nature. When Jace joined him in these recreated woods, they shared a creative vision, able to revisit memories of the past like tourists.

Victor smiled. "This was also the night that you got those mosquito bites on your butt."

"We will *not* be reenacting that," Jace said, his face youthful again. "School was the worst. I had to find creative ways of scratching myself so that nobody would notice."

"The memory cheats and so can we," Victor said. "We'll leave out that detail. But the rest…"

Jace sat upright, like he was ready to skip to the best part. Then he stood and turned around, his eyes narrowed in concentration.

Victor recognized that expression. "Ben?" he asked.

Jace nodded, features apologetic. "He needs me. I have to go."

Victor settled back. "Cool."

"You don't mind that he's interrupting our date night?"

Victor laughed. "Our entire existence is one big date night. I'll be okay."

Jace rolled his eyes. "Could you at least pretend to be jealous? Just this once?"

Victor shook his head. "Never going to happen. Why would I make you feel guilty for wanting to express love, or for acting on selfless concern? If I was that sort of person—"

Jace held up a hand to stop him. "You're infuriating, and I love you. I'll be back as soon as I can."

Victor nodded. "You know where to find me."

Jace walked to the edge of the clearing. He looked back just before he faded into the shadows. He didn't really need to walk anywhere. Jace could have simply disappeared, but there was a certain bittersweet beauty to a slow departure.

Victor flopped onto his back, deciding that he would make the leaves fall so he could see the moon. Before this could happen, he felt a jolt. He too was needed elsewhere. The timing was an odd coincidence. Jace might be calling for him, depending on what he had discovered. That seemed most likely. Victor searched himself to find the source, willing his mind to go blank. It filled again. With the clearing.

"Already there," he said, making another attempt. The answer remained the same.

The clearing.

A third try brought the same result. Victor was needed where he already was? Now he wished Jace hadn't gone. He was better at these things. Victor got to his feet, the sensation still pulsing in his center like a ringing phone that demanded to be answered. Whatever this was, the intensity was unusual, the frequency unrelenting. *The clearing, the clearing, the clearing.*

Of course! Where he stood now was just a constructed representation. The real clearing, depending on how one chose to define reality, was in the land of the living. His final resting place. But why would he be needed there?

Only one way to find out. Victor closed his eyes and focused, imagining himself standing in the same spot, except on a different plane. One physical and inflexible. He felt a pull, and when he opened his eyes, he was there. Almost. Victor was surrounded by woods. He could tell from the daylight streaming between the trees that he was in the mortal world. Just not exactly where he expected to be.

"Bad landing," Victor said, spinning to reorient himself and find the clearing. It was impossible to miss, despite being far away. Light flooded from it, impossibly intense, and yet he didn't need to shield his eyes. The light was too perfect for that, the vibrations it gave off strangely familiar. Gentle, stalwart, patient, and strong.

"Jace?" he said, still not understanding.

"This is stupid," a deep voice grumbled.

Victor spun around, the glowing clearing instantly forgotten. Nathaniel, his son, was standing not far away, trying his best to glare away tears as he kicked at a fallen tree.

"It's just a place!" Nathaniel growled. "What do I expect to happen? Being here won't make a difference. We could have gone to McDonald's instead."

"I always preferred Burger King myself," Victor replied, knowing he wouldn't be heard. Or seen. What a world it would be if ghosts could interact with the living. Politics would get a lot more interesting. He would like to hear what the founding fathers would say to—

"Or better yet, Burger King," Nathaniel said. Then he pulled his shirt over his stomach self-consciously and sighed. No fast food today then. It wasn't hard to guess why.

"Where's Kelly?" Victor asked. "I like him. Never afraid to speak his mind." He looked to the clearing and back again. "What are you doing here? You don't know about this place."

Jace did. And so did one other person. Ben. The pieces rearranged themselves into a completed puzzle. There had been a wedding not too long ago. Jace had gone, Victor hadn't, but afterwards he learned that Ben and Nathaniel had connected with each other. And evidently realized the distant connection they shared because now they were both here, in the most sacred of places. It was obvious why Ben would want to visit the grave of his husband. As for Nathaniel...

"Are you here for me?" Victor asked with a grin, despite the sorrow he felt inside. "I'm flattered! Really. You're far from home. Then again, you do have family here, but I don't think your grandparents ever set foot in these woods."

Nathaniel didn't answer. He sat on the fallen log with a moody expression. Victor sat next to him, concentrating on the distant clearing. No doubt about it. That mysterious light felt like Jace. He watched until it blinked out of existence. Nathaniel heard the footsteps first, standing and brushing himself off. Together they watched Ben approach. His eyes were red and wet, but he was smiling.

"All done," Ben said. "Do you know the way?"

Nathaniel nodded. "To both the clearing and the house, yeah."

"Okay. I'll meet you by the lake." Ben took a deep breath, as if gathering up the strength to say goodbye. "Take your time. All you need. I mean it."

"Thanks," Nathaniel said.

Ben patted him on the arm before stepping over the fallen tree and continuing on his way. Sweet kid. Victor had never struggled to understand why Jace loved him.

"Okay," Nathaniel muttered under his breath as he began walking. "Let's get this over with."

"I won't take that personally," Victor said as he followed. "I always felt a little uneasy about visiting my mom. I love her, don't get me wrong. I just knew when entering her house that I'd have to give up some of my independence. Those old roles always reassert themselves and you become a kid again. That's the nice thing about being an absent parent. We never had that sort of relationship. I'd rather get to know who you really are. That's more interesting than telling you who I want you to be." He nearly stopped in his tracks. "Is that why you're here? You want to get to know me?"

Nathaniel carried on, completely unaware of this conversation. Shame about that. Technically there *was* a way of getting through to the living. A sort of symbolic whisper, but it never made a lasting impression. A fleeting thought at most.

The light that had filled the clearing was gone when they arrived there. Only filtered daylight illuminated it. Victor found himself wishing for a physical body again so he could bask in the sun and warm his skin. That too was possible in the afterlife. Not here though. Not for him. He no longer belonged to this world.

"Okay," Nathaniel said, reaching the center of the clearing and spinning around. His voice was laced with expectation when he spoke again. "I'm here."

"And I'm glad," Victor replied, "but there's not a lot I can do. Or anything, really. I'd love to make a stick float around or something cool, but that only happens in the movies."

"Guess I should have brought a Ouija board with me," Nathaniel said.

"Would've been worth a shot. Makes a great party game at the very least."

"I came a long way to see you," Nathaniel said, his face crinkling with despair. "I guess you don't even know who I am. Not really. Brace yourself, because this is going to come as a shock. I'm your son."

Victor smiled, the news making him happy despite having heard it long ago. "I know who you are, and I couldn't be prouder."

"Surprise," Nathaniel deadpanned. He looked around, as if making certain that he was alone. "God this is stupid," he mumbled. Then he sighed, shook his head, and continued. "You're probably wondering what I'm doing here. It's a long story. There's this guy, Ben. You didn't know him either. He ended up marrying your high-school sweetheart, Jace."

Victor tilted his head. "Technically, I wasn't in high school at the time, but I do like how that sounds."

"Anyway," Nathaniel continued. "Ben showed me around town. We went to the house where you grew up. And where you died. We've been staying with Jace's parents while here, and from what I understand, you spent a few nights there yourself."

"Those were good times," Victor confirmed.

"He even gave me old things that belonged to you. Photos that Jace took and a lion that you might have carved. I'm pretty sure you did, because if there's one thing I'm good at, it's research. I can't find another one like it online. Or even off."

"It feels right that you have it," Victor said.

"And this." Nathaniel pulled out a battered old Zippo lighter. "I had to change the flint, but once I did that and refilled it... I figured this would be a better gesture than flowers or lighting a candle." Nathaniel got to one knee so he could brush leaves away to expose bare earth. Then he flicked the lighter open, lit it, and carefully set it down. It fell a few times before he got it balanced, but he soon managed and stood again.

Victor watched all of this and felt moved, his frustration building along with tears, because all he wanted was to speak to his son. Just once.

"I'm not sure what to make of you," Nathaniel said. "I've heard stories from my mom. Star is my mother, if you haven't figured that out already. I don't know how many women you slept with. She claims you were a free spirit, which I suspect is just a polite way of saying you were promiscuous."

"I didn't get around *that* much," Victor replied.

"She loved you though. She still does, so you couldn't have been that bad."

"Thank you."

"Then again, she doesn't have the best taste in men. My father... I have a few, actually. The guy she ended up marrying—the man who raised me and who I thought was my biological father—he's got some serious issues. They seem to have worked through them, thankfully, but... I guess Heath is okay. He tried his best to be the father I needed. A lot of the time, that's how I think of him, even if we don't have much in common." Nathaniel raised his head, staring off into the distance. "And then there's this other guy. Marcello. We don't have much in common either. But I love him. A lot. He's a free spirit too, in about every imaginable sense. He talks a good game, which I'm told you were famous for. He treats rules like a personal offense and does everything in his power to break them. Sometimes I wonder if you and him are alike. He feels like a father to me. I think of him that way more than I ever let on. Is that because of you? Is there some deep-rooted part of myself that still remembers what you were like, and sees you in him?"

"I've met Marcello," Victor said. "Not formally, but he's often there when I watch over you. Did you know I do that? I'm often there with you, and while Marcello and I are different beasts, I can tell that he loves you."

"To be honest, he's infuriating."

"I've been called that before. Recently, in fact."

"So is Kelly," Nathaniel said, his tone softening. "Maybe the people most worth knowing are the ones who drive you crazy. I wonder what you would think of them?"

"You've surrounded yourself with an amazing family. I'm happy for you. I just wish I could be there too."

Nathaniel exhaled and looked down at the lighter. "I took this trip because I wanted to get to know you. I've never had much to go by. Since I learned the truth, it's become a game of subtraction. I take what I have in common with my mother, remove it from the equation, and wonder if what I'm left with is you."

"Very philosophical," Victor said approvingly. "We have that much in common. And the tendency to brood. That definitely comes from me. I know you've been to some dark places mentally, but your mother's side helps balance that out. Thankfully. I don't want you tipping over the brink, like I did."

"Does it even matter what we would've had in common?"

"You're your own person. That's the important thing."

Nathaniel laughed without humor and shook his head. "Listen to me. I've just told you that I have two fathers, and even though neither of them is biological, that they love me. And yet here I am, fighting off tears while miles away from either of them because apparently it's not enough. I want the man I can't remember to love me too. That's not only foolish. I'm being greedy and entitled too."

"You're not. It's perfectly understandable what you—"

Nathaniel bent over and grabbed the Zippo with a swoop of his hand. "Sorry," he said as he snapped the lid shut. "I'd leave this, but I don't think Ben would forgive me if I burned down these woods."

"I love you," Victor said. "You know that, right?"

"I suppose I could bury it."

"I want you to keep it," Victor said. "As a reminder that you *are* loved!"

"Why bother?" Nathaniel tossed the lighter to the ground and kicked leaves over it.

"Please don't go!" Victor pleaded.

Nathaniel shook his head and turned away.

Victor attempted to grab his arm, but his hand passed through it. He didn't let this dissuade him. He moved closer, brought his mouth close to Nathaniel's ear—a trick that Jace had once showed him—and tried again. "I love you!"

Nathaniel stopped, like he had heard. But then he hung his head and began crying.

"I love you," Victor repeated. This time Nathaniel didn't react. He just kept weeping while breaking Victor's heart, because he felt personally responsible for this pain. In that instant, he regretted who he had been. If he hadn't clung so stubbornly to his ideals, if he hadn't treated every experience like a philosophical quandary, he could have been in a normal relationship with Star. He could have helped raise his son instead of forcing her to play a deceptive game. To finally win him over? To avoid scaring him away? He still didn't understand her reasons, but whatever they were, he was the cause. He should have done everything different. All of it!

Even me?

The voice was Jace's, except it wasn't really there. Just that feeling again. Warm reassurance. Steady unwavering love. The sensation filled Victor, and he saw it all again through new eyes. He didn't get to choose his nature. Nobody did. The genes he was born with had been further tempered by the environment he was raised in. The same could be said for his mother, his own absent father, and their parents too. Victor had never set out to hurt anyone. Neither had Star when she made the decision not to tell him that she was pregnant. That was life, and there was no shame in living it. Not when he knew in his heart that he had done the best he could with what he was given.

"You were a chubby little thing," Victor said. "I did know you. You might not remember it, but I was part of your life. For a while, Star was always bringing you along. Her little brother Nate. That's what she told me. And I loved you. Do you remember the ice cream cone? One of those frozen Drumsticks wrapped in paper? We were down by the lake, and they had this rickety old booth set up where you could buy drinks. Next to it was a freezer full of ice cream, with colorful stickers plastered all over the outside. You saw it and begged for a treat. Star said no. I didn't have any money, so it was up to her. All I remember is your grubby little fingers reaching for the freezer as she guided you away. It was hot that day. I told her I was going back for water. That was free back then. None of this 'healthy' stuff bottled in single-use plastic. I went up to the freezer, took out a drumstick, and waited in line like I intended to pay. When the guy working there had his back turned, I took off running. Star wasn't thrilled when she found out. You were though. Those fat little cheeks of yours were covered in ice cream. It was a mess, and it only made me adore you more." Victor took a shuddering breath, out of emotion rather than need. "Do you hear me? I love you, Nathaniel. If you get one thing out of this trip, you need to know—" The emotion welled up inside of him. Victor gathered it up and set it free in a desperate bid, and even he was stunned by its tangible strength. "**—you are loved!**"

Nathaniel raised his head. He wiped at his eyes. Then he started walking toward the edge of the clearing. Victor's shoulders slumped. He had tried. That's all he could do until the day they met face to face, which he hoped wouldn't happen prematurely. Only then would he finally be able to speak the truth and have it be heard.

"God damn it!" Nathaniel stomped back to the center of the clearing. He got down on his knees, brushing leaves aside until he found what he was looking for. The lighter. Nathaniel stood, rubbing away dirt from the dented surface. Then he put it in his pocket and walked away.

Victor watched him go. Part of him wanted to follow in the hopes of overhearing a conversation with Ben about how the trip had been worth it—how he had left the woods feeling loved instead of lost. Then again, Nathaniel had other fathers to turn to for comfort, and they deserved their chance. Victor would always be there when he felt Nathaniel's need, but he also had faith in his son. They would have their time together. Eventually.

These facts did little to comfort him. Victor was most definitely a brooder. He intended to drown himself in sorrow. He wouldn't lament his own nature, but that didn't mean he couldn't wish that events had played out differently. He could have been a father. He could have made a difference in someone's life.

Victor stood in the clearing, the sunlight passing straight through him, and felt the all-too familiar chill of despair. That is, until a different sort of light returned to the clearing. He spun around, and for a second, he swore he saw an angel with Jace's face. Victor ran to him, throwing himself into reassuring arms, the lips that found his achingly familiar. When he pulled away, the light was gone. Jace stood there in a pilot's uniform, which Victor loved to tease him about since it was the very essence of conformity. Why did pilots need to dress the same way? How did that help the airplane stay in the sky? And yet, he couldn't help but admit that the uniform was exceedingly hot.

"The light I saw earlier," Victor said. "Was it you?"

"Little old me?" Jace said. He shrugged away the question. "You know we're not allowed to speak to the living. It's impossible to do so. Even getting the tiniest message across takes tremendous effort."

"You were watching me?"

"Maybe."

"Is that what you did?" Victor asked. "Did you get through to Ben?"

"Against the rules," Jace repeated, but he wore a subtle smile.

Victor glanced in the direction where Nathaniel had disappeared. "Do you think he heard me?"

"Stranger things have happened," Jace said.

"Speaking of which," Victor said. "I believe we were interrupted."

Jace's eyes sparkled. "Our eternal date night? Are you sure you don't want to stick around? Just to see how things pan out?"

Victor shook his head. "There is no shortage of love in Nathaniel's life. Even if he didn't hear it from me, at least I know he's hearing it from others."

"I take comfort in that myself," Jace said. "Very well. Let's get back to our own lives, in the figurative sense. And I mean it about the mosquitos!"

"Just one," Victor teased. "For old time's sake."

A breeze blew across the clearing, leaves swirling into the air before fluttering down to the ground again, leaving only silence in their wake.

Something Like Stories: Volume Three

Something Like Family

by Jay Bell

Astoria, Washington
May, 2020

Good news, Benjamin! I'll be home earlier than planned. Sightseeing on my own isn't any fun. I used to like it before we got back together, but I had Chinchilla with me then. Now that she's gone, it just isn't the same. I woke up early and drove all morning to reach Astoria. Jason is packing now. It'll be a full house again soon, so enjoy that quiet time while you can. Love you!

Tim sent the text message but didn't lower the phone. Instead he used it to take photos of Jason's apartment. He walked from room to room, documenting anything that had changed since their previous visit, or that he thought Ben would find interesting. This helped reassure him too, since it was clear that Jason and William were doing well.

Gone was the tiny converted motel room where they used to live. Jason had a respectable two-bedroom apartment now, filled with possessions that he and his husband had accumulated over the years. Tim didn't recognize the significance of most objects, but they filled him with warmth anyway, because he knew from his own home how every knickknack represented a memory. The old metal oil can on the living room shelf, for instance. Maybe they had found it at an antique mall, or while exploring an abandoned farm, and took it with them as a souvenir of a day spent together.

Tim grinned when he noticed the framed photo nearby. A group shot of all four of them. Ben was on the far left, his arm around Jason's waist. Tim had their son hooked by the neck, Jason appearing a little overwhelmed by the excess of affection. And on the far right, Tim's other arm was resting on William's beefy shoulders, his son-in-law's cheeks bright red. He always used to blush when Tim was around. Funny how that never seemed to happen anymore. Funny, and also worrying. Tim wasn't getting any younger. Was he finally losing his edge?

A text message popped up on his phone. Ben's response. Tim opened it and was disappointed to only find a string of emojis. All of them were positive, but they weren't as personal as words. He understood. Ben was at work right now. And swamped. A slew of new students with speech and language impairments had been placed into his care this semester. A record amount for the school, forcing them to finally give Ben a bigger classroom. He had his work cut out for him. Even his nights were filled with grading papers, creating plans for individual students, and filling out evaluation forms. Tim had decided that what Ben needed most was a little peace and quiet, so he had opted to make this a road trip instead of a quick flight.

"He's almost done packing," William said, entering the room. "Or to be more precise, he's making sure that I didn't forget anything when packing for him."

"It's a thankless job being married," Tim said. "And yet, somehow it's still the absolute best thing in the world." He tacked on a smile to the end of this, fishing for a reaction.

"You've got that right," William said, returning the gesture. But he didn't blush.

Feeling insecure, Tim casually hit the button on his phone so that the camera was focused on him instead. He looked okay. Were the light bags under his eyes always there, or was the early start to blame? Maybe he just needed to up his game. He was scratching the back of his neck self-consciously when inspiration struck.

"Hey," he said, pocketing his phone. "Do you have scissors?"

"Sure," William said. "In the kitchen."

Tim followed him there, stripping off his shirt along the way. William opened a drawer, took out a pair of scissors, and when he turned around... There it was! The blush!

"This tag on my shirt is driving me crazy," Tim said, keeping his muscles tense as he reached for the scissors. He puffed up his chest when using them to cut off the tag. By the time he handed the scissors back, William's cheeks were bright red.

"Oh god," a voice said from behind. "Whose idea was this? And can we stop a moment to recognize how sad it is that I need to ask?"

Tim turned to face Jason. "I had an itchy shirt tag! It's bad enough normally, but when the back of a car seat is pressing against it for an entire day…" He pulled the shirt over his head again. "Ready to go?"

"Yeah." Jason reached down to touch the handle of the suitcase sitting next to him, but he didn't pick it up. Instead his expression grew hopeful.

"You don't mind my muscles when it comes to heavy lifting, do you?" Tim said smugly as he moved to pick it up.

"Never," Jason said. "Why do you think I married my own set?"

"I've got this," William said, sweeping past him to take the luggage.

Tim was content to let him, understanding how good it felt to be useful. They walked as a group to the curb, Tim opening the trunk of his Dodge Challenger so the suitcase could be placed inside. Then he hugged William.

"He'll be back in ten days," Tim assured him. "In good condition too."

"Drive safe," William said, but not in the casual way that most people did. His words carried extra weight, maybe because of his own history with car accidents, or his near-daily job of rescuing people.

"We'll be careful," Tim said. "Promise."

He got into the car so that William and Jason could say goodbye in privacy, although he did angle the rearview mirror to watch them kissing and hugging. Not for any voyeuristic reason. This was another type of reassurance. He needed to see that Jason was loved and protected. There was little doubt of that with William around, but parents tended to fret no matter how well things seemed in their children's lives. Now he would worry a little less.

"Got everything?" Tim asked after Jason had climbed into the car.

His son nodded, a little quiet in his response. "Yeah."

Parting was never easy. Not when your world revolved around the other person.

"I know what you were doing back there," Jason said a few blocks later, levity having returned to his voice. "Taking off your shirt to get William flustered."

"Hey," Tim said in his own defense. "I'm officially in my forties now. For a gay man, that's the same as turning invisible."

Jason looked over at him quizzically. "What do you mean?"

"I don't stand out as much as I used to. *Everyone* goes to the gym these days. That's how it feels. And people seem to get younger by the day. When I used to walk through the room at one of Marcello's parties, I could feel everyone's heads turning to follow me. Now it's more like—"

"Most of the room instead of all of it?" Jason cut in. "Maybe it's not your age. People get used to you, no matter how… Never mind."

Tim pulled his eyes from the road. "What?"

"You're going to make me say it?" Jason sighed. "Fine. You're handsome, okay? That's something people can't get from a gym, and trust me, being young isn't always enough. You're still something special, but you're also familiar. How long have you been hanging out in Marcello's social circles? Since you were in college, right? That's half your life."

Tim blinked. "Wow. I guess it is!"

"There you go. People have had twenty years to stare at you. They've got it all memorized by now. That's why they don't look as long."

Tim grinned. Then he reached over to ruffle his son's hair. "Who knew this trip would be so good for my self-esteem?"

Jason exhaled. "And yet, I'm feeling drained for some reason."

Tim laughed. "Don't worry, my parents are exhausting too. I'm pretty sure that's normal."

"It is," Jason said, sounding certain. "William and I were talking about this the other day. He said he doesn't feel like he has much in common with his family, and that's why they wear him out. You pick your friends based on shared interests, but you're stuck with your family, no matter how different you are from them."

"That's not always true," Tim said. "Ben is a *lot* like his mom. And when he's having a bad day, he reminds me of his sister. Just don't tell him I said so."

Jason laughed. "What about your parents? What do you have in common with them?"

Nothing. They often seemed like aliens to him, but when he really thought about it… "I have my dad's eyes and build. The rest—hair, skin tone, all that stuff—comes from my mom."

"Sure," Jason said. "But that's only physical. Just because

you meet someone who looks like you, doesn't mean you'll get along with them."

"True. Let's see... My mom is really dedicated. I'm like that with Benjamin. He's my everything. My drive to succeed probably comes from my dad. We're not short on money, but I still need to work every day to feel like I have a purpose. My mom has some of that too, but she was happy to retire. I don't think my dad ever will. I definitely get my spiritual side from Mom, so that's something." Tim glanced over sharply. "Wait, do you feel like you don't have anything in common with Ben and me? Is that what you're saying?"

Jason squirmed in his seat. "Well..."

Tim shook his head as they merged onto the highway. "I'll prove it. You're both musical, right? He sings and you play guitar—two different instruments—but pretty much the same thing. You get that from him. And you're both boy crazy."

Jason snorted. "Boy crazy?"

"Yeah. Sneaking into guy's rooms at night, forcing your way into their lives, upsetting perfectly respectable families with your home-wrecking ways."

Jason laughed. "Okay. Maybe we're guilty of that."

"It's the intensity of your love," Tim said. "You both have amazing hearts."

"Thanks," Jason said. "This trip is turning out to be good for my self-esteem too."

That made Tim happy. The awkward silence that followed, not so much, because a big question hung in the air. What did he have in common with Jason?

"Did you see the newest season of *American Horror Story*?" Jason asked, as if searching for an answer.

"Not yet. I know you think I'd like that but... I'll try it and get back to you."

"It's fine," Jason said. "You're not into scary stuff anyway. How about *Better Call Saul*? You liked *Breaking Bad*, didn't you?"

"Yeah, but the spinoff is kind of slow. I bailed after the first season."

"So did I," Jason said with a chuckle. "William watches it though, so I still catch the occasional episode. It's actually really good."

Was that it? They had both decided to stop watching the same show early on? That wasn't much of a bond. "Did you ever read the Edward Hopper book I gave you?" Tim asked. It was the same one Eric had loaned him shortly after Tim's snowmobile accident. Eric had initially bought the book for himself, but the cover had drawn Tim in. Later, when he asked to borrow it, Eric had made it a gift instead. By doing so, he had passed on one of his interests. Tim had tried duplicating that experience when he gave it to Jason. Not the same copy. Eric had written an inscription in the front, so he couldn't part with it, but he still hoped Jason would be just as captivated by the art.

"Edward Hopper?" Jason asked, as if struggling to remember. "Oh! The book of drawings."

Paintings mostly, but he supposed that answered his question.

"I've flipped through it," Jason said. "It's not the sort of book a person reads, is it?"

Tim had. Front to back.

"Sorry," Jason said, noticing his expression. "I just get busy."

"It's totally fine," Tim said, attempting to sound upbeat. "I was only curious."

"You were trying to find common ground," Jason said. "So was I. It's okay. We love each other. And I don't actually find you exhausting. I was just teasing. I've been looking forward to this trip all month."

"Me too," Tim said. After a moment of silence, he added. "It's hard not to feel a *little* envious of how much you and Benjamin have in common. Can't you—I don't know—start jogging or something? Or hey! Have you ever done one of those paint by numbers? There's still an art to it, and it's really easy."

Jason laughed. "I'm sure I'd manage to mess it up somehow. Don't let what I said get to you. In a way, it makes sense that I'm more like Ben."

"How so?"

"Well... Have you ever done the math?"

Tim shook his head, not understanding.

Jason clarified. "Like how old you would have been when I was born."

That wasn't hard to figure out. Tim simply subtracted his birth year from Jason's own. "Let's see... I would have been eleven."

"Right."

Tim made a face. "I don't see your point. Ben would have been the same age, more or less."

"Yeah, but when did you meet him? How old were you then?"

"Sixteen."

"Exactly! So it's almost like Ben had me before you two met. I'm his child from a previous marriage. That explains why I'm more like him and nothing like you."

Ouch. Tim knew it was a joke, but it still hurt.

"Not as much like you," Jason quickly amended. "Sorry. It was a lot funnier when William and I first thought of it."

Tim mustered a laugh. "It's a funny idea. I get it."

"I love you," Jason stressed. "It doesn't matter how much we have in common. I'm adopted anyway, so if anything, it's surprising that I have *anything* in common with either of you."

"You're not adopted," Tim said. "You're my son." He didn't care if it made sense, or if the numbers added up to realistic ages. It was a truth he felt in his heart. "And I love you too."

"Thanks," Jason said. "You know I've always found it easier to talk to you, right? Especially when I mess up."

"That's for sure," Tim said, shooting him a smile that was surface only. He found it easier to admit his mistakes to Marcello than he did Ben, but that didn't make them family. That made them friends.

"Maybe we can both take up knitting," Jason said. "Doesn't matter if we end up hating it. We'll stick with it, just so we have something we can point to. Pun intended. Get it? Needles? Points?"

Tim let go of his frustration. What he really wanted to do was pull the car over and hug Jason for trying so hard. Instead he reached over to grip his shoulder. "We're family," he said. "That's enough in common for me."

"Same here," Jason said, putting his hand over Tim's before it moved back to the wheel. "I'm really excited about this trip. Did you see very much on the way up?"

"Nah." The original plan was to take his time while driving north, checking out the sights along the way. White Sands National Monument, for instance. The ivory dunes were impressive, but without someone to share in his wonder, Tim had felt lonely and isolated. He was halfway to Mount Rushmore when he decided to scrap his plans and drive directly to Astoria instead. "Nothing sounded as good as seeing you."

"Thanks, Dad. Hey, maybe we can stop somewhere on the way to Austin. Make some memories."

"Yeah?" Tim looked over at him, buoyed by the thought.

"Yeah," Jason said, grinning back at him.

Tim tightened his grip on the steering wheel. "Then we have planning to do!"

They might not share any hobbies, but they had a shared history that could be strengthened by adding to it. With any luck, this trip might end up being exactly what they both needed.

After taking turns driving, they reached their first destination, although neither of them was particularly excited when cruising into Sacramento. Maybe the late hour was to blame. Who wasn't weary after being on the road for so long? Tim pulled into the parking lot of the first decent hotel he saw. He was checking in at the front desk when he noticed the somewhat despondent way that Jason browsed a rack of brochures. He understood why.

Tim had wanted to see Yosemite National Park. Jason would have rather visited San Francisco. Sprawling nature versus a congested city. The two destinations couldn't be of greater contrast, which only seemed to underscore their personal differences. They entertained the idea of visiting both, but with a four-hour distance between each location and still so many miles to go before they made it to Austin, they were forced to choose. So they had compromised and opted for somewhere in the middle. Sacramento. Tim was sure it was a nice city. It just wasn't what either of them desired.

If only Ben was here. He would know how to make this right. He would probably tell Tim something obvious he'd been missing. Tim would feel silly in retrospect, he and Jason would bond again, and everything would be perfect. Maybe that was the problem. What if Ben had acted as the bridge between them all this time? They shouldn't need him to feel comfortable around each other. No, they had to get through this on their own. How hard could it be?

Tim finished checking in and walked over to join his son. "Anything good?" he asked.

"All sorts of options," Jason responded.

"Hey, the Crocker Art museum!" Tim reached for the brochure. "They have a great reputation. We've gotta check them out. The building is supposed to be cool too."

"Oh," Jason said, lowering his arm. "Sure, we can do that."

"What do you have there?" Tim asked, nodding at the brochure that Jason was trying to conceal.

Jason grinned sheepishly and held it up. "The Jelly Belly factory. They give guided tours."

Okay. Forget one of the most prestigious art collections in the state. They were going to see where diabetes was manufactured. "Uh huh," he replied. "That sounds fun."

"It's dumb," Jason said, quickly shelving the brochure. "What else?"

Tim turned back to the options. "How about the California Automobile Museum?"

"Could be neat," Jason said. "Then again, we're already spending most of this trip in a car."

"True," Tim said. He still wouldn't have minded, but he understood why Jason wouldn't find it appealing. "Anything else leap out at you?"

"This one looked promising," Jason said, pulling the brochure free. "The Old Sacramento Waterfront. All of the buildings look like they were built in the eighteen-hundreds, and the sidewalks are made of wood. Isn't that funny? There are a bunch of shops, including art galleries. It's sort of outdoorsy too, since it's right by the river."

Tim nodded. "Anything that you would like though?"

"Yeah! I pulled it up on my phone already. They have a costume shop and weird things like that. Could be fun."

"Okay," Tim said. "That's what we'll do. For now, let's get settled for the night. We can order room service and plan our next stop. I was thinking Vegas."

Jason's face lit up. "Really?"

"Yeah. I've never been."

"Me neither!"

Tim grinned and felt a little better. Their first stop was unlikely to be a big hit. So what? They still had a few more days to get it right.

* * * * *

They started early the next morning, wanting to see as much

as they could before hitting the road again. As it turned out, they were a little too early since most of the shops were still closed when they reached the waterfront. They had breakfast, walked along the river, and stood outside the Railroad Museum, debating about going inside.

"I mean, I like trains," Jason said. "But I don't know if I'm ready for that level of commitment."

"Same here," Tim said with a chuckle. He still found it better than the alternative, which would be...

"The shops seem to be opening," Jason said, spinning around to look in the other direction.

Exactly. Tim enjoyed shopping, but they could do that anywhere. Experiencing local culture was more important to him, but he gave up on those plans when Jason turned an eager expression on him.

"I see salt water taffy!"

"Let's go get some," Tim said, already wishing that he had let Jason take the Jelly Belly factory tour instead. Especially when faced with a bunch of equally weird and chewy flavors of taffy. Kooky candy was obviously something Jason enjoyed, and a factory would have been more interesting than a shop.

"Sss'good!" Jason said as they left the shop, his mouth full of blue goo. "Tase juss like Boo Berry!"

"I'll take your word for it," Tim said. "I'm still recovering from the sriracha one."

"Nrrrg!" Jason said, stopping and nudging him with an elbow.

"Did you bite your tongue?" Tim asked. "Or your cheek? Hard to say which is worse."

Jason shook his head. Then he nodded to an open space next to the nearest building. A white wooden fence separated it from the sidewalk. Beyond this the ground dropped sharply. A framed entrance lead to stairs, the sign hanging above them labeling it as Pioneer Park. A funny name, considering that all they saw below was an empty lot of flattened dirt and a few trees.

"I read about this last night," Jason said after swallowing. "Sacramento used to be built lower down. Then it flooded so bad that they raised the entire city up fourteen feet or something crazy like that."

"Really?" Tim asked, his interest piqued.

"Yeah! A bunch of tunnels still exist beneath the city. There are guided tours, but I didn't think we'd have time."

"I wonder if we can get into them on our own," Tim said. "You interested?"

Jason nodded eagerly. "Let's do it."

Common ground at last! Tim was intrigued by the engineering feat. Jason was probably more into the creepy ambience, but at least they had found a shared interest. He felt optimistic as they descended the steps. Scattered in the dirt were old masonry blocks. Hints of a former foundation. Broken columns remained too, a handful of which still stood.

"This used to be a butcher shop," Jason said, reading from a sign. "It started small during the gold rush and ended up being four stories high."

"I never would have guessed," Tim said, running his fingers along one of the ornate columns. "So down here is the original street level?"

"I think so," Jason said. Then he pointed. "That must be one of the tunnels."

To either side of the stairs was a wall of boards, like a privacy fence, stretching all the way up to the modern-day street above them. The gap between each plank revealed nothing but darkness. The tunnels. Using them they could walk beneath the street and who knows what else, if only they could gain access. Tim was moving toward the wooden barrier to inspect it when he heard a low growl coming from the shadows beyond.

"What the hell was that?" he hissed, halting in his tracks.

Jason banged into him from behind. "What?"

"There's something in there!" Tim said. "In the tunnels!"

"Ha ha," Jason deadpanned. "You're full of it."

"I'm not." Tim took another step forward. Nothing. Another step. Still nothing. One more and…

Grrrrr.

They both heard it this time.

"Holy shit," Jason said, grabbing hold of Tim's arm.

"I told you! Let's get out of here!"

"Wait." Jason pushed past him. He had his phone out as he crept forward. Lower down, toward the corner where one of the planks had rotted away, was a small dingy hole just big enough to squeeze through. A human would never fit in there, probably not even a child, but a creature of some sort could. As if to prove this, another deep growl came from the hole.

"That sounds like a warning to me," Tim said. "Get back here! What are you doing?"

"Looking," Jason said. He turned on his phone's light, moving it along the planks.

"What do you see?"

"Nothing," Jason said, inching closer. "Yet."

He squatted and held his phone in front of the opening.

"Don't do that," Tim said, moving to stop him. "It isn't safe."

The growl intensified. They needed to call animal control, or maybe the Ghostbusters, because this wasn't normal. Whatever lurked in the tunnels had to be a lion that had escaped from the zoo, or maybe some sort of mutant monster, or—

"It's a dog!" Jason said.

Tim froze. "What?"

"For real! Look!"

Jason moved aside and handed him the phone. His concerns momentarily forgotten, Tim took it, got down on his knees, and shined the light into the hole. Sure enough, he saw two green glowing circles. The faint outline of a muzzle too. "You sure that isn't a wolf? Or maybe a coyote?"

"No," Jason admitted. "Can you see the ears?"

Tim moved the light back and forth while squinting. "Yeah. They're floppy."

"Then it has to be a dog."

Tim looked over his shoulder. "What's it doing in there?"

"I don't know," Jason said, expression grim, "but we have to get it out."

"I agree." Tim stood. After handing back the phone, he brushed the dirt off his hands. "Any suggestions?"

"We can try talking to it." Jason started whistling and saying things like, "Here, puppy! Come on out now!"

Nothing happened.

"How about a treat?" Tim said. That had always worked when Chinchilla wouldn't come inside. "I wish we had food on us."

"I have these," Jason said, holding up the bag of taffy.

Tim grimaced. "That's not going to help unless dog food is one of the flavors."

Jason started digging around in the bag, like he wasn't sure. "We have banana dream, frothy root beer, juicy pear, sizzlin' bacon and eggs—"

"What?"

Jason reached in and pulled out a small yellow blob wrapped in wax paper. "Bacon and eggs," he repeated. "Think that'll work?"

"It has a better chance than root beer," Tim muttered. "Unwrap it and see." A few seconds later he added, "Not with your hand!"

Jason was reaching for the dark hole, taffy resting in his outstretched palm. A few inches closer and he could have lost his entire hand!

"Here," Tim said, grabbing a twig off the ground.

He took the taffy from Jason, skewered it like it was a marshmallow ready to be roasted over a campfire, and positioned this in front of the hole. They were both silent as they listened for a reaction. They heard sniffing, then the unmistakable sound of chops being licked. After a long pause, a muzzle poked out of the hole.

"Don't let it have it," Jason said. "We want the poor thing out of there."

Tim pulled back. The muzzle thrust forward, followed by two beady eyes, which regarded them suspiciously.

"Come on, puppy!" Jason said. "Dinner time! Or breakfast, I guess. Come get your bacon and eggs!"

The dog whimpered, as if pleading with them to be reasonable. Tim brought the taffy closer. A strand of drool fell from the animal's mouth, but he pulled away again before it could get so much as a lick.

"It's okay," Tim said. "We won't hurt you."

Another whimper.

"There's no room for negotiation," Tim replied. "If you want a treat, you have to come out where we can see you."

The dog harrumphed in a way so familiar that a flood of happy memories nearly broke his heart. Tim almost gave in, but then they heard paws scurrying against the dirt. The nose and eyes became an entire head. A lot more wiggling revealed the rest of the body as the dog squeezed its way free. Its fur was so matted that clumps of dirt hung off it like mud-caked dreadlocks. The dog's attention was on the twig Tim held, but its posture was poised to flee.

"Now what?" he asked out of the corner of his mouth.

"Let it have the taffy," Jason said. "It's probably not healthy, but anything is better than starving."

"You think it has been?" Tim asked.

Jason nodded glumly. "A dog that size shouldn't be able to fit into a hole that small."

Tim held the twig out, the dog's eyes remaining trained on his, even as its teeth snapped around the taffy and pulled. They watched as it chewed, the dog's head moving up and around with the effort of figuring out this strange substance. Then it spit the taffy out again and looked at them like they were crazy.

"I agree," Tim said with a laugh.

The sound startled the animal, who turned and darted for the hole. Jason was quicker. He threw himself in front of the opening to block it. The dog skidded to a halt. Then it turned and ran in the opposite direction.

"Don't let it get away!" Jason shouted.

Tim was already giving chase. He swiped the air in front of him, his fingertips brushing against filthy fur, but he wasn't quick enough to grab the animal. The dog ran circles around him before deciding to flee. It took off up the stairs, Jason right behind it. Tim grinned. *This* he was good at! The dog might be fast, but Tim had endurance, even if he didn't possess the lung capacity he once did. He took the steps three at a time and—

Tripped.

Tim hit the stairs, bracing himself on his palms, his face a fraction of an inch from the pointed corner of a step. He growled as he pushed himself up, sounding much like the dog he intended to capture. He wouldn't give up so easily. He made it back to street level, looked around, and spotted Jason running down an alley. Tim raced after him and passed his son as the dog went around a corner. He was just about to catch up to it when the damn mutt ducked beneath a delivery truck. Tim didn't slow until he was standing in front of the vehicle. If the dog went the other way, it would run into Jason.

As it turned out, the dog wasn't going anywhere. Tim bent

over to look beneath the truck, where the dog was spread out while panting. It wasn't the only one. Jason was gasping for breath when he finally caught up.

"Not... good," he said, waving vaguely at the vehicle and then the alley.

"He might get run over if the truck moves," Tim interpreted. Around them were the backdoors of various businesses. Any one of them could be receiving a delivery. Or maybe they made deliveries on occasion, and this was their transportation.

"We can wait for the driver," Jason said between gulps of air.

"We might be waiting all day," Tim said. "Even if we get someone to move the truck, if the dog panics, it could be bad."

Jason winced and nodded. "Any ideas? I lost my taffy somewhere back there."

Tim shook his head. "We need better bait. You wait here. I'll see what I can find."

Jason nodded and moved around to the driver-side door. There he sat on the ground, so he could see beneath the truck. He would also be in the way if the driver came back. Smart kid. But not very fast. If the dog made another run for it while Tim was away, they would probably lose it.

Tim broke into a sprint, turning the corner at the end of the block. The first shop was a clothing store. That was useless, unless the dog had a thing for vintage hats. A book store was next, then a candy store, followed by a bakery. Tim almost disregarded this last option, thinking the dog wouldn't want anything sweet, until he saw the window display. Then he ducked inside, and a minute later, was back on the street and pumping his arms, precious cargo gripped in one hand.

"A baguette?" Jason said when Tim made it back to him.

"It's genius," Tim said. "You'll see." He squatted down, pulled the baguette free from its paper sheath, and stuck it beneath the truck.

"I've gotta admit," Jason said with a laugh, "not many foods have that kind of reach. Hey, he likes it!"

"He?" Tim asked. He leaned over to see better. The dog was biting the end of the baguette and scurrying backward until a piece ripped free, which it made short work of.

"It's definitely a boy," Jason said as he watched. "He started licking himself while you were gone."

"I guess anything tastes better than that taffy," Tim joked. "Okay, mutt. The first bite is always free. If you want more, you'll have to come out from under there."

Tim stood and walked to the other side of the truck, where the dog was closest to the edge. He pointed the baguette at the ground and waved it around like a metal detector. That did the trick. The dog came out of hiding, eyes trained on the bread.

"Now what?" Tim asked.

"We need a leash," Jason said. "Or the car."

"Where is it parked? I'm all turned around."

"I marked the location on my phone," Jason said, pulling it out to check. "It's close. Really close!"

"I don't want him running off on a busy street." Tim reached into his pocket for the keys. "Get the car and drive it here. *Carefully.*"

"Be right back," Jason said, catching the keys when they were tossed to him.

Tim decided to sit, hoping the dog would do the same. It worked. The dog settled down and cocked its head.

"Good," Tim said, tearing off a chunk of bread for it. "Let's just relax together and have a meal. We're breaking bread. That makes us friends, okay?"

The dog looked away while chewing, not ready to put a title on anything just yet.

"Holding out for some protein?" Tim asked. "We can do that too. If you don't run off again, I'll get you *real* bacon and eggs. How's that sound? Do we have a deal?"

The dog perked up. It really was a miserable sight. Tim couldn't tell what color the fur was. Gray or brown maybe, but that could just be the layers of grime. The only spot of color came from a bright red wound on one leg, which didn't look too serious. The cut wasn't bleeding, but it was exposed to air. That couldn't be good.

"We'll get you fixed up," Tim promised. "And reunited with your owners. Is there a collar under there somewhere?"

He reached for the dog, who recoiled from him. Tim tore off another piece of bread and waited until it was chewing. Then he tried again. The dog was willing to tolerate him as long as food kept coming. After a few more bites, Tim was finally allowed to touch the animal. He did so gingerly, moving his hand along the fur of the neck, which felt dry in some places and oily in others, but he didn't detect a collar.

The sound of an engine caught his attention. Jason parked the car at the end of the alley and got out.

"I didn't want to scare him," he explained when nearing. "How's it going?"

"Okay," Tim said as he stood. "I think. It doesn't have a collar."

"He," Jason repeated. "That's okay. He might be microchipped."

"Do you have an app for that?"

Jason laughed. "No, but if we get him in the car, we can take him to the nearest shelter. They'll be able to check."

And take care of the dog until the owners were found.

"All right, mutt," Tim said, waving the baguette in the air. "Follow the bread."

He began walking toward the car. The dog kept pace, attention transfixed on the baguette. This was better than a leash! Dogs yanked against those and resisted them. Tim was pretty sure he could walk all the way to Texas like this, the dog never leaving his side as long as there was still bread to nibble. Jason hurried forward and opened the car door, leaning the driver seat forward to expose the back. Tim sighed as he neared, because he knew what he had to do, and what that would result in. He tossed the baguette into the backseat. The dog hopped right in. Jason quickly returned the driver seat to its normal position.

"Okay," Tim said. "You navigate to the nearest shelter. I'll drive."

They climbed into the car and shut the doors. Tim turned the ignition, glancing back to see how the animal reacted. It was fine. The upholstery, however, was already covered in crumbs and dirt. Just as he feared.

"Got it!" Jason said. "Make a left on the street up ahead."

Tim focused on the road. They didn't have far to drive. Just a little over a mile. Once they reached the shelter, Jason got out of the car. "You both stay here," he said. "I'll let them know what's going on."

He shut the door before waiting for an answer. Tim angled the rearview mirror so he could see the backseat. The baguette had been reduced to a soggy stump that was slowly melding with the seat fabric. The dog stared back at him, expression inquisitive.

"You'll have a roof over your head tonight," Tim said. "And real food, don't worry. You'll be better off than me. I'll be feeding money into a slot machine while getting poorer by the second."

The dog began licking its wound, maybe to show that it had bigger concerns than the frivolous dreams of a tourist. Tim returned the mirror to the usual position and stared unseeing at his surroundings, trying not to think much of anything at all.

"No microchip," said Georgia, the woman who ran the shelter.

She was stocky with short hair, her large arms rivaling Tim's own. They must be useful when having to pick up the larger dogs, as he had seen her do with this one. The animal was currently on the exam table and seemed concerned about the two people poking and prodding it.

"Ears look okay," Jason said, peering into a scope he had stuck into one. "Nice and pink."

"The teeth are in good shape as well," Georgia replied after exposing the gums. "He's awfully young. You'd think someone would miss him."

"Do you have a binder we can flip through?"

Georgia nodded. "Mm-hm. Might want to get him cleaned up first, so you can see what you're dealing with."

Jason grinned. "Good idea."

"What about the wound on its leg?" Tim asked.

"Granuloma," Georgia and Jason said at the same time.

They looked at each other and laughed.

"Go ahead," Jason said to her.

"It could be caused by an infection," Georgia explained. "Or more likely, it's a reaction to stress. Imagine a toddler sucking their thumb so long that the skin starts to come off."

"Jesus," Tim breathed. "That's depressing."

"We'll put some ointment on it after he's cleaned up," Georgia said. "It should take care of itself from there."

"We'll pay for everything," Tim said, reaching for his wallet.

"Time is probably the greater concern," Jason said after they heard the front door chime. He turned to Georgia. "Why don't you let us take care of this? Do you have a grooming station we can use?"

Georgia nodded. "You're looking at it. We do the shaving here and the washing in the back. Do you have experience? I thought you said you were in wildlife rehabilitation."

"I am, but before that, I volunteered at a shelter."

"Oh? Where?"

"Austin."

"Texas?" Georgia lit up. "How funny! I used to do wildlife rehabilitation outside of Abilene. When we moved here, there wasn't as much of a need, so I switched."

"We traded places!" Jason said.

"More or less."

Tim was unable to participate in this exchange, but he was proud of Jason for doing so much to help animals in need. He admired that sort of work. They wouldn't leave here without donating a hefty sum.

"Make yourself at home," Georgia said on her way out of the room. "If you need anything, just holler."

"Will do," Jason said.

"Now what?" Tim asked him.

"Um..."

Jason glanced around until he found something that reminded Tim of what an IV drip would hang off, except it clamped to the side of the exam table. A noose hung from it, which seemed kind of grim. Jason put the dog's head through this. Then he opened a drawer where Georgia had indicated the clippers would be.

"What can I do?" Tim asked.

"Just keep him calm. Uh... Here. Feed him these. Slowly."

He took some treats from the counter. That got the dog's attention. It barely noticed when Jason turned on the clippers and started working on the fur mats. He made it look effortless. Tim still fed the dog treats every minute or so, but mostly he watched his son handle himself like a professional sheep shearer.

"Look at you go!" Tim said in awe.

Jason smiled in response. "He's making it easy for me. What a sweetheart. Yes you are!"

The dog wagged its tail in response. It already looked better. Most of the mats seemed to be on its belly and sides. Once they were removed, Jason turned off the clippers.

"We should try a bath now. That'll help us see what I've missed. Ready?"

"Just tell me what to do."

"Can you carry him?"

Tim snorted. "Has it forgotten how to walk?"

Jason cocked his head. "Why do you keep doing that?"

"What?"

"Referring to it—to *him*, as a thing."

"No reason. I just don't want to um...." Tim cleared his throat, which felt tight. "I don't want to get attached. I probably won't be allowed to keep it. Him."

Jason looked surprised. "Do you *want* to adopt him?"

Tim shrugged. "I don't know. It's been a few years since... I'm not sure I'm ready. Even though I love him."

Jason laughed. "This is it!"

"What?"

"Our thing! We're both animal nuts. You've known this dog for half an hour and you already love him? That's so me. No... It's so *you*. I get that from you!"

Tim grinned. Then he strode forward and scooped the dog up in his arms. A wet nose sniffed his face, a tongue lolling out to lick his neck.

"Looks like he loves you too," Jason said before putting on a somber expression. "But you're right. We shouldn't get too attached just yet. Let's get him cleaned up. Then we'll see."

"He's a blond!" Jason said, taking a step back to survey his work.

Tim wiped the water from his eyes to see better. The dog, perhaps noticing this, shook again and sent droplets flying everywhere. Tim didn't mind. It's not like he could get any wetter. He had stripped off his shirt halfway through, and not to show off. Jason had done the same. Their jeans were soaked in the front, all the way down the legs. Neither one of them were complaining. All that mattered was that they had succeeded. The dog looked great. His mouth was hanging open, eyes shining in a way that resembled a smile.

"I think he's a golden retriever," Jason said. "Maybe not purebred, but he has a lot in him. They're smart dogs. Very friendly. High energy too."

"Do they like to run?" Tim asked.

"Oh yeah! Have you forgotten already? My legs still hurt."

Tim started to smile before he forced it away. "I guess we should try to find his owners now."

Jason nodded. He picked up his shirt and handed Tim's to him. "It's good the bread stayed down, but now I want to get a real meal in him. We'll put him in a kennel with a nice big bowl of food, and you and I can go outside to dry off. I figure it won't take long in this heat."

"Good idea."

They went outdoors and leaned against the rear of the Dodge Challenger. Jason let him have the binder, preferring to do a search on his phone. Tim put it on the trunk and flipped through page after page of missing pet posters. Some were printed in color. Others seemed to have been received via fax. Tim forced himself to be fair. Anytime he saw a dog that even vaguely resembled the one they had found, he scrutinized the photo and consulted with Jason before moving on. He would have wanted the same to be done had Chinchilla ever gone missing. She hadn't though. Tim had been too careful. He had done everything he could to make her happy, up until her final moment, which he had almost missed. Thank all that was good in the universe that he had made it home to her in time.

"I'm here, Chinchilla! You're such a good girl. You waited for me, didn't you? I'm so glad you did. It's okay now though, because I can see you're not feeling well and... I don't want you to suffer. Not even for me. I love you too much for that. You'll always be my little princess. There will never be another, I swear. I love you so much..."

Tim swallowed against the painful memory and wiped at his eyes. When he was sure he had himself under control again, he turned to his son.

"Do you think she would mind?" he asked.

Jason looked up from his phone. "Who?"

"Chinchilla. Do you think it would upset her to see me with another dog?"

Jason's response was gentle. "I think it would upset her more to see you turn away a dog who needs a home, just because you're thinking of her. If I found out that you and Ben wanted to adopt again but didn't because you were worried about making me jealous... I wouldn't like that."

"How would you feel about a hairy little brother?"

Jason nodded at the binder. "Keep looking. Even if we find

Taffy's owner, there are plenty more dogs who need homes."

Tim made a face. "Taffy?"

"It's a good name!"

"But he hates taffy," Tim countered. "You saw him. Even when he was starving and desperate, he couldn't stomach it."

Jason rolled his eyes. "What do you suggest we call him then? Baguette?"

Tim shook his head. "That's no good. Although maybe something along those lines. How about Pierre?"

Jason smirked. "You had a British Bulldog with a Spanish sounding name, and now you want to give a Golden Retriever a French name?"

"Why not?" Tim countered. "What country are they from originally?"

Jason consulted his phone. "Scotland."

"Close enough," Tim said. "It's a nice name."

"Pierre," Jason repeated tentatively. "It *is* kind of cute. Think he'd be willing to wear a French beret?"

"We're getting ahead of ourselves," Tim said. "For all we know, he already has a name."

"True," Jason said. "I'll keep searching."

Twenty minutes later, they had exhausted their options. Wherever the dog had come from, they couldn't find evidence that anyone was out there looking for him. The only question that remained was if Pierre had anyone willing to take him in. The decision wasn't an easy one for Tim. The pain caused by Chinchilla's death, the unceasing ache that still haunted him... could he really put himself through that again?

"Why don't you and William have any pets?" Tim asked as he pushed away from the car. "You could use a dog, right?"

"I wish," Jason said. "It's the apartment. Pets aren't allowed. As soon as we have a house, watch out. And if that house has land, it's going be like a farm had sex with a zoo."

Tim laughed. "What if Ben and I help you put a down payment on a place? We can cosign or whatever you need. That way you can adopt Pierre."

"That's ridiculously generous," Jason said, "but it's not the right time. We can't handle another move so soon, and I'm still getting used to the work I do. I want to focus on that. William's schedule is unpredictable so... It's okay if you're not ready. He's a beautiful dog. Someone will take him home. This is a no-kill shelter. There's no rush. We've already done enough by bringing him here."

Tim eyed his son, needing more exoneration than that. "Are you sure?"

"Yeah," Jason said. "Trust me. Golden retrievers always get adopted. What's most important is that he goes to a family that truly wants him."

"He won't have hurt feelings?"

Jason laughed. "He'll be riding a natural high from getting three square meals a day. He'll be fine."

Tim exhaled, feeling relieved. "Okay. Let's go talk to Georgia."

He put his arm around Jason and guided him forward. It had been a strange little adventure, but they had gained so much. Any doubt about their bond had been blown away. They both shared a passion for animals—enough that they were willing to cancel plans and exhaust themselves getting dirty and wet, if it meant helping a furry little critter. No matter what else happened on this trip, in Tim's mind, it had already been a success.

Tim stood in front of the stove, poking at a frying pan and occasionally checking the door to the living room, just in case the love of his life should appear there. It felt good to be home. As much as he liked his car, Tim was tired of being in it. Las Vegas had been a decadent blast, and he'd found the art of Santa Fe inspiring when they stopped in New Mexico, but now he was weary of travel and wanted nothing more than to be at home with his husband. He turned around to check the door again, and this time he was in luck.

Ben stood in the threshold, his hair a poofy mess as he rubbed sleepy eyes. "When did you get here?" he asked.

"Late last night. I couldn't stand the idea of staying in another hotel when we were so close." Tim walked over to give Ben a hug. And a kiss, even though his husband kept turning his head to resist.

"Stop!" Ben laughed. "I have morning breath."

"So do I," Tim said. "Who brushes their teeth before breakfast?"

"Maybe we should start," Ben said after a smooch. He stood

on his tiptoes to see past Tim. "Where's Jason?"

"Still sleeping. He's in his old room. I crashed on the couch. I didn't want to wake you."

"You should have," Ben said. "I missed you. And I can't wait to see him."

"He'll be up soon. For now…" Tim rushed back to the stove. "Have a seat! Breakfast is almost ready."

"How nice," Ben murmured. Then he sat at the table and yawned himself awake.

Tim danced around him, getting everything ready before setting down three plates.

"I'll go get our son," Tim said, grinning at him.

Ben looked just as giddy. As much as they enjoyed their solitude, it was nice to have a full house again. Fuller than Ben realized. Tim went to the living room, but he didn't climb the stairs to where Jason slumbered. Instead he went to the patio door that led out to the backyard. A dog was sitting just beyond, head tilted to one side as if to say, "Aren't I cute? Doesn't that make you want to open the door for me?"

The answer was yes, so he complied.

"Be good, okay?" he whispered. "First impressions are a big deal. Don't mess this up."

Pierre sniffed the air. Then his paws scrambled on the floor before he broke into a run. By the time Tim closed the door and turned to follow, he heard a commotion in the kitchen.

"What in the world?" Ben said. "Oh my gosh! Who do we have here?"

"I can explain!" Tim said, rushing into the room.

Ben was kneeling on the kitchen floor, laughing as his face was licked. "Jason got a dog!" he said.

"More like you got a dog."

Ben looked up sharply. "What?"

"I'm breaking up with you," Tim said. "To soften the blow, I brought you a dog. That's how it's done, right?"

Ben stared at him. Then he laughed. "It seemed like a good idea at the time."

"It was the best idea," Tim said, helping him to his feet. "You know how happy Chinchilla made me. I'm ready for more of that. We have a big home, and we both know it can feel lonely when one of us isn't here so… What do you think?"

Ben smiled. "He's not ours already?"

"Nope," Tim said. "Pierre is only along for the ride, mostly so he can collect on a debt. I promised him bacon and eggs if he didn't run off again. Catching him wasn't easy. I had to resort to bribery. It wouldn't have been fair to leave him in Sacramento without fulfilling my promise, and we were short on time, so we brought him with us. Jason kept insisting that we only feed him healthy dog food for the first couple of days and—"

"You had to bring him home so he could finally get his breakfast."

Tim beamed at him. "Exactly."

"We take promises very seriously in this household," Ben said meaningfully. "Don't we?"

"That's right."

"Just promise me you didn't set three plates at the table because you want him to—"

"Sit here?" Tim said, pulling out one of the chairs.

Pierre hopped up instantly and shoved his muzzle into a plate.

Ben groaned.

"He's a sophisticated dog," Tim said in his defense. "Although he does have some bad habits we need to discuss."

"Is he house-broken?" Ben asked, sitting guardedly in front of his own plate.

"He is," Tim said, taking a seat across from him. "But that's not the issue. Pierre has a gambling problem. He lost a lot of money in Vegas."

Ben fixed him with a stare. "How much?"

"Five hundred," Tim said sheepishly. "The first night."

"You were only there one night!"

"Yeah, but the next morning, he thought he could win it back."

Ben sighed. "What's the damage?"

"A little over a thousand. He's sworn off gambling forever though, I swear. I mean, he swears. Right, Pierre?"

The dog raised his head, a strip of bacon dangling out of one side of his mouth. He turned a pleading expression on Ben.

"You're forgiven," Ben said. "But only if he promises not to do it again."

The dog resumed scarfing down food.

"He takes after you," Ben murmured.

"Funny how that works. You should hear him sing. He gets that from you."

Tim started howling. Pierre wasted no time in joining him. Jason padded into the kitchen shortly after, Tim rising to make breakfast for him. Pierre sat next to Tim during this, assessing his cooking techniques, while Ben subjected Jason to a barrage of questions and hugs. They always had a happy home, although on certain occasions, it felt like there was even more love than usual. Enough that their hearts were bursting at the seams.

―――――

Something Like Goodbye

by Jay Bell

Austin, Texas
2033

Your order is currently being packed and prepared. We will update you when it leaves our warehouse.

Your order is currently out for delivery. Your driver, Johnny G, will ensure that it arrives safely at the intended destination. We will update you with an estimated timeframe.

Johnny G is now heading toward your delivery address and should be arriving within the next half hour. To track their progress, please visit...

Tim tore his eyes away from the text messages and swore. He had lost track of time again while painting. He hadn't noticed the phone's attempts to get his attention until a car door slammed outside his studio. After glancing at the hour, he realized lunchtime had come and gone. That explained why his stomach was growling. He folded the phone and slid it into his pocket. If he was quick, he could meet the delivery guy before the dogs caught wind of him and—

Too late. A chorus of barking had already begun. He could already imagine Pierre at the back gate, the golden retriever jumping in an attempt to scale the fence and defend the house. Boris, his little cohort, would no doubt be nearby and watching, the pug's black eyes shining in admiration. The Terror Twins, Ben called them, and for good reason. Tim hurried to leave the large shed he used as a studio. The moment he was outside, he shouted, "Enough!"

That did the trick. The dogs stopped barking. This probably made it seem like he treated his animals roughly, when in truth, Boris and Pierre considered him to be the alpha dog of their pack and were more than happy to obey. By contrast, they never listened to Ben, which pleased Tim to no end.

He turned his attention to the car in the driveway, recognizing it from the previous delivery. His eyes moved to the front door of the house, where a skinny guy with blond hair stood and waited awkwardly. Johnny G, presumably. Tim remembered his sheepish smile from last time. He flashed one of his own as he approached.

"Sorry!" he said. "My dogs make a lot of noise, but they're harmless. Even if one managed to get out, all they'd do is lick you. And maybe help themselves to some food." He nodded at the bags of groceries already sitting on the porch. While he and Ben sometimes went to the store themselves, most of the items on their list remained the same from week to week, and having them automatically delivered was irresistibly convenient.

"It's okay," Johnny replied. "I love animals. Maybe I could meet them sometime?"

"Be careful what you wish for," Tim said. "They're sweet dogs, but not very well-behaved."

"I wouldn't mind."

Johnny sounded a little breathless. How old was he? Twenty? Younger? He looked like a baby to Tim. Still, it was nice to know that—even in his fifties—he still caught someone's eye on occasion. Tim grinned experimentally. Sure enough, Johnny's face flushed. Sweet, but he already had someone who reacted like that.

"Need me to sign anything?" Tim asked, knowing that it wasn't necessary. He simply wanted to bring this exchange to an end.

Johnny shook his head. "No. Do you want to um... Check to make sure the order is right?"

"I trust you," Tim said dismissively.

"It's just that I didn't pack it," Johnny stammered, "so you never know."

"I trust the warehouse boys too," Tim said. "Unless there's anything else you need, I better get these inside. To my husband."

Johnny didn't look too disappointed. If anything, he seemed even more excited. Maybe because now he could fantasize about Tim without worrying about anything actually happening. Or maybe it just made him happy to deliver for a gay couple. Either way...

"You got your tip, right?" Tim asked. "They let you keep the entire amount?"

Johnny nodded eagerly. "Yes. Thank you! If there's anything else you need, just let me know."

"Will do." Tim kept his expression neutral until he had entered the house. Then he let himself smile openly.

"Oh good," Ben said, coming down the living room stairs. "You got the delivery. Why do they wait until the second you're on the toilet before ringing the doorbell? Every single time, I swear." He noticed Tim's face when taking a bag from him. "Don't tell me. Another admirer?"

"Still got it," Tim said cockily.

"Just as long as you don't give it away. To anyone else, at least."

Ben sounded proud when saying this, maybe liking that his man was still in demand, when really, of the both of them, Tim felt that Ben was aging better. Sure he had a few more lines on his face, and his hair wasn't as thick as it had once been, but Tim found him just as irresistible as when they had first met. Even more so.

"I know that look," Ben said. "Are we going to put these groceries away, or do you want me to go out front with them and pretend to be the delivery boy?"

Tim chuckled. "That's a great idea actually. Next time though. There's ice cream and some other stuff that needs to go in the fridge."

"I made you a sandwich," Ben said as they went to the kitchen and began putting things away.

"Good! I'm starving."

"I didn't want to disturb you. I know you've been in the zone lately."

"I'm really feeling the new series," Tim said, kneeling in front of the refrigerator and moving items around to make space. "I'm thinking it's time for another exhibition."

"Really?" Ben asked. "Wow! It's been years."

"I know, but I didn't want to follow up the last one with anything that wasn't better, or at least as good."

"You're too hard on yourself." Ben neatly folded the reusable bag he'd just emptied. "I'm excited to see what you've come up with."

"Soon," Tim said. "I promise." He unpacked a bottle of champagne and tried to put it in the usual place before he noticed the spot was already occupied. He stared at a bottle foggy with condensation. Then he shrugged, finished unloading the rest of the items, and stood.

"You still need to eat," Ben said. "I could pack you a lunch before work tomorrow. Would you like that? I'll make it a sack lunch, like back in our school days. You can take it with you to the studio."

"Sounds fun. I'd love that!"

"It's a deal. I only wish I'd thought of it before we got this delivery. I would have ordered some juice boxes to make it more authentic."

Tim laughed while opening the pantry. He intended to put the champagne there but stopped when he saw another bottle already waiting. Tim frowned at this. Then he placed the bottle on the shelf next to the other, making them a pair, and turned around.

"When's the last time Marcello stopped by?"

Ben exhaled. "A week or two maybe? I can't remember."

Tim couldn't either. They had seen each other at the most recent charity fundraiser. Marcello had opted for a medieval theme, redecorating the ballroom to resemble a royal castle, complete with a throne for him to sit upon. He had made everyone approach him to pay tribute to their king, dressing the part from the crown on his head down to the regal purple robes. Marcello had been gracious though, passing out deeds to imaginary lands and titles to those he most adored. Nathaniel had been made prince regent of the Kingdom of Maltese, and Tim had been given a dukedom—the territory map he was presented with resembling the state of Kansas. It had been a good night, although very different than those that had come before. Marcello hadn't been as animated as usual. He hadn't risen from his throne at all, except to give a quick speech. Tim had thought Marcello was taking his role as monarch seriously, but now…

"Something's wrong."

"They messed up the order again?" Ben asked, coming over to see.

Tim held the pantry door open for him. "Two bottles here, and another in the fridge. Marcello has never let that happen before."

"He's probably been busy," Ben said. "You know how he

likes to stay active with the studio, even though he's supposed to be retired."

"That's just it," Tim said. "If Marcello likes to keep busy, why hasn't he been over to see us?" He nodded at the bottles again. "Even when he was running things full time, he still stopped by each week."

Ben thought about it. "You're right. It is unusual. If you're worried about him, why not bring a bottle to him instead?"

"Good idea!" Tim gave him a quick smooch. Then he went to the refrigerator and pulled out the cold bottle. When he turned around, Ben was standing there, holding a plate and sandwich.

"Eat something first," he said.

"Can I get it to go?" Tim asked.

Ben stared at him. "You're really worried, huh?"

"I'm sure it's fine. Marcello probably started a new project, that's all. You know how often he talks about building another company."

Tim grabbed the sandwich and took a bite to appease his husband. He could feel mustard on his lips, and maybe a few crumbs, which motivated him to go in for another kiss. Ben resisted. Tim chased after him, and by the time he finally landed his kiss, Ben was laughing, like they didn't have a care in the world. Good. For some reason, it helped him to know that Ben wouldn't be worried while he was gone. Tim still couldn't shake his concern though, so after finishing the sandwich in record time, he left the house to check on his best friend.

Tim entered Marcello's palatial home without needing to knock. He had been given his own key ages ago, along with an access code to the outer gates. That was then. These days he had a small round fob on his keychain that, once pressed with his thumbprint, would make the doors and gates open like magic. Despite this unfettered access, Tim never managed to surprise Marcello by dropping in spontaneously. He was always aware of Tim's movements, or anyone else who neared his home, thanks to an extensive surveillance system. Probably. It was either that, or Marcello possessed psychic powers. After knowing the man for decades, that didn't seem so far-fetched.

Tim paused in the entryway, considering his choices. He decided to try the living room first and was moving toward it when a large body blocked his path, but not the one he'd been seeking.

"Tim!" Nathaniel said, sounding more relieved than surprised. "I'm glad you're here."

"Why?" he asked guardedly.

Nathaniel scratched at his beard, an eyebrow raised, like he was trying to find the right words. Then his attention moved down to the bottle of champagne. "He's not supposed to drink alcohol right now. Doctor's orders."

Tim's stomach sank. "I knew it. What's wrong with him?"

Nathaniel shook his head. "I promised I wouldn't say. But if anyone can drag it out of him, it's you. Come on."

Tim followed behind, and when he realized they were heading toward Marcello's bedroom, he tried to brace himself for what he might find. Especially since this was the private room that visitors were rarely invited into. The bed was too small for more than one person, although Marcello would probably disagree. As they neared the doorway, Tim couldn't help but think of Eric, and how sickly he had appeared in those final days, the cancer having ravaged all but his spirit. He couldn't imagine Marcello so emaciated and weak, but he tried to anyway, if only so he'd be more capable of hiding his shock.

Despite his concerns, Tim nearly laughed in relief when they entered the room. Marcello was sitting up in bed, looking very much like his usual self. He wore lavender silk pajamas instead of his usual suit, but he wasn't pale and fading. A number of tables had been positioned around his bed to support tablets that streamed different news networks, the volume muted on each. A glowing laptop screen rose up from beneath stacks of paper, and three different books were open to various pages. Marcello was anything but idle, which helped reassure Tim that there wasn't an emergency.

"Ah!" Marcello said, clasping his hands together when he spotted Tim. "How wonderful to see you again. You'll have to forgive the state I'm in. I've been positively buried in work lately. Let me greet you properly."

Marcello moved the blanket aside, as if he intended to stand. Nathaniel quickly swooped in, holding him at bay with a hand while trying to cover him again.

"Don't be silly," Marcello snapped.

"You're not supposed to get up unless it's absolutely necessary," Nathaniel grumbled in response.

"I can't hug one of my dearest friends?" Marcello cried.

"No!"

Tim took a step back, surprised by the sudden tension in the room. Then he hurried forward. "I'm actually delivering my hugs today," he said. "No need to get up. And hey, speaking of which, you've got to hear about this delivery boy that was giving me the eye earlier."

"Oh?" Marcello said, pausing in his struggle.

"Yes. He was adorable. I think he wanted me to invite him in."

"And did you?" Marcello asked.

"No, but he got me riled up enough that I decided to come see you."

"Flattery will get you everywhere," Marcello said, opening his arms. "Including this bed. Shall I scoot over to make room for you?"

"Keep wishing, old man," Tim murmured warmly. When pulling away from their hug, he added as casually as possible, "How are you feeling?"

"Better by the second," Marcello said, grabbing the bottle from Tim's hands. "How thoughtful of you!"

"Absolutely not," Nathaniel said, snatching it away. "You know you're not supposed to drink."

"At least let me look at it," Marcello protested. "Put it on the desk over there. I'm sure that, should I have a moment of weakness, you'll rush in here the split second after the cork pops to deprive me of what few pleasures remain."

Nathaniel rolled his eyes but complied.

"What's going on?" Tim asked.

"Nothing of importance," Marcello said, tapping the mattress. "Come! Sit next to me so I'll have two pretty new things to ogle."

Tim did as requested, but not before shooting a concerned glance in Nathaniel's direction. The man looked tired. He wasn't nearly as skilled at hiding his emotions as Marcello. Something was seriously wrong.

"Will you be staying long?" Marcello inquired.

"I have all day," Tim assured him. "Just kick me out when you get bored."

"Never," Marcello said firmly. Then he turned his attention to Nathaniel. "Why don't you return home? I'm sure your husband is dying to see you. Tell him to come visit me soon. I do miss that sharp tongue of his. Kelly always keeps me on my toes, and considering how tired I am of sitting on my backside, that would be a welcome change."

"You sure you won't need me?" Nathaniel asked.

"Quite. I know how insufferable I've been lately. I'll rest easier tonight knowing that you're taking a break from all my nonsense. When's the last time you slept in your own bed?"

Nathaniel didn't answer. He merely swallowed and managed to look even more worried.

Marcello's sigh was gentle. "I'll finally tell him. Agreed? Tim will call you if anything should go wrong."

He wanted to demand an immediate explanation, but Tim forced himself to be patient, because this clearly wasn't an easy decision for Nathaniel. Besides, he could guess what was going on and wouldn't mind living in denial a little longer.

"I'll take good care of him," he assured Nathaniel. "I have your number, and you have mine. Call if you need to. I'll send updates, even if you don't."

Nathaniel finally seemed to relax. "If you're absolutely sure…"

"We both are," Marcello said. "Don't bother saying goodbye. I've always possessed impeccable timing, and I assure you, the moment isn't upon us yet."

Nathaniel gathered up his things. Tim hadn't noticed when entering how the old writing desk was cluttered with photos from the studio and another laptop. These were all cleared away. Nathaniel hovered in the doorway afterwards, as if he might change his mind and stay, but in the end he nodded at them and left.

"The poor boy," Marcello said wearily. "I do hate burdening him so."

"What's going on?" Tim pleaded. "Tell me. Please."

Marcello took a deep breath, but for once, he didn't have an elaborate speech planned. "I'm dying."

Tim swallowed and tried to respond, but his throat was too tight for words to escape.

"Not you too," Marcello said, patting his hand. "You must

have known this was coming. I am, after all, a few years older than you."

"No you're not," Tim said, spluttering laughter. "I was at your fiftieth birthday last year. That makes you younger than me."

"I suppose it does," Marcello said, clearly amused by the thought. "In that case, I'm afraid I have some shocking news. Despite being in the prime of my life, I've been told with great authority that my future engagements will be severely limited."

"How much time do you have left?"

"Hard to say," Marcello said, lifting a hand to study his fingernails, "but people have been underestimating me my entire life. I have no reason to think this will be any different."

"Cancer?" Tim managed to grunt. The word alone reminded him of the pain he felt when Eric died, and the fear he'd experienced during his own close call.

"Nothing so common," Marcello said. "At least I don't think so. The symptoms were severe enough that I knew something was amiss, even before visiting the doctor. When he passed me off to a specialist for more tests, I decided to entrust Nathaniel with the results. All I wanted was the prognosis, not the diagnosis."

"Huh? Why?"

Marcello pursed his lips before answering. "The circumstances surrounding my entrance into this world are unknown, even to me, and it seems fitting that my inevitable exit should also be shrouded in mystery."

Tim was confused enough that his grief was momentarily forgotten. "So you don't know why you're dying. Only that you are."

"Precisely!" Marcello said, sitting upright. "At my age, one must savor what few surprises remain. I could wager a guess, of course. I have my suspicions, but I'm not certain. Will my heart give out? Or will I stop breathing in my sleep? Perhaps blood will shoot from my tear ducts. Isn't it exciting? Anything could happen! Now then, kindly open that bottle. I'd be going mad if not for the opiates. Do you know how difficult it is to find a doctor willing to prescribe those anymore? Harold has also been kind enough to bring me treats from the dispensary, which I've enjoyed, although I was starting to fear I'd never have another drink."

"But Nathaniel said—"

"I'm dying, Tim," Marcello repeated. "I did make sure to ask when he first delivered the news, and I rephrased the question until satisfied that I understood the answer correctly. So if you don't mind, I'd like to continue this conversation over a drink, and if a glass of champagne is what finally kills me, I can't think of a more fitting end."

Tim rose and went to the old writing desk where the bottle still sat. He took his time peeling the foil off the cork, keeping his back to the room so he could process everything. Marcello was right. This wasn't a complete surprise. He might not know his friend's exact age, but Marcello was much older than him. Tim had started worrying about this long ago, but that didn't mean he accepted it.

"There must be treatment plans," Tim said as he spun around. "Options that will keep you around for as long as possible. Even if they're experimental, surely that's worth trying!"

Marcello smiled. "I spoke similar words to Eric once, and even back then, I knew I was only thinking of myself. Would you have extended his life, Tim? At the very end, when it all became so dreadful, would you have wished for Eric to live longer than absolutely necessary?"

Tim frowned. "No. In fact, there were times that I was tempted to—" He chewed his bottom lip rather than say it aloud.

"I entertained such thoughts myself. Now then, about that drink…"

Tim was suddenly feeling thirsty too.

"Bottom drawer on the right," Marcello said after the cork had popped. "You'll find two glasses there. And an empty flask. Perhaps you could take it with you and refill it for me? Nathaniel has been horribly diligent about removing all alcohol from this house. Had he been placed in charge of Prohibition, the entire country would still be dry."

Tim didn't trust himself to reply as he slowly filled two flutes. Having gone through this before didn't make it any easier. He was young when Eric died. Tim had been unprepared for just how bad it had hurt. That friendship, while still incredibly close to his heart, had only lasted a few years. He and Marcello had known each other for decades now. More than half of Tim's life. The thought of him not being in the rest made his insides ache.

"Now now," Marcello said when Tim turned around again. "Don't give into despair. If you must grieve, please wait until I've departed. If there's a surefire way of ushering someone into an early grave, it's treating them like they're already dead."

"Sorry," Tim said, his throat tight. He returned to the bed, sitting in the plush armchair that Nathaniel had likely been camping out in. He handed a glass to Marcello, and after raising his own, lowered it again without taking a sip. "Does it hurt?"

Marcello tilted his head to one side. "Perhaps a bit, but I've borne much worse. To witness the suffering of someone you love while being powerless to alleviate it... *that* is the most excruciating pain of all. Why else do you think I waited this long to tell you?" Marcello raised his glass. "Let us instead celebrate the time we have left."

Tim steeled himself. Then he nodded and clinked his glass against Marcello's. "Here's to making more memories together, because I don't think I could ever have enough. Not with you."

Marcello smiled his appreciation. Then he took a dainty sip, and after smacking his lips, drained the rest in a single go. After burping discreetly, he held out his glass for a refill and said, "When reunited with a former flame, passion takes precedence over moderation. Another, if you'd be so kind."

Tim rose to fetch the bottle, deciding to spare himself further trouble by bringing it back with him. "So what's the deal?" he asked while pouring a refill. "You can't get out of bed for some reason?"

"I'm not supposed to," Marcello explained. "I get winded easily. I don't have as much energy as I once did—an easy problem to solve if I hadn't sworn off uppers in the eighties. I don't suppose you know anyone?"

"If I ever wanted anything like that, I'd ask you."

"Ha! And rightly so. I do know a few shady characters, but I'm only teasing. I'm quite content with my old standbys." Marcello took another sip, this one more modest. "I must admit that I'm tiring of this bed and this room. I'm beginning to feel like a prisoner in my own home."

"Sorry, man," Tim said sympathetically. "I guess this isn't how you would have chosen to go."

"Oh?" Marcello smirked. "What sort of final bow do you think I would have preferred?"

"I don't know. Something more scandalous."

"I like the direction you're drifting in. Entertain me! Delve into the deepest darkest corners of your imagination and design for me my ideal death. How would it occur?"

"You'd be in a bigger bed than this," Tim said, "surrounded by naked men of all colors, sizes, and ages."

"Wouldn't be the first time," Marcello said dismissively.

"*And* you would choke to death. Deep throating gone wrong. Your tombstone would read: 'Twelve inches too many. The others didn't notice until they'd finished filling him up.'"

"Splendid!" Marcello said, tittering happily. "There may be hope for you yet!"

Tim finished his first glass, mostly to help banish the image from his mind, but at least Marcello was smiling. "So what's the real answer? How would you prefer to die?"

"Hmm," Marcello said musingly, watching as Tim poured himself another. "I hate to disappoint you, but my death wouldn't be of a sexual nature. I'd rather become weightless and float into the air, no longer burdened by physical restraints. I'd slip through a window and up into the blue of the sky, never to be seen again. Or perhaps I'd simply disappear. Like the Jedi."

Tim snorted, champagne almost shooting out his nose. "You mean *Star Wars*?"

"Certainly! I always enjoyed the grand scale of those movies. Do you remember how, when the Jedi die, all they leave behind is their robes? One moment they are alive, the next they are a pile of clothing. I remember being disappointed when the three ghosts shown at the end of *Return of the Jedi* were somehow dressed again. What sort of afterlife is that? The Bible claims Adam and Eve were nudists before being cast out of the Garden of Eden. Surely, when we return to paradise, we'll discover that Heaven is clothing optional at the very least."

Tim laughed. "Fair enough. Although I'm having trouble picturing you as a rule-enforcing Jedi. I bet you would have worked for the other team instead."

"The dark side!" Marcello said with a villainous hiss. "Yes, perhaps that would suit me better. I shall drape myself in a black cowl and utilize sinister sorcery to extend my life unnaturally."

The smile slid off Tim's face. For a brief second, he had almost forgotten the gravity of the situation. "Is there anything I can do for you? Anything at all."

"*This* is exactly what I need," Marcello said. "Your company and good conversation. I know you have the gallery to tend to, and your marriage—"

"All of that can wait," Tim insisted. "The gallery practically runs itself, and Ben will understand. Hell, I'll bring him with me next time."

"I'd like that," Marcello said. "Please do. The more the merrier! I said my goodbyes to most of my associates during the previous fundraiser, whether they knew it or not, but you and your family are treasured by me. Do you think Jason would be willing to fly down?"

"He'll insist on it. His husband and kids too. You know they think of you as their great-grandpa."

"As agreeable as I find them, I wish they wouldn't call me that. Speaking of young William," Marcello got a naughty gleam in his eye. "Do you think he'd mind donning his Coast Guard uniform for me? I've never seen him wearing it in person, and you do know how patriotic I can be."

"Perverted is more like it," Tim said warmly, "and yes. There isn't a request you can make that we won't be willing to grant."

"Be careful with promises," Marcello said, settling back into the bed. "Especially whom you make them to."

Tim knew exactly who he was dealing with. If the devil was ever foolish enough to meet Marcello at the crossroads, he'd walk away having sold *his* soul instead of the other way around. Tim loved that about him, along with each and every flaw, which were vastly outnumbered by his redeeming qualities. That's why he would make this work. Marcello was his best friend, and while facing his death wouldn't be easy, Tim would be there for him until the very end.

Marcello's chest rose and fell, the old man softly snoring. Tim was grateful for that. Eric had been a quiet sleeper, and there were moments in those final days that he had seemed to stop breathing altogether, Tim experiencing a jolt of panic each time. He hadn't thought about that in years. Surprising how many of those little details were coming back to him as he lived through this once again.

It had been a good day regardless. They caught up with each other while finishing the bottle of champagne. Marcello talked him into ordering more, although it wasn't Johnny G who delivered it. Just some other kid who probably hadn't seen anything of death except for a flushed goldfish or two. Tim felt like dragging the guy inside to show him what awaited everyone, if only to make him appreciate life more. Then again, why rob him of blissful ignorance, or waste a second on anyone other than Marcello? Tim savored each moment with him, the hours passing quickly as they laughed over old memories. As their buzzes waned, they both grew tired, but Tim forced himself to remain awake so he could keep watch over his friend.

"How's he doing?" a voice whispered.

He turned, surprised to find Nathaniel standing in the doorway. "Totally fine," Tim answered. He stood and stretched, his muscles stiff from sitting in the same chair for so long. "Didn't you get my text?"

"I did," Nathaniel said, "but I..." His eyes moved to the bed.

Tim made sure his expression was sympathetic. "I know how you feel, but it sounds like you've been neglecting a lot for him. Marcello was happy that you were taking a break."

"I need to be here," Nathaniel grumbled. "Just in case."

"We can take turns," Tim suggested. "You've been staying the night here, right?"

Nathaniel nodded.

"How about we switch every other day? You can still check in whenever you want, but I'll be here taking care of him when you're not." Tim glanced over his shoulder at the bed. "What's wrong with him anyway?"

Nathaniel took a deep breath, sounding frustrated when answering. "He won't let me tell anyone. Including him."

"I heard. I was hoping you'd make an exception for me."

Nathaniel seemed tempted, but in the end, he shook his head. "I promised."

"It's cool. Just tell me this: Will there be a sign that he's getting close?"

Nathaniel thought about it. "Probably."

"Okay. In that case, if I'm on duty and anything changes, I'll call you right away. Sound good?"

Nathaniel nodded grudgingly. "I suppose."

Tim didn't take his terseness personally. He knew beneath the stony surface there flowed a river of emotion. "Are you planning on staying the night again?"

"I'd like to."

"That works for me. I need to get home and explain everything to Ben." He turned to collect his things, noticing the two empty champagne bottles, and moved to pick them up. "Sorry," he said. "I know you said we shouldn't but—"

"It's fine." Nathaniel looked down at Marcello's slumbering form. "I want him to enjoy the time he has left. It's hard not giving him whatever he wants. I'm too selfish though. I know he's going to die anyway, but if not drinking means I get an extra day with him, or even just an hour…" Nathaniel turned a grateful expression on Tim. "It's good you're here. I wanted him to tell you sooner. He needs a friend. I'm more like a…"

"A son?" Tim suggested.

Nathaniel nodded, his chin trembling before he got himself under control.

"I'll be back tomorrow," Tim said. "For a full shift. You'll have the entire day off. But do me a favor. Call me if anything changes. Or if you need someone to talk to. Okay?"

Nathaniel nodded his appreciation. Then he sat in the chair, placing a hand over Marcello's as he resumed his vigil.

Tim returned to Marcello's home the next day, a man on a mission. He brought a case of champagne with him, stowing it in the refrigerator before venturing deeper into the house. There he found Nathaniel sprawled out in the chair next to the bed, fast asleep. Marcello was sitting upright, a pair of half-moon reading glasses perched on his nose as he reviewed documents and made changes with a red pen.

"Ah!" he whispered when he noticed Tim. "Could you help me, please? I thought together we could lift Nathaniel and place him on the mattress. Extra points if we can get him into my pajamas. I want him to wake up thinking that we switched bodies."

Tim laughed. He couldn't help it. This was enough to rouse Nathaniel, who snorted, grumbled, and pushed himself upright. Then his head whipped around in concern to the bed.

"You all right?" he mumbled.

"I will be if you renegotiate these subsidiary rights," Marcello replied. "A mere fifteen percent across the board? I realize this is a privileged client, but under these conditions, you're tempting them to circumvent the main purpose of the contract."

"Sure," Nathaniel said, rubbing at his eyes, "but they're still paying us for the initial work. And you know how advertisements are woven into entertainment these days. We're part of the final product, and that could mean that we're entitled to—"

"Guys," Tim said.

Nathaniel held up a hand to ward him off. "I don't expect to get fifteen percent of their total revenue, but we need to underline the value we bring to each production and ask for a cut on *all* royalties they receive. When I push the lawyers for that, I want them in an amiable mood."

"I see." Marcello nodded musingly. "In that case, I recommend introducing terms designed to upset the lawyers, rather than anything so favorable at first glance."

Tim sighed as loud as he could, even if it did end up sounding like an imitation of a cheering crowd.

"Good point," Nathaniel continued. "That way, we have something to offer them in return."

Marcello nodded. "And we might end up where we always intended to be."

"Nice talking to you both!" Tim said, pretending that he was about to leave. The truth was, he was more than used to this sort of behavior. Marcello and Nathaniel shared a love for business that he didn't possess, although it was endearing to witness how they worked together as a team.

"My apologies," Marcello said. "We're almost finished here." Addressing his protegee again, he added, "Everything else I reviewed is perfection. I couldn't have done it better myself. I recommend you meet with our lawyers today to further develop your strategy. Decide what terms you would like the client to agree to and work backward from there."

"Thank you," Nathaniel said as he stood and gathered the papers.

Tim often assumed that Nathaniel was doing Marcello a favor by keeping him involved. The business was now his after all, but he seemed genuinely appreciative of the feedback. Especially now, when he must realize how much valuable insight would be lost when Marcello was gone.

"Lunch is in the fridge," Nathaniel said to Tim on his way out the door. "All you have to do is heat it up. Don't let him talk you into having anything delivered. The doctor has him on a strict diet."

"Deprivation!" Marcello chimed in. "That's what I want listed as my official cause of death. I've been deprived of all joy in life!"

Nathaniel ignored him, lowering his voice. "Don't indulge him too much."

"No promises," Tim said, "but I'll take good care of him no matter what."

He waited until Nathaniel had left before he turned to face the bed.

Marcello was sitting up, legs dangling over the edge. "I'm sure I can make it to the restroom myself," he said, "but if Nathaniel forgot something and returns to find me exhibiting even the slightest independence, they'll have to dig an extra grave next to mine."

"I'm happy to help," Tim said, hurrying forward. Marcello put an arm around his shoulders. Together they stood. He seemed stable enough on his feet. They made it to the attached bathroom without incident, but once in the narrow room, Marcello stumbled. Tim reacted instantly, wrapping his arms around the other man to stabilize him.

"You okay?" Tim asked.

"I'm feeling better by the second," Marcello said, his hands wandering. "Have you always had such defined hips?"

"Yeah," Tim said. "Since before I was *married*."

"I've never let a wedding ring stop me."

"I bet," Tim said, slowly disentangling himself. "If you're looking for a cheap thrill, I'm sure Noah could hook you up with someone."

"My current craving is for forbidden fruit," Marcello purred, "although I did ask him if the Gentlemen's Agreement Club employed shirtless nurses. He said yes and sent a photo of the bustiest woman you could ever imagine."

Tim laughed. "Serves you right. You know that objectifying employees is frowned on these days. I'm surprised you've managed to get away with it for so long."

"Because I have justifiable cause. Shirtless waiters are my service animals. They provide me with emotional comfort. If I could, I'd take them everywhere I go."

"Even in here? Because I'm starting to feel weirded out hanging around the bathroom with you."

"Ah yes. I should be able to manage on my own now. Thank you."

Tim shut the door behind him on the way out. He was willing to wait in the hallway rather than the bedroom, just to give the man extra privacy, but he also expected to be called back in. He was surprised when the bathroom door opened again and Marcello was on his feet. His friend seemed fine, waving away an offer of help, but when he reached the bed, he practically fell into it.

"Are you okay?" Tim asked. "Should I call Nathaniel?"

Marcello shook his head. He didn't speak though. Instead he grabbed an oxygen mask from the nightstand, twisted the nozzle on a metal tank, and held the mask to his face. Once he inhaled deeply a few times and set aside the mask, he offered an explanation. "Shortness of breath, that's all. The resulting dizziness causes me to lose my balance."

"Why don't you get a wheelchair?"

"Aside from my pride? The doctor doesn't want me to become overstimulated, which apparently includes anything other than the errand I just completed. Besides, what need have I for transportation when such handsome young men cater to my every desire?"

Tim couldn't remember the last time someone called him young, but he wasn't about to argue the point. Especially now. With the older generation dying out, he couldn't shake the feeling that he was moving closer to the front of the line.

"Speaking of fun," Marcello said. "Did you refill that flask like I asked?"

"Not yet," Tim said, "but there are six bottles of champagne in the refrigerator."

Marcello appeared ready to leap out of bed. "Then what are we waiting for?"

"For it to be later than eight in the morning," Tim said, checking his watch. "And besides, I have a deal of my own I want to negotiate."

"Oh?" Marcello said, sounding intrigued.

Tim nodded and sat in the chair. "When Eric was dying, it made me realize how little I knew about his past. So we talked about it. He told me his entire life story while I painted him."

"You've already painted my portrait," Marcello replied. "It's on prominent display in the living room."

"I know that," Tim said, "but—"

"Do you know how much I had it insured for? Quite the princely sum. I consulted an appraiser first, wanting the paperwork to back up my claim. Would you care to know what your work was valued at?"

"Well yeah," Tim said. He quickly shook his head. "No! You're trying to distract me, like you always do when I ask about your history."

"Because none of it is important. When presented with a luscious cake, do you pick up a fork and sample a bite, or do you seek out the chef to ask where the eggs came from, and if the hen who laid them is content with her work?"

"I mean, it *is* important where the eggs come from. The free-range ones taste way better and—"

"That's the problem with your generation," Marcello tutted. "When I was young, we were happy for any solid meal that came our way. We certainly didn't lose sleep wondering if the sugar was refined or not."

"Were you hungry a lot when growing up?"

"Not really. Food wasn't scarce exactly, but it was much more basic and..." Marcello blinked. Then he smiled. "Well played. You almost had me."

Tim groaned in frustration. "Oh come on! If your past doesn't matter, then why are you so tight-lipped about it? We talk about pointless stuff all the time!"

Marcello thought about it. "Remember when you called me, upset that you didn't know what sort of music Eric preferred?"

Tim nodded. "Ben mentioned how he sometimes listens to bands that Jace liked even if he's not into them, because it feels like reconnecting with him. It seemed crazy that, as much as I love Eric, I couldn't name a single artist he liked."

"A single *musician*," Marcello corrected. "You know the painters he admired most."

"Hopper, Lautrec, Schiele," Tim said without needing to think. He could easily name a dozen more.

"And you know these names because they were important to him. I also wasn't particularly familiar with his taste in music, although I did call Gabriel on your behalf, and he reported back with the answer you so craved. Did that information make you see Eric in a new light?"

"No," Tim admitted.

"Because it wasn't a crucial part of his identity. It might be with Ben, or even Jason, but music wasn't a cornerstone of Eric's world. That's the point I'm trying to make. You know the important facts about me already."

Tim crossed his arms over his chest. "I don't care. I want more."

"How flattering."

"I mean it! This is my last chance. I have tons of questions about Eric that I never asked you because most of it only he would know. So here's the deal: Champagne is in the refrigerator, but it's not cold yet. We have a few hours to kill before it'll be ready. It's up to you how slowly the minutes crawl by."

"You're withholding alcohol from me?"

"Worse," Tim said. "I'm withholding conversation. There's only one subject I'm interested in." He chose a blank spot on the wall, which wasn't easy with all the art surrounding them, but he found one and began staring at it.

"Be reasonable!" Marcello pleaded.

Tim didn't reply.

"Did I tell you that Corey called me the other day? He has exciting news. I think he wanted it to be a surprise, but he did give me permission to tell you myself, if I couldn't wait."

Tantalizing bait, but Tim ignored the bobbing hook.

"I suppose we can discuss that some other time," Marcello said, sounding disappointed. "In other news, I've had a few thoughts about what I'd like to leave Jason, but I'm not sure if you'll find the idea appropriate."

Tim sniffed, as if disinterested.

The next ordeal was weathering an awkward silence. Tim wasn't sure how long it lasted. Maybe only a few minutes. All he was certain of, was that only one of them could go long stretches without talking.

"Very well," Marcello said. "I'll answer *one* question of your choosing."

"Awesome!" Tim said, leaping on the opportunity. "How did you and Eric meet? No wait, I already know that. Um… What happened to your biological parents? Although I don't actually care about them, so that's no good." He snapped his fingers. "Got it! What's your real name and why did you change it?"

"That's two questions," Marcello said. "You'll have to choose between them."

Tim gnawed on his bottom lip while debating within himself. "I'd rather know why."

Marcello studied him. "An interesting choice. May I ask how you reached your decision?"

"Because the first option would only give me a name. The other will be a story. I hope."

Marcello took a deep breath. "For the record, I consider the name you're familiar with as the real one. Why should any legitimacy be given to a name concocted by people who didn't stick around to discover if it suited me?"

"You were adopted, right?"

"I was abandoned," Marcello said. "For decades I knew nothing of my parents except the name they left me with, and it wasn't particularly elegant. You know what would be fairest? I understand the need to give a child a name, but when they are old enough to decide for themselves, that name should become the middle one, allowing each individual to choose how they'll be addressed for the rest of their lives."

"I take it you don't like your given name."

"Correct."

"Is that why you changed it?"

"No." Marcello's smile was subtle. "I'll tell you the events that led to the actual reason, but I won't go into excessive detail. If my life was made into a movie, I wouldn't allow a flashback to that era, or introduce a cast of heroes and villains that helped shape who I would become, because that man already died. He had to. But I will, in fewer words than I am normally prone to, tell you about him in the broadest of strokes."

He already had the full attention of Tim, who didn't dare respond, worried it might send him off on some other tangent.

"I was born into an era of limited resources," Marcello began. "Not just for the orphanage that would care for me initially, but for the entire country. I possess little knowledge of my biological parents. When I was old enough and had the funds, I hired a detective to learn what I could of them, but even he reported back with precious little. All that's certain is my parents had their own reasons for giving me up immediately after my birth. I try not to resent them for it. Even without them, I did have something that resembled a family. More than one, in fact. I'm sure from your conversations with Jason that you've heard the multitude of reasons a child might be returned to an orphanage, although unlike him, I was eager to please. I wanted nothing more than approval. Not only from potential parents, but society in general. I felt that my dreams were best attained by gratifying others while ignoring my own needs. It's not a phase I look back on fondly."

"So you changed your name?" Tim asked.

"The reasons are more convoluted than that." Marcello shifted to make himself more comfortable. "As a gay man, you know the toll that self-denial can take, how it can snowball until you feel as if you are playing a role rather than living a proper life. I reached a breaking point in mine, as so many of us do, and it was a costly one. I lost everything. Socially and financially. Did these hardships color my current convictions? Perhaps. I've experienced how difficult life can be at the bottom, and I long ago stopped judging anyone who goes against societal norms to survive. Especially those who meet their needs by helping others fulfill their own."

Tim could read between the lines. He knew that Marcello owned multiple homeless shelters. Tim had also suffered plenty of lectures about 'mutually beneficial exchanges between consenting adults' as his friend so often put it. Marcello might be speaking from personal experience. If so, and he didn't feel like discussing those difficult times, Tim would respect that. But he still had questions. "Is that when you started over and buried your past?"

"Not quite. I was still in a transitory state. The person I knew least of all was myself, so I began a journey—both literal and figural—to find him. I ceased shutting out those I deemed beneath me and instead opened myself to everyone and everything. I drank deep of the world, eager for any lesson it could teach. That hasn't changed, although in the early days, I quickly realized that certain experiences were inaccessible to me."

"Such as?"

"Determining if I could cover a pair of twins from head to toe with a single jar of lemon curd while they were stretched out on the deck of my yacht."

"Humble dreams," Tim said ruefully.

"Precisely. And not to spoil the ending, but I discovered much later that the answer is yes. Depending on the size of the jar, of course, and how thickly you apply the layers." Marcello reached for his laptop. "I have photos, if you'd like to examine the evidence."

"No way," Tim said, deftly using the tip of his shoe to push the laptop out of Marcello's reach. "You still haven't answered my question. Why did you change your name?"

"Oh, that's easy," Marcello said. "Because of the Mafia."

Tim's mouth fell open. He barely managed to shut it long enough to ask, "What?"

"During my travels, I'd managed something of an education," Marcello explained. "Nothing so official as a degree, but I had the benefit of private school for some of my formative years, and I've always possessed a curious mind. A talent for numbers too. That added up to very little on a resume, so the only jobs available to me were of—shall we say—a somewhat questionable nature. I had returned to the East Coast at this point, where my talents had caught the attention of a certain organization."

"Wait," Tim said, shaking his head. "You were *in* the Mafia?"

"My goodness, no. There are, believe it or not, some paths even I am unwilling to wander down. But I did stand at the head of that trail while staring down its length and saw the potential to be adopted yet again, but my aversion to family served me well in this instance."

"Doesn't matter," Tim said. "That you worked for the Mafia at all—even as a contractor—is super cool."

"I wish I could agree with you," Marcello said. "The truth is, at this point in history, many men had contact with the Mafia if they frequented gay bars. Such establishments weren't allowed to exist officially. States would shut them down on the grounds of moral indecency. The Mafia circumvented this by opening what was called a bottle club—an organization where members were allowed to bring their own liquor to consume. This wasn't the reality, of course. The Mafia supplied all the drinks, watered down and marked up to exorbitant prices. Please don't imagine a charming speakeasy, or comfortable tables and seats surrounding a stage. Conditions were dire. These establishments didn't have proper plumbing, or the basic infrastructure one would expect from a bar, which meant glasses were often as filthy as their surroundings. Hepatitis outbreaks were common. As was blackmail. The Mafia would extort money from the wealthier patrons, or anyone who was in the public eye. I've heard gay men claim, with misty-eyed romanticism, that the Mafia helped usher in the gay rights movement. While they did play a pivotal role, the Mafia did so with indifference and greed. We were nothing but voiceless victims they could exploit, and they did so ruthlessly. The Mafia certainly didn't offer us protection during the frequent police raids."

"Were you at the Stonewall riot?" Tim asked.

"No," Marcello said, "but I salute those who were angry enough to stand their ground, because they did so with few allies and little hope for improvement."

"If you hate the Mafia so much, why did you work for them?"

"Indifference and greed," Marcello said with a heavy sigh. "I wasn't the same man back then. I was fed up with being poor and had few legal options available to me. You'd be surprised how much crime still occurs in this country for those very reasons. The job seemed simple enough. The Mafia needed an accountant, but they didn't want to use one of their own. I didn't realize at the time how unimportant the running of the bars was to them. The neglect should have tipped me off, I suppose. I later learned that the Mafia often earned more money from blackmailing patrons than they did selling stolen liquor and cigarettes to us. What they really wanted from me was help in catching a thief. They were an organization of crooks, mired in a culture of paranoia, unable to trust even themselves. So they sought out someone of unwavering moral character."

"Ha!" Tim said.

"Ha indeed. I took the position anyway. It didn't sound complicated. They suspected that money was being skimmed off the profits. Aside from themselves, of course, or the cops who demanded frequent payoffs. The first bar they sent me to was without discrepancy. Only the authorized leeches were bleeding it dry. After I made sure the accounts were in order, they moved me to another location." Marcello paused. "Hmm. I've already done more talking than I expected to. My throat is parched."

Tim rolled his eyes and laughed. "You really want me to open a bottle of champagne?"

"No," Marcello said after a moment's thought. "Water will be fine."

Tim waited for a punchline, or a playful wink. Neither manifested. Marcello toyed with the blanket that was pulled up to his waist, folding a narrow strip of it down and brushing it smooth. He seemed pensive while doing so.

"Be right back," Tim said, leaping up and racing to the

kitchen. He took his time while there, wondering if he was asking too much of Marcello by making him revisit the past. If not now, when would he ever have another opportunity? After pouring a glass of sparkling water, he returned to the room to find Marcello in higher spirits.

"I was tempted to go looking for you," he said. "That's how much I value your company."

"Thanks." Tim sat again after handing over the glass. "We don't have to continue, if you don't want."

"I promised you a story," Marcello said, "and it is a simple tale. We've nearly reached the end. When I arrived for my next assignment, it immediately became clear to me that someone was embezzling funds. There were few suspects other than the manager or the bartender. No one else had opportunity to handle the money. As you can imagine, any thieving ceased when I arrived. It wasn't until two weeks had passed that it resumed. Little detective work was required to discover that the manager was to blame."

Tim leaned forward. "So what did you do?"

"I told him the real reason I was there. He suspected as much. Imagine a bar without running water that had its own accountant. What a farce! After I warned Charles—" Marcello swallowed. Then he cleared his throat. "After I warned the manager, he ceased embezzling. That's when I began to indulge in it myself."

"What?" Tim slapped the arm of the chair. "Are you crazy?"

"I was young and imagined myself invincible—the very definition of crazy. You must understand that the Mafia wasn't breathing down my neck for results. I was there to cook the books, as much as I was meant to audit them. I was providing the Mafia with a service, and they were pleased enough with the results to leave me to my work. The manager had been skimming ten percent off the top. When he stopped, I took that ten percent for myself. I only did so for a brief period, but it was enough to build up a small nest egg."

"How much?" Tim asked.

"Around ten thousand dollars. Adjusted for inflation, that's well over fifty thousand now."

"Holy shit!" Tim said, laughing madly. "That's amazing. I didn't know gay bars could be so profitable."

"Keep in mind that the Mafia was making money off more

than just drinks. Prostitution and illegal drugs also contributed to their wealth. Even the jukebox was owned by them, with no royalties paid to the performers, of course. These bars might have resembled pits, but for a select few, they were gold mines."

"Weren't you scared of getting caught?"

"Of course, but unlike the manager, I knew when to quit. I stopped embezzling and reported back for my next assignment, assuring my bosses that the problem had been corrected. I tried my best to be vague, calling it a clerical error. I even convinced Charles to give back a token amount of the money he had squirreled away. This didn't satisfy my bosses. They wanted a name. I resisted until their suspicions began to focus on me, leaving me with no other choice."

"So you told them?"

Marcello exhaled through his nose. "Almost. I gave them the bartender's name instead." He shook his head as if chastising himself. "I swore to myself never to speak of this, but deathbeds *are* where silences go to be broken. The truth is, I had fallen for the manager, Charles, and loved him with all my heart. We were in a relationship. I was concerned for him more than myself, not that it justifies my actions. I knew someone had to take the fall, and I wasn't noble enough to sacrifice myself. What good is love if you aren't alive to give or receive it? I had hoped my employers would fire the bartender, or maybe rough him up. He really was an insufferable man, but looking back on it now, he was exceedingly young. He must have been in his early twenties. Who isn't an asshole at that age, at least some of the time? He didn't deserve..." Marcello steeled himself. "He didn't deserve to die."

"They killed him?"

Marcello nodded. "I'm afraid so. I've often wondered if there is blood on my hands. I may not have murdered the bartender, or wished him dead, but would he have died if I kept my mouth shut? Even if I had maintained silence, someone would have paid the price, if only as warning to others. Since I remained useful to the Mafia, I believe the victim would have been Charles. I tried to console myself with the knowledge that I had saved him, the man I loved. This became harder to do when he disappeared shortly after, along with the last of the money he had stolen."

"Are you sure the Mafia didn't kill him too?"

"I'm certain. He had the decency to leave me a note. It wasn't fake, but I did find it inspirational."

"How so?"

"I'd seen enough to know that I wanted out too. I reported to my next assignment and completed it, but shortly afterwards, I wrote my bosses a letter. I claimed that the bartender had been my lover and that life had lost all meaning without him. I disavowed the Mafia in the harshest words at my disposal, exorcising all the resentment and hate that had been festering inside of me. And I assured them that they would never hurt me like they did him, because I was taking my own life so he and I could be together again."

"Then you ran?"

"No. First I killed myself. I left behind enough planted evidence to convince them, if they ever came looking. I doubt they really cared though. I was a small player. Insignificant. I'm certain they would have gleefully ended my life had I made it easy for them, but they were probably thankful I spared them the effort. In many ways, it felt like I truly had died. My heart was broken, I was beside myself with guilt, and life had lost most of its luster. That's when I learned an important lesson: You can let the hardships of the world dent and dull you, or you can sharpen yourself against them like a knife. So that's what I did. I gave myself a new name and made promises to myself that I've never broken. I became the man I felt I was destined to be. I was reborn."

"Wow," Tim said, leaning back. "Is that when you moved to Austin?"

"Indeed it is. I became politically active and did my best to fight the injustices of the world. As for the money, I felt it was too dangerous to keep, so I gave it to a hopeful young man to invest for me."

"Eric!" Tim covered his mouth with both hands. Then he let them drop again. "So basically, your entire fortune began with money you stole from the Mafia."

"I'll ask you not to repeat that. There's little to worry about so many decades later, but I hate to think that Nathaniel would be targeted for any reason. Or that he might feel morally compelled to give my money away, once it becomes his."

"Your secret is safe with me, but I have to ask. Did Eric know?"

"Do you think he would have come anywhere near that money had I told him of its origin?"

"Later on, I mean."

"I alluded to the truth on occasion but nothing more. I never wanted to put him in any danger. I also tried to make amends. In the mid-eighties, the Mafia was actively targeted by federal prosecutors for a variety of reasons, including the skimming of money from gay nightclubs. As you can imagine, bringing down such a massive beast required additional funds. And eyewitness testimony."

"You got involved?"

"I wasn't a hero by any means," Marcello said. "What little assistance I was able to provide did nothing to erase my previous sins. I spoke a lie that cost a man his life. That's a fact I will never be able to change, no matter how much I wish I could. At least I'll be able to apologize to him in person soon, and face judgement, if need be. You know, I think I will have that drink now."

Tim rose to get it for him. He found orange juice in the refrigerator and decided to make mimosas, since that would be both healthier and colder. When he returned with the two glasses, Marcello was so lost in thought that he took one without enthusiasm. He didn't even glance down to notice the added juice.

"Thank you," Tim said. "I can see now why it's difficult for you to talk about your past. I'm grateful that I got to hear one of the most interesting stories."

"I wouldn't say that." Mischief returned to Marcello's expression. "I'm not sure that story would even make it into my top ten."

"If anyone else said that, I wouldn't believe them." Tim raised his glass. "Here's to happier times."

Marcello blinked in surprise. "Is that what this is?"

"Yeah," Tim said. "I don't mean the whole dying thing, which sucks, but you've come so far since those days. Look at everything you've accomplished."

"I'd rather focus on this moment, although I do have to admit, had I gazed into a crystal ball all those years ago to see how my future would unfold, I would be pleased. Especially with the quality of people I chose to surround myself with."

"Thanks," Tim said with a tight throat. He placed his hand over Marcello's to squeeze it. "I feel the same way."

* * * * *

Tim cruised through Marcello's house, cackling to himself as he urged the wheelchair to go faster. Especially when he reached a corner in the hallway. He wanted to push the machine to its limits and test its promises. Sure enough, the wheelchair took the corner with the superior engineering of a race car. The door to Marcello's room was cracked, Tim extending a foot to shove it open the rest of the way. The scene was the same as it had been all week, except Nathaniel wasn't present this morning. Marcello was. He was sitting up in bed, but he didn't seem pleased to see Tim, or the gift he had brought along.

"Take it back," Marcello said, his palm a flat wall, his face turned away.

"What?" Tim cried, bringing the wheelchair to a halt. "Why? This thing is amazing!"

"I won't end my life bound to a chair."

"Like ending it in a bed is any better?" Tim stood and tugged on Marcello's pajama sleeve. "Just look at this thing! It's state-of-the-art. You can program it with a destination and it'll do all the driving. It also turns on a dime, *and* I talked the dealer into deactivating one of the safety features so it can go ten miles an hour."

"That doesn't sound very fast," Marcello said, eyeing the wheelchair with open disdain.

"Wait until the wind is blowing through your hair as you zip down the street. You're going to love it. I'm sick of this room, and I've only been here a week. You have to be going crazy."

"Some of us are capable of taking voyages of the mind," Marcello said, but his demeanor had softened. "It does look like something out of *Tron*. Do you remember that movie?"

Tim scrunched up his face. "Isn't that the one with Daft Punk in it?"

"Close enough." Marcello threw aside the blankets. "I suppose it wouldn't hurt to try."

"Check this out," Tim said, tapping the touchscreen a few times. "Go ahead and stand up. You can handle that on your own, right?"

"Let's hope so." Marcello slid out of bed, and while he didn't seem very steady, he managed to stand.

"Now turn around," Tim instructed.

"Oh my!" Marcello declared. "Just promise me you'll be gentle."

"We both know you like it rough," Tim teased. "Ready?"

"And willing," Marcello said from over his shoulder.

The chair rolled forward without any assistance, slowing as it neared and gently nudged the back of his legs.

"All on its own?" Marcello asked as he sat. "What a clever machine!"

"I'm telling you," Tim said, "this thing is pure class. If anyone sees you riding in it, you'll get an instant status boost."

Marcello experimented with the controls, the wheelchair lurching back and forth. Then his eyes rose to the bedroom door, a wild smile breaking out. "Let's see what it can do!" With a sudden burst of speed, Marcello shot from the room.

Tim watched in shock as he disappeared out the door. Then he laughed and gave chase. They raced around Marcello's home with careless disregard, but the machine was too well designed to allow an accident. No matter how recklessly Marcello drove it, the chair always slowed and stopped before careening into a wall, or most recently, before plunging into the pool.

"Can I keep it?" Marcello asked, turning pleading eyes on him.

"It's yours," Tim said. "I'm glad you like it. Doesn't it feel good to be outside again?"

They were still behind the house. A gentle breeze made the leaves in the trees flutter, the water lapping against the edge of the pool tranquil and soothing.

"Yes," Marcello said, shielding his eyes against the sun so he could consider Austin's skyline in the distance. "I feel I've been given a second chance at life. I never expected to see the city again. Not in person."

"Day trip!" Tim declared. Then he reined in on his enthusiasm. "Do you think you can handle it? I know you're not supposed to get over-stimulated."

"I've spent my entire life seeking stimulation," Marcello said. "I've been training for this very moment, whether I'm ill or not."

Tim wished he understood the underlying condition better. Then again, maybe it was better this way. Nathaniel had said that Marcello needed a friend. That was Tim's role. Let others worry about keeping his body healthy. Tim was more interested in keeping him sane.

"Of course," Marcello said in tones that sounded harmless

but were anything but, "I can't let the public see me in these." He pinched the leg of his pajamas, pulling at the silk before releasing it. "I'll have to change. Do you think this wheelchair can help with that?"

"I'm sure you can sit on it, *alone*, while pulling on your underwear," Tim said, already rolling his eyes. "I'll do the rest. Please tell me you've had a bath today."

"You needn't trouble yourself with that," Marcello said. "I have the most beautiful Puerto Rican nurse who comes by every morning to assist me. The things that boy can do with a sponge!"

"I don't want to know," Tim said. Then he reconsidered. "Okay, I kind of do. You can tell me about it on the way into town."

They smiled at each other before reentering the house. They both needed this. Marcello wasn't meant to fade away while confined indoors. If he died while screeching down the road in a high-tech wheelchair, at least it would make a good story.

Half an hour later, Marcello was dressed in a white tracksuit, which matched the chair's aesthetic perfectly. "Dear lord," he said after rolling out the front door. "This simply can't be." He placed a hand over his chest in alarm as he looked to Tim for an explanation. The object of his dismay was a brown minivan parked in the driveway. "You've become a soccer mom!"

"Tell me about it," Tim groaned. "I booked a Mercedes SUV, and when I got to the rental place, this is what they gave me."

"Some things never change," Marcello said. "What a ghastly vehicle. If you'd like, I can make a few calls and have it taken away. We'll have it crushed at the nearest junkyard while we watch. I'm assuming you bought full-coverage insurance?"

"Of course. Maybe on the way home though. I'm eager to get going."

"Very well."

The wheelchair was able to extend upward a few feet, high enough that Marcello could easily transfer himself to the passenger seat. After the wheelchair was folded and stowed in back, they were free to go wherever they pleased.

"Simply drive," Marcello said. "I want to see it all."

That surprised Tim. He had thought Marcello would want to go out to eat, or maybe visit the studio that still carried his name. Instead he was content to stare out the window as the world whizzed by, commenting on what he saw. No quips or shrewd observations. Instead he seemed to take pleasure in the simplest of sights.

"I can't imagine having to walk three dogs simultaneously. Taking care of them once home again must be an effort, although I bet her bed is warm at night." Or "Such a beautiful couple. Look how they swing their arms while holding hands, like teenagers despite both of them being gray. They must adore each other." The minivan drove through the downtown area and back out again to the quieter neighborhoods. It was here that Marcello finally asked Tim to pull over, next to a school.

"Let's go for a walk around the block," he suggested.

Tim complied, getting the wheelchair out again.

"What a lovely area," Marcello observed as they idled down the sidewalk. "So many lives, nestled together. I know you prefer your home to be surrounded by as much land as possible. I always valued my privacy too, although being here now, I imagine it must be nice to have neighbors that you see regularly. Even if you don't speak to them, you would still catch glimpses of their lives, building stories about each in your imagination. Do you ever miss that?"

"I don't know," Tim said. "I haven't lived that close to anyone for a long time. Since the frat house, I guess. I don't really miss any of those guys, but I did like the sense of community. I was never alone, which could be irritating. Mostly it was nice. Kind of like belonging to a great big family, you know?"

"Not really," Marcello murmured, "which might explain why I felt compelled to join a cult."

"Now *that's* a story I need to hear," Tim said.

"Really? I found the experience rather boring. I expected the cult leader to secretly drug our food and force us into a massive polyamorous relationship with him. Instead he preached abstinence of all things, except for when it came to procreation, which he insisted I participate in. Beatrice was my wife's name. She was the fiercest dyke I had ever met. We got along tremendously well."

"Wait." Tim pinched the bridge of his nose while shaking his head. "You were married to a woman?"

"Only by a madman's authority. The ceremony wasn't legally binding, and the marriage was never consummated, although we did delight in bragging about the development of our child. After a few months, when the cult leader asked us why Beatrice wasn't showing any signs of pregnancy, she placed a hand on my stomach and in perfectly serious tones asked, 'What do you mean? I just felt the baby kick!'"

"I bet the cult leader loved that."

"I'm afraid not. He had his own frantic sort of charisma, but sadly, no sense of humor. I quickly tired of his rules, and when announcing my intent to leave, I promised a free meal at McDonald's and drinks afterwards for anyone who wished to join me. He lost half his flock that day."

"What about Beatrice?"

"She left with me. Last I heard, she had joined an anti-whaling organization. I provided her with legal assistance after she bit off a man's finger so he would drop the harpoon. A truly ferocious woman. I couldn't have married better. Ah!" Marcello caught sight of something. "That takes me back."

They had circled around the block to the school again, except now children filled the fenced-in yard, participating in sports, climbing over playground equipment, or simply chasing each other around while shouting. Marcello seemed content to park his chair and watch them, eyes shining.

"Do you ever wish you had kids?" Tim asked him.

"Not really. I was too career-driven to truly focus on them. Throughout the course of my work, I managed to guide many young lives, so I don't feel I missed out on anything. I've been a parent in my own way. I don't believe the more traditional route would have suited me."

"Do you have any regrets at all?"

"Surprisingly few. I've had many appetites in my lifetime and fed them all with gusto. It pleases me that, at long last, each of those cravings has been satiated. Well... just about."

Tim went rigid. Then he sighed. "Could you please take your hand off my ass?"

"Spare a thought for a dying man and his final wishes!"

"If you get written permission from Ben," Tim said. "I'll let you touch whatever you want."

"Bah," Marcello said, pulling his hand away. "Ben has always been stingy when it comes to sharing you. Not that I can blame him. I would have conducted myself in the exact same manner had I been lucky enough to win the title of Mrs. Tim Wyman."

This made him laugh. "So you don't regret not getting married? Aside from Beatrice, of course."

"Not at all. I have very few misgivings about that, or anything else in my life. Although I do regret never founding the boy band I had once envisioned. They were going to be called A New Direction, because really, who doesn't like A New Direction? Just imagine five of them on stage, bouncing around to the music for everyone to see. That's what this country really needs, and what each of us craves—A New Direction, penetrating our tender insides with stunning vibrations."

Tim finally picked up on the homonym and shook his head. "You really are hopeless."

"Thank you."

"And I never learn. I was hoping for some words of wisdom before you go."

"Then I shall do my best to accommodate you," Marcello replied, clearing his throat. "They say that only the good die young, which is why I have always endeavored to be as indulgent as possible. That is the secret of my longevity."

"Ha ha," Tim deadpanned.

"I'm quite serious." Marcello nodded to the playing children. "It fills my heart with joy to see them so carefree and caught up in the simplest of pleasures. I spent too much of my youth worrying about what other people thought. I tore myself down repeatedly when not holding myself to impossibly high standards. I was miserable, and the sad truth is that nobody was as concerned about my appearance or status as me. I tortured myself for nothing, but there *were* brief moments of abandon, on the playground for instance, where I allowed myself to simply be. That was the state of existence I aimed for when reinventing myself. I didn't create a new persona. Only a name. The rest was me disrobing. All the imagined expectations and superficial standards were stripped away, one by one, until all that was left was me."

"I can relate to that."

"Which is why you don't need my advice," Marcello said, smiling up at him. "You're one of the happiest people I've ever met, because you no longer pretend to be what you thought others wanted to see. You're Tim Wyman. Considering that you're the only one capable of being him, it would have been supremely tragic if you didn't embrace that persona fully. No one else could have filled that role."

"There will never be another you either."

"Let's hope not," Marcello said, rolling his chair forward again. "You've got me thinking. When I first learned I was dying, I tried concealing the fact for a variety of reasons. I didn't want anyone to see me diminished, or for them to suffocate me with their pity. Had I kept hiding myself away, I would have missed out on the recent memories we've made. With that in mind, let me run an idea by you. How do you think my closest friends would react if I asked them to move in with me? Just for the remainder of the time I have left. Would you be willing? Would Ben?"

"Yes," Tim said. "Absolutely. Jason is flying in this weekend with his family."

"They are welcome too," Marcello declared. "Nathaniel, Kelly, and even that little scamp Buttercup... I'd like them to join me as well."

"Do I get to bring my dogs too?"

"Of course! I know Harold will be willing to stay, Noah accompanying him of course."

"What about that guy you're dating?"

"Peng? I haven't told him yet. Isn't that awful? I've been keeping him at arm's length, claiming I'm too busy. I really must make amends."

They stopped at the corner of the block, beneath the shade of a tree. They could see the school better from here. And be seen. A little boy had noticed them and was sticking out his tongue while crossing his eyes. Tim looked down to gauge Marcello's reaction and noticed the man flipping the bird. To his absolute horror, when Tim looked up at the kid again, he also had his middle finger on display.

"There we go!" Marcello said proudly. "Now he'll have something to show his mother when she asks what he learned at school today."

"You're terrible."

"He's wonderful," Marcello said, attention still on the child. "I appreciate his audacity. We'll invite him to stay with me too."

Tim laughed. "Sounds like you might already be booked up. How many rooms do you have exactly?"

"More than enough."

A thought occurred to Tim, and he was unsure about broaching the subject, but Marcello was right. Time on this world was limited. For everyone. Why spend it being anything but honest and open? "What's going to happen to your house when you're gone? I can't imagine Nathaniel wanting to live there. He's too humble, and you've made sure that everyone else you care about has a home of their own."

Marcello shrugged. "I'm not overly concerned with the house. You can lock the doors with my remains still inside. Let it become a future tomb for some enterprising archeologist to unearth and raid."

"You're kidding, right?" Tim said. "You should sell the house and use the money for a good cause. Otherwise it would be wasteful."

"Is that how you see my decisions?" Marcello asked. "As wasteful?"

Tim winced. "You *can* be a little loose with your money."

"I know that my life must seem excessive to most people, but I was never wasteful. It's true that I'm no stranger to frivolous spending. I like to think I balanced that out by being equally generous with my love. And my gratitude. I rarely shied away from risks, or refused experiences out of blind fear. I left myself open to whatever the universe had in store for me, wanting to accept its gifts with grace. Of all the opportunities I've had to experience pleasure and pain, to bask in the companionship of a friend or lover, or to wage battle for causes I believe in, I never let one go astray without good reason. I've lived to the fullest, and in that regard, I've never felt wasteful."

Tim placed his hand on his friend's shoulder. "It's beautiful the way you speak. Almost as good as listening to Ben sing." He swallowed against rising emotion. "I'm going to miss you."

"Not yet, you won't," Marcello said, reaching up to place his hand over Tim's. "I'm not gone yet, and we still have the entire day ahead of us. I'd like to visit your gallery next. And afterwards, we'll find ourselves a bite to eat. How does that sound?"

Tim still couldn't speak. Instead he squeezed Marcello's shoulder and gestured for him—as so often before—to lead the way.

* * * * *

Tim woke up in a bed that wasn't his own, but the man lying not far away certainly was. Tim belonged to him just as much, so he pulled Ben close and held him for as long as they could. Then they rose along with the rest of the house. The previous week had been intense but gratifying. All of Marcello's closest friends had traveled to be with him, filling the massive house with life, the rooms echoing with laughter. They had even settled into a sort of routine, gathering around the dining room table for each meal and taking turns caring for Marcello when need be, but the man needed little help. He seemed revitalized by having so much company. Marcello even joined Tim on his evening jogs, racing down the sidewalk in his wheelchair and clearing it of any unwary pedestrians.

Today was the grand finale. Marcello had chartered a bus that would take them outside the city to a vineyard. There they would continue their celebrations, surrounded by nature while still every bit as intoxicated. Marcello always saw to that. Even those who didn't drink would find themselves acting sillier than normal, their reservations abandoned. He had that effect on everyone, like the embodiment of Bacchus himself.

"Ready to go?" Tim asked when entering Marcello's bedroom. The older man had made his usual appearance during breakfast, and after excusing himself to get ready, hadn't been seen since. That's what made it so confusing that he was still in bed and wearing his pajamas. Although the guy seductively draped over him helped explain the delay.

"Sorry!" Tim said, when he saw that it was Peng, an Asian man in his early thirties who was a ceaseless chatterbox, but Marcello seemed to find him invigorating. "I didn't mean to interrupt."

"We're all done here," Marcello said to his boyfriend. "Aren't we? Do you feel better now?"

"Yes." Peng nuzzled noses with him and stood. "I'll finish getting ready."

"Very well. I'll see you in a few hours."

Tim nodded at Peng, then stood aside so he could leave. "Everything okay?" Tim asked once they were alone.

Marcello nodded. "He's concerned about being left out of my will."

Tim made a face as he walked over and plopped down in the chair. "That doesn't bother you?"

"Why should it?"

Tim gritted his teeth. "Because it makes him seem like a gold digger."

"Perhaps he is. Some people are attracted to money and power. I've never minded that. As handsome as you are, my friend, you were born that way, so it's hardly an achievement. Although you do deserve credit for taking such good care of yourself." His eyes moved over Tim. "Likewise, I feel I deserve credit for what I've made of myself. The money I've managed to accumulate represents who I am—my personality, intelligence, and ambition—more so than any genetic features I happened to inherit. So gold diggers, as you call them, shouldn't be judged any more severely than those who have a strong preference for an athletic physique or a refined sense of humor. That having been said, I'm sure you've met people who only care about your body and not your personality."

"Tons of them."

"That's fine for a fling, but when it comes to lengthier engagements, I select those who enjoy my company, as well as my money."

"Then why have I been sitting here the last couple of weeks instead of him?"

"Because I love you, darling boy, in a way that I do few others."

Marcello wasn't usually so direct about his feelings. Tim could only respond with the obvious truth. "I love you too."

"Good." Marcello pressed his lips together and narrowed his eyes, as he often did before getting down to business. "While we're on the subject of inheritance, you should know that I'm leaving you an endowment, Tim."

"You don't need to do that."

"But the thought pleases me," Marcello said, smiling naughtily. "I want you to finally have a big endowment."

Tim scoffed. "I already do, thank you very much."

"And now I got you to admit it. You wouldn't have if I'd asked directly."

"I hate you."

"Really?"

"No. Not in a million years."

Marcello reached over to pat his hand. "Then the matter is settled. You'll accept the money?"

Tim shook his head. "We have enough already. What do I need more for?"

"That's your decision to make. Give it away if you like."

"I will." Tim sat upright. "We'll start a new grant through the gallery to support artists. That seems fitting, considering the other one is named in Eric's honor. Would you like that? You and him sharing a legacy?"

"I can't think of anything that would please me more, aside from getting to see him again." Marcello smiled. "We have a unique opportunity in that regard. Is there a message you'd like me to share with Eric?"

Tim's head spun at the thought. He felt like crying, but in overwhelming happiness, because it was as if someone had invented a phone that could contact the dead. "Make sure he knows how I feel about him. And that he always stayed part of my life, even after he was gone."

"Will you carry me with you as well? How fortunate I would feel, to be a constant companion during the adventures that await you."

That did it. Tim cried, but only a few sobs before he got himself under control. "You really need to ask?"

"No. Your tears are answer enough."

Tim wiped them away. "Do you really think there's more? After this life. Ben doesn't. Not really. He always says he hopes there is, but I think that's his way of appeasing me. I hope he's wrong, but what if it is all a story we tell ourselves to make death less scary?"

"If so, nothing could be more human. We are all storytellers in the way that we communicate, creating a plot each time we describe the events of our lives, relying on beginnings, middles, and yes, even endings. That's why I must face my own, so my story can finally be complete. As for what lies beyond that final page, well, wouldn't it be wonderful if we were allowed to help craft the destinies of mortal men? If I should find myself in such a position, I will write for you the most loving of stories with the happiest of endings." Marcello reached over to pat his knee and left his hand there. "There might be a few racy scenes as well."

Tim chuckled. "Lucky for me, you're not the author of my story just yet. Better get dressed. People are already on the bus."

"Change of plans," Marcello said. "I'll be joining you later. I've skipped one too many doctor's appointments, and Nathaniel demands that I remain for this one."

"But you've been doing great!"

Marcello sighed. "Nathaniel is the sort of man who insists on good news being confirmed. This will set his mind at ease. I will join you all in celebration afterwards."

Tim stood and stretched. "Sounds good. Are you really feeling okay?"

"Yes. Why do you ask?"

"Just trying to figure out if you can handle me doing this." Tim dove into bed, tackling Marcello and hugging him. He kissed the old man on his thinning hair a few times, then once on the cheek, before he rolled out of bed on the other side, landing on his feet.

"I don't know what inspired that," Marcello said breathlessly, "but I think we should make it a daily tradition!"

"You've got it," Tim said, shooting him a wink before sauntering toward the door. "See you soon."

He wandered the house until he found Ben. Together they collected Jason and his family, and once they were outside with the other guests, Tim explained the situation to them. He made sure everyone got on the bus but didn't take a seat himself.

"Do you mind if I stay?" he asked Ben.

His husband seemed confused. "Is everything okay?"

"Yeah! I want to be here to help Nathaniel if he needs it. He worries so much that he barely lets himself use the restroom until I show up to relieve him." Tim winced. "Relieve him of duty, I mean. That sounded weird."

"I understood what you meant," Ben said, fighting down a smile.

"I also want to hear what the doctor has to say, you know? Even if that means pressing my ear to the door."

"We'll take good care of Ben," Jason said from the seat behind them. Then he nudged his daughter, "Right?"

"Only if I'm allowed to drink."

"Too young!" William said from behind her, sitting between a pair of boys to keep them from fighting.

"I'm almost twenty!" Daisy complained. "What difference will a year make? And besides, it's not like I haven't been drunk before. Plenty of times."

"Too young!" William repeated, sounding panicked.

Jason sighed. "They grow up so fast."

"I remember when you were that age," Tim replied. "And if I recall, you begged us to buy wine for your picnic with William."

"I think it was prom night actually," Ben chimed in.

"See?" Daisy said, turning to her dad. "It's a family tradition."

"Call your mom and try explaining that to her," Jason retorted before shooting Tim an incredulous expression.

"Looks like you've got it all under control," Tim said. "Have fun."

He leaned over to kiss his husband, did a quick head count, and walked up front to tell the driver that everyone was on board. Then he left the bus and went back inside the house. He stopped by the kitchen first for a glass of water and some much-needed solitude. Then he sat in the living room and called his parents. He had been too busy to do so recently, but he thought of them often, Marcello's condition a frequent reminder that his mom and dad wouldn't be around forever. After catching up with them, Tim stood, intending to check on Marcello.

He had just reached the hall when he found someone coming down it from the opposite direction.

"You're still here?" Nathaniel asked.

"I thought you might need some help."

"I appreciate that," Nathaniel said. And yet, he didn't move out of the way, or turn so Tim could follow him. Instead he appeared to be searching for the right words.

Tim felt a jolt of panic. "Is he okay?"

"Yeah," Nathaniel said. "You caught me in an awkward situation. Marcello asked me to get him a drink."

Tim needed a second before he understood. "Like, a *real* drink? You've finally given in?"

"He was supposed to be at the vineyard already, so it only seems fair."

"I'm surprised you didn't make him wait until later." Tim turned and walked with him to the kitchen, where he watched Nathaniel uncork a bottle. "Do you think the doctor will have anything good to say?"

"I doubt it. He won't be here long." Nathaniel seemed pensive. He was halfway through pouring a glass when he set down the bottle. "To be honest, I was hoping for some alone time with Marcello. With everyone being here this past week—"

"I get it," Tim said, raising his hands. "I was only trying to be useful, but I totally get it. I was just complaining to Marcello that I've been around more than his boyfriend has, but in truth, I prefer it that way. I don't want to share him much. Not now. So you enjoy some time with him. I'll head to the vineyard and make sure everyone is having fun."

"Thank you," Nathaniel said. "I'll take care of the dogs."

"Awesome. See you soon."

Tim went outside to his car. The latest in a long line of vehicles that he loved. The dumb minivan had been returned to the rental agency. It felt good to be back behind the wheel of a real car. He even allowed himself to activate the sound kit once outside the city limits, so the engine would growl whenever he pressed down on the accelerator, despite it running in perfect silence otherwise.

Tim had just reached the vineyard and parked when his stomach dropped. He didn't know why. Through the windshield, he could see a garden patio. The people gathered there seemed to be enjoying themselves. Ben and Jason were deep in conversation, kids running around their legs before chasing each other through the crowd. They nearly knocked over a man who was pouring wine, Daisy flirting with him and probably hoping to increase her chances of partaking. Everyone seemed in high spirits. The scene was inviting, and Tim wanted nothing more than to join it, but he remained in his car, the hollow feeling in his chest refusing to leave. He checked the vehicle's display but didn't find any texts. Everything was fine. If that was the case, why did he feel so strange?

Swearing under his breath, Tim put the car in reverse and tore out of the parking lot. The drive to the vineyard had passed so quickly. The return trip took ages, or so it felt. When he finally arrived back at Marcello's house, he expected to see ambulances outside, or maybe a coroner. Aside from the cars that everyone had brought with them, there were no other vehicles in the driveway. The house appeared tranquil, so he forced himself to calm down as he went inside. How was he going to explain this?

He'd say he forgot something maybe, or just eavesdrop while still in the hall until he heard the reassuring sound of Marcello's voice. That shouldn't take long. Funny then, that the hallway was so silent. The bedroom too, when he pushed open the door. Even the bed was unoccupied. Sort of. Marcello's silk pajamas were still there, the blankets pulled up over them, as if he had simply disappeared.

Like a Jedi.

Tim put his hand to his mouth to hold back laughter, but the sound that came out was haggard and wounded. This wasn't a joke. That would be too cruel. He had asked Marcello how he would prefer to go, and this is exactly what he'd described.

Tim could barely see anything past the tears that began to fill his eyes. Instead he remembered the sound of a husky laugh, a boisterous voice, and the endless jokes that had made his sides ache. Or the complete disregard for his personal space, which sometimes had resulted in groping—not that he ever truly minded—but had also rescued him from the darkest moments of his past. He thought of a gift for gab that made even the ugliest aspects of life sound like poetry, and a keen eye for the beauty not only found in nature and art, but in each and every person that Marcello met. Most of all, he grieved the loss of his best friend. Who would he turn to when needing to make sense of the world? Who else could conjure up impossible miracles in times of crisis? Tim felt lost, forever condemned to walk through the remainder of his years without the perverse wisdom of a crazy old fool who was somehow, inexplicably, the most rational person he had ever met. In other words, his heart was breaking yet again, but he didn't try to resist the onslaught of emotion. He simply placed a hand over the ache in his chest and wept.

"Sorry," a voice said behind him.

He spun around to see Nathaniel, his eyes red and his cheeks still wet. Tim couldn't get the words out to ask what he needed to, wanting to be sure, but Nathaniel understood anyway. He nodded silently. Then he began to weep. Tim grabbed him, pulling Nathaniel close. Their bodies shook as they cried, their howls uncontained as the grief came pouring out. Eventually they let go, looking anywhere but at each other. Tim turned to face the room. He noticed the empty champagne glass on the nightstand and choked back more tears.

"What the hell?" he managed to croak, gesturing at the scene.

"He thought it would be funny," Nathaniel said. "Or poetic. I'm not sure there was a difference in his mind. When the others get back, I'm supposed to put dry ice in his pajamas so they're smoking, like he just disappeared."

"He planned all of this?"

Nathaniel nodded. "This is what he wanted. He left notes for everyone. We're supposed to read them later. And there's this." He walked to the small writing desk, picking up a journal that was worn around the edges, many of the pages sticking out at an angle.

"What's that?" Tim asked.

"He said it's the truth. All of it. I haven't worked up the courage to open it yet."

Nathaniel held the book out, like Tim might be willing to do so for him, but he shook his head.

"I already know who he was," Tim explained. "And so do you. Marcello was a good man. The rest is only details."

Nathaniel lowered the journal. "Is it wrong that I still want to know?"

"That's why he left it for you," Tim said. "I know he wanted to learn the full truth about his parents and was frustrated that he never could. I bet he didn't want to put you through that. Not again. You never got to meet your biological father, did you?"

Nathaniel shook his head, his face crumpling again.

"The journal is Marcello's answer to any questions you might have. I don't think he would want anyone else to see it. Not even me. You were special to him, Nathaniel. You gave him the one thing he didn't already have."

"Family," Nathaniel spluttered between sobs.

Tim went to him, holding the large man while he cried again. Once he was calmer, Tim took a step back. "Is everything taken care of?"

Nathaniel nodded.

"Good," Tim said. "You know, when Chinchilla died, it was Marcello I turned to."

"Same here with Zero," Nathaniel mumbled.

"We don't have him anymore, but we do have each other. Understand? You have Kelly, and I have Ben, but there are times when you don't want them to see how much you're hurting."

"Because you know it'll hurt them too," Nathaniel said.

"Exactly. When that happens, come find me, and I promise to do the same."

Tim's relationship with Marcello hadn't truly begun until Eric's death. Losing the most important person in both their lives was the initial bond, but the friendship that came later was based on so much more. Tim had always liked Nathaniel. Now he hoped they would become even closer. When their husbands tired of the endless recollections of Marcello that were sure to follow, they would always find a willing audience in each other.

"What now?" Nathaniel asked.

"We cry as much as we need to," Tim said. "We get it all out of our systems, because when the others come back, we're going to make sure they celebrate one of the greatest men who ever lived. Agreed?"

Nathaniel wiped his nose. "Agreed."

"And we're going to scare the hell out of them with Marcello's smoking pajamas, because we both know he'll stick around to see their reactions. He's exactly the sort of person to keep the afterlife waiting, just to find out how well one of his stunts goes down."

Nathaniel managed a laugh. Then he gave into misery again. Tim put an arm around him, reminding himself that when one story came to an end, there was always the chance for another to begin.

"This is going to sound ridiculous..." Ben shook his head. "Never mind."

Tim waited. He felt no need to pressure his husband. Ben always made his thoughts known eventually. Tim flopped instead onto his back, stretching out on the blanket while staring up at a perfectly blue sky, a few lazy clouds drifting across it. On the edge of his vision, a tree waved branches thick with leaves, as if in greeting. The weather was gorgeous. It was the sort of summer day that asserted, in no uncertain terms, that life was at its peak and thriving. How ironic then that they were in a graveyard, surrounded by the dead.

"It's just that," Ben said, making a second attempt, "when it comes to Marcello, you never know what to expect. What if he had to fake his death again? That would explain why he told you the crazy story about the Mafia. So you would know. And I bet that Beatrice person is who we're supposed to contact, because she'll be able to tell us where he's hiding."

Tim thought about it. Then he laughed. "Wishful thinking."

"Are you sure? Is there even a body beneath us? Because I never saw one."

"I know what you're doing." Tim let his head roll to the left, so he could look at the neighboring grave. It belonged to Eric, and didn't make as nice of a picnic spot, too covered in wildflowers. That had become something of a tradition in their family. Samson and Chinchilla had received the same treatment. Marcello's grave would bloom eventually too, but not yet. There were still too many visitors who would trample the flowers. Tim often met people he knew when visiting here, and plenty that he didn't. Because of that, the grave was always covered in bouquets and wreaths, even months later. Tim had once imagined himself being laid to rest in this very spot and had bought the plot next to Eric's for that purpose, even before reuniting with Ben. Marcello hadn't made any plans or requests in regard to his remains. Nathaniel had been too upset to make any decisions. So it was up to him, and this seemed the most appropriate place. Two friends, reunited in this world and the next. "You're trying to bring him back."

"How so?"

Tim sat up to look at his husband. "By coming up with any explanation other than the truth. He's gone."

"I know," Ben said glumly. "I wish he wasn't."

"You and me both. I did the same thing when Eric died. I watched him go. I was there when it happened, but there were times when I'd be out in public and catch sight of someone who looked kind of like him, and I'd start entertaining crazy fantasies. Even though I knew they weren't real."

"Same here," Ben said. "I did that with Jace, and now Marcello. *But—*"

Tim chuckled. "Here we go."

"—you have to admit that it is kind of weird. How did Marcello time his death like that, when he knew we'd all be at the vineyard?"

"Never ask a magician to reveal his secrets," Tim said.

"Even when the person asking is batting their eyelashes? Like this?"

Tim watched as Ben put on the most adorable expression he could manage, which of course won him over instantly. "I asked Nathaniel the same thing. He said that Marcello left this world on his own terms."

"You mean assisted—" Ben's mouth clamped shut. Then he nodded. "That makes sense. Do you know what happened to his body? Was he cremated or…"

"You saw for yourself. He disappeared in a puff of smoke." He held up a hand before Ben could protest. "I don't know. Marcello wanted it to play out the way it did. Nathaniel took care of the rest. All I did was give him this plot."

"Which was very sweet of you," Ben said. "I know you planned on being buried here, but this will make Jason happy. He wants to keep our ashes. He says he's going to put us in the same urn."

"Gross," Tim said, sticking out his tongue.

"You love the idea and you know it," Ben said with a smile. "Just imagine being all mixed up with me for the rest of eternity."

"I guess that might be okay," Tim said. "Not so different than how we are now. Hey, what time is it?"

"Almost four. You need to get going?"

"Soon, yeah." Tim had to be at the dog park. He went to the same one, at the same time, every single day, so he could meet Nathaniel. There they would walk their dogs together, usually while talking about Marcello, although lately the subjects were more varied. They had enough in common that their friendship felt natural, and just enough differences to keep it interesting. Much like someone else he used to know.

"You have a good heart," Ben said, his brown eyes shining in approval.

"I'll take whatever credit I can get," Tim said, "but to be fair, it's just as therapeutic for me. Marcello left behind a very big hole when he died." He snorted and looked skyward. "I know what you'd say to that," he called out, "and I'm definitely not looking for that hole to get filled. Not like that anyway!"

Ben laughed. "I guess we better finish what we came here to do."

"Yup." Tim stood. He dug around in the basket they had brought with them, pulling out a glass and the bottle of champagne that had been sitting untouched in their pantry.

The other he had put in the refrigerator, where he intended it to always remain. Just in case Ben was right about that Mafia theory. As for this bottle, Tim popped the cork, took a glass, and poured. He didn't hand it to Ben or take a sip. Instead he placed the glass in front of Marcello's tombstone, which he read again.

Marcello Maltese
1983-2033
Friend, Father, Fiend
"God has enough angels. He needs a successor."

Those were the last words Marcello had spoken. Tim wished he could have heard them in person, but he took comfort in the knowledge that someone else did. Nathaniel had been there, which in a way, was the greatest gift Marcello could have given him—entrusting his chosen son with those precious final seconds.

Tim took a deep breath, swallowing against the tears. "I know you prefer not to drink alone so…" He turned and reached into the basket, pulling out another glass, which he also filled. This one he set next to Eric's tombstone. "I'll leave the rest here," he said, placing the bottle between their graves.

He felt Ben's hand in his, which made him feel secure enough to cry. His husband didn't offer any soothing words, or need to, because they had both mourned before. Ben standing at his side was all the comfort he needed.

"Hey," Tim said. "You know those stories you write?"

"It's just a hobby," Ben said dismissively.

"You should let them be more than that. They're really good."

"Thanks."

"Could you make sure a few are about Marcello? I don't want him to be forgotten."

"Of course," Ben said. "I'd love that. Let me ask you something. Do you think he can see us right now?"

"Marcello?" Tim hesitated. "I know you don't believe in that sort of thing."

"I know what I think. I'm asking what you believe."

"Yeah. He's probably watching us."

"Good."

Ben planted a kiss on his lips, but it didn't end there. He lifted a leg and wrapped it around Tim's hip before leaping. Tim was forced to catch him, stumbling back while doing so, Ben still smooching him forcefully and making it impossible to maintain balance. Tim staggered around before falling backwards onto the blanket, holding Ben close so he wouldn't be hurt. Then he laughed while tightening his arms around his husband.

"We are *not* going to have sex on Marcello's grave," he said.

"Sorry," Ben shouted over his shoulder, addressing the sky. "I tried. Maybe next time!"

Tim laughed again and rolled over on top of him, looking down and seeing everything that was good about this world. Love and companionship. Marcello's favorite pursuits. What better way to pay tribute to him than by making sure the rest of their days were filled with both? Tim stood and offered his hand. Ben accepted it, and after collecting their things, they walked away together, the sun warming their path and catching the glasses they'd left behind, the spirits glowing with a joyful golden light.

Something Like Heaven

by Jay Bell

The Afterlife
2066 (relative mortal time)

Ben's eyes shot open as he sucked in air, having returned from a deep dreamless sleep. No, that wasn't true. As a flood of memories came rushing back, he remembered a party filled with everyone he had ever loved, each reunion making him weep with joy. The dream was one of the best he'd ever had. He knew from experience how quickly the details could fade if he didn't commit them to memory, so he rolled over to tell Tim about it and felt momentarily disoriented. The man in his bed wasn't Ben's husband. Except he was. Jace was sitting up while reading, Samson snoozing on his stretched-out legs.

Ben pushed himself upright, squinting as he adjusted to the morning light. He was safe in the house that they had saved so long to put a down payment on. That was a relief, but it didn't explain the confusing memories. "Somebody must have spiked my drink," he mumbled. "I feel weird."

"It'll pass," Jace said, setting the book down on the nightstand. "Just relax."

Ben copied him by turning a pillow upright to support his back. He sunk into this while considering the day ahead. "Have you fed the dogs yet?"

Samson lifted his head as if offended.

"Sorry," Ben said, shaking his head. "I meant dog." Singular. Which one though? They'd had so many, and even though they swore to never put themselves through the emotional turmoil of losing a beloved pet again, it was never long before Jace brought another one home. Wait, that wasn't right either. Jace wasn't the dog lover. It was—

"Tim!" Ben went rigid with panic. His mind struggled to

rearrange the pieces correctly. The dream had indeed been wonderful, and *long*, spanning decades as he lived together with his high school sweetheart. They had made it to their twilight years, and then… Ben breathed out in relief. He had already been through the worst of it. They had lost each other, but like each time before, they had managed to find each other again in a place he had once thought impossible.

"It's the lack of a physical brain," Jace said gently. "Our memories aren't stored as groups of neurons, but they carry over anyway. Our souls always need time to adjust."

Ben took stock of events again, and this time they made more sense. He remembered dying, but it was such a small insignificant event compared to what came next. Jace. Hours spent only with him, talking and catching up on so much they had missed, even if it was as simple as holding Jace's hand. He reached over to take it now as the rest came back to him. When he had been ready to see the others, Jace had brought him to a party in a ballroom that had once hosted countless charity events. Tim had been waiting there, restored to his youth, and he wasn't alone. Not by far. Everyone that Ben had loved and lost over the years was waiting for him. His mother, father, grandparents, and other relatives. Friends that had passed too soon, and some that had lasted longer than anyone had expected, such as Marcello himself. Ben had shed so many happy tears during the party. He hugged everyone repeatedly, sang karaoke with Tim, and danced endlessly with Jace. That was his last clear memory, being wrapped in those comforting arms and struggling to stay awake, Jace assuring him that it was okay if he needed to close his eyes.

And here he was, in Heaven, although Ben had already been told that the afterlife was so much more than that. From what he understood, it could be anything he desired. Including his appearance. Ben threw back the blanket to expose his naked body. "Yes!" he cried. "Check me out. I'm young again!"

"You most certainly are," Jace said, sounding amused.

"How old am I though?" Ben asked. "I hope I'm in my thirties. That was a great age. Or maybe a little older. Or younger? I need a—"

"Here." Jace passed him a hand mirror.

Ben stared at him instead of taking it. "Can we read each other's thoughts in the afterlife?"

"No," Jace said with a chuckle, "but we do have a term for new arrivals who lived to an older age. We call them mirror gazers, since they're always obsessed with their appearance."

"Nothing wrong with that," Ben said, swiping the mirror from him. Brown hair instead of white, and it was all there! No more bald spot. Just hair so thick and dense that it had resisted styling when he was a teenager. He watched with fascination as the features of his face aged backward. In a few scant seconds, he was sixteen instead of thirty.

"Cute!" Jace said. "I only ever saw photos of when you were that young."

"I just have to think of the age I want to be?" Ben asked. Without waiting for an answer, he aged himself up to eighteen. A little less baby fat on the cheeks, and a build that was more developed, despite being hopelessly scrawny. He hopped out of bed and began strutting around the room, loving how smoothly his body moved. The aches and pains were gone. "Barely legal," he sang as he shook his rump. "Robbin' that cradle! Better not let the neighbors find out, no no nooooo!"

Jace laughed. "Technically you're still an old man, so I'm not worried. But if you insist on being that age, maybe this will make it less weird." After gently sliding his legs free of Samson's weight, Jace got out of bed. In the blink of an eye, his appearance shifted. The blond hair was long now, tumbling all the way down to his shoulders. His expression was more naïve, the eyes wide with the innocence of youth. Jace's body was slender, not having filled out quite yet.

"Oh my goodness," Ben said, his jaw falling open. "That's so freaking adorable. How old are you now?"

"Eighteen," Jace said. "Same age as you."

Ben walked around him, checking out every naked detail, although his interest wasn't sexual yet. He was more curious than anything. This had potential! Now they could pretend they had met as teenagers, even though that would mean... He thought of Tim again. Where was he? Ben wanted to ask, but it seemed an awkward moment to do so.

"Clothes work the same way," Jace said. "Concentrate on what you want to wear, and it'll appear."

Jace was suddenly decked out in his flight attendant's uniform, the one from the photo that Ben had so often stared at and spoken to. His age had changed to match, the hair short again.

Ben felt his heart swell with love. He opted for his favorite bathrobe, not ready to decide on his outfit for today. His only priority was throwing himself into Jace's arms. "This is going to be fun," he said. "I wanted you back for so long. That's already amazing, but I never expected all of this."

"Believe me, it wasn't easy waiting for you to arrive," Jace murmured. "Even though there's enough here to keep me amused for the rest of eternity, it wasn't the same without you to share it with."

"It's all so overwhelming," Ben said when he was released again. "What do we do now? Breakfast? We don't really need to eat, do we? Then again, I just woke up from sleeping, which seems weird."

"That will be optional soon," Jace assured him. "Once you've adjusted. The mind can still get overloaded and need a break, but you won't have to sleep in the future. Meditation works just as well, or there are other techniques, but those are only necessary when there's too much to consciously process. Food isn't required to survive, but eating is still pleasurable, so many people continue to. And yes, I would love to cook you breakfast."

"I better get dressed then," Ben said, moving to pick up the mirror. He remembered how he loved being in his thirties. His body wasn't in decline yet and his mind had become disciplined enough that he wasn't subject to every emotional whim. So that's what he chose. Thirty-five or so. "What do you think?" he asked, turning around.

Jace's expression was hard to read, but he nodded in approval.

"Are you sure?" Ben asked, consulting the mirror again. Then it clicked. "You aren't used to me looking this old."

"I don't mind," Jace said hurriedly. "You look great! And to be honest, I've seen you at every age from your twenties on. I never stopped watching over you."

"Or visiting me in my dreams," Ben said. "Who makes the rules about that sort of thing? Because they need to change. I should have been allowed to remember."

"It's a complicated question, but I'll try to answer it. Over time. There's a lot to learn."

"Good," Ben said, but now it was him making the weird face. He wasn't trying to hide it either. "I know what seems off about this. I'm older than you. At least in appearance. That doesn't feel right."

"If you want, I can change that." The lines on Jace's face deepened, the hair at his temples turning silver, just like his mother's had been.

Ben was blindsided by the emotions this stirred in him. "I wondered sometimes. Especially as the decades went by. I tried to picture what you would look like."

"When I was old? Do you want to see? I can only guess, but I'll try."

Ben licked his lips and nodded. Jace became slightly stooped, his cheeks sagging as his skin wrinkled. His hair was completely silver now, his blue eyes benefiting from it and standing out more. He was beautiful, and it reminded Ben of all they had been cheated of when Jace died so prematurely.

"What the hell?" he complained, wiping at his eyes in frustration. "This is supposed to be Heaven. Why do I still feel sad?"

"Because sorrow is the bleak canvass that happiness is painted upon." Jace tilted his head. "I missed you when we were separated. While you were grieving me, I was grieving the loss of you. I wouldn't want to have been cheated of that, even here."

These words only made Ben feel more emotional, but he didn't want to wallow in the feeling. He'd done enough grieving to last him a lifetime. And beyond. Now he wanted to enjoy being together again and say the things he always wished he could have, no matter how basic they were. "I love you."

Jace smiled. "I love you too. Now let me cook for you. We'll focus on heavier matters later. I don't want you wearing yourself out again too soon."

Ben had nearly forgotten how good it felt to have Jace fretting over him and catering to his every need. He had been one lucky boy. He decided that was the most appropriate age until they could explore their new dynamic together, so he reverted to his twenties. That's how Jace had known him while they were still living. "I'll get dressed and meet you in the kitchen."

"Sounds good."

Once he was alone, Ben jumped in bed and nuzzled noses

with Samson. While petting him, he thought back to some of the favorite clothes he'd owned when alive. A soft cotton T-shirt, jeans that were just the right fit, and shoes so broken in that they felt more like slippers. He had worn each until they had practically fallen apart. Now they too rose from the dead to join him in eternity. The ridiculousness of the situation made him laugh, but he grew serious again when holding the mirror far away to see himself, his eyes lingering on the shirt, which hadn't been his originally. Tim had left it at his house when they were teenagers, Ben feeling like he was being hugged by him each time he wore it.

He set aside the mirror and looked at the bed, where Samson was watching him. In a whisper, he asked, "I don't suppose you've seen Tim around? You remember him. Your other daddy? Or I guess your *other* other daddy. You've had at least three."

Samson purred.

That was all the response he was likely to get. Ben swallowed and went to find Jace, his concerns forgotten as he walked through a home he hadn't set foot in for nearly fifty years. It took him ages to reach the kitchen, since he kept stopping to fawn over details he had forgotten long ago.

"How does all of this work?" Ben asked, joining Jace in front of a sizzling frying pan. He always did make the best omelets. "Is it like our appearance? You just think of a house and—poof!— there it is?"

"It takes more effort than that," Jace said. "Especially if you're working alone. I can teach you if you want. Grab a couple plates for me please."

Ben did so, tickled by their outdated design. Soon he was sitting at the kitchen table with Jace and had just taken his first bite. His reaction was embarrassingly over the top, and not out of nostalgia. "Either the memory cheats," Ben said, "or you do, because your eggs were never *this* good."

Jace's smile was subtle. "I may have taken a few liberties. The best ingredients were always the most expensive, but there's no such thing as money here. Well, aside from in Hell."

Ben snorted. "That sounds about right to me, considering how much trouble it caused back on Earth."

"We could go there today," Jace offered. "Hell isn't the horrifying pit of flames that you're imagining. Most parts of it anyway. There are all sorts of places we could visit. Or, as I offered, I could teach you about how creating works here."

Ben's head was bobbing, but not in commitment. "I wouldn't mind catching up with a few people," he said, unsure how to broach the subject. "It was hard to focus on anyone last night and um... Do people have phones?"

"Anyone in particular?" Jace asked, one eyebrow raised higher than the other.

"Oh, you know. Family or uh..."

Jace started patting himself. "I believe I have Karen's number here somewhere."

"She's still alive," Ben said, before adding with disdain, "Thankfully."

"Your parents then," Jace said, the corner of his mouth twitching. "Who else could you mean?"

Ben's shoulders slumped. "I don't want to hurt your feelings. I know it's been a really long time since we've seen each other, and if anything, I only love you more since then, but—"

"Tim," Jace said with an easy smile. "There's no shame in wanting to see your husband."

"I'm married to you too," Ben insisted.

"Damn right you are," Jace said, "and I don't want that to ever change. But I also have respect for the man who made your life happy during all the decades we were apart. The same one who allowed me to pick you up, have you all to myself, and who very kindly let me continue to hog you at the welcoming party last night."

That's how Ben remembered it too. He had been emotional when seeing Tim again, but they hadn't been alone. Everyone else had appeared soon after, like the best surprise party imaginable, Ben whisked from one hug to the next in a glorious string of reunions. There hadn't been much opportunity to speak alone with Tim to see how he was adjusting to this new life. Or state of existence, he supposed.

"That's what I'll teach you today then," Jace said. "How to find other people when you need them. Would you mind if we finish breakfast first? I promise we have all the time in the world."

Gosh that sounded nice. Ben agreed, able to enjoy the meal more with this worry off his mind, although he still had plenty of questions. "Are you really okay with him now?" he asked toward the end of the meal. "I know you and Tim managed a sort of truce toward the end, but I wasn't married to him then. I was only with you."

"It'll take some getting used to, but I'll try my best." Jace tried to hide an anxious expression behind his napkin while wiping his mouth. "You remember Victor of course."

Ben snickered. "That's right! You and him are... Wow, that's weird. I'm not the only one who's two-timing."

"I wouldn't call it that," Jace said, "mostly because we're both guilty of it, but yes. Victor and I have a relationship. Of sorts. As much as he'll allow anyway. My opinion on the subject has evolved more than his has. Er..."

"I'm loving this," Ben said. He tried to imagine how any of it would work and failed. "As long as we're both happy..."

"That's all I've ever wanted," Jace said. "I just wasn't ready to share you while we were still alive, especially since everything was so limited back then. There were only so many days and hours when we still had to worry about work and everything else it took to get by. Now there truly are no limits." For whatever reason, this made him blush. He shook his head while fighting down a smile, resembling someone enthralled by a new crush.

"Okay, this is going to be an adjustment for me as well," Ben admitted. "You really love him."

"Of course!" Jace said. "But that doesn't change—"

"I know. Believe me, I get it. I've been in love with two men for my entire life. Wait, should I make that past tense?"

"Most of us don't bother," Jace said as he stood. "It feels like our lives have continued here, even if we aren't technically living. Speaking of which, I'll let you get on with yours."

"Should I clear the table?" Ben asked as his chair skidded backward. Except when he looked down, the plates and cutlery were already gone without a crumb remaining. "Wow, this *is* Heaven!"

Jace smiled before changing the subject. "You'll like this too, since it's nice and easy. Especially if you have a strong emotional connection to the person you want to see. Come closer to me."

Ben walked over and stood in front of him, kissing his nose each time that Jace started to speak until he retaliated by planting a big kiss on Ben's lips, followed by an all-too-familiar expression that said it was time to get serious.

"I'm ready now," Ben said. "Really."

"Not that I truly minded those kisses," Jace replied. "Anyway, as I was saying, the stronger the emotional bond, the easier it will be for you to find them. Closing your eyes can help."

Ben did so.

"I want you to concentrate on the center of your being. Think of it as your heart. Not the blood-pumping kind, but the emotional one. Start by thinking about that person—"

"I feel something already," Ben said.

"Oh. Good! So you already feel your love for him—"

"Not him," Ben said, shaking his head. "It's Jason. But he's not here yet. Is he? He can't be!"

"He's still alive," Jace said. "I'm sure of it. This is how I would look in on you though. It's a similar principle."

"He needs me," Ben said. "That's what I'm getting. I think... I think he's in trouble!"

"Stay calm."

Ben was shaking his head. "It's bad. He's really upset!"

"I don't think you're ready to—"

"I need to go to him," Ben said, his panic skyrocketing. "I want to see my son!"

He opened his eyes to plead with Jace just as he felt his entire body lurch. Ben was falling. Or floating. No, he was *moving*. That's what it was. Motion without direction, which was impossible, or should be. The world became a blur before it stabilized again. And he was home. This one fresher in his memory because he had left it only recently. Ben was in the kitchen of the house where he'd spent most of his life, and he wasn't alone. Jason stood not far away, his head bowed, the arms across his chest so tight that he was nearly hugging himself. Ben had no idea how he'd managed it, but somehow he had returned to the land of the living!

"I wish you were here," Jason said to himself with a heavy sigh. "Both of you."

"I'm right here," Ben said, rushing over to him. He tried to place a hand on his son's shoulder, but it went right through. "Great. I'm a freaking ghost. But not the kind you can hear, I'm guessing."

He searched Jason's face for a reaction and noticed how tired he appeared. Were the bags under his eyes more pronounced than usual? Although for a man of seventy-six, he looked fantastic— somewhere in his fifties at most, thanks to advances in medical science that slowed aging to a crawl. Externally anyway, and only for fully matured adults. Lifespans were a bit longer too, but not abnormally so. Thank goodness for that. Ben wanted to be reunited with his son eventually. He would prefer immediately, if that didn't involve death, because he was extremely worried.

"I haven't seen you this upset in ages," Ben told him. "Not since William had his heart surgery."

That medical necessity had gone so well that it was as if it had never happened. No debilitating conditions afterwards, or ongoing treatment past the recovery period. There had been little risk of dying during the procedure, but Ben knew firsthand how even the smallest chance of losing a loved one could result in sleepless nights. "So what's been keeping you up this time?"

"Benjamin!"

He spun around, heart in his throat, because that was a voice he knew better than any other. He felt even more overwhelmed when Tim entered the kitchen, looking absolutely stunning in his forties. That had been the beginning of such a great period for him. He had fully embraced his art, made peace with his family, beat cancer, and tackled the last of his insecurities. Tim had finally unleashed his full potential, and Ben had fallen in love with him more than ever, even though he would have thought it impossible.

They both stared at each other without moving, the same awed expression on their faces. Tim was the first to recover, putting on bedroom eyes and sauntering toward him. "Thirties, huh?"

"Nothing fancy," Ben said demurely. "And look at you! Your hair is still black! Although you know how much I love my white tiger."

Tim growled like he always did once Ben had started calling him that. This never failed to make him laugh, even now.

"I'm so glad you finally woke up!" Tim said, taking Ben's hand and pressing it to his lips.

"Finally?"

"It's been like…" Tim squinted. "A couple weeks?"

"WHAT?"

"In the mortal world, I mean," Tim said. "Don't ask me how

time works in the afterlife. I still don't get it. Anyway, the sleep thing is normal. Most people crash after they get here. Or there. Just be glad you missed the funeral. I was bummed I missed my own, but when I saw yours... They're so depressing." His silver eyes widened and moved to Jason. "Speaking of which, our son needs us."

"That's why I'm here," Ben said, turning around to consider him. "What's going on?"

"I don't know," Tim said, "but someone torched my studio."

"What? They burned it down?"

Tim nodded and gestured for Ben to follow. Together they went to the front door to look out the windows, and sure enough, the converted shed was a smoldering wreck.

"Was it an accident?" Ben asked. "Or an arsonist?"

"I don't think we can blame Daniel Wigmore for this one," Tim said, nudging him. "That's one hell of a callback. Remember him?"

Ben didn't answer. A bicycle had pulled up, stopping next to the wrecked structure. William hopped off the saddle and placed his hands on hair that was darker than it had once been, but he too had staved off the ravages of time. And kept himself in shape. He sprinted to the house and nearly knocked the door off the hinges to get inside.

"Jason!" he shouted.

Ben and Tim scurried backward to make room for him. Out of habit, mostly. Part of the door passed through them anyway, a timely reminder that they needn't worry about being in the way. They followed William as he rushed toward the sound of Jason's voice, meeting him in the kitchen. William grabbed his husband by the shoulders and held him at arm's length to look him over.

"I'm fine," Jason said, managing a weary smile. "So is she."

"What happened?" William asked, voice still laced with concern.

Jason gently freed himself, took William's hand, and led him toward the table where he sat. William did not.

"Morgan got a little upset," Jason explained.

"A *little*," William said in disbelief. He looked toward the front of the house. "Are you sure the fire is out? Should I—"

"The brigade drones were already here," Jason assured him. "Please sit down."

William did so grudgingly. "Where is she now?"

"Lying down in my old room."

William appeared even more panicked. "And what if she decides to set the house on fire? Why would she do this to us? We've been nothing but kind to her!"

"Because she's in pain," Jason said. "She's not the first damaged kid we've taken in."

"No, but this is a much bigger deal than using the refrigerator as a urinal."

Jason covered his mouth to stifle laughter. "I still can't believe Christian did that."

"I'm serious," William said. He glanced behind him and continued in a whisper. "This is dangerous. *Very* dangerous."

Jason exhaled, the sound haggard. "I know."

William reached across the table to take his hand. "So what do we do?"

Jason was quiet. Then he shook his head. "I'm not sure."

"This is hard for me to say," William began, "but maybe we're too old to foster anyone. The other kids have all grown up and moved out. We were just getting used to being on our own again."

"So were Ben and Tim," Jason said pointedly. "They still took me in."

"Yes, but you never tried to burn the place down."

Tim cleared his throat. "He *did* trash my Bentley though."

"He only dented it," Ben said, rolling his eyes. "That car never suited you anyway."

"What are you suggesting?" Jason asked. "That we send her back?"

William pressed his lips together. He clenched his jaw, huffed through his nostrils, and seemed truly conflicted. His answer wasn't direct, but it was clear. "How will I sleep at night or ever leave the house again when I have to worry about losing you in a fire?"

Jason pulled his hand away. Then he stood. "You've rescued enough people in your lifetime. Leave this one to me."

"What are you doing?" William asked, rising to follow him.

"Telling her what will happen if this keeps up." Then he yelled at the top of his lungs. "Morgan!"

"You could have sent her a direct message," William said, still wincing.

"I never did," Ben commented, "and neither did my momma."

"I'm a traditional kind of guy," Jason replied.

Footsteps tromped down the steps to the living room. The teenage girl who appeared had ginger cornrows and creamy mocha skin. Her eyes were red and wet from crying. Ben doubted she was old enough to drive, her boney body a collection of gangly limbs.

"That's an age I never want to be again," Tim commented.

"Same here," Ben said. "I remember Jason talking about her before I died, after they went to meet her."

"What happened to her parents?" Tim asked.

"One of those horrible back-alley splice jobs. Her parents are endorphin junkies." Genetically altered so that their bodies felt a constant high. The side effects could be brutal, and often resulted in a vegetative state. A universal cure hadn't been found yet. Much of it depended on just how botched the initial procedure had been.

"That's rough," Tim said, attention still on Jason.

Their son didn't seem angry. Nor was he very happy. He simply asked Morgan to step outside with him, William following. As a group, they walked past the pool to what was left of the studio. About a third of it remained.

Jason stood there, his gaze moving over the damage, while next to him Morgan squirmed. She couldn't see William, who stood a few paces behind her. That was probably for the best, considering that he looked like he was on the verge of a nervous breakdown.

"You want to go home," Jason said, stating it as a fact.

The hope on Morgan's face was transparent. "Yes," she squeaked.

Jason nodded. "I can't decide which of us had it worse. I was seven when they took me away from my mom. I used to wish it had happened when I was older so I could have gotten to know her better and have made more memories. But I've been thinking lately how it must be for you. From what I understand, everything was good until you were twelve. I know the years that followed weren't as nice, but you still had twice as many years with your family as I did mine. That must make it harder to adjust, and considering how much I struggled with that—" He shook his head. "I don't totally get what you're going through, but I do have a better idea than most people."

He looked over at Morgan, perhaps noticing the way she trembled. And he waited, but she didn't have anything to say in response.

"That's all ancient history to me now," Jason continued, "but you know what's not? I lost my adoptive parents recently. Both of them. And that's been really freaking hard, because I miss them, and as much I still wish I had known my mother better, Ben and Tim were my real family. That's how I came to think of them, and I hate that they're gone. They were old. It was their time. All of that makes sense to me, but you know what? I don't care. Logic can go fuck itself. I miss them so bad that I've also felt like burning something down. So why the hell not?"

Jason walked forward, grabbed a gas can that had been discarded on the lawn, and started sloshing fuel on what remained of the studio.

"Jason," William said, stepping forward.

His husband shot him a look so fierce that William raised his hands in surrender and held his tongue.

Jason turned to Morgan. "Do you have a lighter on you?"

She nodded, pulled it out of a pocket, and handed it to him, her face a mask of disbelief as Jason squatted and set the shed ablaze again.

"There," Jason said, turning his back to it and addressing Morgan. "Now at least we can say we've collaborated on a project. That counts as bonding, right?"

Morgan covered her mouth and laughed madly, her eyes like saucers.

"I'm not your father," Jason said. "Neither one of us is trying to replace your parents, because we can't. Hell, I'm old enough to be your grandfather! But all I want to be is your friend. And that—" He pointed to the house, "is your home, and if you burn it down, guess what?"

"I don't have one anymore," Morgan whispered.

"Wrong. You'll still have a home. It's with us. We would have to find somewhere else to live, preferably with a built-in sprinkler system, but you would still be with us. We aren't going to abandon you. Even if you don't like us, you've gotta admit that we're not so bad. At least I get where you're coming from, and we've been willing to give you your space. With mixed results." He nodded toward the burning shed. "All we want is to take care of you while getting to know each other better along the way. That's not such a raw deal. If your parents ever pull through, I bet they'll be relieved to learn that their daughter is with people who genuinely care about her. They would want you to be happy until then. That might be impossible now, but it won't always be. Trust me."

Morgan broke down in tears, and when Jason wrapped an arm around her, she clung to him. They heard sirens in the distance shortly after, Jason gently leading her toward the house.

"Did I ever tell you about the peanut butter incident?" he asked her as they went. "Foster home number four. They had this ugly tan carpet in the living room, and I wanted to get myself kicked out, so I took a brand-new family-size jar of peanut butter and spread it over the entire carpet, from wall to wall. When my new parents got home from their night out, they were too tipsy to notice and walked right in... and kept on going, leaving peanut butter footprints everywhere."

They heard Morgan laugh as the duo reentered the house. William was busy hiding the gas can and making sure the fire didn't spread, but once the fire brigade drones arrived on the scene and began their work, he did look toward the house with some relief.

"I guess he didn't need us after all," Ben said.

"Yeah," Tim said, beaming proudly. "What a great kid we raised!"

Ben nodded. "And what a great parent he's become. You realize that we might have a fifth grandchild soon. If she sticks around."

"How could she not?" Tim said, draping an arm across his shoulders. "Our house is full of good vibes. She'll come around."

"You're not upset about your studio?"

"Nah. They moved most of my paintings out so it could become her bedroom. And really, it's just stuff, you know?"

"Try telling him that."

They both looked at William, who was sobbing while the drones put out the last of the fire. This time there was nothing left to salvage.

"Maybe he was the one who needed us," Tim joked,

but neither of them laughed, since a weeping William was a heartbreaking sight indeed.

Their son-in-law tried to pull it together when Jason came back outside, quickly wiping away his tears.

"Is she okay?" William asked.

"Yup," Jason said, standing next to him. "She wanted a bubble bath. Water instead of fire… that's progress, right?"

William managed a smile. "Thank you. For knowing what to do."

"I was improvising," Jason admitted. He tore his eyes away from the scene to look at his husband. "Are you okay?"

William nodded glumly. "I was just thinking how I helped Tim build that shed. That's when I really got to know him for the first time. We made other memories there too and—" His voice cracked.

"I know," Jason said, chin trembling. "I didn't want to show her how upset I am, but it feels like we lost another piece of them."

They both started crying, which had Ben on the verge of joining them.

"There has to be something we can do," he said, gesturing at them. "Are we completely useless now?"

"There's so much I haven't figured out yet," Tim said helplessly. "I don't really know."

Jace would. He had already promised to teach Ben all sorts of things, but asking for his help now didn't feel right. He wasn't Jason's father. How would it feel if Tim had to step aside so that Jace could fix what he couldn't? Ben wouldn't do that to him. He needed to find another way.

"What would we have done if we were still alive?" he asked.

Tim shook his head. "I dunno. Group hug?"

"Good idea." Ben grabbed his hand.

Jason and William were holding each other, so Ben brought Tim over to join them. They couldn't touch the two younger men, but they did their best to wrap their arms around them anyway, the space between their elongated hug filled with their two sons. They didn't need to discuss what they did next. Ben thought about how much he loved them both. He could tell from Tim's expression that he was in the same state of mind. More than that! He could *feel* the emotion pouring from Tim, mixing with his own emotions and creating a great big swirl of love. The sobbing subsided as Jason and William grew calmer.

"They're still with us," Jason said, "and always will be. No matter what happens to this house."

"You're right," William said. "I love them both so much. Nothing can change that. I know, because it's the same way I feel about you."

"I love you too," Jason said. "Now let's get inside. I need a nap."

"And I need to file a report with the Emergency Response Service before the fire marshal comes out here to investigate. Can you imagine the legal backlash if they conclude that it was arson?"

Jason took a step back and rolled his eyes. "That'll never happen. As soon as the marshal is out here, you'll start talking rescue stuff, and I'll probably have to set an extra place at the table for dinner."

"I wouldn't mind," William said, almost sounding hopeful.

"You're such a nerd. Come on. And hey, what if we built a pool house? With a guest apartment upstairs, now that my old room is being used again. We could hang a bunch of Tim's paintings in there as a tribute."

"I'd love that," William replied.

"And maybe put some of my books on the shelves too," Ben called after them. "What am I, minced meat?"

"I think they've got their priorities figured out," Tim teased. "Actually, you're gonna love what they did with your books. They've redecorated since we've been gone. Wanna check it out with me?"

Tim offered his arm. Ben accepted it, not hiding his joy at getting to return home again with the man he loved.

One of them anyway.

"What should we do now?"

Tim was standing with a hand on each hip and beaming at him while waiting for an answer. Ben felt like checking the clock, which was crazy, because normally when they were together, he never wanted it to end. He didn't now either, but he worried Jace might be pacing the floor and wondering where he had disappeared to. Ben wasn't sure how to send word to him. Phones didn't seem to exist here, which certainly made it feel more like Heaven, but there must be some equivalent. Considering who he intended to contact, asking his husband about it seemed inappropriate.

"I don't know," Ben admitted. They were standing outside their home. Jason and William's home, he mentally amended, since that's who owned it now. They had toured the house, marveled over the changes, and made sure the occupants were doing okay. Currently they were all inside and sharing a pizza. Morgan had become more animated and was talking to them. Ben had a feeling that everything was going to work out fine. With a day's work done, he had the urge to go home and relax, except they were already there.

"I've got it," Tim said, snapping his fingers. "Close your eyes."

Ben complied. When he was told to open them again, a car was parked in front of him, a dark-haired teenager leaning against it with a cocky smile.

"Too cute!" Ben enthused.

Tim made a face. "Cute?"

"Yes cute. You look like a baby to me."

Tim rolled his eyes and jerked his head behind him. "Recognize the car?"

Ben eyed it and took his best guess. "It's the one you always wanted?"

Tim shook his head in disbelief. "It's the 3000 GT my parents gave me. When we were teenagers?"

Ben laughed. "Oh, *that* one."

Tim narrowed his eyes in suspicion. "Are you messing with me?"

"Never!" For real. Ben had only registered that it had four wheels and was a black sports car.

"I spent so much time building it, just to surprise you." Tim turned around to rub a hand along the hood. "And because I missed it."

"Building it?" Ben asked. "From scratch?"

"Kind of. You have to pour a lot of emotional investment into whatever you're making while visualizing it and such. No assembly required. It's like painting, or in your case writing, except you don't have to rely on tools. If you can dream it, you can create it." He walked around to the passenger-side door. "Hop in. I'll take you for a spin."

His concerns about balancing two relationships momentarily forgotten, Ben slipped inside, flipping down the visor to check the mirror on the opposite side. He aged himself down to sixteen, just as he'd looked when first stalking—*meeting*—Tim. His husband noticed this when settling into the driver seat.

"You know what they call us?" he asked.

"Mirror gazers," Ben replied.

"Not us old folks. They call us mirror geezers, since we're the most obsessed with being able to look young again."

"Really?" Ben flipped the visor shut. "Jace left that part out."

"Ha! I don't blame the guy. It's not the most flattering thing to say to someone you haven't seen in decades."

Ben studied him. He didn't sound jealous or seem like he was putting on a brave front for his benefit.

Tim noticed him staring as he put the car in gear. "I told you when we were living how much I had come to appreciate Jace. That hasn't changed just because we're dead."

"Good," Ben said, not hiding his relief. Jace had also been positive about the situation. Tim was making the effort too. Did that mean there was hope for— "Hey, slow down!"

Tim had floored the gas pedal. They passed through William's abandoned bike as they tore down the lane, reminding him that, as ghosts, they couldn't crash into anything.

"It's okay," Tim assured him. "You're going to love this."

Ben still flinched when they reached the main road and passed through the middle of a pickup truck. Tim yanked on the wheel, making the car spin in a full circle until they were facing the direction they had come from.

"I'd tell you to buckle up," Tim said, "but I forgot to create seatbelts."

Ben didn't get any more warning than that. Tim hit the pedal again, and this time they accelerated at an insane rate. He leaned over and saw that the speedometer was maxed out. The world outside the car was a blur of color. Ben was on the verge of telling Tim to slow down again when he hit the brakes. They both remained in their seats, even though Ben expected to be thrown through the windshield.

"And we're here!" Tim declared.

Ben looked around. They were in front of their old house. What had been the point of that? Except when he climbed out of the car, he noticed the shed hadn't been burned down. Everything was just as they'd left it. The sun was still shining too, the light purer somehow.

"Back in the afterlife?" Ben asked.

"Yup." Tim nodded at the house. "I've been working on this the whole time I've been here. It's not completely done yet, so don't go upstairs. Come on. You're going to love this."

They had just left the physical version of this house. What was the point in visiting a copy so soon?

"Trust me," Tim said, picking up on his doubt. "Hey, want me to carry you over the threshold?"

"Once was enough," Ben said while dodging an attempt to grab him. "Maybe I should carry you instead."

"I'd be up for that. Piggyback ride? It's not like I can crush you to death."

"No way!" Ben said, running for the front door.

Tim chased him all the way into the house, which was exactly as he promised. Reassuringly familiar. Tim took his hand, guiding him through the interior to the glass door leading out to the backyard. "They're all here," he said.

He didn't need to explain. The yard was filled with half a dozen dogs, all of them making Ben's heart swell with affection.

"And guess who the pack leader is?" Tim said as he opened the door.

"Chinchilla!" Ben cried. Literally.

She was all too happy to lick the tears from his face before he was knocked over by Pierre and buried beneath a pile of dog love. They spent ages outside, getting reacquainted with the dogs and each other, Tim showing off by changing the weather and the time of day to amuse him. Ben noticed that their appearances had settled somewhere in their middle age, probably because that's what felt natural for this environment. They had never been teenagers here, the memories they'd made even better than being young. Ben wanted to see the house after all, and on their way in, noticed with concern that the side gate was open.

"They like to wander," Tim explained. "Dogs have their own version of Heaven. It's mostly stuff to pee on or chase, but they always find their way back here again."

One less thing to worry about. Ben was really coming to appreciate the afterlife. "You did a great job," he said when slowly turning in the middle of the living room. "Although I wouldn't have chosen that couch. I know we had it the longest, but I liked the newest one better."

"That's an easy fix. Maybe later though. So uh… What should we do now?"

Ben looked at him and instantly recognized the expression. He had seen it countless times before. "Is that possible here? Does everything work the same?"

Tim grinned. "Want me to show you?"

"Sure!"

Ben watched as Tim undid his pants and pulled down his underwear. Then he stared. And began laughing. "You always impressed me in that department," Ben said, "but it definitely wasn't *that* big. Thank god."

"Can't blame a guy for taking a few liberties," Tim said, flexing and making it bounce. "So should we?"

"Yes, but hold on a second. Can we look like anything we want?"

Tim pulled up his underwear before answering. "Not really. It takes a lot of concentration for the big stuff. No pun intended. Altering your hair and clothes is easy because that's what we did while alive. We're used to it. Everything else needs conscious effort to maintain and doesn't last long. Although some people arrive here looking how they always envisioned. I've met some really happy trans people, for instance. I guess it's all about the mental image we had of ourselves. Most people are boring like us and stick with the default. More or less."

"Uh-huh," Ben said. "And how much concentrating did you do to learn that little trick?"

"There's nothing little about it," Tim said, the bedroom eyes returning. "And to answer your question, I didn't have anyone to hook up with until you got here. So it was more like solitary meditation, if you catch my drift. I'm really curious to find out what sex with another person is like here."

"Then let's see how it goes, although your usual size is fine with me."

"You sure?"

"Well…"

As it turned out, they had endless opportunity to explore the issue, the rest of eternity forgotten as they rediscovered one of their favorite expressions of love.

A black sports car pulled up to the small house Ben and Jace shared, the brakes screeching as the vehicle came to a stop. Ben looked out the passenger-side window at his home. Then he turned toward the driver to express his opinion of the situation. "This is ridiculous."

"This is awesome," Tim countered. "I feel like I'm dropping you off at your parents' house after one of our secret dates. Want me to walk you to the door?"

"No!" Ben said instantly. "Better not."

"In that case," Tim said with a shit-eating grin, "tell your old man I said hello."

"Would you stop?" Ben said, fighting down a smile. He did find it hot, just a little, when Tim was bad.

"Seriously though," his husband said, dropping the act. "Tell him I said hey. And that we should grab another drink sometime."

Ben stared. "You went out drinking together?"

"Yeah. Mostly to talk about the guy we both love. I was feeling kinda down. Without you, it was Heaven in name only, you know? Jace gave me a great pep talk about how it would be the last time we'd be apart. He also encouraged me to start working on the house so I'd have something to show you."

"So the incredible time we just had—"

"Was his idea."

Ben felt emotion rising. He looked out the window again at the house, the urge to rush inside to see Jace almost unbearable.

"Go on then," Tim said. "We'll see each other again. You know where to find me."

Ben only lingered to give him a kiss. Then he was out the door and rushed toward another. He paused when reaching it, watching Tim's car tear around the corner and disappear. Once it had, Ben turned the knob and pushed, praying that someone was home.

"Ben! Hey!"

There he was, Jace himself, rising from the couch. That still felt like such a miracle. Ben didn't let him finish standing. He ran to Jace and pushed him back down, placing a knee on the cushion to either side of his lap. Then he took Jace's head in his hands and kissed him. Repeatedly.

"Okay, okay," Jace said while laughing. "I'm happy to see you too, but I'm also dying to know what the emergency was. It took every ounce of my willpower not to interfere."

"Oh that." Ben flopped over on the couch. He put a pillow behind his head and draped his legs over Jace's lap. "Jason was having a rough time with this new girl they've taken in." He continued his story and didn't stop until he reached the part where he and Tim had gone back inside after playing with the dogs. "And then we uh, had a nice time catching up with each other."

"I bet you did," Jace said with a knowing expression. "What did you think? It's so intense here. The sexual pleasure melds perfectly with the emotion you feel. They're almost indistinguishable."

Ben realized his jaw was hanging open and snapped it shut. "You're not the same man I once knew."

"I am," Jace said with an easy smile, "but I didn't stop growing as a person when I came here. Neither will you. Anyway, I blame Victor. Not simply because we're able to be together again. I'm not saying it's suddenly okay that we each have someone else, now that I've got another option too. As much as I hate to admit it, I think he was right about a few things. Or maybe all his damn lectures have finally worn me down over the years. Either way, I'm not as jealous as I once was."

"I never would have described you that way," Ben said. "Committed, yes. Jealous, no. And considering what I put you through..."

"Ancient history," Jace said dismissively.

Ben reappraised him, excited that there were new sides of Jace to discover. He had spent a lifetime with the same photos and trinkets, which couldn't evolve and change on their own. They had new territory to explore, not just everything that surrounded them, but who they were as people. Ben had certainly changed since they had parted ways. It made sense that Jace had too. "Sounds like we also have some catching up to do."

"Most definitely," Jace said while massaging his feet.

Ben didn't remember taking off his shoes, another example of how subconscious desires seemed to manifest here. "If I'd known you were so chill about everything," he said, testing the waters, "I would have invited Tim inside."

Jace's hands froze. "I'm not a saint. I still want time alone with you, and I don't plan on sharing *everything* we do with him."

"Of course not," Ben said hurriedly. That still left him wondering how he was going to juggle two separate lives, but he would worry about that later. "What are we going to do today?" The thought alone made him smile. How often had he wished for one more day together, or even just an hour?

Jace resumed the foot massage. "I figured we could tackle whatever is on your list first, and if we get through that, I have plenty that I'd like to show you."

"There's still so much I'd like to learn," Ben said, "like how I can get around on my own. I'm still not entirely clear on how to contact people. And I'd like to see my parents again."

"We can have lunch with them. I'll invite mine to join us."

"Yes! That sounds great. Hey, is there any way of telling how much longer it'll be before Allison gets here? Because I already feel like I need her."

"Everything okay?" Jace asked.

"Yeah. You know how we are. Attached at the hip. It feels weird not being able to call her or whatever." He could certainly use some of her advice, but mostly he just wanted to see his best friend.

"There's no way of knowing when she'll get here," Jace said. "Not until that's much closer to happening. But we could still check on her."

"Like I did Jason? That would be awesome!"

Jace's hands had moved to Ben's legs and were slowly working their way upward. "Sounds like we have a full day ahead of us. What should we start with?"

Ben wanted that too, but having sex with Jace right after the marathon he'd run with Tim seemed disrespectful. "Is there such thing as a shower here?"

"Of course, but you can also think yourself clean. It's that easy."

That didn't sound sufficient. Maybe he was still clinging to mortal rituals, but Ben wanted something more involved than that.

Jace read his features and gently lifted Ben's legs to slip out from beneath them. "I know exactly where we'll go. But first, I'll tell you the basics of getting around here."

As it turned out, the process was similar to the leap he'd made to reach Jason. Most of it had to do with connections to places and the ability to visualize them fully. Getting home would be easy since he was intimately familiar with the details and possessed the right kind of emotional investment. Other places he would have to travel to the old-fashioned way until he established a connection. That sounded ideal. As much as he loved the house he'd shared with Tim, after so many decades of living there, Ben became bored with the drive into Austin and back. Always the same roads and the same scenery. That would never be an issue here. He could still explore and discover new locations too.

"You need to be mindful of the realm," Jace said. "Some have different rules. And some have none at all, like in the Astral Wilds, where Victor lives."

Ben shook his head, feeling overwhelmed. "Before we talk about any of that, let me figure out how things work here."

"Good call," Jace said. "Should we head out?"

"Where to?"

"For that shower you wanted. I know just the place."

Ben stood, excited to see what he meant. It could literally be anything. A Japanese bath house, a Turkish steam room, or a natural hot spring tucked away in a valley somewhere. "Show me what you've got!"

"That's the idea," Jace said wryly. "Do you want the scenic route, or the quick way?"

"Quick," Ben said, because he already felt like he could go another round.

"Then you better stay close to me," Jace said, wrapping arms around him.

Ben settled into that hug, nestling his cheek against Jace's chest. His eyes were closed when he felt a lurch, the sound of roaring waters making them open again. What he saw left him speechless. They were standing on a stone disc ten feet in diameter. That was the only ground beneath their feet or anywhere within sight. All around them were roaring waters, rivers of varying hues spilling into a circular hole that plummeted farther than the eye could see. The place they stood was floating above the center of this abyss, the rising mists every color of the rainbow and some he had never seen nor imagined. Above them, in a perfectly clear sky, were six golden suns.

"Beautiful," Ben managed at last, embarrassed by how inadequate the word was. "Did you make this?"

"No," Jace said. "This is the work of an artist. You'll be amazed at what people have created here. I was so overtaken the first time I saw it that I nearly wept."

"I'm out of tears at the moment," Ben joked, even though a few were already rising. "Look at us! We're travelling again. You're showing me the world, just like you used to."

Jace smiled. "It's nice to know that not everything has changed. Ready for that bath?"

"You mean down *there*?" Ben crept to the edge of the platform to peer over the edge. "How far down is it?"

"About twenty miles. That's nearly a ten-minute freefall, since the rules here use Earth gravity, although I have a way of making it last longer. But first..."

Jace moved close to him, pulling up on the hem of Ben's T-shirt, their lips meeting as soon as it was over his head. Ben began undressing him too, and by the time he was finished, they could have been standing in a broom closet for all he cared, because he only had eyes for Jace. As they kissed, Jace slowly walked forward until Ben felt the heel of his foot reach the edge of the platform.

"Do you still trust me?" Jace asked when he saw Ben's panicked expression.

"Yes," he answered, his features relaxing.

"Good." Wings unfurled from Jace's back, gigantic enough to cast a shadow over them both. The feathers were purest white, and as they wrapped around Ben, they felt just like one of Jace's amazing hugs.

"You're an angel now?" Ben asked.

Jace shook his head, eyes seductive. "You won't call me that by the time we reach the bottom."

He took another step forward, Ben clinging to him as he fell in love all over again.

Busy. That summed up Ben's week. He was barely finished with one husband before the other came around. Any downtime that remained was filled with family. Friends too. He had lunch with Marcello, who was currently dating Oscar Wilde, and even though Ben was thrilled to meet someone so famous and laughed himself silly during the meal, he barely got a word in edgewise.

Occasionally he managed to sneak away to check on Allison. She was doing well, although he wished she could see him so he could flaunt his newfound youth. They were going to have so much fun together when she got here. For now, he was glad she was still on Earth. Allison was helping Morgan overcome her issues and connect with her new family. That was so like his best friend. Even when they were separated by death, Allison was still finding ways of helping him.

"It's good you're keeping those counselling skills sharp while I'm gone," he told her during his most recent visit, even though she couldn't hear him. "I need you now more than ever."

He wasn't struggling through hard times. The opposite in fact. Everything was so great that he could barely find time to breathe. That was optional now, so no big deal, but he still needed to process it all. Ben had decided to take a day off for himself so he could. When leaving the house, he had to turn around to remind himself which one it was, because he honestly couldn't remember where he had been and who he had stayed with.

"Meditation," Jace had told him recently. "Or good old-fashioned sleep. You have to let yourself process what you've been experiencing."

Ben had spent enough time in bed recently, although not sleeping. He wanted a change of scenery. As he wandered through what others had created for themselves, or built as a community to share, he cleared his mind and dealt with each thought as it arrived. This helped put everything into perspective. Two happy husbands, two happy homes. What was the issue? He honestly wasn't sure.

Allison would've had it all ironed out by now. He wondered if he could do what Jace had and visit her in a dream. Then again, it would be lame to counter her emotional reaction to this with, "Yes, yes, nice to see you too. Now please fix everything for me." He worried briefly that her version of Heaven wouldn't include him at all until he remembered how much she enjoyed meddling in his life. Thank goodness. Until they could be together again, she deserved a break.

Ben found himself in a park, the trees making music each time wind shook their leaves. He leaned against one of the trunks, singing along with their song as he continued to search his soul. He concluded that the problem was a familiar one. He had a divided heart. Except that wasn't quite right anymore. He loved both men with the *entirety* of his heart... which was being pulled in separate directions. So far neither Jace nor Tim had reacted with jealousy or possessiveness, but they still inhabited two very separate worlds, and Ben was exhausted from leaping back and forth between them.

If only he could combine both relationships into one life. He had fantasized about such things in his youth but didn't have any practical experience. He considered asking Marcello, who most certainly did, but the man was preoccupied at the moment. Eric had seemed both sweet and wise when Tim had introduced them, although Ben got the impression that he was more traditional in his views on love. There had to be someone else he could turn to, but nobody on his mental list of contacts had the right experience or availability. Ben felt discouraged. Enough that he dramatically entertained the idea of giving it all up to live in this park as a hermit.

Victor! Not only did he have a unique perspective, but he had been instrumental in getting Jace to rethink his own views on love. He would be the ideal person to ask, under the circumstances. Ben just needed to figure out how to find him. There was no calling random people in the afterlife. You had to be familiar with them, and if you were, you could send a sort of mental nudge. If Tim wanted to see him now, for instance, Ben would experience a pang that carried the emotion with it, and he'd know who it originated from. Seeking people out through other means was possible too. That's what he would have to do.

Where to find him though? Ben didn't have much to go on. Victor lived out in the Astral Wilds, wherever that was. Ben approached some friendly souls to ask how to get there, and once they pointed him to the nearest border, he conjured up his old Rollerblades. A car was still too complicated for him to create. Tim was a natural at making things, probably because of his background in the visual arts. Ben was simply happy that he could go as fast as he wanted on his skates without having to worry about balance. He zipped through Heaven until he reached a meadow where the land gave way to clouds, and beyond them...

"Space," Ben said in a dramatic voice. "The final frontier."

Ahead of him was absolute darkness filled with stars, but there was so much more: incomprehensible swirls of color, sounds which triggered memories that weren't his own, vibrations that made him feel different flavors, and objects he couldn't seem to focus on. Little of it made sense, but there was something appealing about it too, in a primordial sort of way, like he was facing the raw soup that not only life, but all of existence had sprung from. How was he supposed to find Victor in that mess? And more pressingly, was he safe? Jace hadn't mentioned anything that he should be wary of. Nor had the people who had given him directions here. Ben couldn't die, but he could get lost. If so, he would send out nudges asking for help and hope for the best.

Now if only he had a spaceship, or one of those flying cars from *The Jetsons*. Ben felt he should take precautions, so after making sure no one was around to witness it, he managed with some effort to create a giant plastic hamster ball and climbed inside. Then he pushed against the rounded interior until the ball fell over the edge of Heaven. And floated. Good! That's what Ben had imagined would happen. Maybe that made the difference. He laughed at the silliness of the situation as he slowly rolled out into the void. Until he glanced back and saw that only darkness surrounded him. Heaven was nowhere to be found. Fighting off a jolt of fear, Ben tried sending a little "I love you" nudge to Tim, figuring he would be the least likely to worry and come chasing after him. A split second later, he felt the response.

Love! Now?

Later Ben sent back, along with the feeling of excited anticipation.

Assured that he wasn't cut off completely, Ben was braver in moving forward, and although this resulted in wondrous sights and memorable sensations, he didn't seem to be getting anywhere. Intent was key. That's what Jace had taught him. Ben needed to focus on finding Victor by using whatever connection they had. There wasn't much to go on. Ben had never met him, but they both knew Jace. As soon as he concentrated on that, the ball turned around and went in the opposite direction. Toward

Heaven? Probably because he was thinking of Jace, who he had a stronger connection to than most people. So that wouldn't work. He thought instead of Nathaniel, Victor's biological son, and the ball went in a different direction. That was hopeful, so Ben kept that train of thought going, remembering the trip they had taken to Warrensburg so that Nathaniel could visit the clearing where Victor's ashes had been scattered. It had been an equally emotional trip for him and—

The hamster ball hit something solid and stopped. A tree! Ben looked around and found himself in a forest. He couldn't be sure, but it did resemble the woods that began behind Jace's childhood home. Ben worried that he had accidentally returned to the mortal world, but when he made the hamster ball disappear, he saw that the stars were much too bright in the night sky for that to be true, the air free from the constant noise pollution of distant vehicles and airplanes. All he could hear was the crackling of a fire, which he followed to its source.

He recognized the clearing he entered, but never had he seen it when the lean-to was still standing. Or while a fire was blazing. Sitting in front of it, staring into the flames, was a young man no older than twenty. His hair was cropped short on the sides with a long strip down the middle. Ben knew this person from the photos Jace had left behind, and to his surprise, he was recognized as well.

"Ben!" Victor said, leaping to his feet. He rushed over to take his hand and pull him into a hug. Not a casual quick embrace and a pat on the back, but a serious squeeze that smooshed their bodies together. He still gripped one of Ben's shoulders when taking a step back. "It's good to finally meet you. I feel like we've known each other for ages, although that's bound to be one-sided. Sorry I wasn't at your welcoming party. I've never been one for big social affairs. Especially when it would have been impossible to have a satisfactory conversation with so many people competing for your attention. This is exactly what I was hoping for."

"Hi!" Ben managed. Then he laughed. "Jace warned me that you like to talk."

"I *love* it," Victor said, shooting him a wink. "Listening is even better. I'm just excited to finally get my time with you."

"Gosh," Ben said, "I feel like a celebrity."

"More like a legend. Jace never stopped talking about you."

"My goodness." Ben pantomimed like he was fanning himself. "I don't know if I can take this much adoration. That's what I came here to get away from, to be honest."

"Oh yeah?" Victor returned to the fire while gesturing for him to follow. "Tell me what's been going on. I'm dying to hear your impressions." He snorted. "Literally, considering what it took for us to finally meet."

"Totally worth it," Ben said, willing to flatter him back. "I often wondered what you would be like in person, because if there's anyone who's a legend…"

"Stop," Victor said, grinning at him. "I promised Jace I wouldn't fall in love with you, but you're not making it easy."

"Did he really say that?"

"Not exactly. That was mostly an attempt at charm. Although he did recently *inform* me that I was going to love you."

"We'll see about that," Ben said. "I'm afraid I came here for selfish reasons. I could use some advice."

"There's nothing selfish about wanting to better oneself. If you're successful, everyone around you will benefit. I can't promise you answers, but I do have plenty of opinions."

"Sounds good to me," Ben said as they settled down next to the fire.

He described what his new life had been like since arriving here, making sure to emphasize how happy and appreciative he was. He didn't want to come across as an entitled brat who was never satisfied. Too much of a good thing didn't describe it anyway. He simply wanted…

"—to share my life with both of them," Ben finished, "instead of them having to share me. If that makes any sense."

Victor smirked, but not at his expense. "Maybe I shouldn't have talked Jace out of his mega bed."

"His what?"

"That little house of yours that he recreated? The bed used to be extra wide, and at one point, it even had all of our names engraved in the headboard."

That seemed vaguely familiar, Ben wondering if he saw it during one of the dream visits, but he was more interested in chasing down the implications. "So at one time, Jace was planning on all of us being in one big relationship?"

"I wouldn't say that." Victor took a cigarette from behind his ear and leaned forward to light it off the campfire. Not a trick that would be recommended while living. Victor's hair didn't catch fire, but his eyes did dance with flames as he considered Ben. "Jace recognized that you and Tim would spend the rest of your lives together and knew he couldn't ask you to end that when coming here. So if anything, he was trying to make room for you both."

"That's sweet," Ben said, still not willing to abandon the idea, "but what if we went back to that concept? Except instead of living together—"

Victor held up a hand to stop him. "Not my style. I have no problem staying with Jace on occasion, but this is my home."

Ben made a face and glanced around. "Here?"

"This is where I felt the most at peace while living, so yes."

"It's a gorgeous forest," Ben said, "don't get me wrong, but aren't you lonely? Eternity is a very long time."

"It certainly is, and no, I don't get lonely. I'm not *always* here. I visit my mother sometimes, or my grandfather's tribe. I wasn't waiting here when you showed up either. I was out fishing with Bernie. We never catch anything. We just go for the view and to shoot the shit. I only came back here because I felt someone approaching." Victor paused to take a drag. "I also like to visit libraries. You should check out the Mouseion at Alexandria. The famous library still exists here. If I'm lucky with my timing, I get to meet some of the great thinkers of the world while there and learn from them. That's why I've chosen this age. I'd rather look like a grizzled old fox, but I haven't earned that yet. So I make myself appear young, like someone who hasn't completed their studies, out of deference to them. And yeah, when I've stuffed my head with more knowledge and experience than I can take, I come back here to digest it all in perfect solitude. With the occasional welcome guest to break up the monotony." He flicked away his cigarette, the butt transforming into sparks that floated harmlessly into the air. "Anyway, whatever your heart's desire, the options here are limitless."

"What about the desires of others?" Ben asked.

"Meaning?"

"I can't help thinking that if Jace got to know Tim and fell in love with him…"

Victor's chuckle was good-natured. "Things aren't *that* different here. Hearts remain just as obstinate in this world as in the previous."

"Sure, but you've already changed the way Jace loves. He said as much himself."

Victor shook his head. "He did all the work himself. I only talked him through it. Jace *wanted* to find a solution. He worried about how the dynamic would work between you three. So you aren't alone there."

"Can't you talk him through this too?"

"I wouldn't want that kind of power, and thankfully, it's unobtainable."

Ben's shoulders slumped. "So it's impossible."

"Not necessarily. There's no reason Jace and Tim couldn't fall in love. They already have something in common. You're very important to them both."

That was flattering, but more importantly, gave him renewed hope. "If they both love me, then they'll probably love each other. If given the chance."

"Could be. Then again, you can love someone without liking their friends. That's a common story."

True. Ben felt he had good reason to be optimistic anyway. He thought back to a time, after Tim had broken up with Ryan, that all three of them had become friends of a sort. Tim was no longer attempting to steal him away, and Jace had trusted Ben not to make the same mistake. He loved those memories. They would have Tim over to watch a movie or be invited to his house for dinner. Everything had almost been perfect, until the attraction Ben and Tim felt for each other became unbearable. They had called it off for the sake of his relationship with Jace. That was no longer an issue. Not only could they all be together, but they could all be *together*.

"If you really want to pursue this," Victor said while studying him, "then you should stop keeping them separate so much. Give them the opportunity to explore if they have that kind of potential."

Ben nodded slowly. "Yeah... That could work. Hey, you're good at this! Ever thought of pursuing a career as a counselor? Because if so, you should stick with me. I'm personally responsible for training one of the most successful counselors in

Austin. She gained endless practical experience from being my best friend, and I never charged her a thing."

"A tempting offer," Victor said with a smile, "but I'm happier playing therapist to myself. Although if you ever want to stop by, you're more than welcome. I won't keep you any longer. I can tell you want to get started."

"Jace always said you had a gift for reading people." Ben remained where he was. "You aren't wrong, but I've waited a long time for this, and I have so much I want to know about you."

They huddled next to the fire and spoke with each other until daybreak, sharing stories about their lives and asking questions to deepen their understanding of each other. When it was time to say goodbye, Ben initiated the hug and felt strangely emotional when leaving. Partially because he knew that Nathaniel wouldn't be disappointed when finally getting to meet his father, but also because he was glad that Jace had chosen someone so thoughtful and kind to fall in love with.

"When you mentioned that we were going on a double date," Tim said while standing in front of the bathroom mirror, "I thought Jace would be bringing Victor along."

"Nope!" Ben said cheerfully. "Just the three of us. Fun, huh?"

"Sure," Tim said without actually sounding certain. "Do I still get to drive?"

"I don't think he'll mind. Is that the appearance you're sticking with?"

Tim consulted the mirror again. He was in his mid-twenties, although dressed more nicely than he would have been back then. Currently he wore a black button-up shirt and dark-gray slacks. "I figured it would set Jace at ease if I was the age when he knew me best. You don't like it?"

"I love it! You're always handsome, but do you feel like trying something new with your hair?"

"Yeah, okay. What did you have in mind?"

"Keep the sides short," Ben suggested, "but do a sort of mohawk in the middle."

Tim laughed as if liking the idea. His hair shifted, becoming a row of gelled spikes down the middle. "Nice! I look like a total badass!" His eyes moved to consider the reflection of Ben's uncertain expression. "You're not feeling it?"

"It's good, but maybe without the styling product. And make the actual mohawk longer. Yeah, like that, but now let it fall over to one side naturally. Perfect!"

"Uh… Okay. I guess I could try this."

"Cool," Ben said. "One more thing. You're both so tall. My neck is going to hurt from staring up at you both all night. Would you mind being a little shorter?"

"I never knew that bugged you," Tim said.

"It doesn't. Usually. I never thought about it much, because it wasn't optional. Now that it is…"

Tim shrugged. "Have it your way." He slowly scaled himself down until he was Ben's height and frowned. "This feels wrong."

"Are you sure? Because now that we're the same height, kissing will be even easier."

They were both eager to test this theory, and when they pulled away, Tim was smiling. Until he looked in the mirror again. "Sorry, Benjamin, but this hairstyle is too weird for me."

The gelled and spiked mohawk returned. Probably for the best. The other version was too on the nose. And if he was honest, he preferred Tim's personal style. Ben was only trying to stack the odds in his favor. Jace seemed to have a thing for shorter guys, and with their similar skin tones and hair colors, he thought he could make Tim resemble Victor a little. He knew there was more to attraction than physical appearance, but that was the soil where love most often took root.

Ben decided not to worry much about his own appearance. After a cursory glance in the mirror—he was wearing a burgundy long-sleeved shirt made of a netted material that showed plenty of skin and skin-tight slacks the color of dark chocolate—he rushed them out of the house, excited to get started. When they arrived at his other home, Jace met them at the door. His blond hair had undergone a change too, wavy and styled to one side. That's how Ryan had worn it, if Ben remembered correctly.

"Are you feeling all right, Tim?" he asked. "You look a little… little."

"Says the guy who's wearing pink lipstick," Tim replied, crossing his arms over his chest.

"It's lip gloss actually," Jace shot back, raising a shirt sleeve to his mouth, "and I'm not crazy about it either."

"Don't rub it off!" Ben protested. "We're all trying something new. Check out my freaky outfit. Isn't it fun?"

They both ignored him.

"I do like the punky hair," Jace said.

"Thanks!" Tim replied. "I've gotta be honest though, your usual style suits you better."

"That's a relief," Jace said as his hair popped back into shape.

"You both look great," Ben said, giving up the game. Either they had chemistry or they didn't. Both were so naturally handsome anyway. Jace was wearing an ivory V-neck sweater, the fabric light, and olive slacks which cupped his bulge nicely. Was it always that big though? Whatever made him feel comfortable in this situation. "If my husbands would care to escort me, I'm ready for our big date."

"No kiss?" Jace asked. Then he looked to Tim. "Or is that too weird?"

"I got mine before we left the house," Tim said, not sounding upset. "Go for it."

Jace smooched Ben, and while it was more reserved than usual, Tim seemed to take it in stride. Mostly. "Okay, that *was* a little strange," he said, "but it's not the first time. I caught you guys snogging during that charity ball way back when, and a couple times when I visited your house."

"I've seen you two kiss as well," Jace said pointedly.

Tim thought about it before his eyebrows shot upward. "Oh shit! At the water park!"

"That's right," Jace growled. Then he winked and laughed. "To be honest, there's very little I haven't seen you do together. Sometimes when I'd pop down to Earth to check on you, my timing wasn't the best."

"No way!" Tim said, covering his face. "Oh man, I am so sorry."

"Would you apologize to a Peeping Tom for catching you in the act? I only had myself to blame."

"I would've done the same if the situation was reversed, except that would have made me a Peeping Tim."

So far, so good! Ben turned around and bowed his arms. "I'm ready if you are, husbands!" They each took one and walked him toward the car. "Where are we headed first?"

"We each agreed to choose a place," Jace said. "Although for mine, we won't need the car."

"I want to do mine last," Ben said. All part of his masterplan.

"I can go first," Tim offered. "I want to drive us through the Martian Colony. The living version. They've made so much progress in the past couple decades. I can't wait to check it out in person."

"We can't really drive to Mars," Jace said carefully.

Tim shrugged. "No problem. We'll do the *Back to the Future* jump."

"Huh?"

"Go real fast and appear somewhere else," Tim explained.

"That's how he does it," Ben said with a chuckle.

"I see." Jace cleared his throat. "Well, if you don't mind me making a suggestion, my plan involves something that will let us enjoy the approach to Mars."

"How so?" Tim asked.

Jace took a deep breath, his forehead crinkling in concentration. Then he nodded. Ben and Tim turned in the direction he had indicated and saw that a four-seater airplane was now parked behind the black sports car. While it was small compared to jumbo jets, it positively dwarfed Tim's car.

"Do you really know how to fly that thing?" Ben asked in awe.

"I'm sure we can figure it out together," Jace said with a wink. "We'll do some sightseeing here in Heaven and then head to Mars. If everyone is agreeable to the idea."

Ben looked at Tim to gauge his reaction and noticed that he had reverted to his previous height. Hard to blame him, considering the circumstances. "I'm super-hyped about Mars," Ben said, wanting to give Tim's self-esteem a boost. "This will be a fun way of getting there. And then we can switch to your car, right?"

"Sure," Tim said, managing to muster some enthusiasm. "Let's do it."

"Great," Jace said, extending an arm to guide them toward the plane. "I'm afraid there are only two seats per row, but if you give me a moment, I can redesign the interior."

"Naw, it's all good," Tim said. "I'll take the back now if you take it when we're in my car."

"You've got it," Jace said, bumping fists with him.

Ben's heart echoed this by bumping against the inside of his ribcage. This was going better than he had dared imagine. By the time they returned home, who knew what might happen?

Tim climbed into the back of the plane. Jace stood by the front passenger-side door, holding it open for Ben. He had switched to a dapper pilot's uniform.

"What?" he said innocently when Ben looked him over. Then he added in a quiet voice, "You always did have a thing for uniforms."

Ben stifled a laugh. He certainly didn't mind them fighting over him somewhat, but mostly he was glad they were making the effort to get along. "You okay?" he asked, twisting to face the backseat while Jace walked around the plane.

"Yeah," Tim said, glancing around the interior with shining eyes. "This'll be fun!"

Jace settled into the pilot's seat and flipped a bunch of switches. "I don't know what they actually do," he admitted, "but I love the sound they make."

"What about those buttons?" Ben asked.

"Go for it," Jace said.

Ben started poking them with reckless abandon. Before long Tim was stretched out between their seats so he could toggle switches and jab buttons too.

"Never gets old," Jace said with a chuckle. "Now then…" His voice took on the odd cadence that only pilots seemed to use, which was punctuated with long drawn-out syllables. "Welcome aboard ladies and gentlemen. We ahhhhhh are about to begin our take off. Theeee weather is looking nice today, sooooo we don't expect any turbulence. It should be ahhhh nice and steady ride. For now, kick back, relax, and enjoy the five-star service. Thank you for ahhhh choosing Samson Airlines. Flight attendants prepare for take-off."

Tim was howling with laughter. Ben was just excited. As the plane moved forward, carefully pulling into the middle of the street, he reached over to take Jace's hand. His grip tightened as they accelerated and the propellered nose tilted upward. Soon they were cruising above the neighborhood, Austin spread out beneath them. Ben had learned that other people who chose to live in a facsimile of the city had gathered here as a community, everyone contributing to its recreation. Although many of the details were idealized. Nature thrived within the city limits, extra space being inserted where necessary. The Colorado River was wider too, the waters pure. But not everything had changed.

"I'm glad they didn't mess with the skyline," he said. "It wouldn't feel the same if they did."

"The community comes together to make decisions like that," Jace said. "Currently they only add buildings when they are constructed on the Earth version. That way it doesn't look like it's stuck in the past. Although if you're into history, there's a place for that too. Do you want to see?"

Ben shook his head. "Show me more of Heaven. I haven't gotten a feel for it yet."

Jace was happy to comply. They passed through low clouds, and when their view was unobscured again, Ben was astounded. There was so much! Landscapes that appeared to be painted by Van Goth, crystalline mountain ranges, sparkling seas filled with every imaginable kind of ship, and cities made of pulsing light, spiraling shells, and even food.

"The Leaning Tower of Pancakes?" Ben asked as they flew past it.

"Everyone has their own idea of Heaven," Jace said, bringing the plane lower so they could see the people and animals gathered around the base. They were trudging through syrup and tearing chunks of pancake from the base to shove into their mouths.

"I'm told that the tower usually suffers enough structural damage to fall over by noon," Jace said. "That's when the real feast begins. The next day they build it back up and start over."

"Now I know what I want for dessert," Ben said. "Or better yet, we should fill up one of the bathtubs at home with hot cocoa. I could soak in that all day." Especially with Jace and Tim as his marshmallows. Oh yes! This fantasy was tarnished somewhat when trying to figure out which home it would take place in, but he set those concerns aside, already working on the solution.

"If you really want to experience decadent eating," Jace said, "then we should visit Hell sometime. There's still more I'd like to show you here though."

The tour continued, Ben barely able to comprehend it all. They passed over a city where everything seemed to be made from golden metal, giant robots turning into vehicles to race along the raised streets, and another land where furry creatures dressed in clothing and walked upright. When a giant waved at them as they passed by, Ben turned in his seat to check on his other husband, who was barely able to pull his attention from the window.

"This is amazing," Tim breathed. Then he addressed Jace. "I thought we couldn't fly in the afterlife without special status or permission?"

"Depends on the region."

"Besides," Ben added, "this isn't the only pair of wings he's got."

Tim groaned. "Don't tell me you're an angel."

"I'm not," Jace said, "but if you want to see what they look like…"

He pulled back on the wheel and the plane tilted upward again, passing through layer after layer of cloud. When they finally rose above them…

Ben gasped. This was the Heaven that he and every other child had drawn in crayon. The land beneath them consisted of vast plains of bulbous clouds, an ivory palace with countless towers and spires ahead. All around them, the perfectly blue sky was filled with flying forms. Angels were most often depicted as white guys with even whiter wings, but here the diversity was infinite. Not just in terms of skin color and gender, but the variety of feather patterns as well. A heavy-set black woman zipped across their path on massive parrot wings that were red, yellow, and blue. She was accompanied by a young boy who was covered head to toe in freckles, his wings raven black.

"Oh my god," Ben said, covering his mouth. "Look over there! Is that a dog? *With wings?* I can't deal with this!"

"Think we can get a pair for Chinchilla?" Tim asked. "She's always been my little angel."

"Anyone can become one," Jace said. "It didn't used to be this way, but things really changed after The Great Reunification. I'll spare you the history lesson, or else we'll get off topic, but I'll say this: Becoming an angel takes serious dedication, and results in a tremendous amount of responsibility. Similar to becoming a surgeon back home, but more intense. It's a real commitment. I was always too distracted to go down that path." He looked at Ben meaningfully.

Ben was about to reward him with a kiss until he remembered they weren't alone and checked the backseat. Tim had his arms crossed over his chest and was scowling.

Jace noticed too and said, "You okay back there?"

"No," Tim grumbled, "I think you're an absolute bastard. How am I supposed to compete with this?" He shook his head. "You just had to go first, huh?"

Ben tensed until both men started laughing.

"I'm done showing off now," Jace said. "Let's go see Mars. I was just as intimidated by your idea."

"You were not."

"I was! The first human colony in space is a lot more substantial than a pancake tower."

"Thanks," Tim said. "Hey, do you think..." He leaned forward to whisper in Jace's ear, holding Ben at bay with an outstretched arm when he tried to listen in.

"Yeah," Jace said. "That'll work. Let's head there now."

The airplane gained altitude, the blue sky darkening until it turned black and the stars came out. Then, after a now familiar lurch, they were elsewhere in existence. Ahead of them was a creamy orange planet with mountain ranges the color of a bruise. They were coming in quick, breezing through the atmosphere. The colony was visible on the surface now, a series of domed structures interconnected by covered roads. The world's nations had joined together to build this new outpost, the project advanced enough to allow civilian life. Seeing it from this vantage point made Ben so hopeful for the future of humanity that he sobbed once before he managed to get himself under control.

"See?" Jace said, addressing the backseat. "You had nothing to worry about. I went first because I knew I was outgunned."

"You're way too generous," Tim said, but he clearly appreciated the sentiment.

"I think we're about ready," Jace said as the plane continued to descend.

He abandoned the controls to twist around in his seat and grip Tim's hand. Then, with a flash, he was no longer sitting next to Ben. Tim was there instead, grabbing the wheel of his sports car which had replaced the airplane. Ben made sure Jace was safely in the backseat and not drifting behind the car in space before he faced forward again to look out the windshield. He instantly regretted it. The ground was fast approaching, the car angled toward it in a downward trajectory.

"Are we going to be okay?" Ben asked, grabbing onto his seat.

"No idea," Tim said. "I only know that it won't be fatal. Uhhh... Jace?"

"I've got this," he said from the backseat.

Shortly before they hit the ground, the front of the car lifted, the angle gentler now. Tim yanked the wheel to the right, hit the gas, and cackled madly as he aimed for the spaceport runway. The tires grazed the tarmac a few times, and even went *through* it a few times, before finally settling on the surface so the car could cruise along the runway.

"So badass," Tim said, glancing in the rearview mirror. "Thanks for the assist!"

"My pleasure," Jace replied.

Ben breathed out, but only after shooting his second husband a glare. That was his intent anyway. He simply ended up staring when he saw that Tim's hair had reverted to the shorter style he had preferred in college. Jace was back in his original outfit instead of the pilot's uniform as well. Ben didn't comment, content to let everyone choose what made them the most comfortable. The car turned toward the nearest building, only slowing so they could ogle the parked spacecraft along the way. Then they pulled into a nearby hangar to disembark.

As ghosts they had an all-access pass to wherever they wanted to go. Any door marked with "Official Personnel Only" was walked through as if it had no substance, even though the reverse was true. They snooped and poked around, and when they grew tired of the spaceport, hopped back in Tim's car to drive elsewhere. Ben felt privileged to be here, and finally understood why it had been such a frequent dinner table conversation in their home.

The new colony had been an interest of Tim's late in their lives. Jace had apparently gone through a phase where he read any book he could find about astronauts, especially the early explorers from more than a century ago, so the two men had plenty to discuss. Ben let them talk so he could stare in wonder at the latest terraforming efforts, or the massive greenhouses that provided the colony with food. Mostly he liked people-watching, especially in the civilian areas where life played out with surprising normality. Somewhere here might be another young man who was sneaking out of his assigned habitat to secretly watch a space recruit that he couldn't stop thinking about. Love amongst the stars. Wouldn't that be something?

Ben let himself dream of what it must be like to live here, and when he grew bored with that, he let the others walk ahead so he could do a terrible imitation of David Bowie and sing *Life on Mars?* Although when the other two noticed, he began belting it out, not stopping even when Tim covered his ears.

"I prefer your usual singing voice, Benjamin," he said.

"Really?" Jace said. "I thought it was an improvement."

"I'll decide later which one of you I'm angrier with," Ben teased. He made it up to them by singing a much less shrill rendition of Elton John's *Rocket Man*, which was better received.

After two glorious hours spent on Mars, it was time for Ben's portion of the date. He had given careful consideration to the location, struggling to find a place that would be significant to them all. Then he changed tactics and decided that somewhere neutral would be better. He consulted with Victor, who tipped him off about a series of secluded islands. Ben chose the smallest of these, which was only the size of a sports stadium... of some sort. He had never paid much attention to such things. He only knew that the island suited his needs.

Jace flew them there. Compared to all they had witnessed so far, the surroundings were humble, little more than a beach and cluster of tropical trees. Excellent. Ben looked around in satisfaction as they left the plane. He wanted them to focus on each other rather than be distracted with sightseeing.

"This is nice," Tim said, letting himself fall backward into the sand.

"Peace and quiet after all that stimulation," Jace added. "Perfect."

"They're called the Meditation Islands," Ben told them. "They must have been created for that purpose. I thought it would be nice to have a picnic together and unwind. Please don't laugh if I got it wrong, but I tried making something special for this trip."

"That's great!" Jace said.

"Let's see what you've got," Tim chimed in.

Ben scrunched up his face in concentration. He had learned

that, once creating an object here, it could be called on and sent away again with relative ease. Sort of how inventory worked in video games, or instant access to files uploaded to cloud storage. Performance anxiety made this more difficult than it had been in practice, but after a renewed effort, he felt the handle of a picnic basket materialize in his hands and looked down to see that he had succeeded.

"Nice!" Tim said as he sat up.

"Let's see if it's all still in there," Ben replied. He set down the basket and opened the lid, pulling out a large blanket. The guys took this from him and spread it out over the sand. "And then there's this," Ben said, pulling free a large purple umbrella with a six-foot pole. It couldn't possibly fit inside the basket but physical laws didn't apply here. "It was easier to shove it all in there rather than having to recreate each object."

"That's a popular building technique," Jace said. "You're a fast learner."

They worked together to set up the umbrella so they would have shade to relax in.

"There's more," Ben said, "but I thought we could go for a swim first."

"Hell yeah!" Tim said. He snapped his fingers and was wearing only a pair of blue swim trunks.

Jace and Ben switched into swimming gear too. That meant they were all practically naked, which brought back memories of Splash Town, but he wasn't about to remind them of that trip again, especially considering how it had ended. Instead he yelled, "Last one in has to reincarnate!" before running for the waves. He tripped along the way and lost his lead. Tim picked him up around the waist and ran with him the rest of the way in.

"If you're reincarnating," he said. "I am too."

That was sweet, until he released Ben, dropping him into the water without ceremony. There was nothing to fear, though. Without the need to breathe, their bodies glided through the water like mermen as they explored the ocean floor, a shimmering wonderland surrounding them. They only resurfaced again when ready to. The creator of this place favored realism, the sand sticking to their wet bodies as they walked toward the picnic site, but all it took was a thought to have it fall off their skin. They settled onto the blanket together, Ben reaching for the basket again. "Good news," he said. "I cooked!"

He narrowed his eyes at the concerned look that Tim and Jace exchanged. "You're both in so much trouble. I actually became a fairly adequate cook toward the end of my life. Tell him, babe!"

"Uh..." Tim said, scratching the back of his head sheepishly.

"Then I guess you don't want this," Ben said, pulling out a six-pack of beer.

"Ain't no chef better than my Benjamin," Tim amended quickly. "Couldn't stand to eat anywhere else. That's how good he got!"

Ben smiled and handed him the beer. "And for you," he said, addressing Jace, "I made this."

"Airline-sized bottles of vodka?" Jace laughed as he took them. "And look, they're even made from crummy plastic. You thought of everything!"

"Had to keep it authentic," Ben said. "Be honest when you try these. Please."

Of everything he had created for this date, he was most nervous about the drinks. If he had simply imagined what each drink tasted like and nothing more, the alcohol wouldn't have any effect. For the consumer to feel any sort of intoxication, each drink had to be imbued with will, intention, and other complicated things that he wasn't sure he fully understood.

"Mine packs one hell of a punch," Jace said. "And kicks in fast!"

"The beer goes down nice and smooth," Tim said. "And yeah, I'm already buzzing. We better take it slow."

"Too strong is better than nothing at all," Ben said, feeling pleased.

He settled down between them on the blanket and tried not to force anything. They enjoyed the cool breeze while chatting and staring off into the horizon. The vibe became relaxed enough that Jace placed his hand on Ben's back, rubbing it up and down and making his skin tingle. Tim reached over to take Ben's hand. Neither guy seemed to mind. Conversation continued. Ben's heart and hormones were both going wild, so he decided it was time for the next stage of his plan.

"I know we don't actually need it," he said, "but you can't have a beach picnic without this."

Ben took a bottle of sunblock lotion from the picnic basket. "Who wants to go first?"

Tim leaned forward to consider Jace. "Rock paper scissors?"

"You're on!"

Jace threw a rock, Tim chose paper. Not that it would matter for long. Ben scurried behind Tim, squeezed lotion onto the brown skin of his back, and began rubbing it in. He checked on Jace during this, but the other man still seemed relaxed. Perfect.

"Actually," Ben said to him, "could you take over real quick? There's something else I made, but I just remembered that I forgot an important detail."

"It's all good," Tim said. "I can wait."

"You won't want to," Ben said, handing Jace the bottle. "Not when you find out what great massages he gives."

"Oh," Tim said. "Really?"

Ben's expression was pleading. Jace humored him, took the bottle, and moved behind Tim. Ben lingered long enough to make sure he began. Jace focused on massaging Tim's shoulders, but he couldn't imagine any gay man remaining there for long.

"Be right back," Ben said before retreating to the cluster of trees.

He didn't actually need to work on anything. Instead he watched Jace continue to massage Tim's shoulders. After some muted words, his hands moved farther down Tim's back. If they ended up rolling in the sand while making out, Ben decided he would be totally okay with it, because this was weirdly hot! He thought that was about to happen when Jace set aside the bottle of lotion and moved so they were sitting next to each other. After more exchanged words, Tim flexed an arm. Jace felt it. He was hooked! He had to be. Jace flexed his own arm in return. There was laughter. And then... More talking.

"Come on, you guys," Ben hissed in frustration. "Keep going!"

He waited, but all they seemed interested in was socializing, so Ben rejoined them.

"All done," he said. "I was going to serve ice cream, but I changed my mind and came up with something more personal."

He took three plates from the picnic basket. On each was a slice of *tres leches* cake topped with a red fortune cookie. "Best of both worlds," he explained, hoping the hint wasn't too subtle.

"Fuck yeah!" Tim said. "I love *tres leches* even more here, now that I don't have to worry about the calories."

"It's your mom's recipe too," Ben said. It had taken years of begging to get it from her, but she had relented. Eventually. "And

I used my old recipe to make the fortune cookies," he told Jace.

"I never had any complaints about those," Jace said, cracking his open. He tossed half the cookie in his mouth but stopped chewing while reading what the fortune said. He looked at Ben and raised an eyebrow when swallowing.

"What's yours say?" Tim asked, already holding his own fortune.

Jace reread his a few times like he was trying to make sense of it. "'The lover of my lover is also my lover.' Hmm. Does that mean I'm my own lover?"

"No," Ben said, laughing nervously. "It's like that old saying: 'The enemy of my enemy is my friend.'"

"Interesting." Jace said carefully.

Tim snorted and read his aloud. "'Three is only a crowd if the bed isn't big enough.' Are these supposed to be racy? Or funny?"

"Let's read mine and find out," Ben said, starting to panic. "'Today you can have your cake and eat it two. Or three.' Except look, see how I misspelled 'too' on purpose. It's a play on words. Get it?"

"I'm beginning to," Jace said. "Remind me again why you wanted to go on a double date?"

"Haven't you both enjoyed yourselves?"

"Yeah, for sure," Tim said, "but I didn't realize that you wanted us all to hook up. Is that what's going on?"

"I mean, it could be." Ben looked back and forth between them. He was the only one smiling. Tim was blushing. Jace seemed downright uncomfortable. "Or not. I made a mess of it, didn't I?"

"That depends," Jace said. "Maybe you should tell us what it is that you hoped for."

"I thought it would be nice if you fell in love with each other," Ben said. "I know how ridiculous that must sound, but today was really nice. Especially when disregarding my stupid schemes. I had a great time. Didn't you?"

"Yeah!" Tim said. "It was very chill, and that made it easy. But this..."

"—feels forced," Jace finished for him. "I like Tim. Even before I saw what a great husband he was to you. When we got to know each other back in Austin, it was good too. But I never felt it should go further than that."

"Same here," Tim said. "I wanted to hate you, man. I really

did. But I can't. You're an awesome guy, and the way you loved Benjamin and took care of him, that's what I kept thinking of when I finally got my chance again. You were my inspiration."

Jace seemed moved. "Really?"

"Yeah. And I never felt anything romantic toward you either. Maybe because you were still the competition. It was good to not have that hanging over us today. So I mean... Maybe someday. If it happened naturally."

"I think that's the key," Jace said, turning to Ben. "Today was a great idea, but you have to let us get to know each other. Even then we can't promise anything. If we end up being more than friends, we'll explore that when it happens. And if it doesn't..." He shook his head. "Are you unhappy?"

"No!" Ben said. "Trust me, I've never been happier. It just gets so complicated."

"What does?" Tim asked.

Ben thought about it and took a deep breath. "I'll explain it to you both, but can we go home first?"

"Sure," Jace said, starting to stand.

"Should I drive?" Tim asked. "Wait, which house do you mean?"

Ben remained silent.

Jace was the first to understand. He sat again. "That's what bugs him."

"Huh?" Tim said before realization dawned. "Oh. It's like when things took off for me in Japan. The bigger I became there, the happier I should have been, but it only made me feel like I was being torn in two."

"Exactly," Ben said. "I love you both so much, but I'm constantly forced to choose. For everything, from the first meal of the day to who I settle down with that night. I'm always worried about one of you getting hurt feelings. You've shown me today how incredibly mature you've both become. Maybe I have some catching up to do—"

"I've always loved your antics," Jace interjected. "Most of the time."

"You always kept me on my toes," Tim added. "I don't need that to change."

"And I don't want either of you to, unless it's what you want, because I love you for who you are. But I'd still like to find a solution."

"Then we will," Jace said. "Together."

"Damn right," Tim said. "We've got this, Benjamin. I promise."

Ben exhaled in relief and smiled gratefully at them both. He still didn't know what the solution would be, but at least now he wouldn't have to figure it out on his own.

Ben was the first to awake. He stretched and yawned before kicking off the covers to cool down. Tim was still snoozing next to him. The past few weeks had been so filled with activity—research, planning, building—that even Jace had exhausted himself. They agreed to deal with it the old-fashioned way and sleep it off. That meant one of them had to go his separate way. After a game of rock paper scissors, which had become the standard way of making these decisions, Tim had won. Ben returned home with him to their secluded property in west Austin and quickly lost consciousness.

Now he felt refreshed. And embarrassed by the clumsiness of his recent plan. He should have let himself sleep sooner. His rested mind could see with perfect clarity how his scheme had been doomed to fail. Then again, considering how long it had been since his dating years, Ben hadn't done so bad. His marriage with Tim had found a nice steady rhythm in the second half of their life together. Ben had forgotten how complicated the game of love could be, especially when more than one guy was involved. As he slid out of bed, he felt hope for their combined future. Maybe not in the way he had envisioned on his own, but this was better. They were working together. That was the correct first step.

He went to the nearest window, which overlooked the front yard. The studio near the pool reminded him to check in on Jason and William soon. More pressing was the scratching sound that kept attracting his attention, so he went to the hallway to investigate.

Chinchilla was sitting in front of the linen closet and pawing at the door. She'd always been such a clever girl. "You want in there?" he asked. "I hope you don't need a towel. Or a change of sheets."

She harrumphed like he was being silly, which of course he was. Ben opened the door for her, but the shelves that had divided the shallow space were no longer there, replaced by another door. This one was already cracked. Chinchilla pushed on it with her nose, stubby tail wagging as she went inside. Ben followed her, feeling a familiar lurch, and found himself in another home. The little one that he and Jace had saved up for. It too had a linen closet that was absolutely useless in the afterlife, so they had given it a new purpose. The doors now connected their two homes. They could have simply chosen one house and all dwelled there together, but he was emotionally attached to both homes and didn't want to lose either. His husbands felt the same. And this way there was less pressure for Tim and Jace to combine their lives or be anything but cordial to each other. Luckily they were already more than that. Ben felt it was safe to describe them as friends. He wouldn't pressure them to be more.

"I think I know what you're up to," he said as he followed Chinchilla. "You want to be the first dog to potty in the backyard here. Gotta mark your territory, right?"

That was another nice detail. Each house was still in its respective neighborhood, which was important to them all.

"Wrong way if you want to go outside," Ben said.

Chinchilla didn't listen. She marched down the hall to the bedroom. He soon saw why. Jace was sitting up in bed and reading, hair still messy from sleep. Samson was snoozing on one corner of the mattress, but he raised his head as they entered. Then he meowed excitedly and sat up to begin kneading the bed. Chinchilla went to him and made demanding noises until Ben came to give her a lift. Once up on the bed, she settled down next to the cat.

"They were always doing that," Ben said with a chuckle. "Not at first, but once they got to know each other, they were inseparable."

"How sweet," Jace murmured. "I never wondered if Samson would like a companion."

"Why would he when you give such great cuddles?" Ben said, crawling into bed himself.

Jace lifted the covers to invite him in. Ben nestled against the curve of his body, their bare skin pressing together. He remained facing the rest of the bed so he could continue to watch Samson and Chinchilla curl up together.

"Feeling better?" Jace asked.

Ben knew what he was referring to, and the answer was an easy, "Yes." If he wanted to see either of his husbands, it felt like they were under the same roof with him, despite being in separate houses. Any tough decisions could be handled with a simple game. There would always probably be more for him to want, but that was okay too. He didn't need everything, especially when he already had so much. "Does the new arrangement work for you?"

"Yes," Jace answered after giving it thought. "I'd feel even better if we could talk Victor into joining us. I keep telling him that there could be a door in one of his trees, or maybe a little hatch in his lean-to that he could crawl through."

Ben laughed at the mental image. "We should at least invite him over, just to hang out. Small steps. That's how it's done. And we do have those woods behind the other house…"

"What a wise old man you've become," Jace said, starting to tickle him.

He stopped suddenly when someone in a bathrobe filled the bedroom doorway.

"Oops!" Tim said, shielding his eyes. "Sorry. I heard Chinchilla grumbling in the hall but was too tired to get out of bed. Then I couldn't find her and… Sorry!"

"It's fine," Ben said. "We weren't doing anything."

"Oh." Tim dropped his hand. He noticed the bundle of fur filling one corner of the bed and smiled. "That brings back memories. I'm glad they like the new setup, although we should keep the doors closed until the other dogs get used to Samson."

"He can handle them," Jace said.

"Believe me," Tim said with a chuckle, "I know. It's the dogs I'm worried about. Chinchilla already learned who the boss is, but they haven't."

"Yet," Ben said.

Tim's gaze took in the rest of the scene with transparent longing. "Okay, well, I'm going to start breakfast I guess, if anyone feels like eating. But uh, take your time and I'll—"

"Do you want in on this?" Jace asked.

Ben's eyes went wide. So did Tim's.

"We're only cuddling," Jace said, helping to alleviate the tension.

Tim's grin was wild. "Hell yeah!" The bathrobe disappeared. "Nothing you haven't seen before," he said while hustling to the bed. "Where do I fit in?"

"Right here," Ben said, opening the covers in front of him.

After some shifting and adjusting, they found the right arrangement. Jace was still spooning him while Ben wrapped an arm around a muscled torso. He had never dreamt of wanting to be a sandwich until this moment, but now he hoped it would never end. It felt too good. Jace's fingers stroked his hair, while Ben pressed his lips against the back of Tim's neck and breathed in the familiar scent of his skin.

"Thank you," he said with a swallow.

"For what?" Tim asked.

"Being here with me. Neither one of you had to go this far. It's more than I ever could have asked for."

"And yet you did," Jace said playfully.

Ben spluttered laughter. "Yeah. I suppose I did. I can't help myself."

"That's why we love you," Tim said. "Don't we?"

"That's right," Jace said, draping an arm over Ben. His hand came to rest on Tim's shoulder and remained there. "We love you. Nothing will ever get in the way of that again."

No more disastrous misunderstandings, no more painful separation, and—thank all that was kind and merciful in the universe—no more death. Ben began weeping with joy, but he didn't need to explain why. And when he spoke next, he wasn't forced to choose who he addressed, because they both knew it was true.

"I love you too."

A rectangle of light moved across the bed, the sun warming the bodies that clung to each other. The passage of time meant nothing to them as they chatted idly, remembering exploits from long ago, or making plans for a future wide open with unlimited potential. They had nothing to fear, the possibility of loss nonexistent as they found harmony together, three hearts finally beating as one.

Also by Jay Bell
Straight Boy

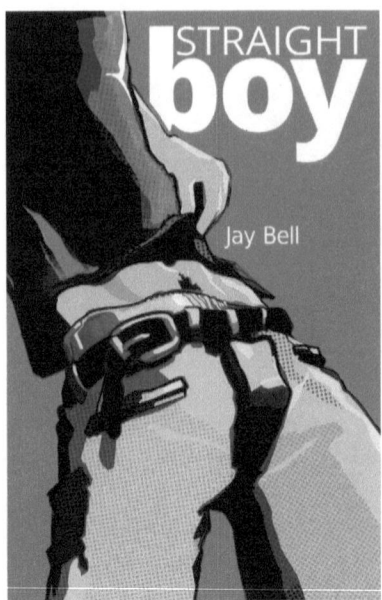

I love him. And I'm pretty sure he loves me back… even though he's straight.

When I first met Carter King, I knew he was something special. I imagined us being together, and we are, but only as friends. Best friends! I'm trying to be cool with that, even though I know he has secrets, and there have definitely been mixed signals. I don't want a crush to ruin what we already have. Then again, if there's any chance that we can be together, it's worth the risk, because Carter could be the love of my life. Or he might be the boy who breaks my heart.

Straight Boy is Jay Bell's emotional successor to his critically acclaimed Something Like… series. This full-length novel tells a story of friendship and love while skating the blurry line that often divides the two.

Something Like Summer has been reimagined as an ongoing web comic series! Join us on this new adventure at www.gaywebcomics.com

Also by Jay Bell:
Kamikaze Boys

True love is worth fighting for.

They say Connor, the one with the crazy eyes and creepy scar, tried to kill his old man. Lately he's been seen hanging out with David, the gay guy who always eats lunch alone. They make an odd pair, the loser and the psychopath. Even stranger is how bad things happen to the people who mess with them. Not that Connor and David are looking for trouble. Even when taking on the world, they seem more interested in each other than fighting.

Kamikaze Boys is a Lambda Literary award-winning novel about breaking the chains that bind you and using them to strike down anyone who gets in your way. Better yet, it's about holding hands with the guy you love while doing so.

Hear the story in their own words!

Many of the *Something Like...* books are available on audio too. Listen to Tim's tale while you jog with him, or ignore your fellow airline passengers while experiencing Jace's story again. Find out which books are available and listen to free chapters at the link here: www.jaybellbooks.com

Also by Jay Bell
The Cat in the Cradle

To set out into the world, to be surrounded by the unknown and become a stranger. Only then would he be free to reinvent himself. Or fall in love.

Dylan wanted one last adventure before the burden of adulthood was thrust upon him. And to confront the man he hadn't spoken to since their intimate night together. Stealing a boat with his faithful companion Kio, their journey is cut short when they witness a brutal murder. A killer is loose in the Five Lands and attacking the most powerful families. Dylan—a potential target—seeks sanctuary from an unpredictable bodyguard named Tyjinn. Together they decide to turn the tables by hunting the killer down. Along the way, everything Dylan thought he knew about himself will be challenged, but if he survives, he stands to win the love he never dreamed possible.

The Cat in the Cradle is the first book in the Loka Legends series and features twenty-five original illustrations created by Andreas Bell, the author's husband.

Also by Jay Bell
Hell's Pawn

John Grey is dead… and that's just the beginning of his troubles.

Purgatory should have been a safe haven for souls that belong neither in Heaven nor Hell, but instead John finds himself in a corrupt prison, one bereft of freedom or pleasure. Along with his decedent friend Dante, John makes a brave escape, only to fall straight down to Hell and into the arms of Rimmon, a handsome incubus. John is soon recruited as Hell's ambassador, visiting the afterlife realms of other cultures to enlist an army strong enough to stand against Heaven. As interesting as his new job is, John's mind keeps returning to Purgatory and the souls still trapped there. Somehow John must stop a war he doesn't believe in and liberate Purgatory, all while desperately trying to attract the attention of an incubus whose heart belongs to another.

Winner of a Rainbow Award for Best Gay Fantasy, honorable mention as Best Gay Novel of 2011, and two wins in Goodread's M/M Romance Member's Choice Awards for Best World Created and Most Surprising/Unique Plot Device.

www.ingramcontent.com/pod-product-compliance
Lightning Source LLC
Chambersburg PA
CBHW031053080526
44587CB00011B/668